STEEL PHOENIX

STEEL PHOENIX

The Fall and Rise of the U.S. Steel Industry

Christopher G. L. Hall

St. Martin's Press

ISBN 0-312-16198-0

Library of Congress Cataloging-in-Publication Data

Hall, Christopher (Christopher G. L.)
Steel phoenix : the fall and rise of the U.S. steel industry / Christopher G.L. Hall.
p. cm.
Includes bibliographical references and index.
ISBN 0-312-16198-0
1. Steel industry and trade—United States—History. I. Title.
HD9515.H28 1996
338.4'7669142'0973—dc 95-46909
CIP

Design: Acme Art, Inc.

First Edition: February 1997
10 9 8 7 6 5 4 3

CONTENTS

PREFACE AND ACKNOWLEDGMENTS

Any study of a rapidly changing industry runs the risk of rapid obsolescence. This book attempts to cover the North American steel industry in the 25 years between 1970 and 1995, during which time the industry underwent dramatic and traumatic changes. While steel was certainly not unique in its transformation during this period, it was distinctive for its size and impact on the entire economy; for its high public and political profile, reinforced by its geographic concentration; and by its ultimate success in overcoming adversity and in "reinventing" itself.

A number of historical studies of the industry have preceded this. The indispensable five-volume history of the U.S. steel industry to 1970, *Economic History of the Iron and Steel Industry of the United States,* is by the Reverend William Hogan of Fordham University (Lexington, MA, 1971). Father Hogan has also published supplementary studies in less depth at intervals since then. The best historical study of a limited time period, covering the years 1945 to 1960, is Paul Tiffany's *The Decline of American Steel: How Management, Labor and Government Went Wrong* (New York, 1988), essential background reading for anyone seeking to understand the mind-set of traditional Big Steel. Other important studies have been published by respected consultants working in the industry, especially Donald Barnett—for example, his and Louis Schorschs *Steel: Upheaval in a Basic Industry* (Cambridge, MA, 1983)—and Robert Crandall. However, the most readable studies, for people not immersed in the industry, are probably those by journalists who have tracked the human and economic tragedies of the closings of major mills. The best of these are John Strohmeyer's *Crisis in Bethlehem: Big Steels Struggle to Survive* (Bethesda, MD, 1986), focusing on Bethlehem Steel; John Hoerr's splendidly titled *And the Wolf Finally Came: The Decline of the American Steel Industry* (Pittsburgh, 1988), which focuses on U.S. Steel and its Pittsburgh-area plants in particular; and Mark Reutter's *Sparrows Point: Making Steel* (New York, 1989).

The other side of the story, the construction of a Nucor minimill, is chronicled in Richard Preston's *American Steel* (New York, 1991), a best-seller that was paid the accolade of being serialized in *The New Yorker*. My debt to these writers, and others, is evident and great.

The industry is well served by a small number of publications of record, notably the daily newspaper *American Metal Market*. The monthly *Iron Age/New Steel* and the British-based *Metal Bulletin* are also essential reference sources. For broader trade, employment and political issues, I have primarily used the *New York Times*, which gave excellent coverage of the steel industry through the 1970s but which has subsequently much reduced its focus on this industry. Technical issues are, unfortunately for the layman, critical to an in-depth understanding of much of the transformation of the industrys economics. The best recent primer on overall industry processes as well as trade is by Peter M. Fish of the industry economic consultants MEPS in Sheffield, England; this was published as *The International Steel Trade* (Cambridge, 1995). Finally the industry benefits from a number of directories, notably the annual *Directory of Iron and Steel Plants* published by the Association of Iron and Steel Engineers in Pittsburgh; and the 1995 *Pipe and Tube Mills of the World*, edited by Douglas Preston Yadon, publisher of the *Preston Pipe Report*. I used each of these frequently for reference while writing this work.

I have worked in different segments of the steel industry since 1980, primarily in steel distribution. As a vice president at Levinson Steel and Thypin Steel, and as a consultant to a range of firms in the industry, I have watched the markets, processes, and players steadily change and witnessed the failures of those who failed to adjust to change. I have also taken pride in the industrys accomplishments in the environmental field, where the steady move toward a recycling-based industry has been slowly accompanied by the adoption of a philosophy that pollution represents the wasteful loss of potentially valuable material. Although uneven, the progress in this direction is remarkable for an industry traditionally identified with the smokestack.

I am grateful for the support and assistance of a large number of colleagues and friends in the industry, and to try to name them all would be impossible. In particular, though, I must thank David Lloyd-Jacob of Butte Mining PLC; Larry Gilbert, Stuart Oltchick, and Richard Thypin of Thypin Steel; Ernie Lantagne of the Congdon and Carpenter Company; Robert McAleer of Edgcomb Metals; Gary O'Neill of International Products Company; George Trainor, formerly of Bethlehem Steel; Ben Teplitz, publisher of American Metal Market; Ned McMahon and Bill Wechsler. My editor, Michael Flamini, has been a great and patient support. Most of all it is my spouse, Jackie Wardell, who has made the book possible.

Christopher Hall
Bristol, Maine, 1996

INTRODUCTION

A Tale of Two Industries

On the Saturday before Thanksgiving, November 18, 1995, the heart of the steelmaking city of Bethlehem, Pennsylvania, stopped beating. The "hot end"—the iron and steel furnaces of Bethlehem Steel Corporation's home plant, where steel had been produced since before the Civil War—was permanently closed. The Bethlehem steel mill had produced the steel beams from which were built the symbols of the American century—the Empire State Building, the launch pads at Cape Canaveral, manufacturing plants, and freeway bridges. Now, after years of attempts to find partners to invest in modernization, years of slow cutbacks and union concessions, Bethlehem Steel decided to cut its losses and cease steelmaking in Bethlehem. Eighteen hundred steelworkers lost their jobs. Once again, television and newspaper reporters filed familiar stories about a steel mill closing, stories that were given prominence because of the fame of Bethlehem. It seemed as if the same story had been running every few months for twenty years.

A "hot end" like that in Bethlehem makes powerful images, for television or for those who work in or live by the plant. Even if much of the smoke has been eliminated by modern pollution controls, the fire and molten metal seem to have a life of their own, and the contrast with the silent, rusting hulk of a shuttered mill is especially poignant. For the residents, facing silence in most of the five-mile long complex that stretches along the Lehigh River through the center of Bethlehem, it felt as if a close relative had died. Yet the images belied the truth, about the steel industry and even about the Bethlehem Steel Corporation. The media largely ignored the surprising success story of steel in North America in the 1990s. Overlooked in most stories was the fact that steel beams would still be produced at Bethlehem, although rolled from recycled scrap metal melted down at another plant of the Bethlehem Steel Corporation. Most significantly, many news reports repeated the familiar litany that cheap foreign steel was eliminating American jobs—at a time when the Bethlehem mill's U.S. competitors were successfully exporting American-made beams. A distorted picture was created by the combination of the medias need for simple and dramatic stories, and the convenience to both company and union of not refuting the old cry that imports were to blame for any cutbacks. The complex truth is that the North American steel industry in the late 1990s is once again viewed as the world's leader, although its leadership is not expressed in terms of tonnage but of profitability, entrepreneurial risk-taking, technology, and labor and environmental practices.

This book is about steels two great industrial success stories and about the four decades of failure and anguished change that separate them. It describes two very different industries: the American steel industry of the late 1950s, the world's preeminent producer of the major raw material commodity of industrial society; and the American steel industry of the late 1990s, the world's leading recycling business and an efficient supplier of one of the materials competing for manufacturing and construction use in an information-based economy. Both the 1950s and the 1990s industries set an example followed by others around the world. Both industries share some—a few—of the same corporate names and locations; both, of course, sell steel. They have little else in common.

The quintessential symbol of America in the late 1950s was, and remains, the automobile—large, finned, chrome-ornamented, perhaps convertible; nearly two tons of steel with a gas-guzzling V-8 engine. Americas self-image, and its international appeal as a role model, was as the worlds preeminent manufacturer. In wartime, the "arsenal of democracy" produced ships, tanks, and aircraft; in peacetime, its factories produced literally millions of cars, refrigerators, and televisions. As a model, it was outstandingly successful. Its steel-based manufacturing techniques and middle-class living standards have spread through much of the world; but as the demand for cars and appliances became satiated, industrial societies developed new appetites.

The quintessential symbol of the 1990s economy is the microchip—even though few people would actually recognize one or be able to describe its working. Like steel, a microchip is a commodity whose value depends on its applications. Based on the microchip, Americas economic leadership today is concentrated in fields such as software; television, film, and music production and dissemination; higher education; and the "information superhighway." The information-consuming society appears to have as much global cultural appeal as its predecessor the car- and appliance-acquiring society, although the new era's consequences for income distribution and social intercourse remain uncertain.

In each industrial era, the U.S. steel industry came to reflect the demands of the economy and society, often in spite of attempts by government, unions, management, and investors to make it something different. In the 1950s, the steel industry emphasized production: tonnage shipped was the measure of success, while quality and cost were secondary matters, and the environmental impact of the industry was not even considered. In the 1990s, the steel industry emphasizes cost and quality, to compete with substitute materials such as concrete, aluminum, and plastics. The average annual consumption of steel in the United States has changed little from business cycle to business cycle since 1975, and real (inflation-adjusted) prices per ton of steel, after rising steadily throughout this century to 1974, flattened out and then dropped by over 50 percent to their 1993 levels. Meanwhile the weight of steel used in a typical application has fallen by as much as a third, as thinner but higher-quality steels are used to cover the same surface area in, for example, auto bodies.

As images of the American economy, the V-8 convertible and the microchip are separated in time by other images: the Apollo moon program of the 1960s, for example, and the shuttered factories of the "Rust Belt" in the 1980s set against the rise of McDonald's, the ubiquitous hamburger chain associated in the popular mind with unskilled work and minimum wages. Like any metaphor, these images both reveal some important truths about the U.S. economy and grossly oversimplify the underlying complex reality. However, each one reflects something of the contemporary public image, and indeed self-image, of American industry in general and the steel industry in particular.

In the 1960s steel believed itself to be invincible, destined to grow in size and profits with the achievements of the U.S. economy. As the Apollo moon landings got under way, Bethlehem Steel was preparing to open its vast new integrated steelmaking complex at Burns Harbor, Indiana. Industry executives worried about how to meet future demand

and prepared plans to build more integrated steel mills in Ohio and California; while under the prosperous surface, the industry was losing its technical edge, its cost competitiveness and markets. Just as pride in the space program faded as society grappled with the more lasting legacies of the 1960s—civil rights, Vietnam, the environmental movement, and the changed role of women in the economy—the steel industry's pride came before a fall.

By the 1980s, the steel industry faced wholesale plant closures, job losses, and financial hemorrhages as its output plunged to only 48 percent of capacity in 1982. The stark images of idled or abandoned steel mills in depressed Rust Belt cities such as Youngstown, Ohio; Buffalo; or the Pittsburgh region, epitomized the failure of American industry to compete with Japanese, European, or Third World manufacturers. American workers appeared doomed to low living standards as hamburger-flippers at McDonald's. Again, though, the image ignored new realities of successful steel businesses thriving in previously unlikely places. Specialty steel companies, making stainless and complex alloy steels; new minimills in the South and upper Midwest; and downstream steel processors and service centers, undertaking value-added and distribution functions the mills could no longer afford to do, made money and expanded. The major steel mills, in going through the trauma of organizational and financial restructuring to survive, shed their complacent, even arrogant, management culture and began to refocus on their core competitive strengths.

Today the U.S. steel industry may no longer be the driving force in the overall economy that it was until the 1960s. It is, however, still a good reflection of the state of the U.S. economy as a whole. Steel has become a very diverse industry. Small is beautiful; although some major new companies have emerged, firms and business units typically specialize in one or two types of steel product rather than the full product line of the historic steel companies. The functions of raw materials supply, steelmaking, fabrication operations, distribution, mill maintenance services, and technical research and engineering are generally separated as companies have retreated from vertical integration. It is an industry that has become more internationally integrated, as steel trade and investment has spread worldwide. It is moreover an industry whose internal social structure, although conservative by contemporary American standards, now reflects the patterns of individual mobility among companies during a career. The decline in unionism has been matched by the rise of participative, delegative management styles in the workplace. Finally women and minority-group managers, while still rare, are no longer remarked upon.

The resurgence of the American steel industry has been portrayed in the simplistic terms of the rise of the minimill, the small scrap recycler, and its victory over the unwieldy iron ore–based giant. While the minimills are a major part of the story, the successful resurgence of the industry is also the story of the turnaround of the historic steel companies; the remarkable feats of some of the "born-again" integrated steel mills, cast off as hopelessly unprofitable orphans by the major steel companies; the technical and management successes of the specialty steel companies; and the dynamic growth of the processing and distribution sector. This multifaceted new industry has weak players and strong; fast-growing companies and those barely clinging to life; but it is an industry that has come to embrace change and, in consequence, to profit from it. Although its profitability swings wildly with the business cycle, it is now in aggregate highly profitable, especially by international standards for "basic industry," and it is thereby attractive to investment capital both for new ventures and to update existing plants. It leads the world in applying electric furnace, scrap-recycling technology; but it has also pioneered the application of new management techniques to make steel more cost-effectively from iron ore. This complex success story, and its Phoenix-like origins in the ashes of the first U.S. steel industry, is the focus of this book.

1

THE PRODUCTION OF STEEL

WHAT IS STEEL?

Iron, the most abundant and cheapest of the Earth's metals, is found in differing concentrations almost everywhere, amounting to about 5 percent of the Earth's crust. It could, in principle, be extracted from any soil or rock; but economic ores of iron have an iron content ranging from 70 percent down to around 20 percent. Unfortunately iron is not, by itself, very useful. It is too brittle to be worked into useable shapes and too weak to carry weight. To be used in the manufacture of goods iron must be alloyed with other minerals, including in all cases the element carbon, also found universally but most concentrated in organic matter such as wood and coal.

Iron is usually alloyed with carbon to make either steel or cast iron. Traditionally, iron ore—directly from the ground if sufficiently rich in iron content, or in a concentrated form—is reduced in a blast furnace with coke and a limestone flux. Costing less than half as much as steel, pig iron contains about 4.5 percent carbon. While still too brittle to be worked mechanically, pig iron is strong enough to be remelted and poured ("cast") in foundries into finished product shapes, ranging from pipes to engine blocks. The foundry industry produces and uses different types of cast iron, known as ductile iron, gray iron, and malleable iron, but more than 95 percent of pig iron is further refined to make steel. Steel is generally defined as an alloy in which iron predominates and that normally has a carbon content below 2 percent. The characteristics of steel are determined by modifying the percentage of carbon contained in the metal and by adding quantities of other metals—normally small quantities of silicon, manganese, and phosphorus. Ninety-two countries around the world produce steel, and on a tonnage basis, it accounts for around 90 percent of the world's consumption of all metals.

Terminology in the steel industry varies slightly from country to country and is often somewhat misleading. However, steels are everywhere divided into at least three broad categories—carbon (or unalloyed) steel, stainless steel, and alloy steels. Although, strictly speaking, all steels are alloys, they are classed as alloy steels only if they contain metals other than manganese, silicon, and phosphorus, introduced as deliberate additions to the iron/carbon base material.

Carbon steels account for around 90 percent of all steel produced—over 500 million tons a year worldwide. Carbon steels can vary considerably in strength, formability, machinability, and weldability; they are produced in a range of grades, each containing specified ranges of the elements that determine these characteristics.[1] However, all carbon steels are susceptible to rust on exposure to the air and to more rapid forms of corrosion when exposed to water, changes of temperature, salts, acids, and so on. Carbon steels are commonly coated with paint or epoxy or with other metals when used in exposed or corrosion-critical applications. The most common metal coatings of steel contain zinc (or compounds of zinc with iron or aluminum), to form galvanized steel; or tin, used in tinplate for food and beverage cans. For reasons of historical accident, steel mills in the United States and Canada typically will add metal coatings to their flat-rolled steel for sale, but not to steel in other forms; and they do not add paint or other coatings; these are added by independent steel processors or by end users.

Stainless steels were created to resist corrosion. Rather than simply coating the surface of carbon steel, which only limits corrosion while the coating is intact, mills include the alloying element chromium, with or without other alloying metals. A metal is termed a stainless steel if it contains at least 50 percent iron and at least 9.5 percent chromium.[2] Stainless steel is always protected by a naturally occurring chromium oxide film on its surface. Chromium oxide films are inert and, unlike externally applied coatings, are self-repairing; if a stainless steel is cut or chipped, its protective cover is immediately re-formed by exposure to oxygen in the air. A wide variety of stainless steels has been developed, but the commonest class of stainless steel by far are the Austenitic, or type 300 series, steels, which contain significant amounts of expensive nickel—usually 8 to 12 percent—for additional corrosion resistance to salt and acids. Used in a wide range of corrosion-sensitive applications from food processing (and cutlery) to petrochemicals, stainless steels are produced in about 30 countries worldwide and account for about 2 percent of steel production by tonnage (far more by value) produced in the United States.

Alloy steels are often defined, poorly, as all steels that are not carbon or stainless. Around 10 percent of U.S. steel production is reported as alloy steel, but this includes large tonnages of high-strength, low-alloy carbon steels. Worldwide, about 5 percent of steel production contains alloying metals other than manganese, silicon, and phosphorus. Sometimes a single alloy element is added, but more often several are used for a beneficial combination of effects. One notable characteristic of alloy steels, unlike stainless or carbon, is that they are produced most often in bar or plate form, rather than as flat-rolled sheet or coil. This reflects their applications; they are used for products such as shafts, machined parts in machinery, pumps, tools, gears, and other critical components. Although the range of alloy steels is very broad, some common if arbitrary divisions are used. "Low alloy" steels contain less than 5 percent of all alloying elements (including carbon, silicon, and manganese); "high alloy" steels contain more than 5 percent. Special categories of alloy steels include tool steels, which usually contain vanadium, used for applications ranging from dies for the extrusion or forging of metals (hot working tool steels) to shear blades and hand tools (cold working tool steels). In addition, high-speed steels are alloy steels containing molybdenum, tungsten, vanadium, and sometimes cobalt, used for metal-cutting drills, taps, and reamers in machine tools. The catch-all term "specialty steels" is sometimes used to group together stainless, high alloy, and certain carbon steels such as spring steels.

A STEELMAKING PRIMER

Steelmaking is a mature industry in which technology evolves slowly. Because the industry's product, steel, changes little over the course of a decade or a century, the industry does not go through the constant changes of technology, production process, and plant location that drive an industry such as computers or customer electronics. However, steelmaking has undergone a steady process of technological change in the last twenty-five years; evolutionary rather than revolutionary, but dramatic nevertheless. Three major areas of technical development stand out, although economics, rather than the availability of a given technology, has driven the change. The three areas are the growth of electric furnace steelmaking, driven by changes in the costs of scrap-based relative to iron ore–based steelmaking; the widespread adoption of ladle refining, which has improved steelmaking efficiency and product quality; and the development of continuous casting of shapes ever closer to the finished product. To follow the changes that the industry has undergone, some understanding of the different production processes is necessary.

The three major classes of steel—carbon, alloy, and stainless—can all be produced in similar processes. Generally speaking, the production techniques differ according to the source of the metallic iron used for steelmaking and according to the product form into which the steel will be rolled rather than the grade of steel to be produced. In this chapter I describe only the two main processes by which steel is made in North America, known for convenience as integrated steelmaking and electric furnace steelmaking. Further detail of rolling and finishing processes may be found in the appendix at the end of this book, where a description of each process accompanies a listing of U.S. and Canadian plants by product.[3]

FIRST GET YOUR IRON . . .

As a product of iron, steel can be manufactured from iron ore, from iron and steel scrap, or from a mixture of the two. In an integrated steel mill, iron ore is reduced to pig iron in a blast furnace. At a traditional integrated mill in the United States, three separate, large plants together produce iron for the steelmaking process: the sinter plant, the coke ovens, and the blast furnace. Each is large, expensive to build and operate, and prone to spewing out pollutants.

At the sinter plant, crushed iron ore—brought from the mine in a form close to powder ("fines")—is mixed with coke powder and a limestone flux and heated to a temperature at which the materials bind into a porous cake known as sinter. Coal is baked in coke ovens to a temperature of 1000°C, then quenched with water. Then the sinter and coke are crushed to size and fed into the top of the blast furnace, so named for the blast of very hot air blown through the sides of the furnace onto the coke burning near the furnace bottom. In a continuous process, the heat from the combustion of the coke causes the oxygen from the iron oxide ore to combine with the carbon from the coke, leaving iron in liquid form; the balance of the iron ore mixes with the flux and the residual coke ash to form slag. Both the liquid pig iron and the slag are "tapped" out of the bottom of the furnace, while new sinter, coke, and flux are added at the top.

An alternative to the use of sinter plants is to supply the blast furnace with iron ore pellets, which are typically produced close to the iron ore mine. There pulverized ore is upgraded by magnetic separation or flotation, and the concentrate is mixed with coal dust and a binder material (usually hydrated lime) and formed into pellets for transport to the blast furnace. Pellets typically have twice the percentage of iron as unprocessed ore. Pellets are thus a much cheaper form in which to ship iron from the mine to the mill.

Much effort has been put into developing ways less expensive than the blast furnace to produce iron. A number of techniques have been developed for the direct reduction of iron from ore, using either gas or coal as fuel and reducing agent. The oxygen in the iron oxide combines with the carbon in the reductant, just as in the blast furnace; but the reduction to pig iron is not complete, leaving a metallic sponge iron product that is 80 percent or more iron. The process is not continuous, nor does it produce iron in a liquid form. Most such sponge iron is charged directly into an electric furnace in place of scrap, though it may be further refined in the recently developed COREX process. In this, sponge iron is transferred to a second furnace known as a melter gasifier, where it is heated along with coal to higher temperatures than in the direct reduction stage. The impurities in the iron combine with the carbon monoxide and hydrogen gases liberated from the gasified coal, and molten iron is left similar to that produced by the blast furnace.

The problem with each of the direct reduction processes is that they are very energy-intensive. They have been commercialized most successfully in countries with large supplies of cheap gas or coal that is not suitable for coking, such as Venezuela and India. Direct reduction had a false start in the United States and Canada in the late 1970s. Five commercial-scale plants were built using natural gas fuel, but three were mothballed when energy price increases made them uneconomical compared to the cost of buying scrap. Plants in Mexico have had better economics, because of both lower prices of natural gas and less availability of scrap.

NEXT MELT YOUR STEEL . . .

Once metallic iron is available, whether as pig iron, some form of directly reduced iron (DRI), or scrap, it is charged into a steel furnace. Three major types are used in the world, although one, the open-hearth furnace, is obsolete and now confined to a shrinking number of facilities in China and Eastern Europe. Open-hearth furnaces dominated steelmaking in North America until the 1960s, but the last ones in the United States were closed down in 1991. Although the open-hearth furnace had the advantage of being able to accept a variable mix of either pig iron or scrap, it also had the disadvantage of taking a much longer time, and consequently more energy and labor, to produce a given volume of steel than either of its rival methods, the basic oxygen furnace and the electric arc furnace.

The basic oxygen furnace (BOF) uses liquid pig iron plus a percentage of scrap (up to 20 percent) as metallic inputs. A post–World War II development of the earlier Bessemer converter, a BOF converter is a pear-shaped vessel holding up to 300 tons of liquid metal, onto which oxygen is blown at high pressure. This reacts with the carbon in the iron charge, creating great heat and forming carbon monoxide (CO) and carbon dioxide (CO2). Fluxes—lime, fluorspar and magnesite—are added, which foam and trap impurities in the metal in a slag. After approximately forty minutes the "heat" is ready to be tapped into a ladle for casting. BOFs accounted for just over 60.6 percent of U.S. raw steel production in both 1993 and 1994, when the industry operated close to its practical capacity. The Canadian percentage in each year was slightly higher, at 65.1 percent in 1993 and 61.4 percent in 1994. The balance of production in both countries was by electric-arc furnaces.

Electric arc furnaces (EFs) are usually charged with shredded iron and steel scrap, although directly reduced iron (DRI) or iron carbide is an alternative metallic charge. Lime is also added as the slag-forming agent. Electrodes are lowered into the furnace to just above the scrap charge and a powerful current is directed through them. The intense heat of the resulting arc between the electrodes melts the metal. As in the BOF, oxygen is injected into the molten metal to refine it to steel by removing excess carbon as a gas and other impurities in a slag. The slag is poured off the surface of the liquid metal, and the refined steel tapped into a ladle as from the BOF.

EFs have the advantage of greater flexibility in steelmaking, because the electric current allows greater control of the process. Steelmakers frequently use analogies to cooking when they refer to the refining process; BOF steel is like a baked product, where the ingredients are charged once and placed in the oven to cook, while the EF is more like a stewing pot, where the mix can be sampled, alloys added, the steel further refined by forming and removing extra slags, and so on. The first EFs were small furnaces used for making specialty steels, where great care had to be taken to get the mix just right. By the 1960s, however, EFs with capacities up to 400 tons—bigger than the largest BOFs—were developed for producing carbon steel.

Due to slow but steady growth of the electric furnace, by 1996 a little more than half of all iron inputs are recycled scrap (including scrap charged into BOFs). The proportion of steel being recycled in this way is likely to continue to increase over the next several years, but the future availability and price of increased quantities of scrap causes uncertainty for the industry.

ALLOY TO TASTE, AND SIMMER UNTIL READY . . .

The second important evolution in steelmaking goes under a number of names, including secondary steelmaking and ladle refining. In each case the term refers to a range of things done to the steel *after* it has been fully melted in the furnace and *before* it is cast into a solid shape. There are really two separate processes, both involving the ladle, the vessel that carries the liquid steel from the furnace. In one, the ladle is used to maintain or increase the temperature of the steel, by the use of a ladle furnace. Ladle furnaces resemble electric-arc furnaces, but with lower power as the steel is already at a high temperature. Secondly, the ladle may be used to perform alloying, stirring, and mixing operations to fine-tune the chemistry of the steel; this is called ladle metallurgy. Separating the melting operation from these finishing operations has a number of advantages. It allows much more efficient use of the (higher-power) melting furnace, which can produce more heats per shift when the time-consuming fine-tuning is done off-line. Also, more precise control of the temperature and chemical properties of the heat is possible in the ladle than in the BOF or electric furnace. Finally the use of the ladle to maintain the temperature of the heat of steel allows flexibility in sequencing steelmaking with casting. Melting is a batch process, while continuous casting is (or should be) a continuous process; on the other hand, casters have the unfortunate habit of going off-line just when a melt of steel is ready to be poured. Briefly, then, ladle furnaces allow greater efficiency, while ladle metallurgy allows greater quality.

Common ladle metallurgy processes include vacuum degassing, where the ladle is placed in a vacuum chamber and the steel stirred. Gases such as nitrogen, hydrogen, and oxygen dissolved in the steel are dissipated into the vacuum. For stainless steel production, a ladle refining process known as argon-oxygen decarburization (AOD) is commonly used. A mixture of argon and oxygen is injected into the metal at the base of the AOD vessel. The oxygen oxidizes excess carbon in the melt while the argon prevents chromium being lost to the slag. Regardless of the grade of steel produced, degassing, decarburizing, and alloying operations are now mostly undertaken at the ladle furnace or secondary steelmaking stage. The only major group of steel mills that have not adopted some form of these processes are those producing the lowest-quality steel commodities, such as concrete-reinforcing bars (re-bar).

. . . THEN POUR TO SHAPE

Liquid steel is cast into a solid shape by pouring it into molds. Traditionally, most liquid steel was cast into ingots, solid blocks of steel that would be transported to a rolling mill for reheating and rolling into a finished shape. Ingots are usually square in cross section (occasionally rectangular or octagonal) and are tapered along their length for ease of withdrawing the cooled steel from the ingot mold. A small proportion of liquid steel is poured directly into casting molds, that is, finished product shapes, usually of quite complex forms that would be difficult to produce by rolling and cutting steel. Casting molds are generally made in sand from a pattern of the required product. Steel use for castings in the foundry industry accounts for less than 1 percent of U.S. steel consumption.

Since the 1960s, ingot casting has been largely replaced worldwide by continuous casting. In a continuous caster, liquid steel is poured into a tundish, a funnel-like vessel large enough to hold temporarily the volume of steel being poured from the ladle; from the tundish, the steel drains slowly down a mold with the cross-sectional shape in which the steel is required. Because the steel cools and solidifies as it moves, it must be pulled through the curved mold at a steady speed to make room for additional steel entering at the top. At the bottom of the mold the solidified shape is cut into lengths suitable for the rolling mill.

Continuous casting effects major cost savings in a number of ways. It eliminates the necessity of an intermediate process known as roughing, in which ingots are rolled into a shape suitable for feeding into the rolling mill selected to produce the final product. For example, to feed a hot-strip mill that produces flat-rolled steel, ingots are first rolled into rectangular slabs in a slabbing mill, and the slabs then fed to the hot-strip mill. A continuous slab caster, in contrast, produces slabs of dimensions that can be fed directly to the hot-strip mill. At each rolling stage, significant costs are incurred in reheating the steel to a temperature at which it can be worked more easily, not to mention the labor and capital costs associated with each mill. Another area of savings is in the increased yield of finished steel product from each ton of raw (liquid) steel, which is improved by at least 5 percent with continuous casting; in addition, the quality of the steel is improved through a more consistent internal grain structure.

The advantages of continuous casting are so clear that by 1995 more than 90 percent of steel made in the United States was cast by a continuous process, compared to less than 10 percent in 1970. By 2000, only a very small number of specialty steel mills will continue to ingot cast, producing small lots of alloy grades that are difficult to cast continuously or that must be subjected to extra hot-working to provide desired metallurgical properties or workability.

THE CAST PRODUCT: HALFWAY THERE

After all the complex processes leading up to casting the steel have been performed, the end product is still something that only a steelworker could love. The product of a continuous caster is a semifinished steel shape known as a slab, a bloom, or a billet, depending on its size and cross section. Ingots must be reheated and rolled into one of these same shapes. None is of much use in itself. They all are simply raw materials, although they have greater value added than materials produced further upstream in the sequence.

Slabs, used to roll plates and coils of flat-rolled steel, are of rectangular cross section and must be at least twice as wide as thick. Typical slab sizes are from 4 to 10 inches thick and from 34 to 100 inches wide. Blooms, used to roll heavy, long steel products such as beams and rails, are of square or rectangular cross section; if rectangular, the width must be less than twice the thickness or the product is classed as a slab. Billets are smaller-size blooms; by definition, they are semifinished shapes with sides of less than 6 inches, or 150 millimeters. Blooms and billets are sometimes cast with a round cross-section, notably for use in the production of seamless tubing.

As continuous casting technology develops, the aim is always to cast the liquid steel into a shape that resembles as closely as possible the finished product, thereby minimizing the amount of rolling that must be done before the steel is sold. In 1996 several companies around the world were experimenting with direct strip casting, attempting to produce a thin sheet of steel without rolling, but this technology is not yet fully commercialized. The most advanced casters in commercial service are thin slab casters, used by the new flat-rolled steel minimills to produce slabs less than 2 inches thick; and for long products, near-net-shape casters produce a shape whose cross section is sometimes described as a dog bone, a shape roughly resembling the outline of a finished steel beam.

Semifinished shapes are traded between steel companies, but are not normally sold to customers like manufacturers or steel fabricators. To be transformed into a usable product, the semifinished steel must be heated once more and worked into a shape known as a steel mill product. The great majority of steel mill products are produced on hot rolling mills to the finished shape demanded by the market. About one-third of steel products are also subsequently cold worked, to produce fine tolerances or sheets thinner than about 0.05 inches, or 1.25 mm.

Although rolling is by far the most common hot working process for forming steel, about 2 percent of steel products are formed by extrusion or by forging in hydraulic presses, usually to produce complex shapes or to process steel grades that are difficult to form by conventional casting and rolling processes. The forging industry, like the foundry industry, is generally independent from the steel mill industry in North America today, although one major company, Bethlehem Steel, retains a large forging subsidiary.

A third specialized hot forming process—the seamless tube mill—has remained within the mainstream of the steel industry. Unlike welded pipes and tubes, which are formed over rolls from strip steel or plates and welded closed along a seam to produce the finished shape, seamless pipes and tubes for use in very high pressure applications are produced from a solid cast of steel to avoid the potential weak point of the weld seam. Seamless tubes are manufactured by the hot piercing process; a heated round billet is pierced in its center by a mandrel and the billet drawn lengthwise over the mandrel by the pressure of rotating rolls shaped to the external circumference of the billet. The resulting "rough" tube is then rolled to the desired inside and outside diameters, again using mandrels for the inside of the finished tube.

ROLLING MILLS: ONE INDUSTRY OR MANY?

Until the 1970s, major steel mills in North America typically operated a range of rolling mills to produce a variety of shapes of steel mill product. Steel was cast into a single semifinished form—ingots—and then transported to product departments, which would transform the ingots first into the appropriate semifinished shape—billets for bar mills, slabs for flat products, and so on—and then, with further rolling, produce the actual bars, sheets, and other hot-rolled products. Many mills then went further and produced, within the one large complex, cold-rolled, drawn, or welded products. In the 1960s U.S. Steel's Gary Works in Indiana, for example, converted around 8 million tons of ingots a year into finished steel products including plates, hot- and cold-rolled coils, galvanized sheets, tinplate, rails, tie plates, a variety of cross sections of bars, both seamless and welded pipe, and forged products such as railroad wheels.

However, during the 1980s this picture was radically transformed as major steel mills, such as the Gary Works, closed essentially all their finishing mills except those producing flat-rolled steel. Gary today continues to cast around 7 million tons of steel a year, but all of it is finished as plate or sheet products. The reasons for this specialization include both the effects of competition, as minimills drove integrated companies out of many product lines, and also of technology, as continuous casters forced mills to select which semifinished shape they would cast.[4] When ingot casting was eliminated, an expensive stage of the rolling process was cut out, at the cost of flexibility by which almost any finished products could be rolled from ingots, given enough breakdown rolling into the right rough shape.

Very broadly, two types of hot-rolled products are distinguished in the steel industry—flat products and long products. Each of these can be subdivided into families of related products, such as bars (which might be of round, square, flat, hexagon, angle, channel or more unusual cross sections, but which can all be rolled on the same type of mill given the appropriate finishing rolls). In the 1990s, very few steel mills produce more than a single family of products. The exceptions tend to roll closely related families, such as plate with sheet products, or bar with structural products or rails.[5]

FLAT PRODUCTS

In North America, a little over 55 percent of finished steel is rolled on a hot-strip mill. This percentage has remained broadly stable over the last thirty years. The forty hot-strip mills operating in Canada, the United States, and Mexico at the beginning of 1995 were of a wide variety of capacities, widths, and vintages. Six of these were smaller-capacity mills, used to produce either stainless steel, skelp (the narrow strip that is used to produce welded pipe and tube), or narrow strip for special applications. The remainder are large-scale production facilities, with capacities ranging from 1 million to 5.7 million tons per year. All but one are located at or close to the steelmaking facilities that supply them with slabs.[6] Most of their output was coiled sheets in widths from 36 to 96 inches, in thickness from 0.054 to 0.175 inches, and weighing from 5 to 40 tons.

In a hot-strip mill, the slab passes through a number of sets of powered rollers known as stands, set in line, with each set reducing the thickness of the material until the finished dimension is reached. Mills may be continuous, with a single pass through each stand, or semi-continuous. In semi-continuous mills, the first stand is a powerful reversing stand through which the steel makes a number of passes, each of which reduces its size, before it is sent through the remaining finishing stands. An alternative type of semi-continuous mill, the Steckel mill, has a single finishing stand through which the steel makes a number of passes to roll the strip down to size. At each end of the finishing stand is a coil box, in which the strip is coiled and uncoiled as the operation continues, while in each box a reheating furnace maintains the strip at a hot enough temperature to allow easy hot rolling.

Plate mills are also supplied with slabs. Any flat steel 3/16 inches or thicker is defined in North America as a plate; however, hot-strip mills can roll coils of steel plate up to ½ inch thick, usually known as coil plate, continuous mill plate, or strip mill plate. Plate mills roll heavy plate and wider plates than can be produced in coil form from a strip mill, usually using one or two reversing stands to roll slabs down to thinner and wider plates.

LONG PRODUCTS

Structural and bar mills are used to roll long products—structural shapes such as beams, channels, and angles; bars with round, square, rectangular, or hexagonal cross sections; and special shapes such as piling and for applications in the truck body and mobile home industries. Depending on size, the semifinished steel is in the form of blooms or billets. As in hot-strip mills, there are a number of mill stands of powered rollers, usually but not always continuous; the heavier the input and output, the more likely the mill is to have one or more reversing stands. Thus mills producing heavy wide flange beams, known as structural mills, or rail mills, their close relatives, have two or more reversing stands; while smaller bar mills, which also produce structural shapes, but in smaller sizes, may have as many as sixteen stands for continuous operation. These stands are typically in a straight line, but certain bar mills have stands set side by side; they are known as "cross-country mills". As the bar is rolled down from billets toward the finished shape, it is bent through guides that loop the steel around through 180$ and direct it into the next stand of the mill. In this way the same drive can power three or more stands of the mill, and the building can be shorter in length.

A special type of bar mill is the rod mill, producing wire rod that is then drawn down into wire. Unlike bars and shapes, which are commonly cut to lengths of 12, 20, or 40 feet, wire rod is coiled in lengths of hundreds of feet, necessary for drawing wires that can run to many thousands of feet. Sometimes a bar mill contains a rod block, for coiling wire rod, as well as shears for cutting bars and shapes; in other mills, dedicated rod mills produce nothing but wire rod. Thirty years ago most wire was produced by the same steel mill that rolled it as wire rod. However, today most wire is drawn from rod at independent wire companies or at least at separate divisions of the same company, so the steel industry could be said to produce the wire rod rather than the wire.[7]

VALUE-ADDED PRODUCTS: TO ADD OR NOT TO ADD?

The steelmaking and hot-rolling processes described so far produce the steel mill product forms—strip, plate, bars, beams and so on—that are the basis of all subsequent processing and fabrication of steel. Value is added to these basic steel mill products in a number of ways before they are sold to manufacturers or construction industry contractors. However, the question of whether steel producers *should* add value to their products is widely debated. It is possible to argue either for specialization by process and keeping a tight focus on a company's core expertise in steel melting and rolling; equally it can be argued that it is foolish not to sell the highest-value product practicable and therefore to perform downstream operations in-house. Both arguments have merit and can be supported by pointing to successful company strategies. In retrospect, the decades of the 1970s and 1980s were clearly a time of deintegration in the industry, with established firms leaving their peripheral downstream businesses and the rise of specialized downstream firms as well as specialized upstream minimills. In the 1990s, however, there are signs of a contrary trend gathering pace, as minimill companies become more sophisticated and as global competition in basic steel products shows no sign of relaxing.

Successful strategies for adding value to steel mill products tend to be as much about controlling captive outlets for steel tonnage as for increasing overall margins or return on investment. Thus because Nucor's bar mills supply Nucor's joist manufacturing operations, a significant base load of tonnage not sensitive to price competition is guaranteed to the steelmaking operation. Similarly, a traditional integrated mill such as Wheeling-Pittsburgh has grown its downstream operations converting sheet into corrugated steel culverts and prefabricated metal buildings, for example, thus providing a cushion in lean times against having to endure cutthroat price competition for every ton. Perhaps because of this tendency to subsidize the steel mill indirectly, though, there is no evidence that the addition of downstream operations increases total returns on the combined investment and, in fact, some evidence that it does the opposite.

Some value-added processes are conventionally considered to be within the scope of the steel industry, while others are considered to be outside it at steel processors or steel fabricators. The distinction can be very arbitrary and has many gray areas; and it changes over time. Today three types of downstream processing of steel are normally considered to be part of the steelmaking, or steel mill, industry: cold working, including cold rolling, drawing (except for wire), and surface grinding; coating with metallic coatings such as zinc and tin (but *not* normally paint or plastic laminates); and forming and welding into pipe and tubing (but *not* normally other forming and welding operations). Each will be described very briefly here, and more detail can be found in the appendix.

COLD ROLLING AND FINISHING

Over 60 percent of all sheet steel produced as hot-rolled strip in the United States is subsequently cold-rolled. Cold-rolled strip is sold in that form or it is further processed by galvanizing or tinplating for sale as a coated product. Strip that is not cold-rolled can be sold as hot-rolled product or formed into pipe and tube products, but it is not normally galvanized or tinplated.

Strip is cold-rolled on continuous mills that maintain the steel in coils but reduce the thickness of the strip while maintaining close dimensional tolerances and producing a smooth surface finish. Cold-rolling mills are commonly four-high mills—having two rolls above and two below the strip, but with only one of each in contact with the strip. Where great force is needed to compress the steel, for stainless and some specialty steels, more rolls are added that do not touch the strip. The most common proprietary make of these "cluster mills" is the Sendzimir mill. The work rolls on each side of the strip are supported by the non-contact rolls, which absorb the force of compression of the steel and concentrate the power of the mill's motors onto the (often quite small) work roll.

Other cold-working processes include cold drawing of wire, bars, and some pipes and tubes; and the cold-finishing of bars. About 10 percent of steel bars are cold-worked, either by drawing through dies to produce a bar with tight dimensional tolerances and a bright surface finish, or, more often, by turning, grinding, or polishing to improve dimensional and surface characteristics. Specialist companies and some steel mills that hot-roll bars perform the operations of cold drawing and finishing of bars. Commonly the bars to be cold finished are hot rolled with great care. They are part of the category of SBQ, or special bar quality, bar products normally specified for demanding applications in vehicles or machinery. MBQ, or merchant bar quality, products are sold without additional processing to steel fabricators for general purposes in construction or assembly.

COATINGS: TINPLATE AND GALVANIZED STEEL

Steel has a major disadvantage. For all its strength and low cost, iron corrodes (rusts) much faster than most metals in both air and water. There are a number of ways to slow down the process of corrosion. The most expensive, but most effective, method is to alloy the steel with chromium or other metals that inhibit corrosion, as in stainless steel. When this is not cost-effective, or when the alloying metals reduce other desirable properties, such as formability, the alternative is to cover the unalloyed steel with a corrosion-resistant coating. This coating can be something as simple (and short-lived) as paint; plastic or epoxy (more expensive but more resistant); or another metal. Tin and zinc are the two metals most widely applied as coatings by steel mills. The resulting products, known as tinplate and galvanized steel, are used to combat two different types of corrosion. Tinplate is used where the acids of food and beverages could dissolve steel used in containers, thus spoiling the food and threatening health. Galvanized steel is used where steel is exposed to the elements, where rain and humidity would dissolve steel over time, and where paint alone is too short-lived a solution.

Tinplate is a very thin and malleable sheet steel product used for forming cans. After cold rolling to very thin gauges, the steel is coated with a very fine layer—only a few molecules thick—of tin to prevent the steel surface of the can and its contents from coming into contact with each other. Chromium is used as an alternative plating metal to tin in some applications and is applied on the same electroplating lines or "tin mills"—giving rise to the name "tin-free steel." Tin mill products have declined in importance and in absolute tonnage over the last thirty years as aluminum cans have taken away most of the beer and soft drink market from steel. Tinplated steel is still the predominant material in food cans, however, and renewed use in beverage cans is possible given the relatively high cost of aluminum in the 1990s.

When steel must be protected against atmospheric corrosion, in exposed applications such as automobiles and metal buildings, metallic coatings of zinc or zinc alloys such as zinc/aluminum are commonly used. About 30 percent of steel sheet produced in the United States is "galvanized", or zinc-coated, using one of two main processes: electrolytic galvanizing—electroplating in a similar manner to tinplating—and hot-dip galvanizing. Hot-dip galvanizing, as the name suggests, is a process of immersing heated steel in a bath of the molten metal coating. The thickness and evenness of the coating is regulated by spraying air or steam over the strip surface as it exits the bath. Galvanizing is most often applied to cold-rolled, lighter gauges of sheet, although heavier-gauge, hot-rolled sheet is also galvanized (often after being corrugated) for structural applications such as metal roofs, silos, and culverts.

Steel that has been electrogalvanized on both sides is now commonly specified for automobile body applications, as automakers have improved quality over the last ten years. Until the 1980s, automotive steel was commonly uncoated cold-rolled sheet, or sheet that was galvanized on one (the exposed) side only. The auto industry is a leader in developing new coatings, such as zinc/nickel alloy coating, and in multiple layers of coating, which may include metal, plastic film, and then paint. Nonmetallic coatings are more commonly applied outside the steel mill, at specialist coil-coating companies.

PIPE AND TUBING

The final steel mill product that this overview must touch upon is welded pipe and tubing. These products are fabricated from flat-rolled steel sheet and plate, often supplied as skelp, a hot-rolled strip product sized to the appropriate widths for forming into standard pipe sizes. Pipe is distinguished from round tubing by the most arbitrary of distinctions. If a tube meets the dimensional specifications (outside and inside diameter) of standard pipe sizes, it is a pipe; if not, it is a tube. Tubing also can be formed into square and rectangular cross sections; these are commonly used in structural, load-bearing applications rather than to carry fluids.

Whether pipe and tubing are properly considered part of the steel industry is debatable. I believe that because of the sheer size of the tubulars sector, it must be included. Total pipe and tube sales to end users in the United States amount to about $10 billion annually, about one-third the size of the total steel mill industry. However, such a number includes imports, sales of independent pipe and tube mills, pipe processors and finishers as well as pipe and tubing manufactured by steel mills. Until the 1970s, steelmakers produced most pipe and tubing. And they still do, including most seamless pipe and most large-sized pipes. But a large and growing number of independent companies do not identify themselves with the steel industry but rather with their product's target market, such as automobile parts or building products. Significant additional tonnages, produced by steel mills, are finished by independent companies by cold drawing, coating, threading, and other operations. The pipe and tube sector is therefore hard to measure. U.S. companies that do consider themselves sufficiently part of the steel industry to report their pipe and tube production to the industry's trade group, the American Iron and Steel Institute (AISI), produced nearly 5 million tons of tubular products in 1994; but as much as another 3 million tons of sheet and plate (domestic or imported) goes to nonreporting companies for conversion. Statistics Canada does not report Canadian pipe and tube production as a steel mill product, but Canadian production appears to account for close to another 1 million tons per year.

Pipe and tubing is commonly divided into a number of categories by end use, which largely but not entirely governs the specifications of the product. The AISI uses eight product categories, not including classification by the process of manufacture—seamless or the various techniques of forming welded pipe. Some categories are inevitably arbitrary and overlapping, and differ from the categories used in other countries' statistics or in U.S. trade data. In the appendices the sector is divided into seven sometimes overlapping categories: five carbon steel groupings by major end use or application, plus the specialized product/market categories of seamless carbon steel pipe and tubing, and stainless steel pipe and tubing.

Since 1970, one pipe market in particular has had a major impact on the overall steel industry. The pipe products known as Oil Country Tubular Goods, often shortened to OCTG, includes welded and seamless pipes used downhole in the oil and gas industry, for drill pipe, production tubing, and well casing. The energy boom of the late 1970s and early 1980s led many steel companies to plunge into this market, leading to major losses and overcapacity when the bubble burst in 1982.

SECONDARY PROCESSORS

As a steel product moves downstream—away from the point at which it is first rolled and as it has additional operations performed on it to add value—the steel industry becomes more diffuse and hard to measure. Independent cold finishers, galvanizers, and pipe producers and coaters are examples of companies that are important parts of the steel industry in North America, but which are often overlooked because of the lack of hard statistics about their operations. These companies have grown in their share of the total steel market over the last thirty years, as major steel companies have specialized and shed operations not considered part of their core steelmaking business. These specialized companies are sometimes collectively termed secondary processors, a phrase that invites confusion with the terminology used in nonferrous metals, where "secondary" means recycled metals, as opposed to "primary" metals from ore. Perhaps because the steel industry has always recycled at least its own "home" scrap in its mills, it has never drawn the distinction between "primary" and "secondary" in the same way as in other metal industries. The difference in terminology may, however, reflect a fundamental underlying difference between steel and other major metals industries.

Steel is an "above-ground" industry: money is made by melting and rolling steel, not by mining. The production of copper, lead, zinc, nickel, or the precious metals, by comparison, are "in-ground" industries: the key to success is control of a scarce orebody and a low-cost mining operation. Aluminum has made a transition over time from an "in-ground" to an "above-ground" industry as the recycling of secondary aluminum has grown and as power costs have come to dominate the economics of aluminum smelting and refining. Steel is also an industry that brings together a number of raw materials to a greater extent than other metals, not just the metal ore from which the finished product is derived. Iron ore is essential to integrated steelmaking, but so are other raw materials: coal for coking or direct injection into the blast furnace; fluxes, such as fluorspar, limestone, and lime; manganese and other alloying metals. Although the larger integrated steel companies still own mines that supply much of their iron ore, coal, and flux requirements, other integrated companies do not, and independent iron ore companies have always been a feature of the North American industry.

While this study focuses on the steelmaking segment of the industry, the largest component in terms of value added to the metal, it is important to remember that the steel industry is really four distinct but interdependent industries: raw materials, steelmaking, secondary processing, and distribution. Before proceeding to detail the transformation of the steelmaking segment of the industry and its associated secondary processing operations, a brief overview of the raw materials and the distribution segments of the industry is relevant. Which of these is the front end and which the back end of the industry depends on one's perspective.

IRON ORE

The iron ore mining industry produces a commodity with a low value-to-weight ratio. The value of ore in concentrates or pellets at the mine is typically less than half its value when delivered to a steel mill; the difference is the cost of freight. Because freight looms so large in the economics of iron ore, access to water transportation is critical. Modern integrated steel mills in Japan, Korea, and Europe are located at seaports into which ore carriers of as much as 250,000 cargo tons can bring ore from producers such as Australia, Brazil, and South Africa. In North America, however, only one integrated mill remains located on saltwater, the Bethlehem Steel mill at Sparrows Point, Maryland, and it is limited by port capacity to cargoes of around 65,000 tons. Inland integrated mills can be divided into those located on the Great Lakes (some eleven U.S. and four Canadian mills); those inland but on the Mississippi River system (four mills on the Ohio river system and one in the St. Louis area); and others dependent on rail access only (two in Ohio, two in Alabama, and one in Utah).

Within the upper Great Lakes—upstream of the Welland Canal section of the St. Lawrence Seaway that separates Lake Ontario from Lake Erie—cargoes of about 60,000 metric tons can be carried from Michigan and Minnesota mines close to Lake Superior to lakeside mills in the Chicago, Detroit, and Cleveland areas. The St. Lawrence seaway locks, both at the Welland Canal and on the St. Lawrence River section, limit passage to ships of less than 730 feet, or to ore cargoes of around 25,000 tons; the upper lakes' "1,000 footers" cannot leave the lakes, nor can large seagoing ore carriers enter the lakes. A cost barrier, that reflects the need to transship overseas ore, tends to keep lakeshore mills reliant on lakeshore ores.[8] The major drawback to the lakes as a supply route is the winter closure; typically the lakes are iced over for three months from mid-January. This necessitates stockpiling of ore at the mills or the more expensive use of rail transport during this period.

Mills located on the Mississippi River system have the option of bringing overseas ore—mostly from Brazil, Venezuela, and Canadian ore from Labrador—to New Orleans, then transshipping by river barge. This procedure has proved cost-competitive with bringing Lake Superior ore to Lake Erie ports and then transshipping to rail to the Pittsburgh area, for example. These mills typically source their ores from both overseas and Lake Superior sources and use a variety of sea/rail, sea/barge, lake/rail, and all-rail routes to the mill; still, on average, they face higher ore costs than mills at coastal or lakeside locations due to the transshipment costs.

The least advantageously sited integrated mills are those located away from any water transport. The mills at Warren and Middletown, Ohio, rely chiefly on domestic ores brought either by all-rail transportation or by transshipping from lake freighters at Toledo or Cleveland. The mills at Fairfield and Gadsden, Alabama, at present use a mix of overseas ores transshipped at the port of Mobile, then carried inland by rail or barge and rail combination, plus a small amount of Lake Superior ore by rail. The Geneva, Utah, mill relies on Minnesota ore by rail, plus Utah ore from the company's mines.[9]

Most integrated mills away from lake or tidal water were originally sited close to local sources of iron ore and coal; over time, these reserves dwindled. Of the twenty integrated steel mills closed or "deintegrated" in the United States in the 20 years from 1975 to 1995, only five were located on deep water. The other fifteen may have suffered from a wide range of problems, but clearly high ore freight costs was one factor in a number of closures. In twenty years the North American industry has gone from having twenty-five inland and twenty-one deepwater (lake and ocean) integrated locations, to sixteen deepwater and just ten inland sites.

The ore industry in North America is highly integrated with the steel industries of the United States and Canada. About 80 percent of ore production is from companies controlled by the integrated steel companies. Although two companies, U.S. Steel and LTV, have wholly owned iron ore mining operations, a more usual ownership pattern is for a number of U.S. and Canadian companies to share in joint venture mining operations, sometimes with other nonsteel interests, in the Lake Superior area or in Labrador. Two companies, Algoma Steel in northern Ontario and Geneva Steel in Utah, still operate wholly owned mines at sites close to their steel operations. However, these captive facilities can supply only part of the mill's needs. In 1994, iron ore was produced from twenty U.S. and nine Canadian mines, the bulk of which was agglomerated at ten U.S. and five Canadian pelletizing plants. The Mexican iron ore industry was relatively self-contained, with its mines and five pelletizing plants supplying the needs of its domestic steel industry, which includes three integrated companies and two that use directly reduced iron in electric furnaces.

From 1990 to 1995, U.S. steel mill consumption of iron ore averaged around 70 million metric tons of pellets, concentrates, and direct shipping ore, of which nearly 80 percent came from Minnesota and Michigan. These supplies averaged a little less than 70 percent iron content, leading to production of between 44 and 50 million metric tons of pig iron each year, plus around 400,000 tons of DRI from one operating direct reduction plant.

FEEDING THE BLAST FURNACE

More than half of U.S. and Canadian iron ore production is now shipped in the form of fluxed pellets—pellets in which limestone or dolomite is added to the concentrated iron ore, thus combining two of the three major integrated steelmaking raw materials. Fluxes are used in both ironmaking (blast furnaces) and steelmaking (basic oxygen or electric furnaces), as agents that combine with silicon, phosphorous, sulfur, and other impurities and separate these from the iron as slag. The steel industry uses between 5 and 6 million metric tons of fluxes each year; two-thirds are charged into steelmaking furnaces, the rest into blast furnaces either directly or as a binder in sinter or ore pellets. All contain calcium; the commonest flux is quicklime, or calcium oxide (CaO), formed by calcinating limestone ($CaCO_3$) or other calcium-containing minerals such as dolomite at high temperatures to release carbon dioxide and leave quicklime. Other flux materials are metallurgical-grade fluorspar (CaF_2); hydrated lime ($Ca(OH)_2$) which contains 24 percent combined water; or uncalcinated limestone or dolomite, which are cheap but contain a lower proportion of reactive material. A small proportion of dolomitic quicklime (CaO•MgO) often is used as a way of increasing the life of the refractory brick linings of the furnaces—dead-burned dolomite is a major component of refractory bricks.

The steel industry does not control or dominate the lime or fluorspar industries as it does iron ore production, which reflects its more limited role as just one of a number of users of these products. Steel consumes about 15 percent of fluorspar and 30 percent of lime used in the United States. Although in the 1960s integrated steel companies often owned limestone or fluorspar mines, in the last two decades most of these properties have been sold off. The United States and Canada are essentially self-sufficient in lime production, although they trade between themselves. Mexico is a significant net exporter of lime.

The third major blast furnace raw material, coal, is both an energy source and a vital ingredient in the reaction that forms carbon-bearing iron. Coal in its natural form is not a particularly powerful energy source, it does not burn uniformly, and it has the disadvantage of packing down and clogging the air flow in blast furnaces. It has therefore traditionally been concentrated into coke by baking in ovens at integrated steel mills. In the 1990s, an increasing number of blast furnaces in North America were retrofitted for the injection of pulverized coal directly into the furnace, as a partial substitute for coke.

The disadvantage to coke is the toxic nature of the process used for its production; the gases and tars produced as the coal bakes are valuable raw materials in chemicals production, but the environmental controls required to contain emissions are expensive to install and to operate. U.S. coal consumption in steelmaking has declined steadily since the mid-1970s, from 90.3 million net tons in 1973 to 27.8 million in 1993, reflecting not only reduced use of blast furnaces but great improvements in the efficiency of their use of coke; the growth of imports of metallurgical coke to around 5 million net tons a year in the 1990s, or 20 percent of the total coke used; and a decline in the use of coal to generate electric power at steel mills. Coking capacity in the United States has been reduced by 60 percent since 1973, as many obsolete and polluting coke batteries have been closed and not replaced.

Five major North American steel companies still operate wholly owned coal mines. Others have sold or reduced their interests, reflecting their reduced needs and the generally widespread availability of metallurgical coal in the United States. Canadian coal needs for steelmaking are generally imported from the United States.

ORE VS. SCRAP

In 1993, an average year for steel production compared to the highs and lows of the last economic cycle, 59,393,000 net tons (53,881,000 metric tons) of raw steel were produced at integrated mills in basic oxygen furnaces (BOFs). Producing this steel took inputs of 52,742,000 net tons of blast furnace pig iron, plus 83,000 net tons of directly charged ore and agglomerates and 15,739,000 net tons of scrap (much of it generated within the steel mill), for a total of 68,564,000 tons of metallic inputs.[10] By comparison, electric furnaces consumed 40,499,000 short tons of scrap, plus 150,000 tons of pig iron, to produce 38,524,000 tons of raw steel, or 39.4 percent of the U.S. total. Canadian integrated production was slightly higher in proportion; BOFs produced 10,136,503 net tons in 1993, while EFs produced 5,622,369 tons, or 35.68 percent.

Note that in 1993, as in each year since 1984, more than 50 percent of the iron inputs to U.S. steelmaking—58,515,000 net tons—were in the form of scrap. Scrap is not only the primary raw material for EF steelmaking, but also represents 23 percent of the iron charge on BOFs. While this percentage of scrap inputs to BOFs is close to the economic limit given the nature of the technology, it does challenge the common view that BOFs are inflexible in their materials requirements.

Scrap is commonly divided into three types by origin: home scrap, that is, scrap generated within the steel mill, sometimes known as revert or recirculating scrap; prompt industrial scrap, generated by manufacturing processes such as stamping plants; and obsolete scrap, metal recovered from discarded or dismantled products ranging from cans to buildings. The first two are the most valuable, although only prompt industrial scrap is priced by bids in the marketplace, because in each case the exact content and origin of the metal is known, and the scrap is likely to be in a form that can quickly be fed into the furnace with a minimum of processing. Obsolete scrap comes in a wide range of grades, including stainless and alloy grades; a small amount is generated in steel mills, from sources such as obsolete buildings and ingot molds, but the great majority of it comes from specialist scrap processors and dealers. Some electric furnace steel companies maintain their own scrapyards, primarily for shredding automobiles, to supply a base load of scrap; the bulk of steelmakers' scrap needs are purchased from outside, however, and independent scrap processors sell on average over 40 million net tons of steel scrap a year to U.S. mills while exporting a further 10 million tons. The $6 billion U.S. ferrous scrap business has evolved into a modern and highly competitive industry, and because scrap is very widely traded in a market with no nationally dominant buyers or sellers, the market tends to react very quickly to changes in supply or demand, and prices fluctuate considerably over time.

A perennial question concerning the future direction of the North American steel industry is whether the availability of scrap will permit the expansion of electric furnace steelmaking. Scrap shortages have been predicted at various times over the past twenty years, and each time the market prices of scrap approach the upper ends of the ranges for different grades, new supplies seem to become available. Only one U.S. and one Canadian steel mill have maintained DRI plants in sustained operation in the 1990s, reflecting the availability of scrap at prices below the cost of producing DRI. It is worth noting that U.S. scrap consumption in steel mills was actually at a peak in 1979, with 77,190,000 net tons consumed in steelmaking, or 32 percent more than in 1993. This number is a little misleading in that home scrap generation was far higher fifteen years ago prior to the widespread introduction of continuous casting, but nevertheless the tonnages traded domestically were actually higher in the 1970s than today. Much more scrap was purchased by integrated companies into the 1980s, to supply part of the charge of their open-hearth furnaces and also to supply a significant number of large electric furnaces operated by companies that also operated integrated steelmaking facilities.

The United States has been considered a scrap surplus area since the 1920s, exporting ferrous scrap to electric furnace steelmakers worldwide. As industrialized countries such as Germany and Japan have reached the stage of universal automobile and appliance ownership, they too have become scrap surplus countries, joining the United States and United Kingdom as scrap exporters; fast-developing countries such as Turkey and Korea have become major purchasers of scrap for their growing steel industries.

While some parts of the United States, such as the Northwest, have relatively less high-grade scrap than others, implying cost disadvantages to scrap users located in such states, it appears that the U.S. scrap industry is able to supply the additional 6 million tons of new electric furnace steelmaking capacity added between 1995 and 1997. The relatively strong scrap demand leads to prices that both increase the supply of scrap over time and discourages some export sales, thus maintaining an equilibrium in the market.

Nevertheless, the possibility of sustained higher scrap prices, and in particular the potential costs of high-quality scrap, has caused a number of steelmakers to reexamine options for alternative iron sources. The largest electric furnace steelmaker, Nucor, whose seven mills required around 7 million tons of scrap feed in 1994, opened a plant in Trinidad that year to process Venezuelan iron ore into iron carbide pellets, using cheap local natural gas. By 1996, this permitted delivery of a high-quality scrap substitute to southern U.S. ports for around $100 a net ton, compared with prices for high grade shredded scrap in the $120 to $140 range. Nucor foresaw the iron carbide operation eventually supplying 1.32 million tons a year, which would, in effect, act as a high-quality component of the overall scrap stream of differing grades blended in the steelmaking process. Nucor has also purchased DRI from Russia and elsewhere, and in 1996 a number of companies were planning other iron carbide and DRI plants. The metallics supply choices that steelmakers will face in the next decade are examined in chapter 8.

FERROALLOYS

One other critical raw materials industry that supplies steelmakers is the ferroalloys industry. Ferroalloys are the alloying metals added to steel to confer properties such as hardness, tensile strength, and corrosion resistance. Manganese and silicon are used in small quantities in the production of carbon steels; other metals are used chiefly in the production of alloy or stainless steels. Alloying metals are usually charged into the steelmaking furnace in the form of ferroalloys—compounds of the alloy metal with iron in a known proportion. Ferromanganese, ferrosilicon, and ferrochrome are the three largest ferroalloys consumed in the United States. Using an intermediate ferroalloy product allows for ease of handling metals that are easily contaminated or volatile and allows a precise and pure quantity of the alloy to be added to the steel. Two major alloying metals, nickel and molybdenum, are not difficult to store or handle, and are charged directly into steelmaking furnaces in the form of briquettes, pellets of nickel metal, molybdic oxides, or ferronickel or ferromolybdenum. Another terminological problem arises here, as nickel and molybdenum often are not considered ferroalloys but are analyzed separately. For ease of discussion, I call all metals added to steel for their alloying properties ferroalloys, whether they are added in the form of a ferro-metal compound or not.

Ferroalloys are widely traded around the world, reflecting their high value-to-weight ratio and the fact that, with the exception of silicon, they are scarce metals, found in ore form at few sites around the world. The United States is the largest producer and exporter of molybdenum, and Canada is the largest exporter and producer of nickel. Other ferroalloys are sourced largely from overseas, which led to major concerns about national security in the United States during the Cold War. Ferroalloys were a major component of the U.S. Department of Defense stockpile of strategic minerals, the disposal of which in the 1990s has had a major depressing effect on a number of markets. The much-reduced stockpile program in 1995 still held quantities of alloying metals and continued to pay to refine them into ferroalloys, but the political life of such programs seemed limited. Table 1.1 shows the U.S. consumption of the major ferroalloys used in steelmaking.

Manganese, whose consumption by the steel industry amounts to about 8 pounds per net ton of steel produced, is not mined in North America. U.S. and Canadian production of ferromanganese is from imported ores and concentrates. The largest import sources of manga-

TABLE 1.1
SOME MAJOR FERROALLOYS

Ferroalloy	Steel Uses	U.S. Production 1992	U.S. Imports 1992	1992 U.S. Steel Industry Consumption
Ferromanganese	Carbon, alloy, stainless	48,000^e	304,000	330,796
Silicomanganese	Carbon (especially spring steels), alloy	30,000^e	257,177	102,947
Ferrosilicon	Carbon, alloy, stainless	346,290	247,601	202,397
Ferrochrome	Stainless, alloy	60,945	410,798	346,114
Ferronickel	Stainless, nickel alloys	2,295	13,015	15,053
Other primary nickel	Stainless, nickel alloys	8,962	102,678	20,309
Ferrovanadium	High-strength, low-alloy, tool steels	2,800^e	798	3,581
Molybdenum oxides and ferromolybdenum	HSLA, alloy and stainless	11,916	2,238	9,174

NOTES:
Metric tons of gross alloy weight, except molybdenum oxides and ferromolybdenum, which are metric tons of contained alloy weight.

^{e} Estimated.

nese are the Republic of Gabon, where a major mine is jointly owned by the U.S. Steel Corporation and French interests, and the Republic of South Africa; the largest sources of imported ferromanganese are France, from Gabonese ore, and South Africa. Other countries producing significant amounts of both manganese ore and ferromanganese are Russia and Brazil.

Chrome, the essential element in stainless steel, is also found in chromite ores in very few places in the world. Both the United States and Canada have small identified chromite reserves, but no current production. The largest producers are Kazakhstan, South Africa, India, and Turkey. U.S. ferrochrome production is largely from ores imported from South Africa, Turkey, and the Philippines. The bulk of North America's ferrochrome supply is imported, with South Africa and Turkey again being the major sources.

The structure of the ferroalloys industry, in North America and worldwide, has undergone great changes over the last twenty years. In the nickel and molybdenum industries, dominated by North American producers, mine and metal production have remained located close to the point of consumption. Additional metals producers in Europe and Japan exist using North American ores. Other ferroalloys, whose ore sources are primarily in developing countries, were traditionally converted to metal by producers associated with the major steelmaking industries and without direct ties to the ore producers.

This pattern has changed dramatically as developing countries have sought to add value to their exports, as the cost of electricity in developed countries has risen in a very power-intensive industry, and as the costs of labor and environmental compliance have further penalized ferroalloys producers in developed countries. North America has gone from being an importer of ores to feed a local ferroalloys industry, to being an importer of ferroalloys. The much-reduced ferroalloys industry uses North American ores (nickel and molybdenum); recovers secondary material; or is kept alive by government subsidy, upgrading materials for the strategic materials stockpile.

THE RISE OF THE SERVICE CENTER

At the other end of the process flow in the steel industry, independent steel distribution is another business that has grown in part by the deintegration of integrated steel. Steel service centers, as they are known in North America, or stockholders, as used elsewhere in the English-speaking world, traditionally make money by holding inventory, breaking down bulk loads, and delivering steel to the manufacturer or fabricator in lots too small for the steel mills to economically handle. Carbon steel mills typically cannot handle orders for less than a truckload of steel (20 tons) at a time, and flat-rolled mills would rather see significantly higher minimum-order quantities. There has always been a place, therefore, for distributors willing to order 5-ton and 10-ton coils of steel, level them into sheets, and deliver them one or two sheets at a time to sheet metal workers. This retail type business accounted for around 20 percent of the total volume of steel sold in the United States until the 1960s.

At that time, the steel service center industry was a two-tier industry. At one level, four of the major integrated steel companies owned chains of distribution outlets, as did a number of specialty mills. These acted as captive outlets for their parent mill's products to smaller customers and accounted for perhaps a quarter of the total distributor business. A second tier was dominated by family-owned small businesses, typically with a single location serving one urban area and its hinterland. Although some such businesses could date their origins back to the nineteenth century or even earlier, most had their origins immediately after World War II, and had started out handling military surplus materials and scrap.[11] In the 1960s many such companies were still involved with the scrap business; and others were involved in the shadowy "secondary" steel trade, either buying steel rejected by mills or their customers as not up to "prime" steel specifications, or salvaging used steel for resale rather than for scrapping.

The independent service centers performed important services for the mills not only in reaching the smaller customers but also in handling secondary material—the mills could earn more by selling this material at a discount to distributors, on the understanding that it would not be certified as to its conformity to standards or its origin traced back, than they could make by recycling the steel back into the furnaces. However, the secondary material did represent a sort of gray market with pricing below the level that mills, led by the U.S. Steel Corporation, had tried to maintain in the marketplace through the 1960s. This situation led inevitably to tensions between the mills and the independent distributors, tensions that worsened after the service centers began to look overseas for supplies of foreign steel at times of domestic steel strikes or shortages.

The ambivalent relationship between these two sections of the industry was not helped by their differences in social composition. The independent distributors were small entrepreneurs with little respect for the attempts of the mills to maintain stability of pricing and market shares in the steel market. They had families to feed, needed to make a dollar, and were not too particular about whom they did business with. The mills' sales organizations, on the other hand, were bureaucracies in which people got to the top by selling their quota and not rocking the carefully balanced boat. To compound the tension, the distributors were largely families who had immigrated to the United States in the twentieth century. Any list of names of the industry's organizations from before the 1970s shows a large predominance of Jewish surnames, plus regional concentrations of Italian, Irish, and Scandinavian families. The mills, on the other hand, limited their management ranks very largely to white Anglo-Saxon Protestant males, even while their labor forces came from every ethnic group in America. In an era when membership of country clubs, for example—all-important to middle managers and small businessmen—was segregated by religion, the social distance made it more difficult to establish close partnerships between mills and independent distributors. This situation was to come to haunt the integrated mills as they began to face shrinking markets and increased competition. Unlike in Europe or Japan, where mill-distributor relationships were much warmer and enhanced by preferential credit terms, U.S. distributors welcomed new steel suppliers, whether domestic or overseas. The openness of the distribution system was a major element in permitting both the internationalization of the North American steel industry and the ability of new entrants to thrive in the market.

The steel service center industry in the mid-1990s handles a little over half of all steel sales to end users. Exact data for the industry are hard to establish, but the industry includes a number of identifiable streams of steel. First, domestic steel mills report their tonnage shipments by product to the AISI, and the larger mills report these shipments by destination market. These reported shipments to service centers amounted to 25.4 percent of domestic shipments in 1994, or 24.2 million net tons. In addition, 12.2 million tons (12.8 percent) were reported as "non-classified" by market. This figure includes both secondary shipments by major steel mills and shipments of small mills that do not keep records of their customers by market. The vast majority of both types of shipment are to service centers, the secondary shipments as a matter of policy, the small mills because of the product mix they roll (merchant bar, for example) and their inability to maintain large sales organizations or service large end users. A third category of domestic shipments that go in part to service centers is reported as "steel for converting and processing," which accounts for a further 10.5 million tons (11.0 percent); this category includes both steel to, for example, independent pipe and tube mills, who in turn sell products such as structural tubing through service centers; and also shipments to independent coil processors that may or may not consider themselves, or function as, distributors. Among these three categories, the actual percentage of steel flowing from domestic mills through steel service centers is at least 40 percent; specialized, industry-specific distributors, such as oilfield supply houses, whose purchases of pipe would be considered sales to the oil and gas industry, not to the distribution industry, are not included in this figure.

Steel service centers also dominate the supply of imported steel, amounting to 20.4 million tons in 1994 after deducting imported semifinished steel and wire rods, imported by domestic steel companies and wire drawers for conversion. A reasonable estimate of service center shipments is around 60 million tons in a peak year in the business cycle, such as 1994, or nearly 60 percent of apparent supply.[12] This does not include intrasegment sales among service centers, which inflate the segment's sales by double-counting steel passed through multiple distributors. Today steel service centers are an approximately $40 billion industry in terms of sales, which does not include the nonferrous metals such as aluminum and brass that many metals service centers also sell. Thus it is close in size, in sales terms, to the steel mill industry.

The growth in the size of the service center industry has been matched by a growth in its sophistication. A number of national chains of distributors have emerged, only one of which— Ryerson Tull, Inc. a subsidiary of Inland Steel—remains majority owned by a carbon steel producer; even this company, the largest single distributor with sales in excess of $3 billion, is in no way a captive outlet for the mill's products; it distributes steel from many domestic and foreign steel companies, and also plastics and nonferrous metals. Other major carbon steel distributors are publicly held companies or are owned by overseas steel or trading companies. The distribution of stainless steel is concentrated in a few companies, often linked to aluminum distribution rather than carbon steel.

These chains evolved in the 1970s and 1980s, as many of the family-owned distribution companies went through a generational change in ownership; companies founded in the 1940s saw their owners reach retirement age, while the next generation had no interest in taking over the business. In other cases, reduced margins as a result of pressure from growing chains of service centers encouraged family owners to sell. Those companies that did not go through changes of ownership had to adapt to more sophisticated ways of financing and doing business.

As the major chains grew, their buying power increased vis-à-vis the steel mills, especially as new electric furnace producers entered markets. Forced by financial losses, major steel companies focused more closely on their core business of melting and rolling steel and cut back on their sales and technical support staffs; this led steelmakers to depend on the service centers to reach more and more segments of the market. Meanwhile the new electric furnace producers took the philosophical approach that they had no wish either to control the market or to play favorites within it; they did not try to reach beyond the distributors to end users except in specialized products, such as wire rod and SBQ bar.

Distinctions among the previously separate functions of trading companies, service centers, and processors have eroded as service centers added capital equipment and sought international sources of material. On the other hand, margins have been constrained both by increased competition at the mill and distributor levels of the industry, reflected in declining real prices for steel over time, and by the trend toward more perfect information distribution. Special deals—whether with foreign or domestic suppliers—became harder to maintain, the declining real price of freight reduced protective barriers of distance, and the use of the fax machine in purchasing led to a greater number of companies quoting on any steel order. With such structural and technological changes, the steel service center industry contributed significantly to the overall pressure from steel markets that broke down the comfortable, successful oligopoly that was the U.S. steel industry in the 1960s.

THE DE-INTEGRATION OF STEEL: OUT OF ONE, MANY?

In rapidly surveying a complex industry, one thing stands out above all the technical details. Where once there was a vertically integrated steel industry in North America, combining operations from mine to mill to fabricator under a single corporate umbrella, there is now a range of interdependent, related but separate industries.

At the upstream end of the steelmaking process, five basic raw materials stand out from other inputs (such as electricity, natural gas, oxygen, and a host of lesser supplies) as being distinctively associated with steelmaking. Scrap, iron ore, metallurgical coal and coke, limestone, and ferroalloys are the five basic inputs that historically have been dependent for a market on the integrated steel industry, which in turn sought to control its sources of these five materials through direct ownership or other long-term contractual relationships. In the 1980s, however, U.S. integrated steelmakers sold off almost 70 percent of their raw materials properties other than iron ore. With one exception, interests in ferroalloys were eliminated. Only iron ore remains an industry principally, although not exclusively, controlled in North America by its customers in the integrated steel industry, a last bastion of vertical integration.[13]

At the other, downstream, end of the steelmaking process, an equally significant although not as complete process has taken place. Independent cold rollers and cold drawers, coil coaters, pipe formers and finishers, processors and distributors have all established themselves either in competition with steelmakers or have acquired the cast-off operations of steel companies. The proliferation of such specialized companies makes it more difficult each year to measure or even to talk with precision about the steel industry.

Despite all this, steel remains an identifiable industry, or family of industries. Globally, almost all steel products are produced by companies that do not produce products from other materials, even competing metals such as aluminum. Although individual steelmaking companies have moved away from upstream and downstream vertical integration, the industry remains vertically interdependent, and changes in each segment impact the others. The emergence in the 1990s of a new generation of strong companies such as Nucor at the core of the industry, in the melting and casting segment, even appears to suggest the possibility of a new re-integration of the industry.

Regardless of which sector of the steel industry one examines, the last twenty-five years have been a time of dramatic change. The next twenty-five years are not likely to be less dramatic.

2

THE WASTED YEARS: 1959–1974

A CHANGING ECONOMY

The final years of the Eisenhower administration saw the United States enjoying a prosperity that was historically unprecedented. The 1950s saw a dramatic rise in the living standards of approximately the middle one-third, by income distribution, of families in the United States. An earlier period of sustained economic growth, the 1920s, had established the pattern of what we today call middle-class life for America's small business owners, managers, and professionals: car ownership (thanks to the Model T Ford); suburban housing; annual vacations; and the spread of electrification allowed the introduction of household equipment such as radios, electric stoves, washing machines, and vacuum cleaners, often as substitutes for domestic servants. After the disruptions of the depression and World War II, the resumption of peacetime economic growth spread this lifestyle to a much wider segment of the population. As unions in manufacturing industry drove hourly wages from under $1 an hour toward $3, they drove their membership into the middle class. Car ownership spread in the 1950s to 70 percent of American families; appliances such as refrigerators and, later, televisions became nearly universal. Middle-class Americans came to treat such goods as a fourth category of basic human need, along with food, clothing, and shelter; indeed in the 1950s more than one-quarter of household incomes were spent on such personal machines, including the gasoline and electricity to fuel them.

Earlier waves of industrial growth, in the nineteenth and the earlier twentieth centuries, had been focused predominantly on capital goods that were collectively, not personally, owned and used: railroads, steamships, office buildings, and factories; this infrastructure was used to produce and more efficiently distribute traditional consumer goods such as clothing. Despite the commercialization of new technologies and products in the early twentieth century, notably electric power and the internal combustion engine, the patterns of consumption for most Americans remained broadly focused on products—food, clothing, housing (wooden or brick) that with a few exceptions (such as the growth of steel tinplate cans) did not use metals. Even after car ownership spread among the affluent in the 1920s, the consumption of steel in society was overwhelmingly in the areas of heavy capital equipment and nonresidential construction. In 1947, after the wartime mobilization of the economy had ended, the three major industries transforming steel for personal use—automobiles, appliances, and canning—used only 24 percent of U.S. steel shipments. The bulk went to end uses in construction; defense; agriculture; the newer energy industries of oil, gas, and electricity; and traditional heavy industries such as railroads, industrial machinery and equipment, shipbuilding, and mining. By 1959 the product mix had changed. Automobiles and appliance shipments and tinplate now accounted for 31 percent of the total, while flat-rolled steel overall had grown from 39 to 52 percent, a proportion that would stay steady into the 1990s. The major areas of decline included the rail transportation industry, down from 8.3 to 3.4 percent of shipments, and other traditional user industries of plate and heavy steels, such as shipbuilding and agriculture.

THE 1950s: A DECADE OF TRANSITION

What was perhaps most surprising about this decade of prosperity was that it ended with U.S. steel consumption at a lower level than it had started the decade. Even though the U.S. steel industry had seen great growth in flat-rolled steel consumption, it had invested $10 billion in the decade in new and modernized facilities, and its capacity to produce raw steel had increased by 48 percent in the decade, the level of apparent steel demand had stayed on a plateau through the decade.

The plateau of steel production in the 100 million net tons range, reflecting the sluggish growth of apparent consumption, contrasted sharply with the growth of demand and production in Japan and Western

Table 2.1
U.S. STEEL CAPACITY AND DEMAND IN THE 1950S

(Thousands of net tons)

Year	Annual Capability	% Utilization	Raw Steel Production	Product Shipments	Exports	Imports	Apparent consumption
1950	99,983	96.9	96,836	72,232	3,095	1,077	70,214
1951	104,230	100.9	105,200	78,929	3,543	2,264	77,650
1952	108,588	85.8	93,168	68,004	4,459	1,213	64,758
1953	117,547	94.9	111,610	80,152	3,345	1,670	78,477
1954	124,330	71.0	88,312	63,153	3,158	784	60,779
1955	125,828	93.0	117,036	84,717	4,553	970	81,134
1956	128.363	89.9	115,216	83,251	5,166	1,333	79,418
1957	133,459	84.5	112,715	79,895	6,953	1,155	74,097
1958	140,743	60.6	85,255	59,914	3,449	1,707	58,172
1959	147,634	63.3	93,446	69,377	2,103	4,396	71,670
1960	148,571	66.8	99,282	71,149	3,473	3,359	71,035

Europe in the same decade. While U.S. growth of raw steel from 1950 to 1960 on a smoothed three-year average basis equaled just 0.4 percent, growth in Japan was 16.6 percent (albeit from a very small base); in Canada, 5.9 percent; and in the six countries of the European Coal and Steel Community, 7.9 percent.[1] The United States had become the first industrialized country to see the steel intensity of its gross national product (GNP) begin to fall.

The U.S. economy's steel intensity—the consumption of steel per million dollars of GNP adjusted for inflation—fell by 25 percent during the decade of the 1950s, through a combination of trends. One was the substitution of other materials for steel, such as concrete in construction and aluminum in cans. A second was the start of a trend toward the use of lighter weights of steel in many applications, particularly in all kinds of transport equipment, as lighter gauges of cold-rolled and coated steels became more widely available. The most important, however, was the shift within the economy toward products that were less steel-intensive, as heavy capital goods declined in importance compared to the rise of personal consumption goods. Temporary factors, such as the revival of munitions production during the Korean War years 1951 to 1953 and the fluctuations of the economic cycle, could not mask this radical shift in the economy. By contrast, in the 1950s Japan and Western Europe (with the exception of the mature economy of the United Kingdom) were still growing in the steel intensity of their economies, as they promoted the growth of industrial sectors such as heavy machinery (Germany) and shipbuilding (Japan).

The lack of market growth combined with the expansion of steelmaking capacity to give U.S. companies low operating rates by the end of the decade, leading in turn to declining financial performance. The industry's capacity expansion in the decade, at a cost of $10 billion, could not be financed from earnings except in the boom years 1955 to 1957, when the industry exceeded $1 billion a year of gross profits. Industry long-term debt trebled in the decade to $2.488 billion, still a relatively low level, but the industry raised money primarily from issuing equity.[2]

THE 1950s EXPANSION

Investment in the 1950s was focused in three areas: in securing iron ore supplies, in adding open-hearth steelmaking furnaces to augment capacity at existing plants, and in building new hot-strip mills to meet the growing demand for flat-rolled steel. In only one case did a major integrated company build an entirely new, "greenfield" steel mill at this time, the U.S. Steel plant at Fairless Hills, Pennsylvania, built on the tidal Delaware River between 1950 and 1952. The bulk of the steelmaking investment was geared toward upgrading or "rounding out" facilities at existing mills, in part because rapid wartime expansion had left a number of plants with unbalanced facilities (such as more steelmaking capacity than rolling capacity, or vice versa); in part because some facilities were obsolete or simply worn out by wartime production levels, and needed replacing; but chiefly because incremental expansion was far cheaper than the greenfield route.

The North American iron ore industry assumed its present shape in the 1950s. The high-grade reserves of Michigan and Minnesota were being rapidly depleted, and the major steel companies faced either a search for new ore supplies or the need to upgrade the lake ores. The industry pursued both courses. Although the St. Lawrence seaway was under construction in the late 1950s, offering the Midwest the promise of greater access to overseas ore, the economics of transport and the existing investment tied up in mining operations favored the construction of pelletizing plants to allow exploitation of low-grade domestic ores. The extensive low-grade taconite deposits in Minnesota, adjacent to developed high-grade ores, could be upgraded from 25 to 30 percent iron content to around 70 percent, making them suitable for blast furnace feed without sintering and reducing the cost of transportation.

The pelletizing plants, constructed in the late 1950s, were expensive; the largest project, belonging to the Erie Mining consortium at Duluth[3], cost its participating steel companies $300 million when it opened in 1958, second only to the greenfield Fairless Hills mill in the scale of capital projects in the decade. In 1995 dollars, that sum is equal to about $1.8 billion. Pelletizing became so popular it was extended in the 1960s even to high-grade ores; by 1970 there were thirty-one plants in North America, but 60 percent of their capacity had been installed by 1961.

Coastal steel mills such as Bethlehem Steel's Sparrows Point plant in Baltimore and its Bethlehem, Pennsylvania, mill had long relied heavily on imported ore, originally from company-owned mines in Cuba and Chile. In the late 1940s and 1950s, major new sources of high-grade iron ore were found worldwide, notably in Brazil, Venezuela, West Africa, and Western Australia. Both U.S. Steel and Bethlehem Steel established new mining operations in South America in the 1940s and 1950s, in Venezuela, Brazil, Peru and Chile. Bethlehem Steel also participated with Swedish interests in developing mines in Liberia and Guinea, West Africa. With the wave of economic nationalism that swept through Latin America in the 1960s, the U.S. subsidiaries in each country there were nationalized on terms that amounted to confiscation; the Liberian operations continued until halted by disorder in that country in 1989.

New reserves were also delineated in Canada, on the Labrador-Quebec border. Although these were not as rich as some others, they were closer to the North American mills and appeared to pose little political risk for investors. The four major eastern Quebec and Labrador mining operations, developed beginning in the mid-1950s by consortia of U.S. and Canadian companies,[4] have accounted for over half of U.S. imports of iron ore by iron content ever since. They are relatively high-cost operations, both because of their remote subarctic locations and their need to be upgraded before shipment, having free-on-board (f.o.b.) vessel costs averaging only 10 to 15 percent below Lake Superior ores. This puts them on roughly equal terms with lake ores on a delivered basis to Cleveland or Chicago, because of the need for small trans-Seaway vessels, but puts them at a disadvantage to cheaper ores (in much larger vessels) from Australia or South Africa in European or Japanese markets. The lack of port facilities for large vessels in the eastern United States, the proximity of the mine's Gulf of St. Lawrence port outlets to the U.S. East Coast, and perhaps most of all the ownership interests of the U.S. producers in the Canadian mines meant that the Canadian ores formed a large part of the coastal mills' feedstock.

The expansion of steelmaking capacity in the United States in the 1950s included significant growth in the coastal regions of the country. Expectations about the changing economics and sources of iron ore played a part in this trend, but so did the need to be close to steel markets. While traditional heavy manufacturing, plus the booming automobile industry, was centered close to the traditional steel-producing areas of the Great Lakes and Mid-Atlantic states, the newer industries of aircraft and oil and gas production were located in states such as Texas and California, while demographics were also slowly shifting construction and consumer goods manufacturing south and west. In 1950 the ten states bordering the Great Lakes or the Ohio River, the country's traditional steelmaking region, had nearly 83 million tons of capacity, or 83 percent of the total; the rest of the country had just 17 million tons of capacity, much of it built in a haste in wartime by the federal government.[5] By 1960 the nontraditional coastal and western states had grown their capacity to 28.1 million tons, or to 29.9 million if the coastal Fairless Hills mill, opposite Trenton, New Jersey, is added to the non-traditional total. This total growth of 75.3 percent in a decade is dramatic, but it should be noted that the traditional steelmaking region grew by more in absolute terms, by 42.9 percent to 118.6 million tons.[6] Within the Great Lakes area, the major location of expansion was along the southern shore of Lake Michigan, where plants along the lake from South Chicago, Illinois, to Indiana Harbor, Indiana—a distance of only 20 miles—added some 11 million tons of incremental capacity. Most of the capacity additions were located at existing wartime or prewar steel mills, even in the nontraditional areas, where growth was undertaken at existing plants such as Sparrows Point, Maryland, Geneva, Utah, and Pueblo, Colorado.

Almost all the additional steelmaking capacity was added in the form of open-hearth furnaces. Some 39.3 million annual net tons of open-hearth (OH) furnace capacity was added in the decade, for a total of 126 million tons of OH capacity out of 139 million total capacity in 1959. The amount of OH capacity built was larger than the entire steel industry of Germany or Japan at that time. Although the steel industries of Europe and Japan were investing heavily in the basic oxygen furnace, known in Europe as the Linz-Donawitz (LD) converter, conservative U.S. companies preferred the OH. Over the years these companies had developed the OH to the most efficient level of which the process was capable. Furnace size had grown from an average of under 100 tons per heat in 1950 to a minimum of 250 tons in all the units installed in the 1950s. The introduction of oxygen blowing reduced heat times by up to a half, while the use of better refractory linings increased the number of heats between relines. The OHs could be run on a wide range of iron feedstocks, from 100 percent pig iron to 100 percent scrap, flexibility that allowed mills to utilize their home scrap and to allow for mix changes when, for example, blast furnaces went down for maintenance.

The incremental improvements in the OH technology were not enough to save the process from obsolescence, however. The last new battery of open hearths in the West was built by Bethlehem Steel at Sparrows Point in 1958; construction of OHs continued in Russia and China into the 1960s. The BOF offered savings in both capital and operating costs. The capital cost of a BOF shop was estimated at around half that of a comparably sized OH shop, very largely because the increased speed of refining makes fewer furnaces necessary for the same output.[7] By the time that 300-ton BOFs were developed in the 1960s, it became accepted that two such BOFs could replace a battery of eight or more similar sized OHs, given average tap-to-tap times of forty-five minutes for the BOF versus between six and twelve hours, depending on the amount of oxygen used in the open hearth practice. The reduced number of furnaces also reduced the need for manpower, although not in proportion to the reduction in furnaces. Savings of between 5 and 15 percent of raw steel costs were common, depending on the age of the OH units replaced.

In the 1950s, however, U.S. companies were slow to accept the reality of the new technology's economics. The first small BOF installation in the United States was made as early as 1954, at small McLouth Steel in Detroit, and the first Canadian installation in 1956 at Algoma Steel in Sault Ste. Marie, Ontario. Only in 1957 did a major company install a BOF—at Aliquippa, Pennsylvania, by Jones and Laughlin, still with only 80-ton furnaces. The results from this shop just outside Pittsburgh probably did more than any other reports to convince conservative Pittsburgh executives of the viability of the process. The three largest companies, U.S. Steel, Bethlehem, and Republic, introduced their first BOFs in 1963, 1964, and 1965, respectively. By waiting an extra ten years to introduce BOFs on a large scale, the major companies had been able to bypass the development stage and install a mature technology; but meanwhile they had spent around $600 million (about $3.5 billion in 1995 dollars) on capacity that was already obsolete.

The third major area of investment in the 1950s was in hot-strip mills, to meet the growing demand for flat-rolled steel. Nine new hot-strip mills were built in the decade, with a combined capacity of 11.4 million net tons; in addition, four prewar strip mills with 8.6 million tons capacity were rebuilt. However, the new and upgraded mills were essentially the same as prewar designs, albeit incorporating more power and in some cases with greater width. Of the 37 hot-strip mills in service in the United States and four in Canada in 1959, only four were continuous mills, without reversing roughing stands that slowed down the rolling process. The four continuous mills[8] included the widest and largest capacity mills in North America, but until 1961 hot-strip mills lacked the power to roll at speeds exceeding about 2,500 feet per minute from the finishing train. The capacity of a mill is proportional to its speed of rolling and therefore depends in large part on the power applied to the rolling stands to squeeze the steel through successively narrower spaces. The speed of each roll depends on the thickness of the steel; thus the speed is greatest at the last or finishing roll, where the steel is thinnest. Mill finishing speeds were raised to over 4,000 feet per minute in the 1960s with the construction of what became known as Generation II hot-strip mills.

1959: A TURNING POINT

In 1959, then, the U.S. steel industry appeared to have both great strengths and great potential vulnerabilities. Investment in capacity expansion in the 1950s placed the U.S. industry in a position where it appeared to have retained the global preeminence it had attained during World War II. In 1959 the United States accounted for 27.7 percent of world production, down dramatically from the inflated percentages of the late 1940s, when continental Europe and Japan were recovering from the ruin of the war, but still equal to the output of the European Coal and Steel Community (ECSC) and Japan combined. Investment in the 1950s exceeded, in dollar terms, that of the ECSC, Japan, and the United Kingdom combined. Average size of firms, plants, and individual furnaces and mills were larger in the United States than in either Japan or Europe,[9] thus allowing greater potential economies of scale. Labor productivity was dramatically greater in the United States—three times more man-hours per ton of steel were required in Japan, although labor costs were one-sixth of those in the United States. The U.S. industry had lower raw material costs than either Japan or Europe, due to proximity to coking coal, the North American scrap surplus, and the heavy investments in ore supplies, although there was little difference in the efficiency with which material inputs were utilized between the major steel industries. The U.S. industry had by far the largest internal market in the world for its products, and that market commanded the highest prices for steel in the world, so that there was little need or incentive to export. In the domestic market, the integrated producers, who had been able to put through price increases to pass on increases in costs—particularly of wages—to their customers, scrupulously maintained price discipline. The U.S. Steel Corporation, the largest producer with 30 percent of the market, announced price changes with which the other producers quickly fell in line, and neither imports nor new producers struggling for market share offered alternatives to steel buyers.

On the other hand, the U.S. industry had a number of major problems in 1959, which the oligopolistic pricing structure served to obscure. Foremost among these were the related problems of labor costs and labor unrest. Five times from 1946 to 1959 the expiration of a (usually three-year) industry-wide contract between the major steelmakers and the United Steelworkers of America led to a strike that shut down the industry. Steel customers were forced to stockpile steel in anticipation of a strike, and the stockpile meant that if an early return to work was agreed, few orders would be taken until inventories were brought back into balance. The cost to steel customers, and the economy as a whole, of stockpiling and (during longer strikes) of shutdowns due to steel shortages made government intervention common in steel labor negotiations. In 1952, during the Korean War, President Harry S. Truman actually seized the steel mills and operated them as government facilities for a time until a Supreme Court ruling returned them to the companies. Political pressure to settle almost inevitably meant pressure on the companies to give in to union demands and then quietly pass along the increased costs to customers. Nevertheless, the importance of steel in the economy was such that journalists and populist politicians in Congress could make careers from denouncing steel price increases, and when a powerful and ambitious senator such as Estes Kefauver held hearings in 1958 and 1959 on the industry, it spent much executive and staff time fighting a hopeless battle of public relations.[10]

The triennial labor contract cycle began to impact on international trade in steel in 1959. A strike beginning on July 15 that lasted for 116 days, until an order from the federal government under the emergency provisions of the Taft-Hartley Act caused work to resume pending arbitration by Vice President (and presidential candidate) Richard M. Nixon. Steel buyers, including the increasingly important service center sector, began to look overseas for steel as their stockpiles were consumed, and imports surged from 1.707 million tons in 1958 to 4.396 million tons in 1959, while exports of scarce and expensive U.S.-made steel dropped to a low of 1.677 million tons. For the first time in the twentieth century the United States imported more steel than it exported. The buyers liked what they received: to many user's surprise, foreign steel was acceptable in quality and in many cases actually cheaper than domestic steel. In 1960 imports stayed strong, at 3.359 million tons; and the United States remained a net importer. With each contract negotiation, new surges in imports occurred—to 10.38 million tons in 1965, to 17.96 million in 1968—and each time they did not drop back afterwards. Overseas producers discovered that the U.S. market was lucrative, thanks to the pricing umbrella of U.S. Steel, and contained many distributors happy to buy at least some of their steel offshore if only as a hedge against the day when strikes would make the relationship with a foreign mill invaluable.

The markets most vulnerable to imported steel were those farthest away from the producing mills, especially markets on the West Coast. Peripheral markets, such as tinplate for the Hawaii pineapple canning industry, were lost for good in the 1960s, because the freight from East Coast mills exceeded that from Japan or even Europe. It had long been common practice to ship steel from East Coast mills to West Coast markets via the Panama Canal, ocean freight being cheaper than rail freight from, say, Chicago to Los Angeles. However, the impact of protectionist legislation requiring shipping between U.S. ports to be carried in U.S.-built, U.S.-crewed, U.S.-flag vessels was such that freight from Antwerp to Los Angeles was about $5 a ton less than from Baltimore in 1961. Yokohama was even closer in freight terms. The new, coastal Japanese mills were to be the unintended beneficiaries of U.S. legislation that had originally been promoted by Bethlehem Steel, until the 1960s the largest U.S. shipbuilder.

European mills were the leading sources of imports at first, even on the West Coast, with Japanese tonnage beginning to make an impact after 1962; Japanese tonnage then quickly rose from 596,000 tons in 1961 to 4.85 million, or 45.1 percent of total imports, in 1966. European and Japanese export philosophies differed somewhat: export shipments, although lucrative, were marginal business for European producers, who were directed under the oversight of the ECSC to develop to meet the needs of growing European industries. Japanese strategy, on the other hand, was deliberately export-led, with new capacity being built in the decade from 1957 to 1967 far in excess of then-foreseeable domestic requirements, and sometimes in excess of the desires of the planners of the Ministry of International Trade and Industry (MITI). Both industries were guided by government policy into cartel-like structures with similarities to that prevailing under the pricing umbrella of U.S. Steel in the United States. A key difference, though, was that in the United States cartel-like behavior applied only to pricing and certain key inputs such as labor and iron ore, not to investment or global market shares.

Imports might have remained a marginal, strike-hedging element in the U.S. market if the cost advantages that the U.S. mills held in the 1950s had persisted. A number of factors worked in favor of foreign producers at the start of the 1960s, however. One was the rapid global development of new, low-cost raw material sources and the decline of transport costs as bulk carriers increased in size and efficiency. European and Japanese producers no longer needed traditional sources such as Lorraine and Manchuria. A second was the construction of greenfield steel mills, which not only benefited from coastal sites and new technology such as the BOF, but also gained efficiencies by virtue of their construction on optimum plans, with balanced facilities, compared with the frequently mismatched, "infill" development of existing mill locations. The third, and most glaring element in the comparative cost picture, was the ballooning of U.S. labor costs.

BIG STEEL AND BIG LABOR

In the 1950s and 1960s, labor costs averaged 40 percent of the costs of steelmaking, not including the labor component in delivered raw material costs. Labor costs vary, of course, with labor productivity, measured in the steel industry in terms of man-hours per ton of steel, and with both the costs of wages and of benefits (health care, vacations, pensions, unemployment insurance, and so on). Integrated steel companies in the United States had, until the mid-1960s, the best labor productivity (lowest man-hours per ton) in the world; until the 1970s they showed little interest in changing the way they utilized labor inputs. Instead of looking at the number of labor hours used, the companies focused heavily on the cost of each labor hour, as determined by bargaining with their unions.[11]

Formal industry-wide collective bargaining between integrated steel companies and the United Steelworkers of America began in 1956, after two decades in which U.S. Steel had negotiated contracts that were then accepted, with few modifications, by other companies. Of the integrated mills, only two did not have United Steelworkers representation—Armco's Middletown, Ohio, plant had an independent union, and the River Rouge steel mill of Ford Motor Company was organized by the United Auto Workers. Small specialty and electric furnace steelmakers tended to have separate contracts with lower wages, or no union at all.

The 1956 three-year contract was typical: after a brief strike, the industry accepted a settlement that increased hourly employment costs by 30 percent over three years, including a cost-of-living adjustment (COLA) provision; on the day after the contract was signed, U.S. Steel announced a general price increase of $8.50 a ton. As wages were adjusted upward during the contract, so too were prices, by $21 a ton in total.

When the 1956 contract came up for renewal in 1959, the economy was in much poorer shape, and the steel companies operated, before the surge in prestrike stockpiling orders, at only two-thirds of capacity. The companies therefore held out for much lower rates of labor cost increases, and the deadlock led to the 116-day 1959 strike. The 519,000 workers who struck idled 87 percent of the industry's capacity; by the end of the strike, they had also caused 250,000 workers in other, steel-dependent industries to be laid off as stockpiles were exhausted. The settlement, finally reached in January 1960 under federal mediation, did have much smaller wage increases—39 cents an hour increase in base pay over three years—but it still had a COLA provision for inflation. Furthermore, the settlement improved the rights of workers to severance pay under the supplementary unemployment benefits program and strengthened union members' pension and health care provisions. Union negotiators, aware that steel wages were well ahead of every other industry except automobile assembly, began to focus more and more on creating a system of job security and lifetime benefits. The costs of such promises seemed acceptable while steel was a growing industry. When it shrank, the costs of former employees came back to haunt the companies.

The 1960s saw no major steel strike, in part because both sides had been badly hurt by the 1959 strike and in part because the industry resumed growth that allowed the companies to continue to pay more. Unease about the ability of the steel market to absorb price hikes indefinitely grew, as imports refused to go away and as the political sensitivity of the pass-through pricing grew.

In 1962, the industry reached an early settlement under President John F. Kennedy's auspices; for the first time since the war, agreement had been reached not only without a strike but in time to prevent the costly stocking-destocking cycle. Again, the settlement focused on job security and benefits issues; the COLA was actually suspended, although this was offset by one-time wage increases. Kennedy wanted a moderate, early settlement that would prevent economic disruption and not add to inflation by increasing steel prices. Five days after the settlement was announced, just as voices in the industry were indicating that this "was not the time" for price increases, U.S. Steel announced a $6 a ton increase. The president, who believed he had assurances that this would not happen, was outraged; he was quoted as saying "My father always told me that all businessmen were sons of bitches, but I never believed it until now." The president's brother Robert, the attorney general, immediately launched an investigation of "price fixing" among the steel producers. Within three days, the unprecedented occurred: Inland Steel, the fourth largest company, announced that it would not raise its prices. U.S. Steel, under both government and competitive pressure, withdrew the increase; Robert Kennedy withdrew the investigation.[12] Soon the steel companies, individually and product by product, began to raise prices; but the practice of across-the-board, per-ton price raises by the industry was at an end.

In 1965 no early agreement was reached; steel customers reverted to the practice of stockpiling, and a surge of overseas steel was ordered in anticipation of a strike. President Lyndon B. Johnson intervened this time, to demand that the two sides defer the strike deadline for eight days and continue talking; they did so and reached an agreement three days after the deadline had passed. In the mid-1960s the industry was booming again; the Vietnam War was becoming a major U.S. commitment, with a consequent growth in demand for steel for munitions and military vehicles and aircraft; the interstate highway system was in the midst of construction, boosting demand for bridge girders and concrete-reinforcing bars; and a flood of money into the economy from Johnson's Great Society programs was helping to bring about a major consumer boom and to boost inflation. With the steel industry facing new peaks of demand, a generous settlement was expected and was granted. Wage and benefit increases cost another 50 cents an hour; and steelworkers were guaranteed the right to retirement on a full pension after thirty years' work, regardless of their age at the time of retirement. Perhaps the biggest cost to the industry, however, was the rise in imported tonnage from 6.4 million in 1964 to 10.4 million in 1965, including for the first time significant tonnages of flat-rolled products brought into the domestic industry's heartland, the Great Lakes ports. Imports reached 10.3 percent of total apparent consumption, and their share was far greater in certain regional and product markets—over a third of West Coast consumption of all products, for example, and 49.3 percent of wire rod shipments. The next strike deadline, in 1968, saw yet another last-minute, generous contract and yet another surge of imports to a new peak, of 17.96 million tons, or 16.7 percent of the market. The integrated mills were slowly withdrawing from, or being pushed out of markets in which their production and freight costs now greatly exceeded those of overseas producers.

THE ENA: PEACE AT ANY PRICE

As each strike deadline further eroded the integrated producers' position, the mills adopted two new tactics to fight the threat. One was to lobby for government protection against imports. The second was to try to work out ways of avoiding the strike threat. By this time the strains on the industry's balance sheet from the costs of catch-up modernization and on its market position from import challenges meant it feared that a major strike could be fatal to some of the weaker companies, and highly damaging to all.[13] The steelworkers' union, led by I. W. Abel, was also concerned about the position of the industry; the layoffs following the 1971 contract were a shock to many rank-and-file union members, but the union's leadership, with a sophisticated research department and a good understanding of steel's economics, took warnings of the industry's growing plight seriously. In late 1972 Abel began secret talks with U.S. Steel's labor negotiators that led to a dramatic change in the industry's labor relations: the no-strike agreement known as the Experimental Negotiating Agreement, or ENA.[14]

The ENA governed the negotiations conducted in 1974 and was repeatedly extended until the industry was facing collapse in 1983. Simply stated, the two sides agreed that in future, wages would automatically rise 3 percent a year plus the COLA inflation rate; in return for this, the union pledged not to strike if agreement could not be reached on other contract issues but to put the outstanding issues to binding arbitration. What could not be arbitrated or challenged, though, was the annual wage increases or the standard management "right-to-manage"

Table 2.2
U.S. STEEL CAPACITY,
DEMAND AND IMPORT SHARE IN THE 1960S

(Thousands of net tons)

Year	Annual Capability	Raw Steel Production	Product Shipments	Exports	Imports	Apparent Consumption	Import % of Consumption
1960	148,571	99,282	71,149	2,977	3,359	70,767	4.7%
1961	149,800	98,014	66,126	1,990	3,163	64,953	4.8%
1962	150,400	98,328	70,552	2,013	4,100	68,465	6.0%
1963	151,100	109,261	75,555	2,224	5,446	72,333	7.5%
1964	151,900	127,076	84,945	3,442	6,440	87,943	7.3%
1965	152,700	131,462	92,666	2,496	10,383	100,553	10.3%
1966	153,500	134,101	89,622	1,724	10,753	98,651	10.9%
1967	154,200	127,213	84,123	1,685	11,455	93,893	12.2%
1968	155,000	131,462	91,755	2,170	17,960	107,546	16.7%
1969	155,500	141,262	93,633	5,229	14,034	102,438	13.7%
1970	155,500	131,331	90,800	7,100	13,400	97,100	13.8%
1971	156,200	120,443	87,000	2,800	18,300	102,500	17.8%
1972	154,600	133,241	91,800	3,500	18,200	106,500	17.1%
1973	155,000	150,799	111,430	4.052	15,150	122,528	12.4%

NOTES:
The American Iron and Steel Institute ceased publishing figures for U.S. capacity in 1961 and did not resume until 1975. The figures for capacity are those calculated by Barry Bosworth in *Brookings Papers in Economic Activity,* no. 2, 1976, table 1, p. 304.

clause. The industry had bought labor peace at a high and accelerating cost in wage rates.

Astonishingly, the arbitration agreement was never invoked, as both sides appeared to fear what might result from outside intervention enough to make them settle on their own. However, the 1974, 1977, and 1980 contracts were in essence concerned with issues of benefits and job security, where the companies made seemingly small but ultimately expensive concessions every three years to further add to employment costs. The wage base kept growing automatically—from $4.81 an hour in 1972 to $13.01 in 1982, or real growth of 38 percent on top of inflation of 132 percent.[15] Total employment costs, including the costs of benefits, rose from $7.075 in 1972 to $23.781 in 1982.

To fight imports, Big Steel had doomed itself to be uncompetitive with imports. To quote Donald Barnett and Louis Schorsch, whose critique of Big Steel's productivity in the 1970s was published just after the end of the ENA era in 1983, "In effect, the industry believed its own propaganda; namely, that the periodic threat of a steel strike provided the foundation for ratchetlike surges in the import share."[16]

IMPORTS AND LOBBYISTS

While trying to buy labor peace on the one hand, the integrated companies were looking for other ways to fight the import threat. The major mills could imports of low-value products to peripheral markets, such as wire rod to the West Coast. Once imports began to compete across the full product line and geographic range, however—as, for example, with the growth of flat-rolled steel imports into the Great Lakes in the mid 1960s—the mills faced the first threat to their comfortable, cost-plus oligopoly that demonstrated the seriousness of the problems they faced.

Ultimately imported steel became cost effective because foreign mills' costs became lower than U.S. costs in the 1960s, due to a combination of faster productivity growth overseas and faster cost increases in the United States. However, imports were commercially feasible in normal market conditions only if two conditions were fulfilled. First, on a delivered-cost basis, the foreign mills had to offer a price that was lower than the U.S. mills' price, because of the lead-time disadvantage they faced: ordering from a mill in Europe might require a lead time of two to three months, compared with three to six weeks from a domestic mill. Second, the overseas mills often had to be willing to accept a lower price for their sales to the United States than they could obtain in their home markets, given the cost of freight, a small import duty or tariff, and the lead-time price disadvantage. The quality of foreign steel was initially suspect, which required new entrants to a market to "buy their way in" until the product was accepted; and they also faced the barrier of outright prejudice, notably in the Midwest and South, where many steel distributors had to offer double inventories of the same item; of foreign material at a lower price and domestic material at a higher. This practice became widespread in the distributor industry as first states, then the federal government, adopted buy-American laws governing procurement for construction and maintenance contracts, which were enforced in practice by labor union vigilance.

The two-tier market that emerged in the 1960s left the importers open to charges of "dumping" foreign material in the U.S. market. Dumping is defined in international trade law as the sale of goods in a foreign country *either* at below the cost of production of the goods or at a price lower than that prevailing in the manufacturer's home market. Prior to 1974, U.S. trade law recognized only the latter as grounds for legal action to protect U.S. producers. In practical terms, much if not most of the world's trade takes place on terms that a court could consider dumping. Manufacturers of products that are traded between countries that both manufacture the products tend to price them in their home markets at a level that more than covers their total costs, fixed and variable. If fixed costs are thereby covered, incremental sales in additional countries can then be produced profitably at any price level above that which covers only the variable costs of the extra production. This principle, known as marginal cost pricing, is accepted as appropriate in U.S. law in, for example, the regulation of utilities: when electric power or telephone service is charged at different rates in peak and off-peak hours, such marginal cost pricing is sanctioned or encouraged by government regulation. In international trade, U.S. manufacturers commonly use such pricing strategies in selling extra or marginal tonnage to competitive markets, although the steel companies largely limited themselves to exporting to those markets where they could sell at a price that covered their full costs, such as Caribbean countries that did not have their own steel industries. As the European and Japanese industries added capacity in the 1960s in advance of the forecast growth of demand in their home markets, they sought to maximize sales by exporting at marginal cost-based prices. As in the 1950s the U.S. mills had never tried to use marginal cost pricing to absorb their extra capacity when they had a cost advantage, they were outraged in the 1960s that such strategies were used against them as the balance of costs and capacity availability swung the other way. The U.S. mills' price inflexibility and long-standing use of full-cost-plus pricing not only handicapped them at home, but caused their export sales to shrink as other foreign producers began shipping to third-country markets that, like much of Latin America, had been the preserve of U.S. mills.

As early as 1966, when the import market share was a little over 10 percent, the AISI's Washington-based chairman, L. B. Worthington, had begun to lobby for temporary tariffs.[17] By the end of 1967, the AISI had recruited a number of steel-district senators and congressmen to support a bill, introduced by Senator Vance Hartke, Democrat of Indiana, to impose unilateral quotas to limit steel imports to 9.6 percent of the U.S. market, representing their average share between 1964 and 1966.

The Johnson administration and the majority of both parties in Congress followed the postwar consensus for free trade. The U.S.-sponsored General Agreement on Tariffs and Trade (GATT) and the spirit in which the United States had spent the late 1940s and 1950s promoting and indeed financing the revival of Europe's and Japan's economies, including their steel industries, ran directly counter to the idea of quotas, which like protective tariffs were perceived to be a damaging depression-era relic. On the other hand, low-level tariffs were in force for nearly all traded products and were an important revenue-raising factor for the federal government. Steel tariffs ranged from 6 to 8 percent, depending on product, but were not high enough to discourage trade. Quotas had long been sanctioned in U.S. law for shoes and textiles, in the latter case by a broad multilateral agreement; the precedents existed to show that a politically powerful industry with a large employment base concentrated in key states could overcome free-trade ideology in the practical interest of votes.

As more of the congressional delegations of steel-producing states and their allies coalesced into the alliance that was later formalized as the Congressional Steel Caucus, and hearings were held in the summer of 1968 on steel quotas by the House Ways and Means Committee, the politically sensitive Japanese embassy in Washington worked with MITI and the Japanese steelmakers to defuse the situation.[18] The Japanese industry proposed to voluntarily limit its exports to the United States, a kind of voluntary quota, and to invite other steel-exporting industries to join them in so doing; but they asked that the tonnage limits, at whatever level they were finally set, be raised by 7 percent a year from the agreed initial level. The U.S. industry was placed in a difficult position. A voluntary quota represented a quick and politically painless step toward its goal; but a guaranteed annual growth of imports sounded too much like the inexorable growth of steelworkers' wages! Moreover, because the strict anticollusion provisions of U.S. antitrust law banned private agreements on dividing market shares, the companies were banned from discussing the Japanese proposal between themselves or with the foreign producers. The companies looked on while Japanese and European producers agreed among themselves on a quota of 14 million net tons for 1969, the major shares going to Japan and the European Coal and Steel Community with 41 percent each. The agreement was to last for five years, with annual growth in imports capped at an agreed 5 percent. This growth rate was less than the original proposal but still enough to suggest that imports would account for most of the annual growth of steel demand in the United States. Only the United Kingdom and Canada, both with long-standing but limited exports to the United States, stayed outside the agreement.

The Voluntary Restraint Agreement (VRA), as such quotas came to be known, was successful in defusing pressure for unilateral government action. It also appeared to achieve the U.S. companies' objective of a halt to the steady growth of imports. In 1969, almost exactly the permitted 14 million net tons was imported. In 1970, when an additional 5 percent would be allowed by the VRA, an economic boom in Europe and the consequent demand for steel there made that a more attractive market than the United States for marginal tonnage: U.S. imports actually dropped to less than 13.4 million tons. They then rebounded to a new peak of 18.2 million tons in 1972, as an economic boom in the United States this time moved steel trade back to its former pattern. Not only was the full VRA quota taken up—now over 16 million tons—but non-VRA tonnage, from Canada, Britain, and new producers not covered by quotas, came into the United States to meet unprecedented levels of demand. One of the inherent problems of VRAs, which would recur for the next twenty years, was revealed: increasing numbers of producers increasing steel production and trade around the world. It also revealed the great political weakness of VRAs: that in boom times, steel consumers will demand steel in quantities and at prices that the domestic mills are unable or unwilling to supply, thereby increasing political pressure in favor of imports to offset the political pressure for protection. The 1972 to 1974 steel boom ended the VRAs, because of both demand from U.S. buyers and the unwillingness of the VRA countries to lose the consequent opportunities to new producers. However, the quotas ended in 1974, just as the boom ended; thereafter imports resumed a central political role in the subsequent crisis of the steel industry.

Attempts were made to calculate the economic costs to U.S. industry of this first VRA. The U.S. Department of Labor estimated that the restrictions between 1969 and 1974 caused import prices to rise by nearly 20 percent.[19] A more detailed analysis by Robert Crandall of the Brookings Institution examined pricing on a disaggregated, product-by-product level to eliminate the effects of product mix changes in the import tonnage; much lower import price rises were found, ranging from 6.3 to 8.3 percent, while domestic transaction prices were raised between 1.2 percent and 3.5 percent.[20] Such strengthening of domestic prices undoubtedly helped the steel producers by more than the actual withdrawal of tonnage that might otherwise have come in to the country. However, it did not do what the industry's lobbyists had claimed in originally asking for relief from imports: it did not give the industry "breathing space" that the integrated companies could use to increase their investment and catch up with their foreign competitors. Investment actually dropped by 50 percent between 1968 and 1972. As was to happen repeatedly over the next twenty years, the integrated companies appeared to view protection from competition as reason to relax their competitive efforts, not redouble them. The companies' political responses to competition were to prove much more innovative than their economic responses.[21]

PLAYING CATCH-UP: INVESTMENT IN THE 1960s

After spending $10 billion in the 1950s, largely on obsolete technology, the integrated steel companies spent $15 billion in the 1960s trying to catch up with producers in Europe and Japan that had leapfrogged ahead of them. The world cost leaders to whom the U.S. mills tried to catch up had a number of features in common, no matter their location. They were modern, greenfield mills, with optimal layouts and well-matched component parts. They had been built after 1955, sited at deep-water ports to take advantage of the new, large bulk ore and coal carriers. They had large blast furnaces with hearth diameters in excess of 10 meters, double the average unit size for the United States; steelmaking was exclusively by the BOF method; hot-strip mills were continuous and high powered. Many of the new plants had capacities in excess of 5 million net tons per year.

The new low-cost mills in Japan included six integrated mills built in the late 1950s and six more constructed in the early to mid-1960s, the six major steelmakers there collectively adding 40 million tons of capacity in the 1960s. In Europe, new or greatly expanded integrated mills at coastal locations were built in Italy (Taranto), France (Dunkirk in the North and Fos-sur-Mer on the Mediterranean), Belgium (Sidmar), the Netherlands (IJmuiden), and the United Kingdom (Port Talbot and Teesside). The U.S. mills most comparable in configuration were the newer mills on the south shore of Lake Michigan—U.S. Steel's Gary Works, Inland Steel at East Chicago, Youngstown Sheet and Tube's plant at Indiana Harbor—and the East Coast mills of Bethlehem Steel at Sparrows Point and U.S. Steel at Fairless Hills. In each case, a waterfront location for receiving ore was combined with a spacious layout and a large, recently expanded, capacity. However, these mills had each had significant investment in open hearths in the 1950s, and none would get BOFs until 1966 at the earliest. Instead of concentrating new technology to drive down the costs of their most competitive mills, in the early 1960s the integrated companies chose to update their older facilities.

In 1960 the United States had five BOF installations, with a total capacity of 4.8 million annual tons, which produced 3.3 million tons of steel, or 3.4 percent of total production. By comparison, Japan produced 2.9 million tons, or 11.9 percent of its output; the ECSC, 1.8 million tons, or 1.6 percent of output.[22] In the next decade the BOF tonnage installed in each part of the world was actually comparable; between 1961 and 1971, the United States installed 70.4 million tons of BOF rated capacity, compared with approximately 85 million tons in Japan and 70 million in the ECSC. The U.S. and European producers also kept pace in the decade as to the share of total production from BOFs; in 1970, 48.1 percent of U.S. production was from BOFs, but only 42.9 percent in the ECSC. Japan's proportion was higher, at 79.1 percent in 1970, but not by enough that the BOF alone was the major element in the declining relative competitiveness of the United States.

It is remarkable how many of the plants that were modernized with BOFs failed to survive the coming shakeout. Of the thirty-seven operating U.S. BOF shops in 1971, most of which had been built in the previous five years, only twenty-two were still operating in 1991, and only eight of these under the same corporate ownership that had built them. The question inevitably arises as to how much of the investment in the 1960s was misspent, just as much of the investment in obsolete technology in the 1950s was misspent. Some units that closed in the late 1970s or early 1980s seem in retrospect to have been futile attempts to update a plant built in the wrong place, of the wrong size, or producing the wrong product. Examples include Alan Wood Steel near Philadelphia (new BOFs 1968, closed 1977); Wisconsin Steel, Chicago (new BOFs 1964, closed 1980); or the Buffalo-area plants of Republic Steel (new BOFs 1970, closed 1982) and Bethlehem Steel (Lackawanna Plant, new BOFs 1964 and 1966, closed 1977 and 1983).

It is also possible, though, to point to counter-examples of small units with seeming geographic disadvantages that have survived or even prospered into the 1990s under independent, entrepreneurial management. Two good examples are the former Republic Steel plants at Gadsden, Alabama (now Gulf States Steel) and Warren, Ohio (now Warren Consolidated Industries, or WCI Steel). Both were small 1965-vintage BOF shops, at 1.5 and 2.1 million net tons per year (ntpy) respectively, far below the size perceived in 1970 as being the minimum for efficiency and located away from water transportation. These investments did not save Republic Steel, the weakest of the seven largest steel companies, which was absorbed into LTV Steel in 1984; but once sold off to independent managers, these mills prospered far longer than any industry analyst in the 1970s expected. These counterexamples demonstrate that neither size nor technology alone has guaranteed success or failure in integrated steelmaking. Nevertheless, steelmaking investments in the 1960s were small (an average BOF shop size of a little over 2 million tons); dispersed (35 BOF shops at thirty-two locations of nineteen companies), and in every case but one, located at a "brownfield" or fill-in site, next to the battery of open hearths that the BOF shop would supplement and eventually replace.

The one exception to the brownfield rule was Bethlehem Steel's new mill at Burns Harbor, Indiana, built from 1968 to 1970. The first greenfield integrated mill in the United States since Fairless Hills was commissioned in 1952, Burns Harbor was located on Lake Michigan at the end of the row of integrated steel plants stretching around the lake to Chicago. Bethlehem Steel built the new mill in part because it could not buy a facility in the same area: it had tried to merge with the Youngstown Sheet and Tube Company in the late 1950s, primarily to acquire its Indiana Harbor mill, but the Federal government refused permission on antitrust grounds. In the early 1960s, therefore, the company acquired extensive land on the lakefront and announced its plan to spend $1 billion on the new plant. Until Burns Harbor was constructed, Bethlehem's westernmost mill was at Lackawanna, New York. A presence in the Midwest was deemed essential to participation in the still-growing automobile market. The plant was built in stages, with a hot-strip mill, plate mill, and finishing facilities built between 1964 and 1966 and a hot end with an initial operating capacity of 2 million net tons per year completed in 1970. The steelmaking capacity was soon expanded to 5.3 million tons. Its profitability permitted Bethlehem Steel to survive the red ink of the 1970s and 1980s flowing from its other five plants. Even Burns Harbor, though, as well laid out and efficient as it was, did not have the latest technology for flat-rolled steelmaking. It would be another fifteen years before Burns Harbor would get a continuous caster.

CONTINUOUS CASTING EMERGES

Continuous casting was originally developed for nonferrous metals, with their lower melting temperatures and lower volatility in the liquid state. Experiments in the United States, Canada, and Britain in the late

1940s and early 1950s led to the first commercial-scale caster becoming fully operational in 1956 at the stainless steel sheet mill of Atlas Steels, Ltd. in Welland, Ontario. Specialty steel mills led the way in introducing casting in the 1950s; alloy steels as well as low grades of carbon steel can be "killed" in the furnace to terminate the violent gaseous reactions prior to casting. However, high-grade carbon steels, for sheet production, were cast into ingots still "alive" or oxidized; when poured alive into a continuous caster, it was hard to avoid frequent (and life-threatening) damage to the caster and harder to avoid poor-quality steel with oxygen blow holes. By the late 1960s the problem had been resolved, after much trial and error, either by the use of vacuum degassing or by modifying the carbon, silicon, manganese, and aluminum contents of the steel to produce a superior "killed" steel for casting.

Slab casting presented greater development difficulties than did billet and bloom casting; in the 1960s billet casters became standard equipment at electric furnace long products producers, which were beginning to undergo dramatic expansion. However, European and Japanese mills, by committing sooner to installing slab casters, were the pioneers in finding ways to operate them effectively. Except for U.S. Steel, National Steel, and the pioneering McLouth Steel, the integrated companies in the United States were reluctant to commit to the new technology. In 1971 there were forty-five production-scale casters completed in the United States; only fourteen were at integrated companies' mills, and only four of these were slab casters for carbon steel. The small size of the electric furnace companies' billet casters meant that only 5.8 million net tons, or 4.8 percent of U.S. production in that year, was continuously cast, despite the large number of installations. By contrast, in Japan at the same time, 11 million tons of steel were cast, the vast majority from nine large slab casters; a massive program of investment in continuous casting was just getting under way, with the aim of adding more than 30 million net tons of casting capacity.

In installing BOFs, the U.S. companies had made major efforts to keep up with the changes in steelmaking economics, yet their overall competitive position was virtually unchanged. Now, they appeared reluctant even to make the effort. It is hard to avoid the conclusion that the mills' reluctance to commit to investments in casters was for more reasons than just the difficulty of perfecting a new technology. In Bethlehem Steel, casters cut across the jurisdiction of three departments—steelmaking, transport, and rolling—and threatened a number of management jobs in each area, thus ensuring that the idea had no sponsors within the organization.[23] A combination of circumstances, including competition for investment funds from a range of competing projects, emerging doubts about the wisdom of brownfield investments, concern about prematurely installing a technology that might later be greatly refined, and the conservatism and institutional structure of the companies, combined to make most integrated companies miss the benefits of continuous casting during a critical decade.

THE "GENERATION II" HOT-STRIP MILLS

Among the mixed record of 1960s investment in upgrading old plants, one area stands out as clearly a success: the so-called Generation II hot-strip mills.[24] Eleven new hot strip mills were built between 1961 and 1970, with an average cost of over $110 million each. They can be distinguished from earlier mills by their computer controls, their increased capacity from high-power and continuous operation, and greater quality through better gauge control of flatness. The new mills effectively eliminated the traditional problem of sheets having a "crown," meaning that the edges were rolled thinner than the center. The new mills were also wider—ten were over 80 inches wide—which allowed sheet users such as automakers to use standard coils of 60 and 72 inches, or even 84 and 96 inches for specific applications, rather than the traditional 36- and 48-inch coils.

The new mills had rated capacities in the 2- to 3.5-million-net-tons-per-year range, although in some cases, with optimum scheduling, they have produced as much as 5 million tons in peak years. Indeed, strip mill capacity often exceeds the steelmaking capacity available to feed them; since the mid-1980s, steelmakers have regularly imported purchased slabs as supplementary strip mill feed. Every one of the new hot-strip mills is still, in 1996, the core of an important integrated flat-rolled steel plant. Indeed, two have been major factors in the survival of the plants at Middletown and at Warren, Ohio, the last two midwestern integrated mills not located on water.

Other expenditures were made throughout the decade to modernize and upgrade existing hot-strip mills, retrofitting them with higher power and better gauge controls. Here the record is much more spotty: of sixteen mills rebuilt in the 1960s, nine were still operating in late 1996. In others, trying to upgrade one aspect of an inefficient plant was not enough to remedy the problems of the entire facility.

THE GROWTH OF THE ELECTRIC FURNACE

The widespread adoption of basic oxygen furnace steelmaking left the integrated mills with a surplus of scrap. In 1960 between 25 and 30 percent of raw steel produced was "lost"—returned as home or recycling scrap to the steel furnaces due to losses in each of the subsequent production processes before a finished product was shipped by the mill. Early BOF practice rarely exceeded a 20 percent scrap component in the charge. As long as open hearths were operating, scrap could be consumed easily; but if open hearths were to be fully replaced in a plant or region, mills would have to sell their scrap or find other ways to absorb it. In addition, independent scrap processors that supplied scrap to open-hearth mills faced growing supplies, particularly from scrapped automobiles, which pushed down the price of the resource. The response was the growth of scrap-based electric furnace steelmaking.

In the 1950s, U.S. electric furnace production varied in a narrow range around an average of 7.5 million net tons of production a year, almost half of which was alloy and stainless steel produced in small heats by specialty producers. But EF production grew from 8.38 million tons in 1960 to 20.16 million tons in 1970, then on to 28.67 million tons in 1974. Almost all the growth was in carbon steel, which accounted for over 70 percent of EF steel in 1970. This growth came about in a number of ways—from the adoption of EF technology by integrated mills; from the conversion of small, scrap-based open-hearth specialty producers to EFs; and by the emergence of new, independent carbon steel EF producers—the minimills.

In the 1960s, installations of EF shops in integrated mills were large-scale operations, designed in some cases to be the equivalent of a large BOF shop. Jones and Laughlin converted their Pittsburgh mill from OHs to EFs by installing two 350-ton furnaces with a combined capacity of 1.8 million tons, for example. Bethlehem Steel at Steelton, Pennsylvania, and later at Johnstown, Pennsylvania, also made full-scale mill conversions to EF steelmaking. A different strategy was to combine EF and BOF steelmaking in a single plant, with the EFs absorbing the home scrap and adding low-cost supplementary capacity; installations such as those of Inland Steel at East Chicago and C F & I Steel in Pueblo, Colorado, are in this category.

One integrated company, U.S. Steel, built a new greenfield EF mill with 1.2 million tons capacity at Baytown, near Houston, Texas, in 1970-71. With a slab caster and plate mill, the new facility was intended to supply the growing oilfield supply industry, including offshore structure fabrication, which was centered in coastal Texas and Louisiana. The mill was designed to be a modern, efficient competitor to the independent EF plate mills such as Lukens Steel and Oregon Steel. It survived just fifteen years, closing in 1986, a victim of the oilfield slump and the high wages and overhead costs of U.S. Steel.

A number of smaller, independent carbon steel producers that had never operated blast furnaces but used "cold metal" (scrap-fed open hearths) to produce products such as plate or wire rod converted to EF steelmaking in the 1960s. In this they followed the example of Northwestern Steel and Wire, which in the 1930s became the first steelmaker to use electric furnaces solely for carbon steel, producing structural shapes and wire rod in Sterling, Illinois. By 1970 Northwestern had a capacity of 2.5 million tons, and was the model for both medium-size independent producers such as Lukens Steel of Conshohocken, Pennsylvania, and smaller companies such as Washburn Wire in Providence, Rhode Island, to convert to EF steelmaking.

By 1974 the U.S. had approximately 29 million tons of electric furnace capacity in operation, including 14 million tons at integrated companies and other established carbon steelmakers, 9 million tons at specialty steelmakers (including the specialty units of integrated producers), and nearly 6 million tons in the minimill category.

The story of the rise of the minimills will be examined in detail later, but it is important to note here that about thirty-six small EF steelmakers producing around 5 million tons of steel had, by 1971, demonstrated the profitability of domestic production of the products from which the integrated mills were retreating—the lowest-value steel products, including common grades of wire rod, concrete-reinforcing bar (rebar), and merchant bar. The success of these small, mostly non-union companies attracted new investors to the industry and the attention of existing companies. Many long-established independent producers sought to copy the minimills' operations and management style, and one integrated company—Armco—actually bought two domestic minimills and opened a third in Mexico City. The imitation, the sincerest form of flattery, made it progressively harder to define which EF steelmaker was and was not a minimill; but in 1974 every commentator's list of minimills included about two dozen mills that had started up since 1954. With no historic facilities or work practices to encumber them, these new mills would survive and indeed thrive, although not always under the same ownership, during the steel crises of the next two decades.

THE 1973 BOOM: THE LAST HURRAH

The market for steel, which had stayed essentially flat in the 1950s, began to rise in the early 1960s from the plateau level of a little over 80 million tons of apparent consumption. By the late 1960s a new plateau appeared to have been reached, at a level a little over 110 million tons of products. A growth rate of apparent consumption of 4.3 percent a year for the decade was achieved, the fastest sustained peacetime rate since the 1920s.[25] The integrated mills gained in absolute terms but lost out relative to the overall market: the influx of 12 million tons of extra imports and 5 million tons from the growth of minimills meant that the integrated producers' gains were of the order of 15 million tons each year, or about half the total market growth. Nevertheless, this increase maintained the profitability of the integrated companies and permitted their massive investment expenditure; it also meant, however, that much of the obsolete capacity was kept open alongside the newer facilities, so that the average production cost of a company's output did not show the productivity gains that would be expected from the new investments.

The domestic companies' production held up well during a mild recession from 1969 to 1971, in part because import tonnage was reduced due to the combination of VRAs and the boom conditions prevailing in Europe. In 1972 the U.S. economy recovered, and the last great steel boom of the old steel industry began.

In 1973, the peak of the 1972 to 1974 boom, the U.S. industry reached its historic high for production and shipments and in inflation-adjusted terms for sales and profits. Domestic shipments of 111.43 million net tons from raw steel production of 150.80 million tons were limited only by productive capacity; the industry operated at over 100 percent of nominal capability for most of the year. Imports were limited to 15.15 million tons due to the VRA, accounting for 12.4 percent of the market; minimill and independent specialty producers shipped less than 9 million tons. Shipping 102 million tons of all products, the integrated mills were able to report record profits reaching $ 2.5 billion in 1974. At the same time, a sharp drop in new investment spending after 1970 allowed them to improve their balance sheets, reducing long-term debt and encouraging the belief that they might have entered a new growth era, or at least a new plateau in the range of 125 million tons apparent consumption, nearly double the level of fifteen years earlier.

In the heady atmosphere of these years, each company's dream plans for future expansion were dusted off. Three companies, U.S. Steel,

National, and Bethlehem, had acquired large landholdings in the San Francisco Bay area, for example, against the day when the market might warrant an integrated mill in the West.[26] Now engineering studies were commissioned, further fill-in land parcels were bought quickly and expensively, and companies prepared to finance a third decade of massive capital expenditures—this time with emphasis on greenfield plants. Ground was actually broken by U.S. Steel on preliminary facilities for one new mill, at Conneault, Ohio, on the Lake Erie shore astride the Pennsylvania border. With an initial capacity of 3 million net tons per year, and an ultimate goal of far more, the new mill was to supplement and ultimately replace many of the company's smaller and older Youngstown- and Pittsburgh-area mills. National Steel also planned a new lakeshore mill, by adding new steelmaking facilities to its finishing mills at Portage, Indiana, in the Chicago-Gary-Burns Harbor belt of steel mills. Plans for at least 20 million tons of new capacity were announced, and undoubtedly others were prepared but not released.

The dreams were shattered in late 1974. The economy, battered by the 1973 oil shock and by adjustment to the end of the Vietnam War, entered a deep recession just at a time when VRAs had been terminated and steel users were frantically trying to build up inventories. Mills went from carefully rationing their customers by "allocations" through the summer, to layoffs by the end of the year. A much more acute version of the old strike-hedging stockpiling and destocking cycle took place, but this time there would be no return to "normal." As the seriousness of the situation emerged, the expansion plans were quietly shelved again, and the industry slowly began to face up to an era of declining steel consumption—and the surprisingly rapid decline of the integrated industry.

As the first wave of major plant closings hit in the late 1970s, many asked whether the steel companies could have changed their fate by different strategies in the 1960s. With perfect hindsight one can point out two fatally flawed areas of company strategy: both the integrated companies' investments and their labor relations strategies in the 1960s were geared to maintaining the status quo.

In terms of labor inputs to production, the objective was to hold down the rate of increase of the unit cost (hourly wages and benefits) to the extent possible given the need to avoid strikes. No real attention was paid to transforming labor productivity, and even where new technology made this possible, the potential savings were not realized. Productivity gains were impeded by a combination of "featherbedding" and obsolete work practices that management avoided challenging, and by the practice (due to rising demand) of maintaining obsolete facilities in service alongside new equipment.

Capital investment strategy, driven by memories of the flat growth through the 1950s and by institutional attachment to its historic locations, was focused on brownfield, incremental investments at plants that were already mismatched in terms of the coordination and relative scales of their component parts, and that became more cluttered and inefficient with additional investment. An integrated steel mill, seen as a continuous production process, operates as efficiently as its least efficient production bottleneck. The majority of U.S. integrated plants in 1974 were located on pre-1920 steel mill sites, and resembled almost randomly collected vestiges of different waves of expansion on a confined site plan—prewar, wartime emergency construction, and the 1950s and 1960s waves of investment. Replacement or upgrading of one unit, whether a steelmaking, rolling, or finishing unit, might address one bottleneck but could not address the overall problem of coordination of the several parts. Only at a greenfield site could the components be evenly matched and physically sited in line to minimize handling costs and the buildup of work-in-process inventory.

The example of Burns Harbor showed the mills what could be done on greenfield sites. The growth of the market in the 1960s might have allowed between four and six such new mills. Instead capacity was augmented at existing sites by companies uncertain as to what level of demand lay ahead and anxious to maintain throughput at existing plants rather than take the risk of following markets to the South and West with new facilities. By the time the companies began to believe that the greenfield mill strategy was possible, in the early 1970s, it was too late. The economy in the 1970s was driven by new realities of the cost of energy, new awareness of the environment, new materials, and new information-based ways of generating income that did not consume steel. The very costs and conservatism of the integrated part of the steel industry made steel a less competitive raw material in the new environment and contributed to the erosion of its market and its customers' markets. Imports and minimills were a permanent part of the marketplace and were stronger competitors than the high-cost integrated mills. Big Steel, seemingly so mighty in 1973, was to prove a hollow figure.

3

MELTING DOWN: THE END OF "BIG STEEL" IN THE UNITED STATES, 1975–1989

AN INDUSTRY IN CRISIS

In 1975, 21 integrated steel companies operated 48 integrated steel mills in the United States[1]. Twenty years later, 18 of those 21 companies had left the integrated steel industry, been merged or sold off, reorganized in bankruptcy court, or simply closed. Of the 48 mills, 27 were closed or operated as non-integrated plants. Only 8 of the surviving mills were under the same corporate ownership in 1975 and 1995. Integrated steelmaking capacity (excluding electric furnaces) dropped from around 125 million tons in 1975 to around 70 million tons in 1989 and 65 million tons in 1995. Integrated industry employment dropped from 512,000 in 1974 to 168,000 in 1989.[2]

In 1975, each of the integrated companies sold its products at the same prices; each employed union labor on the same terms. In 1989, the surviving companies had a broad range of labor costs; and although still maintaining similar list prices, in practice they each negotiated differing, competitive prices with different customers. The change in the integrated steel industry in this period is as much one of behavior as of structure.

It is common in descriptions of the integrated steel industry to speak of "the industry" as a unit, as if it spoke with a single voice and behaved monolithically. This assumption of cartel-like behavior was valid in many ways into the 1980s, as the integrated firms acted together, formally or informally, with regard to pricing, labor negotiations, and relations with the federal government. However, unlike the more formal cartel-like arrangements for controlling market shares and capacity that exist with the blessing of governments in Europe and to some extent Japan, the U.S. industry had no mechanism other than the market for allocating capacity and shares of a shrinking market. The story of the industry in this period is in large part the struggle by firms with conservative managements to find new ways to do business in a highly competitive environment, stripped of the protection of cartel-like arrangements that had lasted for seventy years.

Many of the old ways of thinking continued, exemplified by the assumptions underlying the campaigns to limit imports—that price competition was somehow unfair and that the steel industry was entitled to special treatment by the federal government as a strategic national asset. At the same time the industry's situation exposed steel company management to the practices and expectations of other industries, through the wave of 1970s conglomerate mergers and demergers, and to greater discipline from the financial markets as companies found they could no longer finance their capital needs from internal cash flow. New patterns of behavior emerged, exemplified by the selection of executives with a legal or financial background to head the largest steelmakers, instead of choosing men with sales and steelmaking backgrounds who had risen within those companies. The threats to corporate survival generated a wide variety of new corporate strategies. The success of some of these left an integrated steel sector in the 1990s with profits and prospects for a future other than terminal decline.

A CHANGING ECONOMY, CONTINUED

The world's economy entered a severe recession in late 1974, driven by the need to adjust to two major supply "shocks" to the world economy. Between 1972 and early 1974, inflation rates in the United States and Europe jumped rapidly, driven primarily by the acceleration of food and energy commodity prices. Farm prices almost doubled in this period, for reasons as diverse as massive wheat purchases from the West by the

Soviet Union, the disappearance of the Peruvian anchovy stocks from the south Pacific, and belated adjustments to the 1971 dollar devaluation.[3] Similarly, the impact of the formation of the Organization of Petroleum Exporting Countries (OPEC) on oil prices in 1973–74 had a widespread inflationary effect throughout the world economy. Each shock had the effect of a permanent move of the global supply curve for a major economic sector, rather than the normal movements of a demand curve in relation to a fixed supply curve. After President Richard M. Nixon instituted U.S. price controls to help get reelected in 1972, he released them in 1973; a short and dramatic boom in the economy resulted, peaking in the fourth quarter of 1973. For the steel industry, the boom continued into the summer of 1974, as steel users built inventory even as orders were declining.

The subsequent 1974–75 recession was similarly short but dramatic, with about a 3 percent fall in final sales combined with a 3.5 percent, or greater than usual, inventory destocking effect. Although all sectors of the economy were affected, the steel industry's customer base was disproportionately hurt. The impact of energy prices caused demand for automobiles to drop immediately and then to shift to more fuel-efficient, smaller, and lighter vehicles, thus causing a permanent downward shift in the demand for steel. Offsetting movements, such as an increase in demand for oil drilling and public transportation equipment, did not affect steel until two to four years later, given the long lead times for capital spending. The year 1975 saw a drop in steel shipments of 30 million tons, or 27 percent, over 1974. Significant falls also occurred in Japan (14.5 percent) and the European Community (19 percent), but effects of the release of price controls exacerbated the recession in the United States.

With hindsight, 1974 appears to be a turning point in the evolution of Western economies. Up to that point, forecasts for all manufacturing sectors assumed growth based on the same level of materials intensity in the economy. Malthusian fears of shortages predominated in policymakers' debates, and concerns about capital requirements for expansion were widespread at the industry level. After 1974, the trend lines shift downward away from their historic curve; but in 1974, with steel operating at 100 percent of effective capacity and shortages widespread, the industry's policymakers may be forgiven their obsession with expansion. In 1975 the integrated steel companies had plans for about 20 million tons of new capacity in the United States, not including minimill plans or about 3.7 million tons planned in Canada.[4]

Industry observers such as Fordham University's Father William T. Hogan worried that worldwide, at least 300 million tons of extra capacity was needed in the decade.[5]

The hubris shown in reported remarks of steel executives in 1974 makes astonishing reading. At the end of 1973, U.S. Steel's chairman Edgar Speer noted that imported steel was having a diminished impact, and soon the AISI's legal counsel was boasting that "the day may be coming when steelmakers in the E.E.C. [European Economic Community] may be demanding for their protection a V.R.A." to slow exports from the United States. The industry did not protest when the U.S. VRAs, in effect since 1968, expired and were not renewed.[6] The most astonishing claim, perhaps, was by the International Iron and Steel Institute, the Brussels-based association of national industry associations. The IISI's secretary-general, Charles Baker, claimed at the end of 1974 that "the world steel community has placed top priority" on developing nuclear energy for steel production. The "huge sums" needed would require international cooperation, but at least three promising technical approaches should be pursued. Bethlehem Steel's chairman Stewart Cort reflected the consensus about the bright future when he spoke in May 1974 of "a decade of at least relatively strong demand."[7] Next month the orders started to dry up.

THE LEGACY OF THE BOOM YEARS

The integrated steel companies collectively earned a record $2.475 billion in 1974, a 6.6 percent return on sales or 17.1 percent on stockholders' equity. Flush with money, the companies took the opportunity not only to plan for expansion but to settle a series of disputes with the Environmental Protection Agency (EPA) with agreements to spend money on air and water pollution abatement and to agree on a generous labor contract, taking effect on August 1, 1974, the first reached under the "no-strike" provisions of the March 1973 Experimental Negotiating Agreement (ENA). In each area—capital expenditure plans, pollution control agreements, and the labor contract—the companies' decisions were based on the assumption of sustained long-term growth in the steel market, if not indefinite continuation of the boom, that would allow these new commitments to be financed. When the depth of the steel recession in 1975 became apparent, the companies could and in many cases did postpone or cancel the proposed capital investments. However, they could not revoke the commitments they made to the EPA or the labor contract.

After 1975, the strategies pursued by integrated steel companies began to diverge as each sought a means for corporate survival. Strategies differed at the company level of business diversification and ownership; at the level of plant and product mix within their integrated steel businesses; and at the plant level, in differing tactics for investment, management, and production. Many of these strategies will be assessed in subsequent chapters. The industry as a whole did, however, continue to pursue certain common goals through industrywide strategies, through either formal mechanisms (joint labor negotiations), neutral forums (congressional hearings), or the continuation of cartel-like behavior (price leadership/followership). The industry also tended to act in common in investing in facilities where perceived capacity shortages posed threats or opportunities, notably in developing domestic ore capacity in the mid-1970s, in pursuing the mirage of the seamless OCTG "boom" in the early 1980s, and in installing electrogalvanizing capacity for the auto market in the mid-1980s.

The industrywide strategies in pricing, labor relations, resistance to imports, environmental compliance, and investment over the next fifteen years were in large part determined by the consequences of the 1973–74 steel boom and the reaction that set in during the next two years. While import controls are a sufficiently complex and important enough area of both steel economics and public policy to warrant a separate chapter, here we cover the other areas of the industry's behavior in the critical decade and a half in which common, industrywide strategies were pursued, formally or informally. These were labor contract negotiations, pricing, environmental compliance, and, to a degree, capital investment policies.

WAGES VERSUS JOBS

The conclusion of the ENA no-strike agreement in 1973, and the guaranteed annual pay increases that the industry conceded in return for the no-strike commitment, changed the way the industry viewed its labor costs. During the years of the ENA contracts, from 1974 to 1983, the annual cost-of-living adjustments and the minimum 3 percent additional pay increase locked steel management into a spiral of cost increases that forced it to examine its use of labor rather than its unit cost, which seemed out of management control. The ENA framework for guaranteed wage increases also allowed the union to focus on different issues, namely job security and retirement benefits.

Between 1950 and 1974, employment levels in the steel industry had been remarkably stable, with between 500,000 and 600,000 employees in steel-producing operations.[8] Over 75 percent of these were hourly paid members of the United Steelworkers of America, covered by the Basic Steel Agreement industrywide contracts. Labor productivity had tended to increase as industry output rose, more through the achievement of economies of scale in the addition of new capacity than by any conscious use of labor-saving practices or equipment. The same crew sizes, with the same work rules, might be used when a plant replaced a rolling mill with a new mill at double the previous capacity, for example. Thus overall labor inputs stayed stable in quantity while the industry's per-ton productivity rose. As long as the industry grew, management looked good, and the industry and the economy as a whole was able to pay steelworkers a premium over the wages of other industries' workers and other countries' steelworkers, based on the growth of productivity.

The 1973 ENA was modeled in part on an agreement that had governed wages in the auto industry since 1948. The United Auto Workers union had been a friendly rival of the United Steelworkers of America (USWA) since 1945, and had a long-standing deal with General Motors called the AIF, or Automatic Improvement Factor. Intended to tie automatic annual wage increases to the trend of average productivity increase in the industry, the AIF had started at a 2 percent annual increase and was bargained up to a 3 percent level by the 1970s. The AIF and a COLA had put the auto workers slightly ahead of the steelworkers in their "race" to be the best-paid workers in America. The problem with this as a model for the steel ENA was that steel industry productivity growth had never been sustained at 3 percent a year, and in the decade to 1972 had averaged 1.5 percent. By giving automatic increases above this level, the steel industry committed itself to increasing labor's proportion of total costs.

Hourly employment costs in the steel industry stayed stable until 1973 as a percentage of the average for all U.S. manufacturing industry. The premium over the average manufacturing wage stayed in the range from 40 to 50 percent until 1974, then rose rapidly to over 75 percent in 1981.[9] Moreover, the premium paid U.S. steel industry workers moved rapidly ahead of the premiums paid other nations' steelworkers. An agreement originally signed because of fears of imports, motivated by the surges in hedge-buying imports during each contract negotiation, perversely helped imports to grow by locking U.S. producers into uncompetitively high costs. In addition, the one thing the unions gave up—their right to strike—was the one tool they were least likely to use when their members' employment was at stake. The timing of the ENA agreement was doubly poor. It concluded at a time when the steel industry was at a cyclical peak, when management believed that output and profits were likely to continue. It was also negotiated immediately before the impacts on steel of structural changes in the U.S. economy became evident—the "supply shocks" of 1972 to 1974, the emphasis on the environment and materials efficiency, and most important, the rise of inflation.

If the industry's negotiators cannot be blamed for not foreseeing changed economic conditions in 1973 and 1974, it must nevertheless be questioned why the ENA remained in place through two three-year contract renewals in 1977 and 1980 when the changed circumstances were painfully evident. Only in 1982 did the eight companies represented on the industry's contract coordinating committee seek to reopen the fundamental terms of their contract, and in 1983 a new contract was signed incorporating cuts in compensation. In the interim, wages increased by 260 percent and hourly employment levels were cut by 50 percent. The relationship between the two numbers was painfully visible to all concerned.[10]

With wage rises essentially taken care of and layoffs a factor of life in the industry after 1975, the union naturally turned toward matters of job security in the 1977 industrywide negotiations. The new contract increased company contributions to the Supplementary Unemployment Benefit (SUB), and increased the benefits payable to laid-off steelworkers to $125 a week, or $170 a week if state unemployment compensation was not available. For "senior workers," the period for receiving SUB was extended to two years. A $300-a-month pension supplement would be paid to any worker forced to retire before the Social Security qualification age. Pensions were to be increased by $1.50 a month for each year of service in 1977, and another $1 in 1979. Although these appeared to be solid gains for the union, the negotiations took place just after a bitter fight for the presidency of the Steelworkers union, in which the "establishment" candidate, Lloyd McBride, had just beaten off a challenge from the more confrontational Ed Sadlowski. When the new contract was presented to the conference of USWA local presidents for ratification, after delays that dragged on into an Easter holiday weekend, the conference actually voted by a narrow margin to reject the contract as inadequate. After scrambling to bring back supporters who had gone home for the holiday, the McBride team narrowly won a second vote.[11]

The 1977 contract simply added to the costs of making necessary cuts at a time where massive layoffs were becoming inevitable. The first large plant closures were announced later that year, thus requiring the weakest companies—such as Youngstown Sheet and Tube, which closed its Youngstown Plant at year end—to pay the highest share of the costs of the 1977 settlement. However, its focus on employment issues in the 1977 contract, like the 1973 ENA, showed that the USWA had far greater foresight in setting its negotiating objectives than did the companies.

By the time the 1980 negotiations were due, voices in the steel companies were beginning to be raised against the ENA. Especially vocal was U.S. Steel's new chairman, David Roderick—a "numbers man" with a financial training, unlike his predecessor Edgar Speer, a traditional industry "hot metal man."[12] At least one company—Jones and Laughlin—considered the possibility of withdrawal from the collective negotiating arrangements. Nevertheless, many companies, driven by commercial departments that still feared a strike more than any long-term threat, sought to have the no-strike agreement renewed. A summit meeting of company chief executives in San Francisco in January 1980 agreed not to continue the ENA after that year's contract settlement, but to allow its extension for one last three-year term.

The 1980 contract contained few innovations; after a relatively good year for steel in 1979, the companies were reluctant to make demands for concessions from the unions, but the unions, conversely, were well enough aware of the underlying problems of the industry to make new demands. Once again it was agreed that the ENA status quo, with its attendant wage rises, continue for another three years, just as the industry headed into a new slump, the worst to date.

THE EARLY 1980s: THINGS FALL APART

While 1979 saw steel shipments by the U.S. industry pass the 100 million ton mark for the first time since 1974, 1980 saw the start of a slide into the worst trough of the industry's history. Shipments in 1980 fell to 83.8 million tons, rose slightly in 1981 to 88.5 million tons, driven by the energy boom in the Southwest, then fell again to only 61.6 million tons in 1982. That year represented the lowest level of shipments since the 1930s; the integrated companies lost $3.3 billion, or 11 percent of their total equity. After a gentle downsizing of almost 15 percent of the union workforce in the period from 1974 to 1980, the industry now had no option but to close idle capacity and terminate as many workers as possible in a cost-slashing race against bankruptcy.

The 1982 steel recession was brought about by the application of Reaganomics to an economy already weakened by adjustments to dramatic changes in the price of oil. The steady rise in the underlying inflation rate to double-digit levels led the Federal Reserve Bank to increase interest rates in the early 1980s to levels where short-term borrowing could cost as much as 25 percent. High interest rates choked off capital spending and cut back household borrowing to buy automobiles and houses, but they also drove up the value of the dollar, thus making both U.S. steelmakers and steel users uncompetitive internationally. Throughout the period of 1981 to 1985, an overvalued dollar made foreign steel irresistibly cheap, driving imports to a new high of 26.4 percent of apparent consumption in 1984 despite import controls. It also drove up the market share of imported automobiles and capital goods, further eroding the market for U.S.-made steel. The Reagan administration's vaunted 25 percent tax cut failed to provide the intended "supply side" spur to the economy in the circumstances, while it drove up the deficit and therefore added to the pressure on interest rates by increased government borrowing.

The policy-driven recession lingered for steel into the late 1980s. In the words of Stephen Axilrod, the Federal Reserve's staff director for monetary policy: "If you have a lot of demand, you've got to keep interest rates high to keep the demand from overheating the economy. When you're trying to wring out inflation, you have to keep the economy below its potential. The nasty way of putting that is you have to keep unemployment high. If you start from a low enough level, you can still have an economy growing rapidly at high rates of real interest. But you won't have an economy at full employment."[13]

This policy, dubbed "preemptive monetarism," certainly succeeded in squeezing double-digit inflation out of the economy. It did so, however, at the cost of an unprecedented change in the U.S. economy: personal real incomes, for all but the top quarter of incomes, stopped growing. The massive unemployment created—in economic terms, an excess supply of labor—drove down the unit price of labor in the economy to levels below those in much of Europe and Japan by the end of the decade. While this historic change permitted a dramatic revival of American manufacturing in the 1990s, it guaranteed that the changes in the steel industry in the 1980s were permanent.

Compounding the overall recession, at the start of 1982 the one sector of the economy that had seemed recession-proof—the booming energy sector centered in Houston and in the oilfields of the Southwest and Rocky Mountain states—began its own meltdown. Sustained by an OPEC price of $34 a barrel and the removal from the world's market of Iran's 6 billion barrels per day of oil production by the revolution of 1980, drilling reached the unprecedented average level of 4,500 working rigs in the onshore United States in the fourth quarter of 1981. Shipments of OCTG—drill pipe and casing—to the U.S. market approached 7 million net tons in 1981, as footage drilled in the United States accounted for 82 percent of all non-Communist world footage in that year. Although signs of a surplus of pipe inventories began to appear in 1981, the dimensions of the glut appeared only after a collapse of oil prices at the end of 1981. By March 1982 the Rotterdam spot crude price was $26 a barrel, or $8 below the posted OPEC price, and falling. U.S. drilling ventures that depended for profitability on $34 oil (or higher) were closed down. As rigs were idled (and orders for new rigs ceased), it became apparent that over 6 million tons of OCTG inventories existed in the oil patch. The pipe market collapsed to just 1 million tons of new pipe deliveries in 1982.

LABOR IN AN AGE OF CONCESSIONS

In the first six months of 1982, 111,500 steelworkers were laid off, more than one-third of the average workforce in 1981. Major mills such as U.S. Steel's National and Duquesne plants in the Pittsburgh area, producing pipe for oilfields, and Bethlehem Steel's Lackawanna Plant had most operations "suspended" while their owners pondered whether to take the inevitable write-off that a permanent closure announcement would necessitate. Meanwhile other mills, even if they appeared to have bright futures because of new investments or secure markets, laid off high proportions of their workforces as operations were reduced to one shift or by reducing the number of furnaces and rolling mills operated at a plant. Thus Bethlehem's Johnstown mill was down to 2,800 active workers in October 1982, from 13,000 in 1979; LTV's Aliquippa Works, near Pittsburgh, down from 10,000 to under 500; and so on.[14]

Few integrated steel mills were located in regions with diversified economic bases. A steelworker laid off in Johnstown, Lackawanna, or Pittsburgh had few options but to move away and try to make a life elsewhere. The 1982 recession was particularly cruel to many families who, having lost jobs in Ohio or Pennsylvania in the first wave of closures in the late 1970s, moved to Houston to work in the high-paying, booming oilfield. One million people moved to Houston in 1981. In the next two years, most of them faced layoffs and moving for a second time. Because a mill's closure meant having to move to find work, families lost the equity that had been built up in a house as mill town property values plummeted. Skills commanding premium wages were suddenly useless outside the steel industry. The restructuring weighed heavily on the rank-and-file steelworker, however generous the short-term unemployment benefits the union had negotiated. Many believed they would never work again. This fear gave the companies a powerful leverage upon the union. In retrospect, it appears that this leverage was used too little, too late to save a core of jobs by negotiating changes in work rules and labor costs. The union officials, on the other hand, lived in fear of their own radical opponents, whose "no concessions" line was a continuation of a long-standing political opposition to what was perceived as the "establishment" of the union's top staffers. Union leadership was very cautious about concessions, due to its need to keep the support of most local presidents in the face of constant criticism from radicals.

While changes in the contract relationship between Big Steel and the USWA seemed inevitable in the light of the industry's meltdown, achieving them was slow and painful. As with the start of the ENA era, its end was foreshadowed by developments in the auto industry. General Motors, which had given the United Auto Workers (UAW) guaranteed pay increases and the COLA since 1948, asked for contract concessions in early 1982. When the UAW resisted "give-backs," the company announced the closure of seven plants. The union quickly backed down, agreeing to wage cuts that would be "passed through" to the customer in the form of price reductions, intended to increase GM's market share and save jobs. Four of the threatened plants stayed open. Both GM and Ford agreed on profit-sharing arrangements for unionized workers and on various forms of labor-management consultation and cooperation on work practices. With its competitor UAW agreeing to such far-reaching changes in its relationship with the employers, the way appeared paved for the USWA to change course. On May 28, 1982, after a year of informal conversations that achieved nothing, the steel companies formally requested a reopening of the 1980-83 contract.[15]

There were precedents for granting concessions. In November 1981, the union agreed a deal with the Timken Company, a producer of specialty steel and ball bearings in Canton, Ohio, on wage and work rule concessions to persuade the company to build a new steel mill locally rather than move to Kentucky or Tennessee.[16] In January 1982, the union agreed in bankruptcy court to wage concessions at McLouth Steel, the small integrated producer in Detroit that had filed for Chapter 11 protection in late 1981. The union then entered negotiations with a potential investor in the mill, Cyrus Tang, to buy the company and commit the necessary capital expenditure for modernization in return for long-run wage concessions and a profit-sharing plan. In November 1982, the local union members overwhelmingly ratified such a plan, and the company emerged from bankruptcy under Tang's ownership.[17]

Meanwhile in April, the union agreed to concessions at the Wheeling-Pittsburgh Steel Company, a medium-size company with plants employing 12,000 people in the Pittsburgh area that was often described as "the smallest of the major steel companies." Wheeling-Pittsburgh had been one of the eight major companies known as the Coordinating Committee Steel Companies (CCSC) that jointly negotiated the basic steel industry contract with the USWA. This put Wheeling-Pittsburgh in a different class from Timken or McLouth, which had "me-too" contracts, agreed separately from but essentially following each Big Steel contract. Wheeling-Pittsburgh was burdened with debt it had incurred for expansion and modernization in the period from 1978 to 1981, including borrowing for a new rail mill that was guaranteed by the Commonwealth of Pennsylvania and the Federal Economic Development Administration. Wheeling-Pittsburgh gained about $1 an hour in labor cost reductions for eighteen months in return for an Employee Stock Option Plan (ESOP), and in November 1982, the company agreed on a further contract amendment giving wage reductions over the period 1983-84 in return for a profit-sharing plan. While the concessions—including a further extension of the wage concessions in late 1984—were not in themselves enough to save Wheeling-Pittsburgh from a bankruptcy filing in 1985, they signaled that the union was willing to place job-saving above maintaining its hard-won wage levels.

After the presidents of the local unions voted to authorize negotiations, talks opened in July. The companies essentially asked to eliminate the COLA: to suspend it for one year and then cap it at 50 cents an hour, regardless of the inflation rate, in years two and three of a three-year contract. The companies also wanted to terminate a plan for extended vacation periods for senior employees reminiscent of professional sabbaticals and to divert 50 cents an hour of wages into the Supplementary Unemployment Benefits fund. The union was willing to suspend base pay increases and make concessions on benefits, but not to suspend or cap the COLA. The late 1970s years of 10 percent-plus inflation were too recent. The talks were suspended at the end of the month. Although the union had unprecedentedly offered concessions—which it publicly claimed would have saved the companies $2 billion over three years—both sides were haunted by the assumption they both agreed to use, of 8 percent inflation continuing over at least three years. In fact, the recession and the drop in energy prices were so successful in killing inflation that it stayed between 3 and 4 percent for the next four years.

The continued layoffs and losses drove both sides back to the bargaining table in November. By then, smaller firms in the industry were lining up to renegotiate their contracts. Northwestern Steel and Wire, a large electric furnace producer in Sterling, Illinois, and integrated producers CF & I Steel in Pueblo, Colorado, and Interlake (now Acme Steel) in Chicago, sought and gained concessions of from $5 to $7.50 an hour in their labor costs. These financially weaker companies, like McLouth and Wheeling-Pittsburgh, now had a competitive advantage over their larger competitors still tied to the CCSC basic contract. The cartel-like uniformity was crumbling in the face of economic necessity. The November talks reached agreement in two major areas. The COLA would be replaced with a complex profit-sharing bonus plan, which would have meant different rates of pay at each company based on its profitability. The union also agreed to separate the companies' small fabrication and specialty plants, known as the List Three plants, from the basic steel agreement.[18] These operations typically competed head-on with non-union independent operations and were especially hard hit in the recession because of their disproportionately high costs. Each List Three operation would now have to reach its own labor bargain, which—in order to allow many of them to survive—would mean dramatic cuts in pay.

The List Three concession killed the November agreement. The tentative terms had to be voted on by the union's Basic Steel Industry Conference (BSIC), with each local president having one vote regardless of the size of their local. The small List Three locals, who would pay the greatest price, were able to muster a majority to vote down the agreement. The union and the companies were back to square one.

When negotiations resumed a third time, in February 1983, the union was under an additional, more subtle threat. The chairman of General Motors, Roger Smith, had called USWA president Lloyd McBride at Christmas 1982 and given him a gentle threat among the season's greetings. GM needed to know no later than March 1st whether there would be a steel industry strike at the expiration of the contract on July 31, 1983. If it appeared there would be a strike, GM would place orders for steel with mills in Japan and Europe.[19] GM had relationships with European steel mills through its European subsidiaries, and its experience with steel there showed the foreign product not only to be cheaper but better quality.

Under this threat to the largest remaining piece of business the integrated mills had, the two sides negotiated down to the deadline. On February 28, a settlement proposal emerged that effectively fudged both the List Three and the COLA issues. The List Three plants would be covered by the agreement but would be free to negotiate their own alternative contracts—meaning, in effect, that plants threatened with closure could impose lower wages. The COLA would be eliminated in year one, while for year two it would be resumed if inflation exceeded 4 percent, and over the third year it would be progressively restored. Wage and benefit reductions amounting to $2.15 an hour in the first year were agreed, far from the levels that had been conceded to the smaller companies that had renegotiated their own contracts, and over the three years the concessions would be restored, giving an hourly cost at the end of the contract actually $2 an hour above the starting level, due to increases in health costs. The settlement was a poor bargain for the companies.

The 1983 contract was the last industrywide one, and its fate reflected the end of the cartel mentality of the industry. With one company, Wheeling-Pittsburgh, already having broken the united front, the me-too negotiations with smaller companies between March and August were chaotic. Each company tried to cut their its own best deal on wage givebacks and work rule changes, each pleading urgent financial necessity—and usually getting better terms than Big Steel had negotiated. After the Big Steel contract was introduced on August 1, local negotiations were undertaken at a number of threatened plants covering concessions on work rules and staffing levels. Where the local unions would not agree to concessions, operations were closed or sold.[20]

Moreover, a spate of List Three negotiations resulted in separate deals for many of the CCSC companies' smaller operations, to try to save, for example, the rebar-fabricating shops of Bethlehem Steel and the wire drawing shops of U.S. Steel. The industry was finally, slowly, beginning to behave competitively.

The 1983–86 contract, with its failure to achieve the $5 an hour or better cost savings that the companies had sought, led first National Steel, then Allegheny Ludlum, to withdraw from the CCSC in 1984. The remaining five companies agreed to dissolve the group in 1985 and to bargain separately for successor contracts in 1986.[21] By the time negotiations were under way, the industry had been transformed. LTV, including both the former Jones & Laughlin and Republic Steel companies since their merger in 1984, had followed Wheeling-Pittsburgh into bankruptcy. A significant number of Big Steel mills had been sold off—National Steel's Weirton mill to its employees in 1982; LTV's Gadsden, Alabama, mill in early 1986; U.S. Steel's Johnstown plant in 1984; and Bethlehem's Seattle plant in 1984. On the West Coast, Kaiser Steel closed in 1983; its finishing end was restarted as California Steel Industries in 1984 by Brazilian and Japanese investors; U.S. Steel's Pittsburg, California, mill was set up as a separate joint venture operation with Korea's Pohang Steel Company as USS-POSCO in 1985. In each case the new entity threw away the old management-union rule book and tried to find a new way of working together. What is perhaps most remarkable about the old ways of working is that they lasted, in the biggest companies, until 1986, a decade after the harm they were doing to the industry was clear.

THE END OF PRICE LEADERSHIP

The other key area where a comfortable industrywide tradition ended after 1975 was in pricing. As in labor negotiations, the industry had long looked for pricing leadership to U.S. Steel, although U.S. antitrust law constrained the cartel-like behavior.

The first major change in the industry's pricing behavior occurred in the 1960s, when U.S. Steel began to hold back from its previously unquestioned role as price leader. The political sensitivity of steel prices until the 1970s seems hard to imagine just twenty years later; but in an economy driven by metalworking, and with pre-OPEC oil prices low and stable, steel's publicly announced and generally enforced price changes were big news. Steel was viewed as a major determinant of inflation, with its role in the public mind akin to that of oil pricing in the 1970s and 1980s: every price announcement got page one headlines nationally. This prominence made steel vulnerable to government pressures. Managing the economy seemed to require managing steel prices, and U.S. Steel was in an exposed position to be "managed."

The 1962 confrontation between President Kennedy and U.S. Steel over pricing showed the companies how serious the federal government could get. After that confrontation, steel industry executives' telephones were rather obviously tapped by the Federal Bureau of Investigation (FBI); their personal income tax returns were pulled for audit by the Internal Revenue Service (IRS); and they were denounced by politicians, the media, and from pulpits around the country.[22] Between 1962 and 1977, the federal government under five presidents attempted to "jawbone" the steel industry into keeping prices low. Rather than announcing periodic price increases—notably after each new labor contract—U.S. Steel tended to sit back and wait for another producer to announce first and thereby be the one to take the public heat for pushing up prices. After the 1965 contract settlement, in which President Johnson had personally intervened to force a settlement on the two sides, U.S. Steel failed to make a price announcement. The industry waited for four months in a state of leaderless indecision and "crisis" until Armco announced a price increase and the other companies followed with relief.[23] In 1968 and 1971, Bethlehem Steel, as the number-two producer, took over the pricing lead role.

During the Johnson administration's price restraint policy, Bethlehem responded to the 1968 new union contract by announcing an immediate 5 percent price increase. The administration, which had urged restraint on the union during the negotiations, responded angrily. The Department of Defense announced that it would buy steel from only those companies that did not follow Bethlehem's lead. Most companies did follow Bethlehem, until after a week U.S. Steel announced that it would raise its prices by just 2.5 percent, within the administration's price restraint guidelines. Bethlehem then cut back to the U.S. Steel prices and the industry fell in line. Almost identical circumstances occurred in 1971. Bethlehem announced a 12 percent increase, this time during the Nixon administration's attempts to control inflation. Again, the government threatened to stop dealings with Bethlehem and companies that followed it, and again it was U.S. Steel that, after a pause to assess the probable outcome, announced a 6.8 percent increase; the administration praised U.S. Steel's "restraint" and the industry fell into line.[24] In the 1971 case, the emerging economic plight of the industry made it hard for the government to act strongly against the companies, and the decline in Vietnam War spending gave it less direct leverage. However, the industry was simultaneously attempting to get (in 1968) and keep (in 1971) government support for the VRA import quotas. In 1971 the president's Council of Economic Advisors explicitly linked extension of the VRAs to continued good "price behavior."[25]

Meanwhile the list prices, to which such public attention was paid, were beginning to show signs of being undermined by events. Even at the height of U.S. Steel's market power in the 1950s, the industry had found discreet "discounting" during recessions to be an irresistible way of trying to fill idle capacity, even if loud public protestations were made that this never happened. As a rule, the bigger the company, the less informal discounting occurred, although even at the biggest mills there were ways to try to poach a little extra tonnage from the competition by bending the rules; for example, perfectly good tonnage might be sold as secondary, rejected material at a discounted price in order to quietly place more tons with a distributor.

In the industry recession of 1968, with import tonnage exceeding 15 million tons and import prices averaging 20 percent less than domestic list prices, discounting became rampant, although every major company denounced the practice and denied that it did so. To try to restore some meaning to the published prices, Bethlehem took the dramatic step of slashing its list prices in November by $25 a ton—22 percent on hot-rolled sheets, for example. The response of other major companies was chaotic, with price cut announcements ranging from $5 to $30 a ton; over the course of two months, Bethlehem gradually raised its book prices back to the former level; and—due more to a firming steel market, with VRAs imposed in December 1968, than to the salutary effect of Bethlehem's shocking action—discounting became much more limited and discreet again.[26]

The 1968 "price war," as the trade press dubbed it, was no such thing; it was an attempt to enforce the system of administered pricing by demonstrating the power of the major companies to their smaller brethren who were stepping out of line. As such it may have had the desired effect temporarily; but it did not stop importers from undercutting the list price. The VRA did that, by limiting the quantity of imported steel, to make it a scarce commodity and to drive its price up closer to the domestic level.[27]

The control of prices that the industry had maintained for seventy years finally broke down with the 1973–74 steel shortage and its successor, the 1975–78 steel slump. During the 1973–74 shortage, mills put all their customers "on allocation," rationing their sales to established customers according to their historic purchases. In these circumstances, spot prices for steel soared above the mills' list prices; imports entered in record numbers in spite of the VRA, which was ended in 1974 as apparently unnecessary. A highly competitive secondary market developed for such steel as was available, and the smaller mills broke the discipline of the list prices again—this time in an upward direction, selling at a premium. Established supply relationships were strained as steel users scrambled to get extra material, without scruples as to its origin or quality.

When the market reversed in 1975, the strain that the shortages had placed on the price mechanism, combined with the sudden surplus of over-inventoried steel, led to even greater disregard for book prices on the downside. By the end of 1975, every mill had an established, if flexible, policy of discounting from its published prices based not on announced schedules for quantity or location but on negotiated numbers. Depending on a customer's industry, location, order size and frequency, and the vendor's perceived competitors, steel prices could vary as much as $50 a ton from a list price of $350 a ton. The published base prices were no longer base-plus, with tables of extras added for quality, shipping distance, and so on; they were the base from which percentage *discounts* were made depending on the market power of the buyer.

Even under such a regime, the industry still had a residual pricing power; announcements of base price increases did still mean real price rises for customers, because real prices were negotiated in terms of discounts from base. This meant that steel price rises were still publicly signaled by company announcements and still subject to presidential and congressional criticism. As late as November 1976, an industry price move led this time by National Steel, raising the base flat-rolled steel price 6 percent, was criticized by President-elect Jimmy Carter, who accused the steel companies of "trying to maintain normal profits at a time of abnormally low volume."[28] Perhaps the last example of such "jawboning" was the apparent leak of a report of President Carter's Council on Wage and Price Stability in October 1977. The report on steel pricing and imports noted that the steel industry was a source of major inflationary pressure, because its price and cost increases were both well above the average for industry. It indicated that the import restraints the industry sought would "not significantly improve" the industry's position, a point reiterated in an interview by the report's author, Dr. Barry Bosworth, who added that the industry was "not in danger of collapse."[29]

By late 1977, however, the preponderant opinion in government was turning rapidly toward the industry's position. From concern about price rises, the balance of political opinion had come to favor price maintenance as a way of supporting the domestic industry at a time of layoffs and plant closures. The closure announcement of the Youngstown Sheet and Tube mill in Ohio and the consequent formal organization of the Steel Caucus, a group of congressmen and senators representing steel-producing districts, showed a groundswell of political support for measures to "protect" the industry. The final outcome of the debate in Washington in late 1977 over steel imports was the Trigger Price Mechanism (TPM), which will be described in more detail in chapter 4 on trade policy. By setting a (high) reference price as a yardstick for scrutinizing imports for potential dumping suits, the TPM effectively set a price floor for the industry. Although the TPM may not have greatly restrained imports, it did give the industry an unprecedented government sanction to an alternative form of administered pricing.

The net effect of the Trigger Price Mechanism is hard to distinguish from those of more dramatic macroeconomic events, the global economic recovery leading to high steel operating rates in 1979 and the fall of the dollar in 1977 and 1978. In those two calendar years the dollar fell 22 percent against the deutsche mark and 34 percent against the yen, forcing import prices up dramatically—by 45 percent between 1976 and 1979—and allowing domestic prices, helped by increased demand, the same dramatic rise. Robert Crandall estimated that of this rise, about a 10 percent increase in import prices by 1979 could be attributed to the TPM.[30] It appears that the price support role of the TPM was unnecessary in the light of actual events. What the TPM did do was maintain for one more economic cycle the role of the integrated firms as price-setters rather than price-takers.

The ability of the integrated companies to maintain a price umbrella over the steel market ultimately depended on how great a proportion of the total steel supply in the U.S. market was provided by firms that followed the "administered pricing" system in a disciplined way. As long as price-setters greatly exceeded price-takers, the oligopoly could be maintained. Until the mid-1970s, the integrated firms and those nonintegrated firms that followed their price leadership controlled over 75 percent of the supply of steel in the market, which allowed enforcement of price discipline on the greater part of the steel service center community through fear of being cut off by domestic suppliers. Although the system was becoming very ragged, especially in times of recession, it held because there were no major suppliers who behaved as price-takers in a free market without reference to the official base price structure.

From the mid-1970s onward, though, the combined share of price-takers grew rapidly, including imports (17.8 percent of apparent supply in 1977), minimills that behaved as price-takers (at least 5 percent in 1977), and the "leakage" of secondary shipments (about 7 percent of shipments) and other forms of "unofficial" discounting from the major mills. Added to these growing sources of free market steel was the growing role of steel service centers, which controlled the final sale of almost all the imported steel as well as a growing share of domestic shipment—16.8 percent of reported shipments in 1977 (and rising)—plus all the unreported secondary shipments the mills classed as "miscellaneous and other." When the distributor sector, whose share of domestic shipments was growing steadily as integrated mills closed or sold their "List Three" distribution, processing, and fabricating operations, controlled pricing of perhaps 40 percent of end-user steel purchases, mill control of the pricing system was ultimately untenable. By 1977, the growth of a free market in steel had reached a level where oligopolistic price discipline could not be maintained without external, governmental support. The TPM provided that support, but for just one more economic cycle.

The steel slump that began in 1980 and was compounded by the oil drilling slump in 1982 brought about the final end of oligopoly pricing. The surge in imports of steel that drove the import share of the U.S. market from 16.3 percent in 1980 to 21.8 percent in 1982 was brought about by a combination of factors: a weak economy in Europe relative to the United States; a shortage of OCTG for the drilling boom, especially in seamless grades of pipe; and the start of large-scale importing of semifinished slabs and billets by U.S. steelmakers. Although the integrated mills were among the culprits, importing not only semifinished steel but also seamless pipe for their customers to supplement their own production, in public they needed a culprit to explain the return of layoffs, plant closures, and red ink. To be fair, their frustration was undoubtedly great at seeing the increased flow of imported steel when their hopes of lasting recovery, raised by the brief 1979 peak in output, were being dashed.

The failure of the Trigger Price Mechanism to halt the flow of imported steel was ultimately caused by the inflation of U.S. steel prices while it was in effect. With double-digit inflation in the United States and prices further boosted by the strong market in 1979, the trigger price "floor" was quickly left behind, despite attempts to raise it in 1980. World spot prices were well below prevailing U.S. prices after the 1979 price rises, allowing imports to come in above the trigger price but below domestic prices. Between mid-1979 and mid-1980, the composite Antwerp spot price for European steel exports averaged $420 per metric ton, compared to $477 per metric ton in the United States.[31] A fixed floor was attractive when prices were declining but of little use when prices rose. The TPM fell victim in 1982 to renewed lawsuits and threats of lawsuits, by the integrated mills claiming dumping and subsidization of imported steel. From 1982 onward, a return to quota-based import control signaled the end of government intervention in steel pricing. Moreover, the explicit deal between the companies and the federal government, whereby the companies withheld their weapon of price-based trade lawsuits in exchange for the quotas extended between 1982 and 1984 to essentially all steel imports, removed the last pricing constraint from offshore suppliers.

From 1980 to 1996, U.S. steel prices have remained stable in *nominal* terms from peak to peak of each business cycle, while fluctuating by as much as 25 percent from the peak to the trough of each cycle. Thus cold-rolled sheet prices to service centers, for example, exceeded the $500 per short ton mark in late 1981, in late 1984, in 1988–89, and in 1994–95. Peak service center prices faced a barrier at around $520 a short ton. In the intervening troughs, domestic prices for the same material have sunk below $400 per short ton in 1982, 1985, and 1992, with import material typically priced 10 to 20 percent below these levels. In real terms, however, with inflation averaging a steady 3 percent, this nominal price stability translates to a 50 percent real drop from peak to peak.

Although the major U.S. mills have maintained a practice of posting list prices throughout this period, at no time since late 1981 have carbon steel transaction prices approached the integrated mills' list levels. Discounting from list has ceased to be an orderly process, and steel buyers have learned to cut their own best deal without reference to list, while the use of "spot" prices or "offerings," once limited to import brokers, has spread throughout the domestic industry. List prices are no longer even a good signal of price direction changes, as they lag rather than lead the market.

The pattern of steel pricing, then, can be divided crudely into three periods. Until 1974, under the oligopolistic "administered pricing" system, real U.S. steel prices based on cost passthroughs rose ahead of inflation and ahead of world prices as long as the integrated companies could control the market through mutual discipline, the price leadership of U.S. Steel (later shared between Bethlehem and U.S. Steel), and the threat of sanctions against out-of-line distributors. From 1975 to 1981, steel prices rose in nominal terms (in an era of high inflation) but fell in real terms. During this period the system of "base-plus-extras" pricing was replaced with "base-less-discount," but some semblance of pricing order was maintained, in part with the support of the federal government through the Trigger Price Mechanism. From 1982 onward, the market price of steel has fallen in real terms while retaining the appearance of stability in nominal terms. Negotiated pricing has become universal, and sellers as well as buyers have become "price-takers" in an imperfect, but largely free, steel market.[32]

Since the 1970s, certain minimills, led by Nucor, have successfully adopted a policy of posting list prices at or even below average transaction prices in the market and then refusing to discount from them except for published quantity discounts. This strategy differs from the pre-1974 days of list pricing in that Nucor and the other mills do not claim to be price-setting. They see themselves as price-takers responding to world prices and U.S. demand, and do not attempt to enforce their prices on others. However, inevitably as this pattern of list pricing spread, a renewed price leadership role emerged in different product markets for leading minimill players such as Nucor, Birmingham Steel, and North Star Steel. In 1996 it appeared as if this price leadership would continue to follow normal competitive patterns of price-taking, with the minimill companies having neither the market concentration nor the philosophy of seeking oligopolistic stability.

STEEL AND THE ENVIRONMENT

Of all the investment decisions made by the steel industry from 1975 to 1989, the most controversial were those related to environmental protection. The Environmental Protection Agency (EPA) was founded in 1970 to enforce environmental regulations previously assigned to a myriad of overlapping but largely toothless bureaucratic agencies. It immediately began to focus on the steel industry, which was estimated in the early 1970s to be responsible for one-third of all industrial waste-water pollution in the United States, and 10 percent of the total air pollution emissions. [33]

Between 1971 and 1973 the EPA initiated lawsuits aimed at almost every steel producer in the United States to compel reductions in air and water discharges in line with the growing international environmental movement. While the U.S. steel industry was not subjected to stricter standards than those in Japan or most of Europe, it did have a higher proportion of older and therefore more polluting facilities, and consequently faced a higher total cost of limiting or cleaning its discharges. The suits placed the steel companies in a politically difficult position. It was hard to fight the popular environmental regulations, put in place under a supposedly "pro-business" Republican administration, at a time when the industry was asking for help from foreign competition that operated under similar rules. Although the AISI made ritual denunciations of the costs of compliance with environmental regulation, there was no concerted industry campaign against them. When company profitability soared in 1973-74, most of the suits were settled by consent agreements under which the companies agreed to spend specific sums by specified dates to bring emissions to required levels.

In the three peak years 1975 to 1977, the steel companies spent $1.2 billion on pollution control capital investment, or 13.5 percent of their total capital expenditures.[34] None of this expenditure earned a financial return, although it did permit plants to remain open that would otherwise be forced to close. As a percentage of industry sales, these numbers are similar to the pollution-abatement costs in the period for the Japanese industry; they are similar to (if slightly higher than) U.S. industries such as petroleum and chemicals, and lower than those of the pulp and paper industry.

The capital costs alone are only a part of the story. Energy requirements for operating pollution control equipment, for example, were estimated at 2.1 percent of the industry's total energy requirements—again, comparable to other industries, such as cement (2.0 percent) and aluminum (2.8 percent). In 1977, the total estimated contribution of pollution abatement costs to total costs was estimated at 5 percent by the EPA, and 6 percent by the AISI—including capital, operating, and maintenance costs.[35]

Given that competing materials, and competing foreign steel industries, had comparable environmental costs, these costs were not likely to make a material difference to the fortunes of the steel industry.

At a time when the drop in profitability and steel demand caused other capital spending to be cut back, however, the mandated environmental expenditures rankled steel executives, who were conditioned by decades of hostility to the federal government to see this as an unwarranted intrusion into their business. The cost of environmental compliance was often cited as a reason for the closure of facilities in the 1970s, and indeed it was a factor in determining the timing of closures. However, as the most polluting facilities of any given steelmaking process were invariably those that were obsolete and inefficient, they were targets for closure anyway. The EPA became a convenient scapegoat to which inevitable job losses were attributed, but its true role was more accurately that of placing the proverbial final straw on the camel's back.

Examples of major steelmaking facilities whose closures were attributed publicly to the cost of environmental compliance included Kaiser Steel's Fontana, California, plant, closed in 1983 after a buyer had been sought in vain for five years[36]; the open hearths and much finishing capacity at Bethlehem Steel's mill at Johnstown, Pennsylvania, closed between 1973 and 1977[37]; and U.S. Steel's Ensley Furnaces open-hearth battery at Fairfield, Alabama, closed in 1977.[38]

In each case the claims do not bear much scrutiny. Kaiser Steel had spent $233 million between 1977 and 1979 on new facilities to try to make the plant profitable, including replacing its open-hearth furnaces with cleaner BOFs and new bag houses to filter air emissions. Kaiser's decision first to try to sell the plant, then to close it, was based on continued unprofitability even after the new facilities had been installed; the lack of prospects for profitability were enough to make both Japan's NKK and LTV Corporation walk away from detailed negotiations on acquisition of the plant. There were many reasons for Kaiser's high costs (in an import-dominated, low steel price market), including the increasing depth and overburden of the company's remaining local iron ore reserves and the transport cost of bringing other raw materials for integrated steelmaking. Pollution controls, for which the principal capital expenditures had already been made, were a very minor element in the picture.

Bethlehem's historic Johnstown plant, which in the 1870s was the largest steel mill in America, was not as chronically unprofitable as Kaiser Steel. However, the mill, on a narrow strip of land stretched along a riverbank for almost twelve miles, faced many problems of layout and plant configuration. In the early 1970s, it also faced the need to replace inefficient and polluting open-hearth furnaces. In 1972, the EPA set a five-year deadline for the plant to curb its emissions. Of Bethlehem's five major integrated mills, Johnstown was the smallest and oldest but faced the second largest environmental cleanup bill. Bethlehem Steel announced in 1973 what had long been feared in the community: the start of a progressive shutdown of those operations that could not meet the EPA standards by the deadline. The mill then started on a roller-coaster of events.

In 1974, at the height of the steel boom, Bethlehem did an about-face; believing it needed every ton of capacity, the company agreed to build a new BOF shop at Johnstown and upgrade the mill. Then with the 1975–76 slump, as capital expenditures came under scrutiny, the upgrade was scaled back and in November 1976 the plans for BOFs were replaced with plans for electric furnaces, with similar steelmaking capacity but that would allow the closure, rather than the upgrading, of the (polluting) coke plant and blast furnaces. In 1977, a disastrous flood in the town brought about the early closure of the mill's primary end, but Bethlehem chairman Lewis Foy, a native of Johnstown, committed the firm to reopening the mill and continuing with the electric furnaces. It was not until 1993 that the company finally gave up on an operation whose products, bar and wire rod, were dominated by low-cost minimills. In the Johnstown case, then, although the costs of environmental compliance were a prominent element in what became a very public debate over the future of the plant (and community), these costs did not prevent the mill being kept open in the medium term, a decision of questionable economic validity.

In Alabama, U.S. Steel's Ensley Furnaces were one of the oldest parts of its sprawling Fairfield mill complex. In 1973, the company faced an EPA deadline of June 30, 1977, to comply with emissions limits and also the evident obsolescence of the plant's hot end. In the 1974 rush to commit to capital investment for growth, the company committed to modernize the Fairfield mill with a new coke battery, new 5,400-ton-per-day blast furnace, and a new BOF shop, thus making a modern hot end capable of producing 3 million tons of raw steel a year. In 1975, the company began to look for ways to stretch out or cancel its capital investment plans and went to court to challenge the EPA deadline. The furnaces emitted around 3,000 tons per year of iron particles, among other pollutants, into Birmingham's air, and the courts upheld the EPA's deadline despite the company's threat that

300 steelworkers would lose their jobs. U.S. Steel continued the capital investment program, and the furnaces were closed on schedule. Although the BOF shop was not opened until 1978, the plant survived in the interim at a lower production rate on steel brought from other U.S. Steel mills. The Fairfield mill, then, is a case where the EPA actually contributed to the survival (to this day) of an integrated mill, by adding to the pressure to start and then to maintain capital improvements that made the plant competitive.

These examples, which could be repeated many times, were cases of great public and political sensitivity. More commonly, the companies and the EPA negotiated agreements for compliance over reasonable time periods, and the EPA (and state agencies) showed flexibility in interpreting environmental laws when faced with politically sensitive job losses. In 1976, for example, the EPA agreed to let Ohio's Mahoning River, into which six integrated mills in the Youngstown-Warren area discharged waste water, stay polluted rather than have the mills close. Strong lobbying by the towns and their congressional delegations undoubtedly influenced the decision; but the practical effect was negligible as five of the six mills were closed between 1977 and 1982 because of high operating costs and obsolete facilities.[39] Similarly, in 1977, the EPA and Pennsylvania state authorities were willing to waive water discharge rules to encourage companies to take over and restart the shuttered Alan Wood Steel Company mill in Conshohocken (near Philadelphia); steelmaking was not resumed there for economic, not environmental, reasons.[40]

The EPA also made a major concession to the steel industry when, in 1981, it approved the "bubble" concept of measuring emissions from a steel plant. This measured air quality on the basis of particle discharges from the plant as a whole, over a dispersed area, rather than measuring concentrations at individual smokestacks or other sources of emissions. The result was to reduce the costs of compliance significantly for a number of plants.[41]

Cokemaking presented perhaps the greatest engineering and cost challenges in seeking compliance with air pollution standards. To make coke, the coke ovens must be opened intermittently for charging of materials and discharging of coke, gas, and tar by-products; it is therefore a process that has historically contributed much of the air pollution of steelmaking. A battery of modern, environmentally sealed coke ovens with a capacity of 1 million tons per year of coke costs as much to build in 1997 as a complete 1-million-ton-per-year flat-rolled electric-furnace steel mill—around $300 million. The coke plant can, however, recover much of its costs from the sale of power and chemical by-products as well as from its output of coke.

The cost of constructing modern cokemaking facilities, and the practical service life of around twenty-five years for a coke battery without a "pad-up" rebuild, led to a steady fall in U.S. coking capacity from 1975 to 1990. Industry coke capacity figures were not released after 1960, but on the assumption that production was close to capacity in 1973-74 and again in 1979 and 1989, capacity appears to have fallen by about one-third, from 75 million tons to 50 million tons in the first five-year period, and then by a second third, from 50 to 25 million tons, from 1979 to 1989.[42]

This dramatic fall in cokemaking, far greater than the approximately 45 percent fall in integrated steelmaking capacity in the fifteen-year period, can certainly be attributed in large part to the costs of environmentally friendly cokemaking. The steel companies' response to the changed economics of cokemaking has been a mixture of more efficiently utilizing coke inputs; purchasing coke from offshore sources (about 20 percent of the total consumption by 1989); and, in the 1990s, the injection of pulverized coal into blast furnaces as a partial substitute for coke. What has not happened is an industrywide coke shortage, despite regular forecasts of such an occurrence. Three integrated companies, Inland Steel, Weirton Steel and WCI Steel, have managed to operate without coke ovens entirely, using purchased coke that they have had no difficulty in obtaining.

Except in the area of cokemaking, the net financial impact of increased environmental controls on integrated steelmaking seems, in retrospect, to have been minor. While a total reported capital investment of $4.5 billion between 1971 and 1982 hardly seems negligible, much of this expenditure was commingled with other aspects of procurement of modern equipment, and in no year did it exceed 14 percent of industry capital expenditures. While industry appeals (which went unheeded) to be allowed to depreciate environmental investments more rapidly certainly had a logical basis, the industry did not oppose stricter environmental controls in principle. Indeed, by the 1990s, throughout the industry it was recognized that polluting discharges were a form of waste, and recycling of inputs, from pickling acids to waste heat, was accepted as good economics. In the long run, therefore, the EPA helped the steel industry to adjust from a culture of profligacy to one of efficiency.

CAPITAL INVESTMENTS: BIRDS OF A FEATHER . . .

While much of the capital investment expenditure undertaken between 1975 and 1989 is best viewed in the context of individual companies' strategies, many similarities of behavior among the integrated steel companies suggest an industry conditioned to "me-too" behavior rather than oligopolistic collusion.

In light of many of the strategies pursued over the next two decades, it is remarkable in retrospect that in the boom of 1973–74, the steel companies did *not* spend money in a number of ways that might appear logical strategic options for cash-rich steel companies. They did not try (until much later) to diversify out of steel; they did not invest (with one exception) in minimills; and they did not (with two minor exceptions) invest in steelmaking in growing markets overseas.

Diversification outside the steel industry, a strategy pursued with a hint of desperation later in the 1970s, was scarcely considered in the 1973–74 boom. Although both National Steel and Armco had made moves into other metals—titanium and aluminum—in the 1960s, most industry non-steelmaking investments were related to either steel fabrication or to steel's raw materials. U.S. Steel, for example, developed its coal mining and cokemaking operations into a profit center by refining and selling by-product tar, gases, and industrial chemicals. Bethlehem Steel, long a major shipbuilder using its own steel plate, acquired interests in yards in Texas and Singapore that focused on offshore oil rig construction. However, no acquisition in 1973–74 foretold the desperate moves of five years later to acquire insurance companies, savings-and-loan institutions, or retailers; steel and its related operations looked to be too profitable to make diversification desirable and appeared to require all the investment funds the companies could find.

Investment in minimills probably appeared unattractive for similar reasons. Armco Steel did acquire two independent minimills in 1974—Pollak Steel in Marion, Ohio, and Sheffield Steel in Sand Springs, Oklahoma, producing concrete-reinforcing bar and fence- and signposts. At both locations, the steelworkers' union contract was imposed; this, combined with the allocation of corporate overhead from Armco, managed to make the acquisitions marginally profitable at best. Both were sold in 1981. The experiment was not repeated until the 1994 announcement that LTV would build a new flat-rolled minimill. In the 1973–74 steel boom, most integrated mills believed they already had the successful formula for profitability and that adding integrated capacity was more important than dabbling in the minimill business. After 1974, when the relative attractiveness of the minimill method was greater, the problem was how to manage an entrepreneurial and preferably non-union operation under the corporate umbrella of a Big Steel company. The integrated companies may have appreciated what Armco learned by experience, that competitive success in the minimill industry was a matter of company culture as much as investing in the right plant and product configuration.

The U.S. steel companies viewed the rest of the world as either targets for exports or as sources of raw materials. Specialty steelmakers had a rather more international outlook—both Allegheny Ludlum and Crucible Steel had built mills in Europe in the 1960s—and Armco had a long record of fabricating operations in Latin America, going so far as to build a small wire rod mill in Mexico City in the 1960s. For the most part, though, the industry's attitude had been summed up by U.S. Steel's Benjamin Fairless in 1962, when he said, "Even if we were of a mind to do so, such a move [geographical diversification] is hardly feasible for the American iron and steel industry. We can't very well scrap our existing plants, representing an investment of many billions of dollars, and spend more dollars to build new plants overseas." [43] In fact, in 1974 U.S. Steel did commit to its first major investment in Europe, spending $225 million on a new cold-rolling mill in Spain, which opened in 1976.[44] However, the investment was quickly sold and the experiment was not repeated.

Where the major companies did consider investing their windfall profits in 1973–74 was in greenfield plant capacity. Companies believed that the shortages of those years indicated that the market could support significant capacity growth, and that there was a chance to emulate Japan's productivity growth by the same method—building waterside greenfield plants. There was also the recent, successful example of Bethlehem Steel's Burns Harbor mill, built from 1966 to 1970, and a major contributor to that company's profits. At least three major mills were announced and came very close to being built. Bethlehem Steel actually built the first unit of a planned major integrated mill at Pinole Point, on San Francisco Bay; the galvanizing line opened in 1976. U.S. Steel completed the planning and most of the permits for a 6-million-ton-per-year facility at Conneaut on Lake Erie before the project was suspended in 1977. National Steel planned a new integrated mill to complement its existing finishing facilities at Portage, Indiana, on Lake

Michigan. Other sites were acquired by other companies with similar long-range ambitions. Each project fell victim to the slump in steel demand in the mid-1970s, as did many lesser projects for incremental capacity expansion at existing mills. Nevertheless, the momentum of projects committed in the 1973-74 period was sufficient to continue the growth of U.S. raw steel capacity through the mid-1970s in the face of closures of obsolete open-hearth capacity; industrywide rated capacity peaked at 161 million raw tons in early 1977.

Major non-environmental capital projects that were completed reflected the industry's pattern of waves of copycat, "me-too" investment in similar types of facilities. Just as the early 1950s saw a rush to build new open-hearth capacity, and in the 1960s investment in new hot strip mills and in BOF shops was popular, the mid 1970s saw a distinctive wave of investment. This time the major companies focused on electric furnace steelmaking and on expanded iron ore facilities. (See table 3.1)

In addition to building new BOF shops to replace open hearths at Fairfield, Alabama, and Fontana, California, an unprecedented number of large electric furnace steelmaking shops were commissioned at integrated companies' mills. EFs could use the home scrap that was formerly fed to open hearths, and had low environmental emissions and low capital cost. Two major EF shops had been built by integrated companies, Bethlehem Steel at Steelton, Pennsylvania, replacing open hearths, and a greenfield mill by U.S. Steel at Baytown, Texas, from 1969 to 1971. In the period from 1974 to 1981, ten integrated companies built additional large carbon steel EF shops. Whereas EF capacity had previously been concentrated on either specialty steel production or at smaller, limited product-range operations, EF shops were now built to supply core Midwest, flat-rolled product mills. By 1981, six EF carbon steel mills with capacities of over 1 million tons were operated by integrated companies: Houston, Kansas City, Steelton, Johnstown, J&L Pittsburgh, and Baytown, not including the massive independent EF shop of Northwestern Steel and Wire in Sterling, Illinois. In addition, Republic Steel built a large EF shop with over 1 million tons of capacity at Canton, Ohio, primarily for its alloy and stainless steel bar operations, the so-called Canton Alloy Shops. The integrated companies were sufficiently optimistic about the growth of the technology to invest in DRI research and even, at Armco in Houston, to install a DRI plant (replacing an unorthodox arrangement of old blast furnaces being used to supply hot metal to electric furnaces during the 1970s). In total, the integrated companies

Table 3.1
CAPACITY ADDED BY INTEGRATED STEEL COMPANIES, 1973–1981

(Millions of net tons per year)

BASIC OXYGEN FURNACE [BOF] SHOPS

Company and Location	Capacity	Plant Configuration	Status in 1996
Bethlehem Steel, Burns Harbor, IN	1.0	At existing BOF shop	Operating
Kaiser Steel, Fontana, CA	2.5	BOFs replaced OHs	Plant closed 1983
U.S. Steel, Fairfield, AL	3.0	BOFs replaced OHs	Operating

ELECTRIC FURNACE [EF] SHOPS

Company and Location	Capacity	Plant Configuration	Status in 1996
Armco, Houston, TX	1.5	EFs replaced OHs	Plant closed 1984
Armco, Kansas City, MO	0.8	Add to existing EFs	Operating [a]
Bethlehem Steel, Johnstown, PA	1.3	EFs replaced OHs	Operating [b]
Bethlehem Steel, Steelton, PA	1.8	EFs replaced OHs	Operating. EFs replaced 1993
C F & I Steel, Pueblo, CO	0.9	Supplement BOFs	Operating
Ford Motor Co. (Rouge Steel)	0.8	Supplement BOFs	EFs closed 1993
Inland Steel, East Chicago, IL	0.9	Supplement BOFs	Operating
J & L, Pittsburgh, PA	1.6	EFs replaced OHs	Plant closed 1986
J & L, Cleveland, OH	0.8	Supplement BOFs	EFs closed 1990
Lone Star Steel, Lone Star, TX	0.5	Supplement OHs	Operating
McLouth Steel, Trenton, MI	0.6	Supplement BOFs	EFs closed 1992
Sharon Steel, Sharon, PA	0.5	Supplement BOFs	Operating [c]
U.S. Steel, Baytown, TX	1.2	Expand existing EF	Plant closed 1988

NOTES:
a Plant sold 1994 to management and investment group as GST Steel, later GS Industries.
b Closed 1993; mill reopened early 1996 as Bar Technologies, Inc.
c Closed 1992; mill reopened as Caparo Steel, 1995.

owned around 22 million tons of EF capacity in 1981 out of a total of 36 million tons. Most of this investment proved to be wasted.

Twelve years later, with the closing in 1993 of the Johnstown mill and of Rouge Steel's EF shop, just two integrated mills retained electric furnace operations: at the Inland Steel Bar Company division of Inland's East Chicago mill and at Bethlehem Steel's Steelton plant. In 1994, a new furnace was added at Steelton to the early-1970s EF shop, in preparation for the unit's supplying (from 1995) the one surviving structural mill at Bethlehem, Pennsylvania, as well as Steelton's rail mill. Two other mixed-process mills, Lone Star and CF & I, closed their integrated open-hearth steelmaking operations in the 1980s and became dependent on their EF shops.[45] The other installations were closed or sold.[46] Of the two new BOF units built in the period, the second Kaiser Steel BOF shop, completed in 1978, operated just five years before the plant was closed. The other, the U.S. Steel Fairfield shop, continues in operation.

In contrast with the short average life of many of these presumably unprofitable investments of the 1970s, the 1960s investments in BOF shops and large hot-strip mills are still largely operational. Of the 83 million annual tons of BOF capacity installed up to 1973, 62 million tons remain in service as the core steelmaking capacity of U.S. integrated steelmaking today. Every "Generation II" hot-strip mill built in the 1960s operates today as the centerpiece of a modern flat-rolled mill.

There are a number of reasons for the contrast in the apparent success of the 1960s investments in BOFs and the apparent failure of the 1970s investments in EFs. One is the fact that the new BOF technology was first installed in the integrated companies' most profitable plants—those at their core midwestern operations, because that was where incremental capacity was needed most in the 1960s. Thus, for example, U.S. Steel installed BOFs at its plants in Gary, Indiana; Lorain, Ohio; and the Edgar Thomson Works in Pittsburgh by 1971, but the outlying areas at that time still relied on open hearths. Fairfield got its BOFs in 1978, while U.S. Steel never made the investment at its Fairless Hills and Geneva mills, serving the East and West Coast markets.[47] By the 1970s, a second tier of mills was faced with the need for investment, driven by obsolescence in their open-hearth facilities and by the environmental question. These mills were less favored either because of site (away from deep water), product mix (competing with minimills in bar products and plate, for example), or because of the obsolescence of their finishing facilities as well as their steelmaking. Companies closed some of these mills rather than waste money on them: the Youngstown area mills, for example. Others had EF shops installed as "quick fixes" rather than invest in a BOF shop that would also require money for coke and blast furnace upgrades, as at J&L in Pittsburgh and Bethlehem in Johnstown.

From examining similar EF installations at integrated and nonintegrated companies, it appears that the problem was not the suitability of the technology, but its application by the integrated companies. Integrated mills had higher costs than their independent rivals, and they were less committed to the businesses typically supported by EF shops. Thus plate mills fed by EF shops, Armco in Houston or U.S. Steel in Baytown, for example, closed while EF/plate-mill configurations at independents Lukens Steel or Oregon Steel thrived. Similarly in beams, U.S. Steel at South Works[48] and Armco at Houston closed while superficially comparable facilities were operated close by at independents Northwestern Steel & Wire and Chaparral Steel. In each case a mill using integrated companies' management and labor practices failed while a company with a lower cost base survived. In such cases, management of a single-plant company may be far more committed to the plant's survival than the management of a multiplant firm would be to any one unit—except where personal emotion intervenes, as it appeared to do with Bethlehem's decision to continue at Johnstown under chairman Lewis Foy. Another contributing factor in the failure to utilize large-scale EF steelmaking successfully may be the failure to combine the steel furnaces with continuous casting.

Continuous casting, after its hesitant introduction in the 1960s, was slowly applied more generally for flat-rolled as well as long-product steelmaking in the 1970s. The question that must be raised here is why, after the initial units had been "debugged" and had demonstrated 10 to 15 percent cost savings as well as quality improvements, the industry still did not fully embrace the technology.

The first U.S. commercial-scale slab caster for flat-rolled carbon steelmaking was commissioned by U.S. Steel at Gary in 1967, and by 1972 seven more units had been commissioned, with a total capacity of 8.8 million annual tons (around 7.5 percent of flat-rolled capacity, including plate). Between 1973 and 1981, the integrated companies added only three additional slab casters. Two more were ordered in 1981. By that year, the percentage of U.S. steel continuously cast had risen to only 22 percent, including more than 70 percent of all minimill production; thus, integrated producers were still using the ingot-casting method for well over 80 percent of their flat-rolled production. Only one flat-rolled products mill was 100 percent continuous cast, the U.S. Steel Baytown mill after its second caster installation in 1977; this was the EF/plate products mill that was closed in 1986. By comparison, Japan was continuously casting over 60 percent of its steel in 1982. The U.S. percentage only exceeded 40 percent in 1985, and then grew quickly toward the 90 percent mark by 1995. Continuous casting for flat rolled steel only became general practice in the United States in the third decade of the technology's development.

Unlike their hesitancy to invest in new technology such as the continuous caster, the integrated companies plunged into expansion of their iron ore facilities in the 1970s with a vengeance. During the

1973-74 boom, companies feared for their abilities to maintain adequate ore supplies for future expansion, and then in 1974 U.S. Steel's and Bethlehem's Venezuelan iron ore operations were nationalized. The suspicions of international investment at the integrated companies must have seemed confirmed. U.S. Steel's chairman Edgar Speer promised that in future, "no one [overseas] nation will supply more than 5 percent of our ore needs." Immediately a series of investments in expanding North American ore mining were planned.[49]

Although around half of the added capacity could be justified by the need to replace depleted mines, at least 17 million tons of additional annual ore capacity was added at a time when iron ore use was dropping. The increased North American capacity did allow reduced dependence on South American and African ores, but at a higher delivered cost. It is remarkable that, at a time when other capital investments were being canceled or postponed, all of the planned iron ore expansions went ahead. It would appear that emotion, rather than logic, drove these decisions—fear of reliance on imports; and pride, in keeping up one's end of a joint venture. The total expenditure on expanded iron ore capacity in the period, at over $50 per annual ton, came to around $2 billion—enough in 1970s dollars to have brought the industry to 80 percent continuous casting in 1981 at a savings of at least $20 per continuously cast ton. Table 3.2 presents the major iron ore expansions.

CAPITAL INVESTMENT, CONTINUED . . . STILL FLOCKING TOGETHER

The 1980s continued the integrated industry's pattern of capital investment in "me-too" waves. During the decade, continuous slab casting finally became recognized as essential for the survival of an integrated flat-rolled steel mill, and by 1992, every major flat-rolled mill used continuous casters, if not for 100 percent of their production. Between 1983 and 1988, when the industry was at its lowest point of output and write-downs, it nevertheless completed seven major casters.[50]

Two other waves of capital investment in the 1980s were in finishing facilities to meet expanded demand. In the early 1980s, in response to the shortage of OCTG during the drilling boom, companies rushed to add seamless pipe capacity. In the mid-1980s, in response to changing demands from the automakers, was a wave of investment in electrogalvanizing lines. The seamless boom very quickly turned into a

Table 3.2
MAJOR IRON ORE CAPACITY EXPANSIONS, 1974–1981

(Millions of net tons per year)

Company	Operation	New Pellet Capacity (million net tons per year)	Service Date	Partners
Eveleth Taconite	Hibbing, MN	3.6	1976	Oglebay Norton, Ford
Hibbing Taconite	Hibbing, MN	5.4	1977	Pickands Mather, Stelco, Bethlehem, Republic
National Steel	Keewatin, MN	3.4	1977	National Steel, Hanna
Inland Steel	Virginia, MN	2.6	1977	Inland Steel
U.S. Steel - Minntac	Mountain Iron, MN	6.0	1978	U.S. Steel
Québec Cartier and Sidbec-Normines	Fire Lake, Québec	6.0	1978	Sidbec-Dosco, British Steel Corp., U.S. Steel
Hibbing Taconite	Hibbing, MN	2.7	1979	(see Hibbing entry above)
Tilden Mining	Tilden, MI	4.0	1979	Cleveland-Cliffs, Inland, McLouth, International Harvester.
Empire Mining	Palmer, MI	2.8	1980	(as for Tilden above)

SOURCES: *Iron Age*, Mar. 29, 1976, page MP-10; Financial Times *Mining International Yearbook*, 1982; company annual reports.

bust with the collapse of the drilling bubble in 1982. The demand for electrogalvanized (EG) steel, however, continued to grow, so that despite large capacity additions, there were shortages of automotive EG steel in 1994.

Between 1979 and 1982, the U.S. market for seamless Oil Country Tubular Goods exploded from around 1.5 million tons per year to over 4 million, then just as quickly back to under 1 million. With an industry seamless OCTG capacity in the area of 2.8 million tons at 12 companies in 1980, the product was heavily imported in 1980-81, including tonnage brought in for finishing and sale by U.S. producers such as U.S. Steel. Not wishing to miss out on a boom, ten companies announced projects for new or expanded seamless capacity. Three of these were minimills, of which only one (Hunt Steel) was completed (and quickly went bankrupt). Two more, at Timken and Babcock & Wilcox, were at specialty companies; the seamless aspects of their capital programs were quickly cut in 1982-83. Six of the projects were initiated by integrated mills. Two of the projects, Wheeling-Pittsburgh's proposed joint venture mill with Kobe Steel, and Armco's project, for a greenfield seamless mill to be supplied by a new rounds caster at Ashland, were canceled promptly when the market turned. Four major projects were at least partially completed. J&L built a new seamless rounds caster at Aliquippa from 1980 to 1982, to supply its Aliquippa and (expanded) Campbell Works seamless mills, at a cost of over $300 million. The Aliquippa seamless mill closed in 1983, the Campbell mill in 1986, and the new caster was written off. U.S. Steel built new rounds casters at both Lorain and Fairfield, the latter being part of a new caster and seamless mill complex completed in 1984 at a combined cost of over $700 million. CF & I Steel completed a new rounds caster and was halfway through building a new, second seamless mill when the project was put on hold in late 1982. Of the $175 million spent, $76 million was written off in 1984. The completed rounds caster was used to supply the original mill.[51]

As in the case of the iron ore expansion of the 1970s, the industry had spent over $1 billion on capacity to meet a demand spike that was never repeated. In the mid-1980s, the seamless mills collectively operated at less than 25 percent of capacity until a number of companies—Armco, Wheeling-Pittsburgh, Babcock & Wilcox, LTV (including both J&L and Republic's seamless mills), and Phoenix Steel—all exited the market between 1984 and 1988. In the 1990s, U.S. Steel remains the only integrated seamless producer, with a unique market position by virtue of its ability to a supply a size range from 2 inches to 26 inches outside diameter. There are only three other domestic companies now in the market for OCTG sizes of seamless, all EF producers: CF & I, which closed its BOF shop in 1986; Newport Steel's Koppel Steel division, which operates the former Armco seamless mills; and North Star Steel, which bought the new seamless minimill Hunt Steel's assets from bankruptcy in 1985. OCTG prices have never recovered: average 1994 prices, as tracked by the Preston Pipe Report, were only 66 percent of the nominal prices in 1982.

The other wave of capacity additions has had a much happier fate. In the early 1980s, determined to win back market share from Japanese suppliers through quality improvements, U.S. automakers began to press the steel industry for electrogalvanized (EG) sheets. The model years from 1987 to 1991 saw a gradual switch from hot dip (HD) galvanized or simply painted, ungalvanized steels to EG steel (plus some aluminum and plastic) on most exposed surfaces on U.S.-made cars. EG steel has higher rustproofing qualities than HD galvanized and has a smoother surface finish for painting. In 1984, the announcement by each of the big three automakers that they were looking to buy significantly more EG steel for the 1987 model year surprised a steel industry that had only three EG plants. Five new lines were brought on stream in 1986, increasing industry capacity from 550,000 annual tons to 2.2 million. The success of these facilities led to three more lines being built and commissioned, again within months of each other, in 1992. [52]

The expansion of HD galvanizing was also significant, although most of the capacity additions in this area did not start up until the 1990s and will be discussed later. Overall, galvanized steel was the major product success of the integrated steel industry over the last ten years. Total galvanized shipments rose from 6.75 million tons in 1984 to 14 million tons by 1995 and are expected to continue to grow. This increase in tonnage is not additional steel use, but rather the substitution of higher value-added (and, usually, more profitable) steel for less expensive uncoated cold-rolled or hot-rolled sheet. EG sheet commanded a price premium in 1995 of approximately $100 a ton over HD galvanized steel, which in turn sold for approximately $100 a ton over uncoated cold-rolled steel. The galvanized market is a major target of flat-rolled minimills for the late 1990s.

JUST WHEN WE NEEDED A CARTEL, IT COLLAPSED

The period of retrenchment and restructuring in the years 1974 to 1989 was as painful for the European steel industry as for that of the United States, and was not easy for the Japanese industry. The latter industry stopped growing in the early 1980s, as Japanese conglomerates exited the shipbuilding industry and as Japanese carmakers began to move production overseas, closer to their markets. Although still a major net exporter of steel, chiefly to China and other growing Asian markets, the Japanese industry has begun to implement cutbacks in capacity, aided by government assistance and the promotion of market-sharing arrangements under formal (governmental) and informal (market-sharing) agreements. The real changes for Japan's industry appear to lie ahead in the next ten years, as the nation's economy continues to move away from metal-based manufacturing and as export markets become more self-sufficient in steel.

The European industry has undergone a transformation more closely resembling that of U.S. industry. While this is not the place to discuss that transformation, certain key differences in the way the transformation was managed are instructive. Above all, the problems of the European Community (EC) steel producers were accepted from the start as problems that governments would have to deal with, whether they were the owners of nationalized steel companies (as in Italy, France, and Britain for parts of the period) or not (Germany and the Benelux countries). The EC's predecessor, the European Coal and Steel Community, had indeed been founded to restructure the continent's industry on an international scale after World War II. Subsidies were given directly and indirectly to national steel industries to invest in new capacity and to shut down obsolete capacity, notably in the period 1977 to 1984, when around a third of European capacity was permanently closed. Governments shouldered the burdens of unemployment and pension payments, and also intervened to support prices and allocate market shares at times of extreme market recession, as under the Davignon Plan of 1980 to 1983.

The use of these tools, plus the more recent effects of privatization in Britain and Italy, has accomplished a restructuring that has been in some ways more far-reaching than that in the United States. The British steel industry, for example, has gone from twenty integrated mills at the time its integrated firms were nationalized (for the second time) in 1967, to five heavily modernized mills on its reprivatization in 1988 (and four today), while its capacity has been cut by a half.

Regardless of the philosophical merits and demerits of cartels or government intervention, industrywide planning does have the advantage of allowing capacity cuts and investment allocation decisions to be made without having to protect against the competitive reactions of other players. In the 1970s and 1980s the U.S. integrated industry was weakened to a far greater degree than its European equivalent due to both the reluctance of individual firms to close capacity (lose market share) and to poor investment decisions driven by the need to keep abreast of other companies' actions (maintain market share). The failure to persuade the federal government, or the public, that a national industrial policy for dealing with the steel industry's problems—the trade issue aside—condemned the industry to suffer a protracted "free market" transformation just as it emerged from conditions of oligopoly that could, in theory, have been used to allocate markets and capacities. It also condemned millions of lives, and entire regions of the country, to disruption and poverty for up to 15 years until the same free market restored jobs and growth to those regions.

The U.S. industry might also have undergone its transformation more rapidly, and emerged with fewer but more efficient facilities, if it had just five or six companies of the same average integrated company size as in Japan or Europe. U.S. antitrust law, administered by governments accustomed to view the steel industry as prone to anticompetitive, cartel-like behavior, generally precluded mergers except when companies were close to failure, as with the 1979 and 1984 mergers from which emerged LTV Steel. Larger companies would hypothetically have been capable of undertaking the kinds of wholesale closures of marginal capacity that only U.S. Steel, and LTV when in bankruptcy, was able to do from large "portfolios" of facilities. The evidence shows, however, that there is no guarantee that increased company size will lead to better decisions.

The survival in the United States into the late 1990s of 12 publicly traded, integrated steel companies, 8 of which have less than 5 million tons of capacity, would have seemed implausible in the 1970s when numerous studies "proved" that the economics of BOF steelmaking were optimized above 6 million tons of annual capacity. The adoption of entrepreneurial survival tactics, including minimill-like corporate cultures, was one change not used in Europe or elsewhere, because the struggle for survival in a free market did not require it. The other radical change in the industry—the growth of the minimill sector toward dominance of long products markets—has been constrained in Europe by the same measures that strengthened its integrated companies. It is therefore possible to argue that, by allowing the rapid shrinking of the integrated industry, U.S. free market policies have succeeded in giving the U.S. leadership of the world's steel industry once again, by creating the opportunity for growth of the minimill.

4

PLEAS FOR PROTECTION: THE POLITICS OF TRADE

THE IMPACT OF IMPORTS: SOME BASIC ECONOMICS

In any capital-intensive production process, marginal changes in the level of output have disproportionately large effects on profitability. Because fixed costs are a high proportion of total costs, to make a profit plants must operate at high levels of production, usually described in the steel industry in terms of the percentage of nominal annual capacity utilized. Thus a break-even operating rate for a firm or the industry might be of the order of 70 to 90 percent of capacity—although, of course, the actual rate will depend on the market prices attainable and the firm's ability to control its variable costs of labor inputs, power, and raw materials. Firms in a free market with no barriers to entry will typically operate not far above the break-even rate, where they compete for "marginal" or incremental business.

In any such industry, the impact of a new competitor is significant at the margin: if a new entrant captures just 10 percent of a market previously divided between two existing firms, the loss of (say) 5 percent of their output each may alone be enough to drive both existing players below their break-even output level until they adjust their costs or product mix. Worse, the new competitor will probably undercut existing price levels to enter the market, so that overall market prices fall as the existing players struggle to hold their level of market share (and production throughput). As a result of falling prices, the break-even level required for existing firm's profitability rises at just the time when their market share is falling. Conversely, however, the exit of a competitor from a market may have a positive impact on other firms' profitability that is disproportionate to the market share held by the departing firm.

This powerful effect of small changes in market shares means that competitive firms in the global steel industry are continually trying to capture market shares by offering advantages in quality, service, or (most often) pricing. Pricing is a tool that can be used selectively at the margin because once the break-even operating rate has been passed, any additional sales add to the firm's profitability even if they are at low prices—as long as the price received covers the direct costs of producing those extra tons. Thus once fixed costs are covered by a base load of output, the remaining capacity can be used to produce tonnage sold at marginal cost pricing, with profitability being reckoned on the surplus over variable costs rather than the surplus over total (variable plus fixed) costs. Electric and telephone companies use this principle in offering discounted off-peak rates to increase the use of otherwise idle capacity. For a steel company, however, the use of marginal cost pricing offers as many dangers as opportunities. The company's "base" customers may find out that other "marginal" customers are getting better terms, and seek the same pricing for themselves. If so, and the overall price level in the market declines, the firm will be worse off than when it started to buy the extra market share.

To successfully implement a strategy of marginal cost pricing in the steel industry, then, requires that customers to whom marginal tonnage is offered at a lower price are somehow isolated from the majority of base-load customers. Companies can attempt to do this by trying to maintain the secrecy of discounted-price deals; but more often, and more successfully, they do it by pricing at different levels in different geographical markets, where the barriers of distance and differing business cultures allow different prices to prevail.

Because these geographical differences are maintained over time, a classic national strategy for industrial growth is to maintain high domestic prices through tariff barriers while exporting surplus production at lower prices to industrialized countries. Each of the countries that has sought to grow its steel industry through exports has pursued this strategy—whether or not supported by explicit government price support mechanisms. Wherever capacity has been installed in excess of demand in the domestic market, that country has sought to export at lower prices, thus creating a world spot market for steel that (except in times of shortage) operates at below the average selling prices in major markets. Since World War II, first Western Europe (in the 1950s), then Japan (the 1960s), major Latin American countries (the 1970s), then Korea (the 1980s), have pursued export-dependent capacity growth in their steel industries. In the 1990s, the states of the former Soviet Union have diverted capacity to exports as that region's demand has slumped and need for convertible currency has grown; Turkey and the Southeast Asian nations are pursuing the same export-led strategy.[1]

From the 1960s onward, two types of new entrants have captured significant shares of the U.S. domestic carbon steel market: imports and minimills. Both types of new entrants have had essentially the same type of depressing effect on market pricing and the market shares of integrated firms, and both have followed a pattern of starting their inroads with the lowest-cost products (wire rod, bar) and moving up to higher-value, flat-rolled products. However, their timing and strategies in market entry have been somewhat different. The importers began to capture share from around 1959 onward, about a decade before minimills emerged as a growth sector. Their move up to higher-value products was more rapid, both because they did not have to develop technology (for the most part, imported steel is produced by integrated mills) and because their prices were undercut by the minimills.

The presence of individual foreign suppliers in the market has often been transient, depending on the value of the dollar and the relative attractiveness of other opportunities worldwide. Inevitably, overseas suppliers are less committed to U.S. markets than are the minimills for whom the United States provides the base throughput. Importers use marginal cost pricing in the U.S. market, when not constrained by government intervention. This gives foreign steel an advantage in terms of downward price flexibility in weak markets and a disadvantage in stronger markets when the steel may be diverted more profitably elsewhere. Offshore steel may therefore be less appealing as a long-term source for major manufacturing steel users, although Japanese, British, and Canadian mills have maintained shipments to established U.S. customers regardless of short-term trade shifts.

The biggest difference between foreign mills and minimills, however, lies in the simple fact that integrated mills have access to political tools to assist their competition with any non-U.S. supplier. They have no such recourse against new U.S.-based market entrants. The arbitrary nature of national boundaries and the politics of trade may be seen along the U.S.-Canadian border. In New York State, for example, Canadian pipe and light structural shapes are available from low-cost mills, organized by the United Steelworkers of America, located a few miles over the border from Buffalo. Yet because of federal and state "Buy American" legislation, urged by union pressure, government construction work in New York uses non-union pipe and shapes brought at higher cost from as far away as Texas, Louisiana, or Arkansas. Discriminatory sourcing or "Buy American" rules have nevertheless generally had a minor impact on steel trade, serving only to increase the comparative costs of the government agencies and firms that adhere to them (and force distributors to maintain dual inventories of foreign and domestic steel). National trade policy, however, has had a major impact through its constraints on the ability of foreign steelmakers to supply U.S. customers. Trade policy designed to protect the integrated steelmakers had three related direct effects on the steel market: it limited the volume of foreign steel entering the United States; it increased the overall domestic price level of steel; and it forced the foreign steel suppliers to move toward the highest-value segments of the steel market. What it could not do was what the integrated companies sought: preserve the status quo.

THE IMPACT OF IMPORTS: SOME BASIC POLITICS

Between 1968 and 1992, U.S. steel imports were constrained by non-tariff barriers for all but five years. During this period the greater part of the structural adjustment of the U.S. steel industry took place, including the end of the integrated mills' "administered pricing" system, the loss of two-thirds of the industry's jobs, and the exit of integrated mills from essentially all but flat-rolled product markets. Integrated steel followed the examples of the U.S. shoe and textile industries under protection: their decline continued even though—or perhaps because—their customers were saddled with excess costs due to protection. It is easy to conclude, therefore, that trade protection was ineffective as a component of national economic policy; moreover, a number of detailed econometric studies have concluded just that in rigorous detail.[2] Nevertheless, trade protection was maintained for a lengthy period and remains an issue in the mid-1990s, for reasons that have little to do with economics and everything to do with politics.

The pressure on the federal government to "do something," to adopt an interventionist industrial policy in response to structural change in a given industry, depends on at least four variables: (1) the industry's absolute size; (2) its geographic concentration; (3) the nature of public perceptions and exposure to the industry; and (4) the perceived strategic importance of the industry to the country, both in terms of its impact on other industries and on the comparative economic and military standing of the United States. Thus an industry like fast food, similar in sales and employment size to steel in the 1960s, which underwent a dramatic restructuring as traditional diners and soda fountains were replaced with product-specialized fast food chains such as McDonald's, saw no pressures for government intervention. The declining industry segment was large but geographically scattered so that no one politician depended on its votes; its component companies were too small to afford to lobby, it was largely non-union, and it had no claim to strategic importance. The oil industry, on the other hand, fulfills most of the criteria, but government support for it has been constrained by widespread popular hostility to the industry based on memories of price rises, shortages, and exaggerated beliefs about industry profitability.

Steel had the advantages of being large, concentrated in a few key states, and a vital input to much of American industry; it also had few direct enemies as it did not sell its product directly to the public, unlike the petroleum industry. It was, moreover, an industry in which presidents and congressmen were historically happy to intervene on pricing questions and in labor negotiations. Integrated steel was therefore a politically sensitive industry in both senses of the term; its management, although uniformly and adamantly Republican in their politics, knew how sensitive Democrats were to the voting strength and funds of the steelworkers' union.

IDEOLOGY AND BUREAUCRACY: U.S. TRADE LAWS

Until the early 1960s, the carbon steel industry was, on the rare occasions when the question arose, committed to free trade. Only three major integrated companies, U.S. Steel, Bethlehem Steel, and Armco, maintained major export sales organizations. Only Armco, with its fabricating operations and grinding ball plants in Latin America (much of whose business was with the U.S.-owned mining industry), had significant manufacturing interests overseas. Only Bethlehem and U.S. Steel had raw materials properties outside the United States and Canada. Except for certain specialist trading companies, the remainder of the industry operated essentially within North America. An industry operating essentially in a state of autarky—that is, independent of international trade—would not find it hard to change to a stance against free trade once its interests became threatened.

Chapter 2 described the growth of imports in the 1960s. The combination of the triennial threat of strikes in the domestic industry, the growth of capacity in Europe and Japan beyond the immediate level of demand in those markets, and the cost advantage of many overseas producers drove the United States from net exports of steel of 1.7 million tons in 1958 to net imports of 15.8 million tons in 1968. The major surges occurred in years when labor contracts ended and strikes threatened—in 1959, 1962, 1965, and 1968; but the intervening years saw not a return to previous import levels but the maintenance of a new plateau.

As early as 1965, the AISI began to collect data on Japanese and European steelmaking costs with an eye to invoking existing U.S. trade law against "dumped" foreign steel. U.S. trade law is complex, involving the executive, legislative and judicial branches of government, and its complexity allows a politically astute industry many ways of exercising pressure against imports.[3]

In 1934, Congress delegated to the president the power to raise and lower tariffs. By the 1950s, the U.S. Tariff Commission (the future International Trade Commission, or ITC), created as a fact-finding agency in 1916, had acquired authority from the president and Congress to determine tariff policy, including non-tariff restrictions on imports and exports such as licensing or quotas. Today most trade cases are determined by the ITC.

Three main types of cases can bring about action by the ITC to change U.S. import policy. First, at the request of either the president or Congress, the ITC can review an import category for any reason under the so-called escape clause built in to successive trade acts. The second and third types of case, antidumping investigations and countervailing duty investigations, may be undertaken at the request of a firm, an industry association, a union or group of employees, or at the ITC's own initiative. Dumping occurs when goods are sold either below their cost of production or at a lower price in the export market than in the exporter's home market. Given the widespread use of marginal cost pricing by steel exporters, the vast majority of globally traded steel could be found to be dumped under this provision. Countervailing duties are invoked if a foreign firm or industry is found to be subsidized by its government. Given the prevalence of government intervention to promote or protect steel industries worldwide, especially from the 1960s to the 1980s, once again a high proportion of traded steel could potentially be found to be subsidized. The collection of data in antidumping or countervailing duty cases is undertaken by the U.S. Commerce Department, nominally through its commercial attachés at U.S. embassies worldwide.[4] In practice, the department hires teams of consultants, usually including both lawyers and accountants, to visit the foreign producers and assess production cost, selling price, and subsidy data. The foreign supplier usually, if reluctantly, cooperates and opens its books to the visiting investigators; if the foreign entity is not fully open and cooperative, it is presumed guilty of whatever dumping or subsidy allegation has been leveled against it, and the ITC will automatically impose sanctions reflecting the claims, however outrageous, of the domestic petitioner. The Commerce Department reports to the ITC whether, on the basis of its findings, dumping or subsidy has actually taken place and at what level (usually described in terms of a percentage of selling price in the United States) but does not take further action itself.

In all cases, the ITC must review the Commerce Department data and determine whether domestic U.S. firms face injury or the threat of injury from the imported goods. Relief can take the form of increased tariff duties, quotas, negotiated agreements with the foreign supplier, or (permitted but rarely used) adjustment assistance such as loans or tax relief to the petitioner.[5] When a relief measure is imposed, a review date must be specified (after at least two years, and usually three to five years after the effective date) by which the ITC must determine whether removal of the relief measure would cause injury.

These procedures conform in most respects to the international standards set out in the 1947 General Agreement on Tariffs and Trade (GATT; since 1995, the World Trade Organization [WTO]) of which the United States was the major proponent. However, the United States is the only country with an antidumping code that does not require evidence of material injury to domestic producers, as required by GATT; rather than require firms to demonstrate material injury, the presumption of injury is sufficient for the ITC to impose remedies. Given the low spot export prices of most traded steel, the antidumping procedure, then, is a weapon that can be used against almost all imported steel in the

United States, with the domestic petitioner having to prove nothing and the foreign supplier having to prove its "innocence" to the Commerce Department investigators.

As this process is heavily slanted against the foreign supplier, the major recourse for foreign steelmakers from the 1960s to the 1980s was to have their governments intervene to threaten retaliatory action against U.S. exports. The bluntness of this instrument, and the threat of escalation to an all-out trade war, was a powerful force tending toward negotiated compromise. From the late 1980s, however, foreign steel companies became more sophisticated in using U.S. law to challenge trade decisions. Japanese and European companies took to hiring the same consultants who had previously worked for the Commerce Department, to generate their own sets of cost and pricing data to defend their actions and to try to demonstrate the lack of injury to domestic producers. As a result, the success rate of U.S. steelmakers' petitions has declined greatly in the 1990s.

All forms of trade protection, almost by definition, raise domestic prices; "protection" is against not the foreign product per se but against its competitive pricing. The most logical action the ITC could take in response to widespread problems caused by imports would appear to be to raise tariffs, across the board, on the products in question. U.S. tariffs on most types of steel were in the 6 to 8 percent range in the 1960s and have gradually been reduced in successive rounds of trade negotiations to their current average of 3 percent. Tariffs at these levels appear to have negligible effect on steel imports; why not, then, simply raise the steel tariff? Tariffs are simple tools that are economically efficient and subject to a well-understood regime of international law. Under the original 1947 GATT treaty, any government may raise tariffs when an industry is hurt by competition from imports, as long as the tariffs are applied equally to all participating nations (the "most-favored nation" clause) and the government imposing the tariff either allows its trading partners to retaliate or itself makes concessions on other imported products in order to balance its overall trade flows.[6] Both economists and the consensus of international opinion reflected in the GATT and WTO treaties accept tariffs as a second-best alternative to free trade.

Nevertheless, the ITC proposed raising tariffs on steel on only one occasion, in 1984, and its recommendation was quickly rejected by the Reagan administration. The favored alternative, used between 1968 and 1974 and between 1984 and 1992, has been negotiated bilateral agreements known as Voluntary Restraint Agreements (VRAs) to set quotas on U.S. imports from steel exporting countries. VRAs have been used extensively by the U.S. under both Democratic and Republican administrations to protect not only steel but textiles, apparel, footwear, color televisions, machine tools, and automobiles; they have also been used, against Japan, by the European Community.

VRAs have the disadvantage that they require lengthy and often hostile negotiation with (to be effective) large numbers of supplying countries; they generate diplomatic and political hostility that may require trade-offs in other areas to assuage; and they are inherently porous and open to abuse, because they are not universal. Moreover, they generally benefit the foreign suppliers more than the domestic industry. Foreign market shares are frozen and effectively institutionalized, and the limit on growth in market shares and the capacity constraint on foreign suppliers encourage them to raise their U.S. prices, thus transferring funds as profits out of the United States that would either not be earned (under free trade) or would be paid to the U.S. government (as tariffs). The United States as a whole thereby loses from VRAs in the short run, while the mechanism does nothing in the long run to roll back import shares by increasing the competitiveness of domestic suppliers.

VRAs benefit the domestic industry in that they allow prices to be raised without erosion of market share to imports. This argument is usually couched in terms of the need to finance investment for modernization and renewed competitiveness, rather than in terms of the need to charge more to steel customers. Under carbon steel VRAs (and under the specialty steel VRAs), the domestic price level did indeed rise, freed from the threat of losing market share to cheaper imports, and the profitability of domestic companies was thereby enhanced; but the assumed increase in investment did not materialize. Integrated company investment actually fell under both VRAs, for reasons that appear to include both the perception that the industry need not try so hard to compete when protected, and also the fact that outside capital markets viewed with disfavor an industry under a protective government umbrella that might be removed with disastrous effects.

A second method of raising domestic prices by targeting imports was tried once as an alternative to steel VRAs, the so-called Trigger Price Mechanism (TPM) imposed by the Carter administration and effective from 1977 to 1981. The TPM was designed to address the antidumping argument of domestic industry and explicitly to raise price levels to provide companies with the financial means to modernize.

Under the TPM, no quotas were set for imports; however, a threshold price was set below which imports were assumed to be dumped and, therefore, subject to the rapid imposition of punitive antidumping duties that would in effect exclude that supplier from the U.S. market. The trigger prices were set on the basis of calculated Japanese industry costs, on the assumption that Japanese industry was the most efficient producer, and applied to all steel importers. As with VRAs, the short-term effect was to raise the prices of imports and thereby the general level of pricing in the market; however, unlike under VRAs, the foreign suppliers could still ship extra tonnage into the United States. Encouraged by their increased profits, they naturally did so. Industry pressure eventually caused the TPM to be abandoned, under the threat of resumption of the kinds of massive antidumping and countervailing duty suits that the TPM had been designed to forestall.

Ultimately, both the VRA and the TPM proved to be tools that did little to help the domestic industry while increasing the profits of foreign suppliers. A number of studies of the impact of trade restrictions on steel have not found any evidence of new jobs created in the United States; at best, the restrictions slowed down the pace of the restructuring of integrated steel and thereby arguably slowed the growth of the minimill sector. The costs to the rest of the economy in terms of higher steel prices are large and relatively easy to estimate; the costs to the industry itself, in terms of diversion of effort into politics, the prolonged delusion that "normal" times would return or could be reimposed under protection, and the decline of investment under VRAs condemns them as a tool.

It remains a subject of debate among political scientists why such clumsy, and arguably counterproductive, tools were ever chosen (and remain an option advocated by some). There are generally three competing arguments. First, VRAs may be desired by industries that believe they can gain greater protection from freezing market shares, and from limiting competition thereby, than they can gain under the increased pricing but continued competition under tariffs. This argument implies that the domestic industry is powerful enough to get what it wants. Second, they may be a tool deliberately chosen by free trade administrations, knowing their ineffectiveness, to "buy off" protectionist demands in Congress and from industry. Third, the institutional interests of government bureaucracies may be served by the use of non-tariff tools that placate foreign governments, obscure the causes of inflation, and do not harm domestic interests such as ports, importers, and traders.[7]

While each of these arguments has some bearing on the issue, the fact that the domestic integrated steel companies have consistently supported quotas, as opposed to other forms of remedy, appears to strengthen the first argument in the case of steel. The difference between VRAs and the Trigger Price Mechanism, which the industry ultimately rejected, was that competition for market shares continued under the TPM. VRAs have always been seen as a sufficiently favorable alternative to antidumping or countervailing duties for such suits to be withdrawn in favor of the imposition of VRAs. The choice of the VRA as a policy instrument is also consistent with the behavior of an oligopolistic industry striving to defend its practices of "administered" pricing and stable market shares—even though the economic viability of such a continued oligopoly was clearly long past in 1984 and in grave doubt as early as 1968.

THE FIRST VRA: 1968–1974

The 1968 contract negotiation saw the biggest surge in imports to date, from 11.455 million tons in 1967 to 17.960 million tons in 1968, a growth of 57 percent. The growth reflected a rise of 14 million tons in steel demand during the year, largely due to stockpiling in anticipation of a nationwide steel strike. Imports accounted for almost half of the additional demand.

The import surge took place against a background of an artificially high U.S. dollar, tied to gold under the tottering Bretton Woods system; a serious U.S. trade deficit; and the unprecedented growth of federal government spending and activism under the Johnson administration, in areas from social programs, to space, to Vietnam. In January 1968, President Johnson appealed in vain to the Steelworkers for a "no-strike" assurance to help U.S. efforts to reduce imports and curb the outflow of dollars and gold that was straining the world system of fixed exchange rates to the breaking point.[8] In Congress, meanwhile, legislators from steel-producing districts, led by the Democrat Senator Vance Hartke of Indiana and working closely with the AISI, began to press for protection. Unfortunately for the industry, its own numbers made it almost impossible to use the antidumping weapon against imports: in 1965 the AISI calculated that, excluding transport costs, Japanese costs were 29 percent less than U.S. steelmaking costs, and European costs averaged 23 percent less. Moreover, U.S. import prices were significantly higher than Japanese and European prices until the 1970s, so that neither on cost nor on relative selling price grounds would an antidumping suit be likely to be sustained. Earlier attempts to invoke antidumping law, in steel company petitions in 1958 and 1963 on wire products, had been thrown out for lack of proof.[9] Nevertheless the U.S. industry used the rhetoric of "dumping" of foreign steel. There was also the possibility of claiming countervailing duties against subsidized steel imports, but this law had not been used in practice for thirty years and would not be relevant against the biggest sources of imports, Japan and Germany. As existing trade remedies could not help the industry, new legislation would have to be sought from Congress.

The prevailing view in Congress in 1968 was strongly on the side of free trade, as the AISI admitted. Nevertheless, the steel-producing states were powerful enough to cause protectionist proposals to be taken seriously. When Senator Hartke introduced a steel quota bill in March, citing fears for the U.S. balance of payments as much as the threat to the "strategic" steel industry, both houses of Congress scheduled committee hearings. A series of industry and union spokesmen pleaded for relief, even as both sides were locked in labor contract negotiations.[10] Political pressure to "do something" about steel imports in 1968 was well timed to receive a favorable hearing in the Johnson administration. Lyndon Johnson himself was at best lukewarm to both the steel companies—"nickel-bending bastards," as he called them—and to the Steelworkers' union, which had supported John Kennedy over him for the 1960 Democratic nomination for president.[11] The administration was concerned not with votes—Johnson had announced at the end of March that he would not seek re-election—but with the dollar. A widening trade gap and budget deficit were putting increasing pressure on an overvalued dollar, locked into a system of fixed exchange rates based on a valuation of the dollar at $35 per ounce of gold. Under the Nixon administration, the dollar would twice be devalued and then the system of fixed exchange rates abandoned altogether; but the Johnson administration struggled to maintain the fixed value of the dollar against a rising inflation rate—over 5 percent in 1968—while running a record budget deficit. Major tax increases offered a long-term solution; but to postpone the seemingly inevitable fiscal adjustment, the administration was willing to try to shore up the dollar by restricting imports.

Sensitive to the growing concern over imports, the Japanese steel industry unilaterally announced a policy of "orderly marketing" of exports to the United States in March.[12] Essentially this was an agreement among the Japanese mills not to compete to sell more steel into the United States, but to maintain existing market shares and customer relationships. This voluntary self-discipline, in essence a publicity gesture to counter the introduction of the Hartke quota bill, quickly came to nought as U.S. steel buyers clamored for more steel as the August 6 strike deadline loomed. Second-quarter steel imports rose from the first-quarter record level of 3.4 million tons to 5 million, with Japanese companies maintaining their share of the total. Yet the press and the administration seized upon the idea that Japan wished to cooperate. The idea of "voluntary" restraint was to shape the terms of the import debate for the next two decades.

With congressional hearings under way and pressure from the dramatic growth of second-quarter imports, the administration began to discuss more formal but negotiated restraints with Japan in July, via discussions between the U.S. Embassy in Tokyo and the Japan Iron and Steel Federation (JISF). The Senate Finance Committee postponed action on the Hartke bill to allow time for these discussions, but the JISF's first public offer did not please the U.S. industry. It offered to limit its future growth in exports to the United States to 7 percent a year, but wished to maintain its existing market share—presumably that record level it held in the first half of 1968. A steel labor agreement on July 30 took some of the immediate pressure off the discussions, as steel consumers stopped placing new import orders and sought to reduce their stockpiles. However, the steel already on order led to another tonnage record for imports in the third quarter, and the industry was not willing to let the matter drop. To increase the pressure on the administration, U.S. Steel filed a petition with the Treasury Department in October, seeking countervailing duties against subsidized European steel. This case was the first postwar use of the 1930s trade laws against subsidization of imports; it also would set a precedent for the debate over the next two decades. The Treasury Department quickly found that only Italian government subsidies would warrant countervailing duties, but it did proceed with the case against the Italian industry. Countervailing duties of between 10 and 20 percent were actually imposed on Italian steel in May 1969.[13]

In November, the bilateral talks, now extended to European Community producers, appeared to be bearing fruit, even as pressure in Congress seemed to increase. The election of Richard Nixon as president, and a shift toward more Republicans in Congress, was interpreted as increasing the likelihood of U.S. quotas. Japanese and EC steelmakers publicly announced unilateral cuts in their exports to the United States in late November, although once again these announcements were more for public relations than changes in policy: imports had fallen steadily from August on. During December, agreements were actually reached with both Japan and the EC, based on a 14-million-ton-per-year global quota—significantly less than the rate in the second and third quarters of 1968, but well ahead of the 1967 import level of 11.5 million tons. A level of imports that would have seemed unthinkable four years earlier was now being accepted, with relief, as a national U.S. commitment.

The "voluntary" limits were to be in effect for three years, until the end of 1971, with a 5 percent increase allowed in each of the second and third years. Japan and the EC each agreed to limit their 1969 exports to 41 percent of the 14-million-ton global level, the balance being assigned hypothetically to the other sources of imports, chiefly Canada and the United Kingdom. Neither of these countries agreed to join the 1968 VRA system, but the Johnson administration, in one of its last acts before leaving office, signed the agreements with Japan and the EC, believing that a restriction on the sources of 80 percent of steel imports would give sufficient help to both the industry and the dollar.

Imports did stay close to the VRA level in 1969, while in 1970 they actually dropped to 13.4 million tons (compared to a 14.7 million target) due to a temporary steel shortage in Europe. This level represented a cut in import tonnage of 25 percent from the record level in 1968 and allowed price increases by the U.S. integrated companies to take hold, triggering criticism in the press that the industry was "taking advantage" of the quotas—which was, after all, why they had been put in place.

With the end of Europe's boom and with the Big Steel labor contract expiring once again in 1971, import pressure returned to the U.S. market, and 1971 tonnage slightly exceeded the 15.5-million-ton import target. Perhaps more important than the absolute tonnage level under the VRA, however, was the change that took place in the product mix of imports. Since the early 1960s, the proportion of imported steel in higher-value products had slowly increased. From 1969, this shift increased in pace, as the VRAs limited only aggregate steel tonnage by country. To maximize revenue under such a constraint, foreign companies simply shifted to higher-priced products. Not only did the integrated mills' most profitable products, flat-rolled steel and pipe and tubing, account for growing proportions of the total, but beginning in 1969 a marked shift toward specialty steel grades became evident. Many of the largest European and Japanese companies produced both carbon and stainless steel, as did four major U.S. integrated mills in the 1960s. The import share of the apparent consumption of stainless steel, 16.8 percent in 1968, grew to over 20 percent in 1970. President Nixon asked the U.S. Tariff Commission to conduct an "escape clause" investigation into specialty steels in November 1970, after stainless producer Allegheny Ludlum had threatened to file antidumping suits on stainless and tool steel from Japan and Europe.[14] However, the profitability of U.S. specialty steelmakers was such that the commission could find no injury; specialty steelmakers would have to wait until 1976 before they got their own separate quotas.

While imports in 1971 exceeded the 15.5-million-ton VRA target, the steel industry was suffering from the effects of the 1970-71 recession as the inflation of the Johnson years turned to "stagflation" under the Nixon administration and Paul Volcker's chairmanship of the Federal Reserve Bank. In the circumstances, the extension of the VRA for three more years was politically uncontroversial, although the President's Council of Economic Advisers let it be known early in 1971 that they would recommend extension only if the mills' "price behavior" supported the administration's attempts to bring down inflation. Only when the steel boom of 1973-74 that followed the 1970-71 recession led to widespread shortages of steel in the United States, and demands from consumers for more imports to be allowed, did the first round of VRAs expire. In 1974, the mills' record profits and their operation at over 100 percent of rated capacity made it impossible to make a political case for a further VRA extension. Moreover, the recovery of the European economy at the same time as the U.S. steel boom meant that imports during the boom were actually well below the 1972 to 1974 VRA quotas.

What did the first VRA achieve? Clearly the tonnage restrictions—and the threat of them, even before the VRA was negotiated—did reduce the absolute level of imports and cause significant substitution effects. The limits affected pricing. The U.S. Department of Labor calculated the VRA of 1969 to 1974 to have caused an increase of 20 percent in import pricing. However, Robert Crandall took a more detailed approach to the price effect of the first VRA, by estimating results for each steel product class rather than by lumping together all steel mill products, to avoid complications from the shift in import product mix. This analysis produced a much more limited price effect of between 6.3 and 8.3 percent on import pricing; by comparison, domestic prices, which were constrained for most of the period by federal price control policies targeted at the inflation rate, rose between 1.2 and 3.5 percent.[15] Estimates of the transfer effects of the price increases—the extra profits earned by foreign sellers—ranged from $386 million to $1 billion.[16] The direct price level impact of the VRA may be less important than other consequential behavior changes by market players. The importers—overseas mills and trading companies—moved up into more profitable niches. U.S.-based traders began to look for new, non-VRA sources of steel from countries that were not traditionally steel exporters: steel from South Africa, Australia, Brazil, Korea and Eastern Europe began to appear in the import statistics under the first VRA—not in enough tonnage to "break" the VRA by themselves, but enough to interest those producers in the further, long-term potential of shipping to the United States. Meanwhile, the domestic integrated companies appeared to let down their guard. The system of administered pricing, under threat from cheap imports and domestic discounting, survived another six years. Attempts to restructure appeared to come to a halt.

The demand for protection had included public promises that a "breathing space" of relief from imports would allow companies time to invest and improve their productivity. Capital spending actually dropped dramatically, by 50 percent from 1968 to 1972. Only token gestures of industry restructuring took place, either through mergers (Wheeling Steel and Pittsburgh Steel had joined in 1968, National took over Granite City in 1971) or plant closures (U.S. Steel closed its small Duluth open-hearth mill in 1971). After five years the industry was essentially the same as before, with just as many undersized, obsolete plants. Some new hot-strip mills had been built, although they may have added to the duplication of capacity. According to one detailed analysis, the industry actually lost ground in both labor and capital productivity during the VRA.[17]

THE STEEL SLUMP: 1975–1977

Inherent in industry use of political remedies with fixed time periods is the risk that the timing of cycles of the trade restriction, elections, and the economy will not coincide to the industry's advantage. In 1974-75 this happened with a vengeance: VRA renewal was impossible in 1974's boom climate, when one year later renewal would have been certain: by then the industry was mired in its deepest slump to date.

In 1975 and 1976, steel mill product imports entered the United States at lower rates than under the VRA, dropping by almost a quarter, from 15.970 million tons in 1974 to 12.012 million tons in 1975, and recovering only to 14.285 million in 1976. The import share of apparent consumption increased slightly, from 13.4 percent in 1974 to 14.1 percent in 1976; but essentially the degree of import penetration seemed to have been arrested below the 1968 level that had triggered the VRA. What drove the renewed pressure for import controls, then, was not so much the rate of imports in the years 1975 and 1976 as the overall slump in steel demand and the role imports played in finally breaking the shaky administered pricing system.

The shift from sluggish growth to absolute decline in steel demand, and the depth of the recession driven by the Fed's determination to extinguish inflation, brought about the painful retrenchment in the steel industry that culminated in the first wave of plant closures between 1977 and 1979. The combination of losses and layoffs made it imperative that the companies be seen, by shareholders and the public, to be doing something. In reality, little of a short-term, quick-fix nature could be done; but imports were an easy target, and attacking imports was both politically easy and emotionally satisfying. A campaign against imports directed attention away from the companies' own competitive failings, to a scapegoat that (unlike minimills) had no constituency in Washington; built common ground with a union that might otherwise be expected to be hostile to the companies' layoffs; and required the federal government, rather than the companies, to actually do something. It also attacked the competitors that were the greatest threat to the integrated mills' pricing system. Most minimills in the 1970s were content to follow the major mills' price lead, even if they practiced more discounting and deal-making more often and more openly than the integrated mills. The importers, however, often simply disregarded the domestic price and therefore directly threatened the foundation of the industry's oligopoly structure.

During 1975, with the bottom seeming to drop out of the steel market, the companies quickly sobered up from their giddy ride of allocations and extravagant profits. Company profits actually rose during 1974 and into the first quarter of 1975, as the lifting of price controls allowed steel price rises; first-quarter 1975 profits of the ten largest integrated companies were 50 percent higher than in the previous year's first quarter. In the second quarter, profits slumped as prices and tonnage volumes slumped, and they continued to decline steadily through 1977, a year in which many steel companies reported their first-ever losses.[18] Import prices, however, began to fall quickly from early 1975, reflecting a drop in demand worldwide, not just in the United States. The price drop was not sufficient to increase import sales, but it did force down the domestic mills' prices, by something like 20 percent during the two-year period that saw the end of the "list-plus-extras" pricing discipline that had been maintained for seventy years.

In January 1975, the Treasury Department announced that at President Ford's direction, twenty classes of imports, including carbon steel, were to be investigated for subsidies contrary to U.S. trade law. When little progress was made on this investigation, U.S. Steel attempted to put pressure on the administration by filing countervailing duty complaints on EC steel in September. The complaint argued that the EC's Value-Added Tax (VAT) was not paid by European producers on their exports to the United States, but U.S. producers had to pay tax on their sales into Europe. The suit was quickly dismissed by the Treasury, which ruled in October that EC steel was not subsidized; an outraged U.S. Steel Company press release claimed in reply that European steel was subsidized by between $30 and $100 a ton.[19] Nevertheless, the record profits of the steel companies, and the accusations of price gouging, were too recent. It would take two more years of campaigning for the carbon steel companies to win renewed protection.

The specialty steel industry was in a somewhat stronger position. Having failed in 1970–71 to persuade the U.S. Tariff Commission of their case, they joined with the USWA to try again in July 1975, requesting universal quotas from the newly renamed International Trade Commission (ITC). The new case was filed under the revised Escape Clause incorporated in the 1974 Trade Act, which allowed companies (as well as the president or Congress) to request relief where injury was proven, without requiring proof of dumping or subsidy. In January 1976, the ITC made the specialty steel case its first ruling under the new provision and found that the domestic industry was indeed injured by imports of stainless and certain other alloy steels. It recommended to President Ford that a five-year quota of 146,000 tons be imposed on all countries' imports, broken down into five categories of specialty steel. The countries most affected would be Japan, Sweden, and the European Community.[20]

The Ford administration was as opposed to trade restraint as its predecessors, and sought once again to head off unilateral action with negotiation. In March, the president announced that, although he concurred with the finding of injury, import quotas would not be imposed for ninety days pending an effort to negotiate voluntary agreements for orderly marketing—a specialty steel VRA. Although the EC refused to negotiate, Japan did so, and accepted a quota of 66,400 tons in the year beginning with the second half of 1976, compared to Japanese shipments of 78,500 tons to the United States in 1975. The remaining producers had to compete among themselves for the balance of the quota, which became effective at the end of June. As agreed in the discussions with Japan, the three-year quota put in place was for 147,000 tons in the first year, rising by 3 percent a year in the second and third years.[21]

The specialty steel industry achieved its success through a combination of factors. It had lobbied consistently and determinedly for relief since 1970, and could make a plausible case that it had been damaged by the carbon steel VRA due to product substitution. Top executives were personally involved in the campaign, and Allegheny Ludlum's president Dick Simmons and USWA president I. W. Abel met personally with President Ford in 1976. The specialty steelmakers had a far better industry image than did carbon steel; they included a number of competitive, independent small firms as well as some of the integrated majors; their products and costs were widely viewed as being globally competitive. Moreover, there was no recent history of shortages and price spikes to generate hostility, and, indeed, the industry was simply not as prominent and therefore politically sensitive as the carbon steel industry.[22] The specialty industry's success, however, led the carbon steel industry to increase its efforts to regain protection.

In the middle of 1976, imports began to rise from the reduced levels they had maintained since late 1974. U.S. steel demand, while still anemic, was finally picking up with the recovery of the U.S. economy, while Europe in particular remained mired in a deep recession. U.S. prices began to firm slightly, attracting more import tonnage. Meanwhile, the distressed state of the European industry, where the problems of overcapacity were becoming even more evident than in the United States, had led to an agreement between the EC and Japan to limit Japanese exports to Europe to 1.34 million tons in 1976. Coincidentally or not, Japanese exports to the United States rose dramatically through 1976, at the same time that European imports declined. When import figures showed that Japan accounted for 60 percent of all steel imports in the first eight months of 1976, the AISI protested that the Japan–EC agreement was diverting at least an extra 1.5 million tons a year into the United States from Japan. The AISI filed an antidumping complaint against Japan on October 6.[23]

In 1976 as in other election years, the steel industry's plight became subsumed in broader election issues, and protecting steel was not an immediate priority for incoming President Jimmy Carter. The Japanese industry, sensitive to the changing balance of opinion in Washington, asked the Japanese government in March 1977 to approach the U.S. government to restore a VRA; the same month Gilmore Steel (now Oregon Steel), a West Coast plate producer, filed a suit that led to the imposition of antidumping duties against Japanese plate imports. The Gilmore suit prodded the nervous Japanese industry to initiate talks with their European counterparts on a joint approach to the United States for a renewed VRA, but the Carter administration quickly indicated its opposition to quotas. In May, the AISI published a 60-page booklet called "The Economics of International Steel Trade," purporting to show that all steel imported to the United States was dumped, subsidized, or at best produced by workers paid unfairly low wages; the booklet was not clear on whether the AISI was calling for wage increases for foreign workers or wage cuts for U.S. employees. Its claims were ridiculed in July in a counter-report by Merrill Lynch, commissioned by the Japan Iron and Steel Exporters' Association, but the pressure continued. In September 1977, steel imports were blamed by Youngstown Sheet and Tube for the closure of its Youngstown plant; the president expressed his "concern" but still resisted calls for protection. The issue was consigned to an interagency task force headed by Treasury Secretary Tony Solomon. [24]

THE SOLOMON PLAN: THE TRIGGER PRICE MECHANISM, 1978 TO 1982

The report of the Solomon Task Force, presented in December 1977, took a very different philosophical approach to the question of steel imports.[25] The report was the product of a decade in which a bipartisan consensus existed (in Europe as well as in Washington) that governments had as a top priority the control of inflation by direct intervention in wages and prices. Moreover, in a climate of major structural adjustments in the economy, driven by the commodity price shocks of the early 1970s and the end of the fixed exchange rate system, the Solomon Plan was the closest that the United States has come to a full-scale industrial policy for steel.

The task force met in the fall of 1977 in an atmosphere of mounting crisis. The steel industry was announcing its first major plant closures, and the Congressional Steel Caucus was being formed to focus the political demands to "do something." Antidumping suits had been prepared by the major integrated companies against Japanese and European producers on flat-rolled products and wire, and these were filed at almost weekly intervals in October and November to add to the political pressure. The Solomon Plan was the administration's response to this atmosphere. It sought to stretch the boundaries of federal involvement to support an industry, while falling short of direct intervention to resolve the overcapacity and cost problems.

The task force suggested policy changes in numerous areas that had been on the AISI's agenda for years: postponement or reduction of environmental standards; faster depreciation schedules and other investment tax relief; a waiver of antitrust guidelines to encourage mergers; and additional government financing of industry research and development. It also made two more radical suggestions: for federal loan guarantees for steel industry investment and for import protection by price controls rather than quantity controls. Most of the plans suggested were welcomed by the administration but diluted when confronted with bureaucratic inertia and competing interests; fo xample, in 1978 the Justice Department fought the J & L—Youngstown merger just as strongly as it had ever opposed steel consolidation, but was overruled by Carter's attorney general, Griffin Bell. The Environmental Protection Agency (EPA) did become noticeably more accommodating about compliance deadlines under the Carter administration, but did not change its emissions standards. The loan guarantee program and import price protection were put into effect, but both ultimately failed to materially aid the industry.

In 1978, the Economic Development Administration (EDA), a federal agency founded in 1966 primarily to assist the development of poor rural areas, was authorized to guarantee up to $550 million in borrowing by the steel industry for new investment. The federal guarantee would permit significantly lower interest rates and thereby make marginal investments more attractive. However, the idea that the government would in effect subsidize new competitors while companies were struggling to maintain existing capacity was at best controversial. U.S. Steel's chairman David Roderick warned that "loan guarantees are the first step to nationalization."[26] His ire was understandable: the loan guarantees were specifically targeted at medium-sized steel companies, correctly identifying these as the companies in greatest need, but potentially working against the need for rationalization of the industry by the merger or closure of the less efficient players. The EDA did become involved in two major projects. One, by a local consortium in the Mahoning Valley to acquire and reopen the shuttered Campbell Mill of Youngstown Sheet and Tube, ultimately failed to demonstrate the viability of the mill regardless of interest rates. The second, a proposal by Wheeling-Pittsburgh to construct a new rail mill at its Monessen plant, did receive EDA (and Commonwealth of Pennsylvania) loan guarantees, after bitter opposition from the three existing rail producers, U.S. Steel, Bethlehem Steel, and CF & I. The rail mill opened in 1981, the same year U.S. Steel left the rail business; it was closed and written off just five years later. Subsidized interest rates could not change the market fundamentals, which in this case were that the rail market was not big enough to support more than two domestic producers.

The loan guarantee program was ineffective because it was driven politically by the perceived need to create employment. Investment was not needed in new capacity; it was needed in cost-saving equipment such as continuous casters, which would further cut employment and which could for the most part be justified commercially without soft loans. The other significant measure of federal intervention, to address imports through (in effect) price controls, was similarly ineffective because the problem it was designed to address disappeared as circumstances changed.

Like the VRA, the Solomon Plan's import relief measure was designed to head off continuous court battles and to persuade U.S. producers to agree to withdraw their threatened trade lawsuits. Unlike the VRAs, the Trigger Price Mechanism directly confronted the domestic industry's core problem: that imports were sold in the United States at prices well below the domestic producers' price, thus threatening the domestic market share. Using Japanese costs as a reference because the Japanese industry was assumed to be the most efficient (lowest cost) in the world, a base price for foreign steel was set equivalent to the full production and transport cost of Japanese steel delivered to the United States, including an arbitrary 8 percent profit margin for the Japanese mill. Any steel sold below this price was assumed to be dumped and would automatically trigger antidumping penalties. A floor was thereby implicitly set under steel prices in the United States, a move theoretically consistent with the search for price "stability," but in practice perversely opposed to the federal fight against high inflation. It also represented a dramatic change from seventy years of government opposition to steel price increases.

Assumptions behind the TPM appeared to include the probable continuation of the import market share at around the 15 percent level, maintained from the start of the VRA in 1969 into 1977 but already being left behind as imports gathered pace in 1977. This implied that U.S. producers really could compete, or defend their market shares, if steel was not "dumped" at below Japanese full cost. It also assumed that exchange rates would be stable. Neither assumption was valid.[27]

The TPM was set in January 1978 at a level slightly above the offer price of most imported steel entering the United States in late 1977. However, the average of $330 a ton was still $20 a ton less than average domestic prices and $30 a ton below the level demanded by U.S. Steel's Roderick. World export prices of steel had bottomed around the third quarter of 1977 and thereafter rose steadily with global economic recovery. Moreover the recovery coincided with a slide in the value of the dollar, further increasing world steel prices in dollar terms. These factors allowed the domestic producers to raise prices three times between January and June of 1978, by a total of $40 a ton, or around 13 percent. The price relief, plus the recovery of domestic demand, restored profitability to almost all the industry in 1978. The domestic mills had seen little benefit from the recovery during 1977: while apparent supply rose that year by 7.4 million tons, domestic shipments had increased by only 1.7 million tons, with the import share rising from 14.1 to 17.8 percent. In 1978, however, apparent demand grew by another 8.2 million tons, and domestic shipments rose 6.8 million tons. Even though imports still increased, to 18.1 percent of the market, the TPM appeared to be working.[28]

By the beginning of 1979, the Solomon Plan looked as if it could claim to have fulfilled two of its objectives, announced by President Carter in welcoming it in December 1977: to increase industry profitability by $900 million a year and to put idle steelworkers back to work. Industry profits rose from the borderline level of $22 million in 1977 to $1.276 billion in 1978; employment recovered by 16,000 in the year, if not by the full 25,000 increase hoped for by Carter. The reality was, however, that the trigger prices were actually now well below domestic prices, and the spread gave plenty of room for European producers to increase their shipments to the U.S. market and make significant real profits. Only Japanese imports were cut back, due to unilateral action in late 1977 by the Japanese producers who chose to observe voluntary limits of 6 million metric tons, cutting back their market share from 7.2 percent in 1977 to 5.6 percent in 1978; never again were Japanese shipments to the United States to exceed 7 million short tons as in 1976 and 1977. Imports from Japan were down 17 percent in 1978, while imports from the EC rose 12 percent. Japan's industry was beginning to lose its own competitive edge, thus making orderly marketing seem as important to Japanese producers as it was to the U.S. integrated mills. The withdrawal of Japanese plate in response to the Gilmore dumping suit led to U.S. importers buying Korean and East European plate at prices that ranged from $20 to $30 a ton below Japanese prices, themselves $20 to $30 below domestic list prices. Japanese cooperation in supplying cost information, as well as in cutting back on tonnage, led a grateful Treasury Department to halve the antidumping duties on Japanese plate in January 1978. After 1977, Japan effectively ceased to promote steel imports to the United States, leaving the EC and then nontraditional steelmaking countries to take the lead. This change took time to enter the public perception, and into the late 1980s Japan remained a target for public attacks by the steel industry's spokesmen and its unions.

By 1979, it was clear that the trigger prices themselves were of little relevance, but the worldwide economic recovery permitted hopes for a return to the heady days of shortages in 1973–74. December 1978 imports were down 34 percent from the previous December; by March 1979 imports were at 1.1 million tons, compared to 2 million in the previous March. The AISI issued a ritual denunciation of the 1978 year-end import figures, asserting that "the $6 billion deficit on steel trade" could grow to "equal the $45 billion oil deficit by the mid 1980s." However, by the AISI's annual meeting in New York in May, predictions of a serious world steel shortage were common. As early as March 1979, there were suggestions that the TPM might be abandoned; when the three-year specialty steel quotas expired in June 1979, the administration did not renew them. The major outstanding dumping petition still under investigation in early 1979, by Lukens Steel against EC plate, was actually withdrawn by Lukens in June, a recognition of the hopelessness of the case.[29]

The political climate changed once again with the turn of the steel cycle in the summer of 1979. As orders fell away and companies reexamined their plants for places to cut excess capacity, the old complaints returned. In November 1979, U.S. Steel announced its long-expected plant closings and in so doing took the opportunity to criticize the TPM, accuse Japanese and European producers of dumping, and threaten antidumping suits once again. This time chairman Roderick received a public rebuke from the administration. Secretary of Labor Ray Marshall responded that the government would not allow the use of import barriers to protect the industry from the consequences of its own poor judgment.[30]

By early 1980, it was clear that steel faced another recession as deep as that of 1975–76, even while the U.S. dollar rose against foreign currencies in response to the second OPEC "oil shock" of 1979. Imports to the United States fell in 1980 by 11.6 percent to 15.5 million tons, reflecting the falling market, but grew in market share from 15.2 to 16.2 percent. The increasing synchronization of Western economies' business cycles in the 1970s meant that as demand declined worldwide, the consequences of excess production could not be relieved by exporting, and both U.S. and European operating rates sank down toward the 70 percent level even as closures in both regions finally began to reduce steel production capacity. The responses of industry in Europe and the United States were classic cases of opposite potential responses by cartels to market stress. The European industry quickly agreed with government, in the form of EC Industry Commissioner Vicomte Etienne Davignon, on industrywide production cutbacks, plant closures, and price levels, designed to maintain each company's (and nation's) market share; only the three largest German producers objected, as their relative efficiency was, in effect, to be penalized by requiring proportionate cuts of them. In the United States, the industry's concern for market share took the more limited form of demands for limits on imports, with no attempt to gain greater government intervention (especially with Big Steel's traditional distaste for a Democratic administration). Meanwhile, the 1980-81 boom in oil drilling led a number of integrated producers to begin importing seamless tubes themselves while they sought to satisfy exploding demand for that product.

The Carter administration suspended the Trigger Price Mechanism in March 1980 after a massive filing of antidumping suits by U.S. Steel and Bethlehem Steel, which cited essentially every import source of each major steel product. The rise in the dollar's value made it impossible to maintain Japanese costs as a basis for the TPM at a high enough price level to keep imports out, thus rendering it useless in the eyes of the U.S. industry. The Commerce Department, which taken over from the Treasury the investigative role in trade suits in 1979, found preliminary evidence of dumping in April 1980, and the ITC in turn found a "reasonable indication" of injury in May.[31]

The administration was both frustrated by the industry's attitude and embarrassed by the timing of the suits. Trade relations with the EC, always sensitive, were complicated in 1980 by a series of disputes over agriculture, air transport, and ground rules for a new round of GATT talks. Europe's Commissioner Davignon, grappling with the enforcement of painful capacity cuts while Europe was in an unprecedentedly deep recession, was under political pressure to defend European exports; he proclaimed publicly that up to 3 million metric tons of European exports to the United States were threatened by unjustified antidumping claims and flew to Washington to warn of a trade war if steel imports were disrupted. On March 26, President Carter wrote to Roy Jenkins, president of the European Commission, that the steel suits were "not a hostile act of government," effectively disclaiming federal support for them.[32]

With the TPM ended and no successor program in place, pressure from the industry mounted for renewed protection. The USWA denounced the suspension of the TPM, and imports began to rise starting in April and May 1980 after two years of gradual decline. In June, U.S. Steel's Roderick called for a new "government-to-government" "voluntary" agreement, and the Commerce Department opened diplomatic discussions with both the European Community and, in a last echo of its days of unquestioned industry hegemony, with U.S. Steel. Carter and Jenkins cautiously described their meeting at the Venice economic summit of the G7 heads of state in late June as "increasing the likelihood" of a steel trade settlement.[33] Behind the scenes pressure was put on U.S. Steel to withdraw its suits.

When an agreement was announced on September 29, it looked as if U.S. Steel had backed down. The Trigger Price Mechanism was restored, with product trigger prices set between 10 and 12 percent higher, justified—the White House said—by apparent Japanese cost increases. U.S. Steel bowed to pressure and withdrew its trade suits for the time being, and the status quo ante March seemed restored. The pressure on U.S. Steel was to have a dramatic and unforeseen effect: in November, U.S. Steel announced it was to buy Marathon Oil, a company twice its size. U.S. Steel, the spokesman of the industry and symbol of its former might and glory, was forced to look for its future elsewhere.

During late 1980 and throughout 1981, imports surged once again, with a heavy emphasis on products for the booming oilfield—not only seamless pipe but plate and line pipe as well. The import share of apparent consumption, 15.2 percent in 1979 before the second oil shock impacted both the dollar and Western economies, rose to 16.3 percent in 1980 and a record 18.9 percent in 1981. The oil-driven steel market in 1981 saw domestic shipments rise that year by 4.6 million tons while imports rose by 4.4 million. Domestic capacity utilization was still near record low levels, yet imports were taking half of any pickup in demand. Of course, these aggregate numbers did not tell the full story. The categories of semifinished steel, largely imported for use by the domestic producers, and pipe for the oilfield accounted for almost all of the 28 percent rise in import tons in 1981; most domestic pipe mills were working at 100 percent of capacity and could not meet demand. With steel layoffs continuing at sheet and bar producers, imports were still the easiest target on which to vent frustration. Nevertheless, during its first year, for lack of an alternate policy, the new Reagan administration tried to keep the TPM system alive.

The dollar's rapid recovery against European currencies in 1980–81 drove European costs down in dollar terms, meaning that many producers could now claim to have full production costs below the U.S. trigger prices. When the Commerce Department denied requests for "preclearance"—approval to sell below trigger price on the basis of demonstrated low costs—a number of steelmakers in late 1981 began to ship at those prices regardless. In attempts to keep the system alive, the Commerce Department filed antidumping suits against flat-rolled steel from Belgium, France, Romania, South Africa, and Brazil. The Japanese trading company Mitsui was also accused of fraud in evading the TPM, by reporting false prices to the U.S. Customs Service. However, as the world spot export prices of steel sank further below U.S. trigger prices, the TPM's ineffectiveness became increasingly evident. Companies circumvented the TPM when they did not ignore it altogether: U.S. importers established shell companies offshore to buy steel at world prices, then "resell" it to their U.S. parents at the trigger price.[34]

To try to rescue some kind of international agreement, more U.S.-European ministerial level meetings were held in December, but the two sides were far apart on the tonnages and prices for which each was willing to settle. When the talks were seen to be fruitless, U.S. Steel and Bethlehem refiled antidumping and countervailing duty suits in January 1982 against European, Brazilian, and South African producers. The TPM was suspended again, this time for good.

In retrospect, the Trigger Price Mechanism appears to have been doomed from its inception by forces far greater than the power of the U.S. Department of Commerce to police international steel prices. The strength of international steel demand, and most important the strength of the dollar, determined the world spot export price of steel. When the dollar fell, as in 1977-78, U.S. imports fell and import prices rose. The TPM could certainly not take credit for a rise in import prices when the dollar fell in those two years by 22 percent against the mark and 34 percent against the yen, at the same time that world steel demand was rising.

Similarly, when the world (and Europe in particular) faced a glut of steel during the recession of 1980 to 1982, and the dollar bounced back to close to its pre-1977 levels as a result of the oil shock, the TPM could not prevent steel being traded at world prices below the trigger prices set to please U.S. producers. The federal government simply did not have the bureaucracy, the legal authority, or even the desire to police the steel trade effectively. Recognition of this, as the TPM was challenged, evaded, or ignored in 1981, doomed the program. Control of pricing is inherently more difficult in a free market than quantitative restrictions on tonnage imports; in the late 1970s and early 1980s, the United States had finally reached the stage of being a free market in steel, as the practices of domestic oligopoly faded away. In attempting to shore up the domestic producers' position with an import price "floor," the government was shutting the barn door after the horse had bolted.

1982 TO 1984: BACK TO VRAs

The breakdown of the TPM coincided with the start of the deepest period of slump of the steel market in the United States. As capacity utilization sank below 50 percent in early 1982, steel shipments fell 30 percent from the already depressed levels of 1981. Imports fell, especially in the areas of pipe and plate for the oilfield, but so slowly compared to domestic shipments that their market share grew to a new record of 21.8 percent.

Meanwhile, the Commerce Department continued slowly to process the antidumping suits filed in January, while diplomatic contacts were maintained between Commerce Secretary Malcolm Baldridge and European producing states. Japan stayed out of the diplomatic controversy and quietly let it be known it would restrain its exports to the United States by another notch.[35] The deadline for the Commerce Department to make a preliminary ruling on the first cases was June 10, and in the weeks leading up to it, both the EC and the United States made public threats while maintaining private talks about new quotas. In May, Secretary Baldridge pleased the domestic mills by saying that the United States would seek retroactive penalties if unfair trade was proved; at the same time, he was offering the EC a quota equal to between 4 and 5 percent of apparent consumption. The two sides then argued over whether or not this number should include seamless tubulars.

The Commerce Department announced its finding of unfair subsidy against EC, Brazilian, and South African steel on June 10 and recommended stiff countervailing duties to the ITC. The EC quickly announced that it would retaliate, while its foreign ministers, meeting at Luxembourg, delivered a strong protest and announced they would appeal to both GATT and the steel committee of the Organization for Economic Cooperation and Development (OECD).[36] However, behind the public posturing, both sides were eager to secure an agreement and to put the issue behind them. The Reagan administration, in its relations with Europe, was far more concerned with preventing a proposed gas pipeline to supply Western Europe from the Soviet Union; the EC was simultaneously imposing the sharpest ever cutbacks on European steel producers, reducing their production quotas for the third quarter of 1982 by between 35 and 47 percent. Baldridge met with Vicomte Davignon in Brussels on July 9 and was offered an across-the-board 10 percent cut in EC exports to the United States, but rejected this and held out for a more comprehensive agreement. The EC Commissioners quickly agreed, and talks opened in Brussels on July 28.[37]

The steel talks inevitably became complicated by the dispute over the gas pipeline and were delayed by the August vacation period in Europe. Within the EC, the traditional divide between the largely unsubsidized, privately owned industry in Germany and the Netherlands and the state-owned, subsidized industries elsewhere added to the difficulty of securing an agreement. The Commerce Department had found German and Dutch subsidy margins to be zero or less than 1 percent; there therefore seemed to be little for these producers to fear from U.S. trade laws if there was no agreement. Meanwhile, the Commerce Department continued to report on additional steel trade investigations. In August, it found steel from five EC countries and Romania to be dumped at up to 41 percent below "fair value" and Spanish stainless and carbon steel to be illegally subsidized. To add to the pressure, and to the backlog at the Commerce Department, industry prepared additional suits—against rail products from the United Kingdom, France, and Luxembourg, and against stainless from the United Kingdom.[38]

After three months of often acrimonious talks, the sides announced on October 20 agreement on a VRA that looked very similar to what Secretary Baldridge had offered in May—a quota amounting to an EC share of 5 percent of the U.S. domestic market. The German cabinet objected, but the German industry went along for fear of unilateral action if it did not comply. The carbon steel companies agreed to withdraw their trade cases against the EC producers. By the fall of 1982, the seamless pipe question looked moot: the slump in the oil price had exposed the glut of seamless inventories. Specialty steel, however, was not included in the quota. The EC quota represented a sharp drop from the 7.3 percent of the U.S. market it held in 1982. The voluntary Japanese restraint, which was converted into a formal VRA in 1983, was also equivalent to around 5 percent. It looked briefly as if U.S. imports might fall back into the range of around 15 percent that had prevailed before 1976 and under the weak dollar of 1979. It was not to be.

The futility of restricting part but not all of the steel trade became evident within weeks of the EC agreement, as imports from third countries surged to replace the EC tonnage. Canadian, Brazilian, Korean, and Eastern European producers all had excess capacity in the continuing steel slump, costs that were low or hard to measure, and the combined market share of these and other "nontraditional" import sources rose from 6.9 percent in 1981 to 13.3 percent in 1984, more than wiping out any reduction from the traditional sources. Canada faced excess capacity for the first (and only) time in the early 1980s, and agreed to an informal VRA with the United States in 1984. But between 1974 and 1983, seven developing countries—Brazil, Chile, India, Mexico, Korea, Taiwan, and Venezuela—saw their combined share of world steel production rise from 4 to 10 percent. The U.S. market bore the brunt of this new competition.[39]

The frustration of the U.S. producers reached new heights in 1983 and 1984. Even as Japanese and EC shipments fell, imports rose—by only 400,000 tons in 1983, as steel traders adjusted and sought new sources, but by 9 million tons in 1984 as the U.S. economy recovered and the dollar continued to rise. As under the first VRA, European and Japanese producers switched toward specialty steels whenever possible, presenting the specialty industry with a new crisis.

A series of antidumping trade cases on stainless steel led to rulings in early 1983 of dumping margins against EC and Canadian producers. The administration responded in July 1983 with a series of measures that, like the carbon steel agreements, were directed against the most critical problem areas. Tariffs were raised slightly on all specialty steels, while quotas were imposed for three years on stainless steel bar and rod and on tool steel. In addition, talks were undertaken with Canada and Japan to secure voluntary quotas on their stainless exports; the EC refused to negotiate an additional stainless VRA. Once again, the effect was to divert, rather than restrain, steel imports. Stainless flat-rolled products imports rose 60 percent between the first quarters of 1984 and 1985.[40]

During 1983 and early 1984, the stainless industry joined with the carbon industry in a growing chorus of demands for universal quotas. With trade litigation rising in Europe as well as in the United States, many steelmakers in Japan, Europe, and the United States began to seek some kind of global steel trade agreement to head off an impending state of anarchy, driven by the emergence of new steel exporters and global overcapacity, which could threaten either to bring about a full-scale trade war or to end all import restrictions. In the United States the major producers adopted, whether by chance or design, a dual approach to trade litigation. Bethlehem Steel, supported by the steelworkers' union, filed "escape clause" suits aimed at limiting carbon imports globally back to the 15 percent level from the 25 percent of early 1984; while U.S. Steel, with greater legal resources, adopted the deliberate strategy of massive filings under the antidumping provisions, aimed at trying to cover every steel product and every foreign steel producer: entire truckloads of documents were filmed, for maximum publicity, being delivered to the Commerce Department.

In the summer of 1984, matters came to a head just as a presidential election season was getting under way. In July, with a soaring dollar, imports peaked at 33 percent of the U.S. market. Meanwhile, in June, the ITC had begun to issue its recommendations on antidumping tariff margins on its backlog of trade cases. By September, the ITC had recommended to the president that dumping and countervailing duty margins be assessed against products and countries accounting for 70 percent of all imported steel products, and a presidential ruling was required under the law—although the action could be delayed up to three days after the election. To add to the pressure, Democratic candidate Walter Mondale called for limiting steel imports to a maximum of 17 percent while campaigning hard against President Reagan in the hard-hit steel-producing states now known as the Rust Belt. In Congress, quota bills were introduced by members of the steel caucus, but the administration strongly resisted more limits at congressional hearings.[41]

President Reagan's response was an announcement on September 18 that he found the imposition of countervailing duties "not in the national economic interest," and instead directed the U.S. Trade Representative, Bill Brock, to seek VRAs by year end with each country whose exports to the United States had increased in previous years. A target of 18.5 percent of the U.S. market would be set for finished steel products, although an additional 1.7 percent would be allowed in the form of slabs for finishing by U.S. steelmakers. The new program would last for five years in the first instance, from October 1, 1984, to September 30, 1989. The president could claim he was still committed to free trade, having rejected the ITC's proposed tariffs, but in reality the administration had, in the heat of an election campaign, fallen back on "managed trade" through a universal VRA.

Toward the goal of universality, the existing understandings with the EC countries, Japan and Canada were rolled over into the new program, leaving only about 5 percent of the U.S. market—not enough—to be divided among all other producers. Nevertheless, 14 more nations eventually were signed up, for a total of 28, including each of the new steel exporters and the Eastern European steel producers. The implicit offer of a guaranteed annual tonnage of shipments to the United States was a strong attraction, while the threat of unilateral U.S. action remained if the steel producer did not cooperate. Antidumping and countervailing duties that had been placed in effect on certain products over the previous two years were canceled as the VRAs came into effect, and the domestic producers once again withdrew their petitions.

The second VRA initially proved another disappointment to the domestic industry. After eighteen months, in April 1986, imports were still taking nearly 25 percent of a disastrously weak market. Shipments in 1986 of just 70.26 million tons were better than at the low point in 1982-83 but were still the third worst shipping year since the late 1940s. Industry operated at just 63.8 percent of a capacity that had been reduced through plant closures by 27 million annual tons since 1982, and industry employment continued to fall. In both 1985 and 1986, 30,000 jobs were permanently lost. It was hardly surprising, then, that the USWA's president Lynn Williams denounced the new VRA as a failure. The companies, having urged a universal VRA, were slower to condemn it, but expressed disappointment that it was "behind its goals" and urged stricter curbs. [42]

During the summer of 1986, a steady turnaround became evident in the steel market. Once again, as between 1977 and 1979, the United States saw a simultaneous improvement in its economy and a weakening in the value of the dollar. The year 1987 saw domestic shipments rise by 6.4 million tons while imports fell by 280,000 tons—as in 1979, imports and domestic shipments did not move in the same direction. The improvement was sustained until the end of 1990, with the import share of the U.S. market then falling back to 17.5 percent.

After 1985, Japan slowly withdrew from the U.S. market; its shipments dropped from 5.974 million tons in that year (and a peak of

6.630 million the previous year) to 3.652 million in 1989—well below its VRA allowance—and then on down to just 1.783 million in 1993. The steady rise of the yen made exporting to the United States unprofitable in almost any market and was replaced (as in the auto industry) by a strategy of direct investment in U.S. production capacity. Imports from Europe followed a more varied pattern. In general, in the VRA period of 1984 to 1989, there was a rise in shipments from newer suppliers, such as Turkey (which was considered too insignificant to have a VRA negotiated in 1985) and the Eastern European countries, while of the EC producers, only low-cost British Steel increased its shipments, much of which was in the form of a negotiated special allowance of semifinished steel for its subsidiary Tuscaloosa Steel. The VRA probably did restrain shipments in those cases where a producing country's currency was closely tied to the U.S. dollar, as with Taiwan and some Latin American producers.

In the fall of 1988, George Bush made an election promise to extend the VRAs on their expiration in the summer of 1989. In July 1989, their extension for thirty months, to January 1992, was confirmed, but on two conditions. First, that the target import share of the U.S. market for finished steel mill products would rise over the period from 18.4 to 20.2 percent. Second, President Bush was explicit that there would be no further extensions (the two-and-a-half year period would expire before election-year politics heated up again). Meanwhile, during the VRA extension period, the United States would seek to negotiate a global Multilateral Steel Agreement (MSA) to set out rules for orderly steel trade for the future. The ambitious goals for the MSA included abolition of subsidies in exchange for the abolition of quantitative restrictions on steel trade. Once again, the integrated companies got to keep the "safety net" they asked for, but for only half the length of time they wished.

The 1989 campaign to extend VRAs was more muted than previous campaigns. During the five years since 1985, the steel world had changed significantly. First, imports no longer seemed such a threat. When semifinished steel for domestic producers was excluded, imports were back to the 15 percent of consumption level. The change in the value of the dollar not only reduced exports, but it actually led to the growth of U.S. exports. After languishing at around the 1 million-ton-per-year mark since 1982, exports shot up to 2 million tons in 1988 and 4.5 million tons in 1989, the best year for exports since 1974. While still only a quarter of the level of imports, the major companies were beginning to benefit from international trade as well as suffer from it. The companies were also benefiting from their own imports of semifinished steel, notably from slabs for flat-rolled products. With steelmaking "hot end" capacity below hot-strip mill capacity at most integrated companies, imports were a low-cost alternative to maintaining idle capacity just for the occasional cyclical peak of demand.

Perhaps the biggest difference between the 1989 renewal and earlier campaigns for protection was the emergence of a strong body of opponents of steel protection, both within and outside the steel industry. In 1984, only the Caterpillar company among major U.S. steel users dared to speak out against the imposition of a VRA; as a major exporter, Caterpillar opposed anything that increased its costs relative to competing foreign manufacturers. By 1989, with U.S. manufactured exports growing at 10 percent a year since 1986 thanks to a declining dollar, a coalition of steel users opposed extension. Even more telling, the minimill section of the industry, organized for the first time in the newly founded Steel Manufacturers' Association, conspicuously failed to take a stand in support of the VRA, while a number of minimills—led as so often by Nucor's chairman Ken Iverson—spoke out individually against the VRA. Finally, a significant section of the integrated industry was now partially owned by Japanese companies and so kept a low profile—which left U.S. Steel and Bethlehem, still the largest companies and still unaffiliated with overseas producers, exposed. These companies and the USWA appeared for the first time to be simply one special interest group among many competing interests, not the strategic underpinning of American manufacturing that they had for so long portrayed themselves to be.

On the expiration of the VRA in 1992, little progress had been made toward an MSA. The attention of government trade specialists had been diverted by the exhausting negotiations that led to the reform of GATT as the World Trade Organization; and on the North American Free Trade Agreement (NAFTA) with Canada (and soon Mexico). When steel subsidies were discussed between the United States and Europe, it proved impossible to reconcile the desire of many European mills, especially in France, Italy, and Belgium, to have certain types of subsidy accepted as a routine part of doing business, while U.S. integrated producers were adamant that any MSA should give at least as much protection against dumping and subsidies as existing U.S. trade laws. Although discussions on an MSA continued intermittently in 1994 and 1995, no progress appeared likely unless the United States would be willing to compromise on its trade laws and the EC would compromise on subsidies, both of which would require governments to overrule the desires of their less efficient steel producers.

Without the protection of a VRA, and with a mild recession in 1991-92 keeping U.S. steel shipments and imports low, the immediate response of the biggest integrated companies to an era without protection was predictable. U.S. Steel and Bethlehem steel filed massive antidumping and countervailing duty suits on most imported sheets and plates. As in 1968, 1976, 1982, and 1984, the lawyers generated several tons of documents, at an estimated cost this time of $35 million in fees. The 84 flat-rolled cases charged subsidy by thirteen countries and dumping by twenty, covering products that accounted for 5.8 million tons in 1991, or half of all imports after excluding semifinished products. The Commerce Department made a preliminary determination of injury in seventy-two cases, in the subsidy cases in December 1992 and in the antidumping cases in February 1993. Bonds thereafter had to be filed equal to the amount of the estimated dumping margins, which varied widely between producers—from 1.45 to 109.22 percent on plate, for example. The United States seemed to have entered a further area of managed trade, this time represented by the acronym coined by Bethlehem Steel's chairman Hank Barnette—TLR; Trade Law Remedies.

In July 1993, the ITC completed its investigation of the findings of the Commerce Department, and shocked the industry. In 40 of the 72 cases, no injury was found, leaving much of the hot-rolled and cold-rolled sheet markets open to imports. Duties were assessed in a number of plate and galvanized sheet cases, but at generally low levels. In lesser cases in 1992–93, duties were assessed on standard pipes and on free-machining bars from a number of countries, but in cases on rails and special quality bars no injury was found.

The 1992–93 round of trade petitions showed that a new climate existed in Washington. Steel trade cases would be examined on their merits, not from the standpoint of defending American interests. Moreover, the cases were fought for the importers by many of the same lawyers and accountants who had previously worked on the side of the U.S. companies or the Commerce Department; the playing field had been leveled dramatically. However, the integrated companies may still have earned a good return on their investment in legal fees. The short-term disruption to the import market from the original findings of injury by the Commerce Department was enough to firm the market prices of flat-rolled steel and allow the integrated companies to pass two price increases. As always, the real issue was not so much import tonnage but pricing.

After the 1993 case dismissals, the boom years for steel of 1993 to 1995 precluded pressure for more protection. In 1994, imports (excluding semifinished) rose to 22 million tons, or 20 percent of the market, reflecting spot shortages in a number of products and essentially full capacity operation by flat-rolled producers for the first time since 1974. Eight million tons of semifinished were also imported, mostly to boost domestic flat products production. In 1995, the rapid slide of the dollar—by 20 percent against the yen in the first four months of the year—and the easing of flat-rolled shortages saw both finished and semifinished imports fall once again.

In the mid-1990s it began to appear as if the U.S. industry had learned to live with—and compete with—imports, helped by a long-term shift in the dollar's value reflecting the currency's changed global role and the twin U.S. deficits. However, the integrated companies continued to track imports and foreign costs carefully, in the full expectation that further suits would be filed as soon as a market downturn increased the likelihood of an injury finding. A major lobbying effort was undertaken in 1995 to influence the Commerce Department's rewriting of trade regulations to conform with the World Trade Organization's rules. With a presidential election due in 1996, the integrated mills were keeping their powder dry against the day when trade law might again be needed to support prices.

TRADE POLICY, INDUSTRIAL POLICY, AND CONFLICTS OF INTERESTS

The integrated steel industry has consistently pursued the limitation of steel imports for about thirty years, starting around 1965, when the American Iron and Steel Institute began to study Japanese and European steelmakers' costs on behalf of its member companies. The specialty steel industry has also supported, and received, import limitations at various times, but has been less consistent in its pressure for intervention, partly because of its own profitability as demand for its product has continued to grow and partly because of the international operations or aspirations of some of its member companies. Both the AISI and the specialty steelmakers' lobbying group, the Specialty Steel Institute of the United States, plus individual companies such as U.S. Steel and

Bethlehem Steel, have maintained extensive (and expensive) lobbying campaigns in Washington and have sponsored publications and press campaigns nationally to support their positions. The extent of the political effort on the trade issue has led at least one European observer to charge that the U.S. industry was much more innovative in its political response to the import challenge than in its economic response.[43]

Nevertheless, the long-standing and politically successful campaign for protection raises other questions. If the industry was able, relatively easily, to get support from Congress and several administrations for protection even in the face of a broader bipartisan policy and ideology of free trade, why did it not seek other forms of assistance or a national industrial policy for addressing its capacity and price problems, as happened in the European Community? Second, given the failure of protection to restore the industry's position, the costs that trade protection imposed on steel customers, and the ability of a growing section of the industry to compete without protection, why was the campaign so successful for so long?

Industrial policy is a term that means different things to different people, including the advocates of such policies.[44] A reasonable common definition would be the formulation of a strategy by government for the structuring of one or more national industries. Advocates of such policies argue that, much like a large corporation, a national government can select where to invest resources and can_without moving to socialist planning of an entire economy—try to pick "winners" and to stabilize or rationalize "losers." European governments, most prominently France, and Japan are cited as showing successful examples of both types of intervention—for example, to promote the French aerospace industry or restructure the European steel industry. In each steel restructuring case, the struggling industry took the initiative to solicit government aid, rather than it being imposed against the industry's wishes, although inevitably individual firms turned out to be winners and losers.

In the United States, federal government policies have, in fact, played a major role in the restructuring of the U.S. steel industry, but in most cases they have done so almost inadvertently as a result of other federal policy objectives. Industry actions are shaped by federal tax codes, labor law, environmental regulation, antitrust policy, pensions guarantees, the promotion of recycling, improvements in automobile fuel economy, and so on. With the exception of trade protection and the questionable selective advantages of bankruptcy protection, the economic and legal framework within which the integrated carbon steel industry has operated has seemed to be a hostile one. Government actions have appeared to directly add costs to the integrated mills and to indirectly promote their minimill competitors. Yet for all the protests by the integrated companies against specific policies, no requests have been made for a positive, pro-steel industry policy even when the industry might appear to be in desperate need of, for example, assistance in closing excess capacity. The closest approach to a comprehensive package of measures to aid the industry, the 1977 Solomon Plan, was denounced by U.S. Steel as socialistic.

The lack of government intervention, as compared to the support given European integrated companies, for example, probably on balance speeded up the pace of restructuring of U.S. industry, although some policies—notably the antitrust restrictions of mergers—may have had opposite effects. It is remarkable how the U.S. integrated industry has not increased its average firm size through consolidation over a period when the weakest companies—mostly small, single-plant integrated producers—kept a disproportionate amount of their capacity open. The reasons for the lack of calls for restructuring aid, though, seem beyond the logic of self-interest and may lie in the realm of ideology or psychology. Ultimately the integrated companies' managements seem, in this as in other areas, to have suffered either from a failure of imagination, or from an excess of it—excessive fears of socialism and threats to their own jobs. As it was, most of those jobs were never secure; only U.S. Steel, Bethlehem, and Inland survived the restructuring without bankruptcy or foreign ownership. It may be no coincidence that U.S. Steel and Bethlehem continued to lead the industry's thinking and actions in the field of public policy, while their followers were led to their doom.

Trade policy stands out as the great exception to the rule of nonintervention by government in the United States. For nearly 20 years, U.S. Steel and Bethlehem Steel, sometimes supported by other individual companies, always supported by a pliant AISI, persuaded successive administrations and Congresses that their problems could be solved if only the foreign competition, unfair almost by definition, could be sent away. Industry asked for (almost) nothing else; how then could this one request be denied a sector that was going through such difficulties, generating such unemployment among the voters? If voter pressure was not enough, then what about the patriotic picture of this great (and strategic) American industry battling against unscrupulous foreigners? It is remarkable that it was not until 1984 that the first major U.S. manufacturer, Caterpillar, broke ranks to denounce the calls for expensive protection; not until the late 1980s that the minimills organized their own voice in Washington. The integrated companies ran an outstandingly successful political and legal campaign, but they fought against a symptom, not against the problem.

Trade battles may in the long run have assisted, rather than retarded, the speed of restructuring. While trade policy had significant short-term impacts on pricing at the margin, its effects were clearly outweighed by far greater economic trends—the business cycle, exchange rates, world steel export prices, and the growth of the minimill sector. By focusing so much of the attention, energy, and time of integrated company managements on fighting imports, the companies lost opportunities to focus on their real problems and their more dangerous domestic competitors. Fighting imports was a distraction that the integrated companies did not need.

5

THE RISE OF THE MINIMILL

DEFINING THE UNDEFINABLE

The term "minimill" came into general use in the steel industry in the early 1960s and was picked up in the financial and business-journalism community by the early 1970s. When first used, the term was applied to a small number of new electric furnace mills built during the 1950s and 1960s that had a number of common characteristics: they were small (until 1969, having less than 200,000 short tons of annual capacity); they supplied local markets (typically within a 400-mile radius) with reinforcing bars and some light merchant bar products; they were owned independently from integrated steel mills but often with corporate integration backward into scrap processing or forward into fabricating operations; and they had a philosophy of operating with the lowest possible costs, with the minimum of capital investment and corporate overhead. The mills that were held up as exemplifying the new type of operation included those of Florida Steel (now Ameristeel), North Star Steel, Nucor Corporation, and Roanoke Electric Steel.

With the success of the new mills, the use of the term "minimill" began to spread. Problems of definition came about in two ways. First, the concept of small, independent mills melting scrap and rolling a limited product line was not new. Small cold-metal open-hearth mills had a long history, and there was no clear break between these small independent mills and the large integrated companies. Indeed there was a wide spectrum of steel mill configurations in a gray area in between the two. For example, small electric furnace mills were operated by integrated companies to serve distant markets, such as those of Bethlehem Steel at Seattle and Los Angeles; and also independent but large-scale electric furnace operations produced limited product ranges but otherwise aspired to the status of major steel companies, such as Northwestern Steel and Wire in Sterling, Illinois (beams, bars and wire rod) and Lukens Steel in Conshohocken, Pennsylvania (plate). In the 1970s and especially the 1980s, when the problems of the integrated companies became as evident as the success of the minimills, producers in the intermediate gray area began calling themselves minimills. By doing so they hoped to dissociate themselves from the integrated companies in the eyes of the capital markets and also in some cases actually to emulate the original successful minimills.

The second part of the definitional problem also came with the minimills' success, as they grew out of the "mini" part of the term. The first new 500,000-ton minimill, Georgetown Steel, was built in South Carolina in 1969, producing wire rod. In the late 1970s, minimill companies expanded by constructing or buying multiple mills. Four companies—Korf Industries (Georgetown Steel), North Star, Florida Steel, and Nucor—passed the million-ton mark of total capacity, thus approaching the size of the smaller integrated companies. Chaparral Steel in Midlothian, Texas, expanded to become the first million-ton minimill at a single location by 1982. Nucor, with seven mills, passed the 5-million-ton mark in 1993, and growth in the sector looked set to continue toward the end of the decade. In recognition of this growth, a number of attempts took place to replace the term "minimill"; "market mill" and the cumbersome term "independent electric-furnace producer" were tried but never caught on. In 1995, the term "minimill" was still commonly being applied to new flat-rolled mills of 2 million tons of capacity.

Such a mill cannot be described as small, except perhaps by comparison to the handful of 10-million-ton-plus capacity integrated mills in Russia, Japan, and Korea. The term "minimill" survives because certain similarities exist between the small, 200,000-ton rebar producer and the flat-rolled mill ten times its size that allow both to be considered in the same category. The most obvious characteristic is the use of electric furnaces, especially as integrated mills have either closed nearly all their electric furnace capacity or chosen to de-integrate and pursue the minimill strategy. However, as minimills use more scrap substitutes, including iron carbide beginning in 1994 as well as DRI, EF steelmaking may become increasingly "integrated." Moreover, independent integrated mills, such as Acme Steel in Chicago or Geneva Steel in Utah, have adopted aspects of minimill practice or technology that allow them to claim to be minimills themselves. In these cases, it is not so much the technology—although Acme has built a thin-slab caster—as less tangible qualities that appear to justify the use of the term.

Corporate culture is the intangible that is consistently used to differentiate minimills. Firms frequently claim or identify at least five aspects of this. One is a lack of corporate staff and overhead. Nucor takes great pride in its spartan headquarters, located in a suburban shopping mall, with a staff of less than 20 people including the chairman. Although most integrated mills have sold some if not all of their corporate jets, golf courses, and office towers, the contrast remains stark. A second, related feature is the use of low-cost, off-the-shelf technology bought from vendors worldwide rather than the use of custom-built equipment and in-house research. When companies deliberately avoid inventing things, the "not-invented-here" syndrome is avoided; although Nucor, alone among the minimills, has since the mid-1980s pioneered the commercialization (although not the research and development) of new technology. A third feature, perhaps related to the first two, has been flexibility in entering and exiting markets. Minimills have been bought and sold, built and closed, with far greater frequency than integrated mills. This may reflect their low capital cost, but it also reveals a different attitude toward assets and bottom lines. Successful minimill companies have not hesitated to sell profitable operations for a good price (for example, Co-Steel's sale of its interests in North Star and Chaparral) or to buy seemingly distressed assets in quite new product areas at a low price (for example, North Star's acquisition of a bankrupt seamless pipe mill in Youngstown and a structural shape mill in Calvert City, Kentucky). A portfolio of assets has been built, either by geographic diversification or in different steel product lines, at the very time when most integrated companies have been cutting back to just "core" flat-rolled products. A fourth aspect of the minimill culture is labor relations. Minimills are by no means always non-union; nor are they immune from strikes. However, they all attempt to maximize the flexibility with which they use labor inputs, seeking to minimize their total labor hours per ton rather than minimize the cost of labor per hour. As an example, Chaparral Steel uses its security guards to do overnight data entry, light maintenance, and act as paramedics and ambulance drivers as needed, rather than the traditional single-task employee common to integrated mills.[1] Last, but in some ways most important, minimills are price-takers in the marketplace. As a general rule, their operating philosophy has been to sell at a low enough price to fill the mill to capacity and to sell at a transparent pricing structure, with announced and generally available quantity discounts and no hidden deals. Many minimills have a part of their throughput dedicated to captive fabricating plants, such as joist or rebar shops, but the great majority of their output is sold to distributors. There are few secrets in steel distribution, and while the minimills have been aggressive competitors for distributor business, their pricing flexibility has usually been announced to, rather than concealed from, the market.

This corporate culture—the lean, aggressive price-taker—is the rhetorical antithesis of what the integrated mills had become in the 1960s and how they are often still—if unfairly—stereotyped in the 1990s. The emphasis on man-hours per ton meant that minimills shunned labor-intensive downstream finishing and distribution operations, other than captive fabrication operations. As they diversified their products away from the specialized end-use markets for re-bar and wire rod, their growth created opportunities for steel processors and service centers, which grew in size and market share along with the minimill sector. Service centers draw their steel supplies disproportionately from minimills and imports, with whom they may share a common entrepreneurial culture and for whom they provide services the integrated mills often supply in-house. Integrated mills, conversely, have sold disproportionately high quantities of their output directly to end users, whether manufacturers or fabricators, and have tailored their marketing to the large end-user market. Unfortunately, the demands of these customers—for special chemistries or quality, for additional finishing operations, and for metallurgical consulting and after-sales support—have added costs that the supplying mills have not been able to recapture in higher prices. The cost differential between the integrated mills on the one hand and the minimills and imports on the other has therefore been heightened by their comparative marketing strategies, while the selling price differential has been little or nothing.

As the term "minimill" became synonymous with "virtue" in the eyes of the financial community in the 1970s and 1980s, companies claiming to be minimills proliferated but their actual operations and culture differed widely. In 1980, a person asked to define a minimill might say "I know one when I see one". By the 1990s, U.S. steelmakers had gone though such a shakeout that most companies had adopted minimill practices, even if they retained the traditional integrated steelmaking process. The story of the minimill industry, then, is not only the growth of a number of successful companies with their own distinctive variations on a common formula; it is also the story of how that formula was adopted and adapted by a significant section of the preexisting U.S. steel industry.

FROM "INDEPENDENT" TO "MINIMILL": TWO CASE STUDIES

The oldest minimill companies operating in the United States today began steelmaking not in the 1960s or 1970s but almost a hundred years ago. Both Keystone Steel and Wire (Keystone Consolidated since 1968) and Northwestern Steel and Wire began as wire producers in the 1880s, and started making their own wire rod from open-hearth steel in 1910 and 1912 respectively. Atlantic Steel and Newport Steel can claim continuous operations at existing mills since 1901 and 1909, respectively, although Atlantic Steel no longer melts steel at its original Atlanta plant. Today such companies are indisputably in the minimill category. The story of their transformation illustrates much of the success of the minimill concept.

Atlantic Steel, today a division of Canadian minimill and fabrication company Ivaco, Inc., was founded in Atlanta, Georgia, in 1901 as an open-hearth bar producer. In the 1950s, the cold-metal open hearths were replaced with electric furnaces, but the mill remained in some ways a miniature version of an integrated steel company, with an impressive headquarters building, a steelworkers' union contract, and ingot pouring, blooming, billet and bar mills, and wire drawing, nail, and baling tie machines. The company followed the major companies' list prices and thrived by serving regional markets with bar and wire products that the integrated companies operating in the South, notably the Alabama mills of U.S. Steel and Republic Steel, did not produce locally. In the 1960s, the emergence of new minimills in the Southeast challenged Atlantic Steel's dominant regional position, and a change of strategy followed. In 1975, the company built a new and very typical minimill 40 miles outside Atlanta in the small town of Cartersville, with a continuous caster and bar mill for re-bar and merchant bar products. The company was acquired in 1979 by Ivaco, and in 1980 a caster and an upgraded rod mill were installed at the original Atlanta plant, although steelmaking was ended there in 1988 when Cartersville's capacity was expanded. In 1995, the two plants had capacity to roll around 1 million tons of bar and rod a year, although the long-term future of the Atlanta rolling mill—on a valuable site close to the city center—was in doubt. Ivaco reported in 1994 and 1995 that Atlantic Steel was not profitable, and rumors that it might be for sale were reported in the industry.

Atlantic Steel's story as it evolved from independent producer to minimill is typical of much of the nonintegrated industry in the United States. It primarily serves regional markets with bar and wire products, although it ships some less common sizes of bar to national service center markets. Its steelmaking practice evolved to emulate "typical" minimill capacity and configuration. Until 1992, it had captive fabricating operations in the form of the Florida Wire and Cable Company, a wire and wire rope producer, which was sold to minimill competitor Georgetown Steel. Itself briefly a two-mill steel company, Atlantic became part of a larger international North American minimill group.

The NS Group, Inc. (formerly Newport Steel), dating from 1909, has a company history that is almost as long. Its story is equally illustrative, although the company's products are less typical. Located at Newport, Kentucky, across the Ohio River from Cincinnati, Newport Steel operated as an independent producer of sheets and welded tubing under various corporate owners, before being acquired in 1956 by Acme Steel of Chicago, then as now a small integrated sheet producer. Using cold-metal open hearths to supply a prewar, 66-inch, three-stand reversing hot-strip mill with a rolling capacity of just 460,000 annual tons, the company found it increasingly hard to compete with major mills in the sheet market but could profitably use part of its sheet production as the raw material for forming welded pipe. The open hearths were replaced with electric furnaces in the 1960s. In 1980, however, its parent (known as Interlake, Inc., between 1964 and 1986) closed the mill after its Steelworkers local refused to give wage concessions to help the company through that year's steel slump.

The plant's managers obtained financing to buy the assets and reopened the mill in early 1981, reverting to the original Newport Steel name. A second, larger-diameter pipe mill was installed in 1984, allowing the company to produce pipe up to 13 inches in diameter and allowing the full capacity of the strip mill to be utilized for pipemaking operations. In 1986, the company bought a second shuttered steel mill, Kentucky Electric Steel in Ashland, which had been built as a minimill in 1965 to produce specialized flat bar products, and adopted the name NS Group for a holding company for the two mills. In 1987, NS made a further acquisition, Erlanger Tubular Corporation in Catoosa, Oklahoma, a processor and finisher of both welded and seamless pipe for OCTG applications. The company's commitment to pipe, and especially the oilfield, increased still further in 1990 when it bought the seamless pipe mills of Armco, Inc., at Ambridge and Koppel, Pennsylvania, which had been closed in 1985 in response to the seamless overcapacity following the boom and 1982 slump in oil prices and drilling. The two plants included an electric furnace and continuous caster, a large 22-inch round bar mill, and two seamless mills. In August 1994, a second pipe finishing plant for seamless OCTG was acquired in Baytown, Texas, while a line pipe coating plant was announced for Newport, Kentucky.

Reflecting the company's increasing specialization in the oilfield market, the Kentucky Electric mill was sold off at the end of 1992 via an Initial Public Offering of stock. NS recorded a profit of $21.5 million on the sale, having bought the mill in 1986 for just $1 million of its own money and with "soft" state and federal loans and grants. In 1995, NS Group shipped 635,000 tons of pipes and bars, ranking it only number 13 among minimill groups for tonnage, but its pipe products were second only to U.S. Steel for the range of sizes and finishing capabilities offered.

NS Group's history is unusual but not unique in the minimill sector. One other U.S. independent-turned-minimill, Laclede Steel of St. Louis, operates a narrow strip mill to supply a welded pipe product range, as does Canadian electric furnace producer Sidbec-Dosco. North Star Steel operates a seamless pipe mill in Ohio and finishing facility in Houston, as does Oregon Steel at its CF & I division in Pueblo, Colorado, a former integrated mill. Numerous minimill companies have acquired former integrated mill assets, seeming to blur the distinction between the types of company. However, that distinction can be clearly discerned in NS Group's operations.

Prior to the closure of either the Interlake mill at Newport in 1980, or the Armco mills in 1985, the facilities operated today by NS were unquestionably part of "Big Steel," although they were electric furnace operations. Their workforces were not only unionized but operated with the wages, benefits, and work rules of the national Basic Steel Agreement. Corporate overhead ranging from maintenance facilities to large sales organizations, plus the physical scale of the plants' facilities relative to their production capacities, produced an unsustainable cost structure that forced the plants' closure.

The reopened mills under NS management share most of the characteristics of U.S. minimills except for their rolling mill equipment.

Although unionized, the mills operate with less than half the number of people they formerly employed. At Koppel Steel, for example, the union local represents 600 people rather than 1,500 under Armco. The local cooperated with flexible work rules and labor-management committees, and brought only one grievance under the first four years of NS's ownership. As a reward, the company volunteered wage and benefit improvements, including a dental plan and a 401K savings program, for a five-year contract beginning in 1994. While a large percentage of the company's pipe is finished—heat treated, threaded and coupled, or coated—at captive plants, the company nevertheless sells primarily through pipe supply houses and steel service centers, and acts as a classic minimill price-taker in its markets. Its published prices generally reflect the pipe market, with a volume discount structure that the company appears to uphold scrupulously. NS Group has been highly opportunistic in both its acquisition strategy and in its sale of the profitable Kentucky Electric mill. Although pipe businesses have been only marginally profitable in the 1990s, capital investment in cost reduction and quality improvement has been undertaken continually; a 1994 industry capital spending survey listed 22 projects at the company's mills, ranging in cost from $90,000 to $7.44 million.[2] Mills that were written off under integrated ownership have proved to be survivors under minimill management and look set to be viable long-term suppliers.

Atlantic Steel and NS Group are both examples of the survival of steel mills through the turmoil of the industry's restructuring in the last thirty years by adoption of minimill techniques. Neither company has been especially profitable or pioneering, but both have maintained important market positions in limited product or geographic markets. Other examples might equally well be cited of historic independent mills that aspired to the status of major steel companies in the 1950s, but by the 1980s aspired to the status of minimills: Lukens Steel, Laclede Steel, Copperweld and Oregon Steel (formerly Gilmore Steel). The adoption of minimill philosophies by these independent mills helped drive the integrated producers out of additional markets and back toward their "core" flat-rolled product line.

Other independents did not survive the downturn of the steel market in the 1970s; a number of open-hearth producers closed before they were able to adopt minimill strategies. Continental Steel, a large wire rod producer in Kokomo, Indiana, found that the adoption of electric furnace steelmaking was not enough to ensure survival. Dating from 1914, Continental was reorganized from its bankrupt parent Penn-

Dixie Industries, a cement producer, in 1982. The company installed a new continuous caster and expended its rod mill in 1984–85, but it went into bankruptcy for a second and final time in 1986. Many factors contributed to the company's demise, including the highly competitive nature of the wire market and the debt assumed both to buy and to modernize the company; but ultimately, the company simply failed to drive down its costs fast enough to be able to survive in a competitive marketplace. It adopted a minimill plant configuration but not a minimill cost base, and therefore could not survive.

REBAR AND WIRE RODS: THE MODERN MINIMILL EMERGES

The first company identified with the modern minimill concept was Roanoke Electric Steel, which began to produce rebar from ingots poured from electric furnaces in April 1955. The company started with a steelmaking capacity of 50,000 tons per year, using two 15-ton Whiting furnaces. The company's subsequent development set a pattern followed by much of the minimill industry. In 1962, it installed the first continuous caster in the United States, which, combined with an additional 40-ton electric furnace, gave the company a capacity of 150,000 tons and dramatically lowered its costs compared to ingot practice. Expansion and competition brought saturation of the regional re-bar market, and the company moved into merchant bar products, acquiring three bar joist fabricating plants, with rebar eventually being produced only when orders for more profitable bar products did not fill the plant. Equipment was steadily upgraded in the 1970s and 1980s. The rolling mill, originally a cross-country mill typical of many small bar producers, was replaced in stages from 1979 to 1983. A fourth, 100-ton furnace, and larger casters increased annual steelmaking capacity to 600,000 tons, thus exceeding the bar mill's 400,000-ton capacity. In the mid-1980s, the company considered installing a second mill to produce larger structural sections, using the extra steelmaking capacity, but decided against it in the light of apparent overcapacity in that market. Roanoke today sells merchant bar products to distributors throughout the eastern United States, and sells rebars locally and billets to other steel mills. The company is publicly held, although its stock is thinly traded and much is still held by local families involved since the company's founding.

Roanoke set a pattern for new entrants into the industry. Mississippi Steel (Jackson, 1957), Florida Steel (Tampa, 1958), Hawaiian Western Steel (Honolulu, 1958) and Thomas Steel (Lemont, Illinois, 1958) rapidly emulated its success, helped by the rapid expansion of concrete construction in the 1950s and 1960s. Each began as single-product rebar mills, although Thomas quickly added merchant bar products. Also in the late 1950s, as independent wire rod producers such as Keystone and Atlantic Steel converted to electric furnace production, wire producers Ameron Steel and Wire (now Tamco) at Etiwanda, California (1957) and Roblin Steel in Dunkirk, New York, (1959) built the first new minimills dedicated to wire rod production.

The earliest minimills had capacities ranging from 40,000 to 100,000 tons a year, and furnace sizes averaged only 20 tons per heat. In the 1960s, additional entrants to the sector adopted a larger configuration, typically using 35-ton furnaces for an annual capacity of between 100,000 and 150,000 tons; early entrant companies quickly added equipment to bring their capacities up to the same levels. Hawaiian Western Steel remained an exception; its size is governed by the constraint of the state's limited construction market. In other cases, mills found that they could sell rebar economically up to a radius of about 400 miles from the mill, although regional variations in transport costs and construction patterns influenced this. Border Steel, a minimill built in El Paso, Texas, in 1961, marketed its steel up to 750 miles afield, to Houston and southern California, while three mills of Florida Steel, at Tampa (1962), Indiantown (1971), and Jacksonville (1976) sold almost all their steel within 200 miles, to Florida's booming construction industry.

The rebar minimills reflected dramatic changes in construction in the United States. They both benefited from and helped facilitate three major developments. First was the explosive growth in infrastructure spending from the 1950s to the 1970s, including the construction of the interstate highway system. Second, the demographic shift to the Sun Belt states directed growth away from the region in which the traditional integrated producers were located and could dominate the market. Third, concrete construction grew its market share, at the expense of wood and steel, during this period, helped (especially in the Sun Belt) by low-cost inputs of aggregates, energy, and rebar from the new minimills. Regional differences in the economics of alternate types of construction persist in the 1990s, with concrete dominant for nonresidential construction in markets such as Florida, while steel-frame construction remains dominant in much of the Northeast and Midwest. The early wire rod

Table 5.1
CONCRETE-REINFORCING BAR:
IMPORTS, MINIMILLS, INTEGRATED MILLS

(Thousands of net tons)

	Domestic Shipments	U.S. Exports	U.S. Imports	Apparent Consumption	Import %	Minimill %	Integrated Mill %
1959	2,176,927	13,776	851,943	3,015,094	28.26	39	33
1969	3,658,559	86,762	470,818	4,042,615	11.65	71	17
1979	5,303,000	86,281	116,955	5,333,674	2.19	87	11
1989	5,015,000	87,801	233,735	4,693,464	4.98	95	0
1994	4,929,000	106,124	328,015	5,150,891	6.37	94	0

NOTES:
Breakdown of minimill versus integrated mill market shares are author's estimates based on production capability, not actual shipments.

The last integrated mill to exit the rebar business was Bethlehem Steel, upon the closure of its 11-inch bar mill at Steelton, Pennsylvania, in 1986.

minimills similarly focused on low-cost, low-quality wire markets for such construction-related markets as concrete-reinforcing mesh (used to provide lateral strength in concrete paving) and fence wire.

Given these changes in construction trends, the first generation of minimills scarcely needed to make inroads into the markets of the integrated producers. Instead they served markets that had hardly existed before and which were peripheral to the integrated mills' strategies. Rebar and wire rod were, in fact, markets in which imports had a high level of penetration in the 1950s, before imports were perceived as a problem. The import share of the rebar market peaked at 28.3 percent of apparent consumption in 1959 and has since fallen steadily to negligible levels—under 2 percent in the 1990s; the United States has been a net exporter of rebar since the mid-1980s. Wire rod imports grew to 54.7 percent of apparent consumption in 1968, and have since fallen to under a quarter—to 15 percent of the market in 1993, if two-way trade with Canada is excluded. Although the separate reporting of wire rod and wire products complicates calculations of market shares, it is clear that in rod as in rebar the minimill producers have driven back imports. They have also driven out the integrated mills. Bethlehem Steel, once dominant in the product throughout the eastern United States, was the last U.S. integrated rebar producer to exit, in 1986.[3] U.S. Steel remains a wire rod producer through its USS-Kobe joint venture at the integrated Lorain, Ohio, mill; its wire operations were sold in 1986 and are now

Table 5.2
WIRE AND WIRE ROD:
IMPORTS, MINIMILLS, INTEGRATED MILLS

(Thousands of net tons)

	Domestic Shipments	U.S. Exports	U.S. Imports	Apparent Consumption	Import %	Minimill %	Integrated Mill %
1959	4,676,262	29,881	1,282,988	5,929,369	21.64	35	44
1969	4,878,728	143,412	2,275,194	7,010,510	32.45	37	31
1979	5,310,000	72,045	2,153,129	7,391,084	29.13	47	24
1989	5,158,000	273,716	2,649,895	7,534,179	35.17	59	6
1994	5,603,000	253,995	3,272,935	8,617,485	37.98	62	0

NOTES:

Breakdown of minimill versus integrated mill market shares are author's estimates based on production capability, not actual shipments.

To get as close as possible to shares of the final product market (i.e., wire, in whatever form), the following data are incorporated in table 5.2. Domestic shipments are AISI reports of wire rod (i.e., to independent wire manufacturers) plus steel company shipments of wire and wire products. Beginning in 1989, the AISI did not break out steel company shipments of wire products other than drawn wire; these tonnages are included within either rod or drawn wire. Imports and exports are of wire rod, wire, and wire products, excluding industrial fasteners. Total domestic consumption of wire and wire products will be slightly less than the total shown for apparent consumption, due to production losses in the conversion of wire rod to wire at companies other than steel companies. Similarly, domestic wire rod production is somewhat higher than the shipments total shown, due to conversion losses in the conversion of wire rod to wire internally at steel companies.

The last integrated mill to exit the wire rod business was Bethlehem Steel, upon the closure of its Bar, Road and Wire (BRW) division mills at Johnstown and Lackawanna in 1993. USS–Kobe Steel produces rod sizes as small as 5 mm on its new 10-inch mill stands installed at Lorain in 1994-95, though these are considered to be part of the small bar market, not for the wire rod market. CF & I Steel is considered an integrated mill until 1982. Northwestern Steel and Wire is considered a minimill throughout.

the American Steel and Wire division of Birmingham Steel. Bethlehem Steel closed its last wire rod operations at Lackawanna and Johnstown in 1993. Tables 5.1 and 5.2, above, show how the shares of integrated mills, imports, and minimills changed over time.

Between 1955 and 1969, a total of twenty new mills were built in the first wave of minimill construction. In addition, three long-established rolling mills, Structural Metals, Pollock Steel (now Marion Steel) and Steel Company of West Virginia, added electric furnaces on minimill lines. Most followed the pattern set by Roanoke Electric Steel: starting with a small, low-cost facility and then rapidly upgrading as the mill made money in local, niche markets. Profits were plowed back into larger furnaces, casters, improved rolling mills, and broader product ranges. Minimills were quick to adopt the new technology of the continuous caster. In addition to Roanoke's pioneering installation in 1962, twenty-two additional minimill billet caster installations were complete by 1970, including four cases where two casters were installed at a single mill. By 1985, 63 minimill casters were in use, and the percentage of continuously cast steel from minimills approached 100 percent, at a time when the integrated mills were still casting over 60 percent of their raw steel as ingots.[4]

Many first-generation minimills also broadened their bar product lines during the 1960s and 1970s, again following Roanoke's example, as increased steelmaking capacity and saturation of re-bar markets encouraged diversification. By 1969, nine minimills were selling merchant bar products, although the market was still dominated by integrated mills and by larger independent producers, such as Northwestern Steel and Wire. Kentucky Electric Steel, a minimill built in Ashland, Kentucky, in 1964, was the first minimill dedicated to specialty bar products, producing flat bar sizes for spring steel as well as merchant bar. Nevertheless, it followed the pattern of the first-generation minimills: it started small, with one 15-ton furnace; it expanded its capacity and product range using internally generated funds; and it was vertically integrated, in this case backward as its owners were scrap processors.

Although it is risky to generalize about a group of companies with different strategies and opportunities, probably most corporate owners of first-generation minimills did not consider themselves to be steelmakers primarily. Prior to building minimills, they were in the re-bar business—in other words, part of the construction industry; they were wire manufacturers; or they were scrap processors who wanted to add value to their scrap or secure a more reliable outlet for it. Until the 1980s, such vertical integration of minimills was common, and other types of steel-using businesses integrated backward into minimill steelmaking: joist manufacturing (Nucor), mine roof bolts (Birmingham Bolt), fasteners (Ceco). However, at the end of the 1960s, a new trend emerged, toward increased mill size and cost of entry into the business, that suggested that steelmaking could no longer be treated as a convenience or an afterthought in corporate or investment strategy.

A SECOND GENERATION: 1969 TO 1982

In 1969, German steelmaker and engineer Willy Korf built the Georgetown Steel mill at Georgetown, South Carolina. With a design capacity of 500,000 tons per year, it far exceeded the size of the largest new minimill built up to that date, the 200,000-ton-per-year capacity North Star Steel, built in St. Paul, Minnesota, in 1965. Configured with three large (for the time) 60-ton furnaces, two continuous casters, and a continuous wire rod mill, the mill was planned from the beginning to serve national, not just regional, markets and to produce DRI to supplement regional scrap supplies. The adjacent 400,000-ton-per-year Midrex DRI plant, developed by Korf and the Midland-Ross Corporation, became the first U.S. commercial DRI facility on its completion in 1971.

The Georgetown mill represented an investment of around $40 million, including the DRI plant, or around $80 per annual ton of the mill's capacity. This compared with the costs of anything from $5 million to $15 million that the first generation of minimills had cost, or a typical start-up cost per annual ton of $40 to $70. On the other hand, the cost of new integrated capacity at the time, such as the Burns Harbor mill, was around $500 per annual ton. While inflation in the 1970s would approximately double these numbers by 1980, the cost ratio of integrated capacity to minimill capacity remained the same. The relative costs effectively precluded the construction of new integrated capacity; but the cost of a mill on the scale of a Georgetown Steel was beyond the reach of the small rebar or scrap companies that had pioneered the minimill.

In the 1970s, it was still economically possible to build a first-generation–type rebar mill, as was done by the major rebar fabricator Owen Steel in 1974. Owen Electric Steel in Columbia, South Carolina, was a small (100,000-ton initial capacity) mill, most of whose product was consumed by the parent company's fabricating shops. Owen was the exception to the pattern of the decade, however. Of the 20 mills built between 1970 and 1982, the average capacity of the mills at start-up was 255,000 annual tons; and a significant product shift had also taken place. Thirteen of the new mills were primarily producers of merchant bars and light shapes, even if they also rolled rebar. Two were exclusively wire rod producers, and only five were predominantly or exclusively rebar producers.

Also in the 1970s, chains of minimills emerged—companies found that a successful formula at one mill could be replicated in other regions or product markets. Four million-ton companies were built over the decade: Florida Steel, North Star, Korf Industries, and Nucor. The first multiple-minimill company was Florida Steel, whose first small rebar mill at Tampa, Florida, opened in 1958 with a capacity of 60,000 tons per year. Mills in Charlotte, North Carolina (1962), Indiantown, Florida

(1971), Jacksonville, Florida (1976), and Jackson, Tennessee (1981), followed. The Jackson mill brought the company's combined steelmaking capacity to over 1 million tons per year. Florida Steel also acquired the Knoxville Iron minimill (built 1964) in 1987.

Ameristeel, as Florida Steel was renamed in 1996, remains the leading rebar fabricator in Florida and operates rebar fabricating shops in southeastern construction markets from Virginia to Louisiana. Although as much as half of production is still used internally at the rebar shops, the company was quick to diversify into merchant bar products, and in 1985, a wire rod block was added to the Jacksonville bar mill. The Jackson mill was the company's first to roll a majority of merchant bars and light shapes rather than rebar. Florida Steel remained a regional company, and entered a period of consolidation in the 1980s after its rapid growth in the 1960s and 1970s. The 1980s saw increased competition in its markets, and management—which owned much of the publicly traded company's stock—attempted to sell the company in the mid-1980s while its profitability, and market valuation, remained high. In 1992, the Japanese minimill company Kyoei Steel, Ltd., of Osaka bought the company.

Unlike other major minimill companies, Ameristeel has not attempted to diversify away from bar mill products or from the Southeast's construction market. The two other minimill chains that emerged in the 1970s, Nucor and North Star, led the industry in product diversification in the 1980s, but grew in the 1970s on the basis of merchant bars and rebar, as did Ameristeel. The original North Star Steel mill was built in St. Paul, Minnesota, in 1965 as a joint venture between a Canadian company, Co-Steel, and the giant Minneapolis-based grain and commodity trader Cargill. Cargill's commodity interests included scrap processing operations, and the success of the St. Paul mill led it to buy out Co-Steel in 1974 and undertake a strategy of growth in the minimill industry. In the 1970s, this growth was regional and relatively conservative. The St. Paul mill was expanded to 450,000-tons-per-year capacity, and a second mill, already under construction in Wilton, Iowa, was bought in 1977, which produced a mix of merchant bar products and rebar. However, in 1979, a third mill, at Monroe, Michigan, was dedicated to the production of special bar quality (SBQ) rounds for the automotive and cold-finishing markets. In the 1980s, an aggressive policy of acquisitions was pursued that saw North Star acquire three more mills, producing wire rod, structural shapes, and seamless pipe; while in the 1990s, the company resumed new mill construction, with new flat-rolled and bar/rod capacity. Its strategy, facilitated by the financial resources of Cargill, grew out of its success in the 1970s in both buying and building bar mills, and it ended that decade with just over a million tons of capacity.

In 1983 North Star bought one of the largest new minimills, the 600,000-ton-per-year wire rod mill of Georgetown Texas Steel in Beaumont, Texas. This mill was built by Korf Industries in 1976 on similar lines to the pioneering Georgetown mill in South Carolina, although without a DRI plant. The Beaumont mill both benefited and suffered from the roller-coaster of the energy-driven Gulf Coast economy. When the oil market slumped in 1981, the mill was left with empty order books and high interest payments; the mill had been financed by borrowing, and interest rates at their 1981-82 peak exceeded 20 percent. North Star was able to acquire the mill by assuming the debt, which Cargill paid off after negotiating sizable discounts. Thus Korf Industries became one of the first minimill companies to fall victim to a shakeout, which was perhaps inevitable in the 1980s as the minimill industry matured. Dr. Willy Korf's ambitions to become a global leader of the minimill industry were set back, although he retained the South Carolina mill and minimills in Germany and Brazil. In 1983, he sold 51 percent of his U.S. company Korf Industries to the Kuwait Investment Authority, and the company—renamed Georgetown Industries in 1984—thereafter pursued a conservative course. The Midrex DRI technology subsidiary was sold to Kobe Steel of Japan, and local scrap processing interests were sold. The company spent the next decade as a single-mill wire rod producer with a captive wire drawing subsidiary, Andrews Wire, taking part of the output.[5]

The fourth minimill company in the million-ton capacity club at the start of the 1980s was Nucor.[6] Although Nucor has become synonymous with pioneering in the 1980s and 1990s, its growth in the second wave of minimill construction was technically and financially conservative. Its carefully structured approach to marketing merchant bar products made Nucor the most profitable of the publicly held minimill companies in the 1970s. A former mini-conglomerate, Nucor had progressed from automobile manufacture through nuclear equipment to the less exciting but more profitable bar joist business. Nucor's six Vulcraft joist plants were and are the largest suppliers of steel roof joists to the national construction industry and consume large tonnages of steel bars. Like rebar shops and wire drawers before them, Nucor was tempted to control its raw material supply by building a steel mill.

The Darlington, South Carolina, mill, built in 1969 with an initial capacity of 120,000 tons, quickly proved its worth not only as a supplier to Vulcraft but as a seller of merchant bar and rebar, competing with existing minimills within the Southeast. The ability to sell merchant bar profitably out to a radius of around 600 miles meant that Nucor could cover essentially the entire country with four strategically placed bar mills. Using Vulcraft's national operations as a base market, Nucor added plants in Jewett, Texas (1975), Norfolk, Nebraska (1977), and Plymouth, Utah (1981). The mills each differed slightly in configuration, reflecting advances in Nucor's experience and in available furnace and casting technology, but each expanded quickly to over 500,000 tons of annual capacity. Each produced a mix of common bar and light structural products, ranging up to 8-inch channels at the Jewett mill. In 1981, upon the opening of the Plymouth mill, Nucor reached the mark of 2 million tons of capacity, of which less than a quarter was devoted to rebar production. Nucor had establishing itself as the clear leader in the merchant bar products market and began to look for other products to conquer.

One other remarkable minimill deserves mention here as a product of the second wave of minimill expansion. Chaparral Steel was built at Midlothian, Texas, outside Dallas, in 1975 with an initial capacity (quickly increased) of 220,000 tons from a single, large 130-ton electric furnace. From the start, Chaparral targeted a somewhat broader range of bars and shapes than most minimills, and in 1980–82, a major expansion was completed that took the company into wide flange beams. The beam market was dominated by a small number of integrated producers, plus the large independent EF mill Northwestern Steel and Wire. Chaparral initially rolled only the smaller beam sizes up to 14 inches—Bethlehem rolled sizes up to 36 inches for major high-rise columns—but Chaparral shipped nationally, not regionally. In 1982, Chaparral had a rolling capacity of 1.5 million annual tons, the first "minimill" to approach integrated mill size standards. Like North Star in St. Paul, Chaparral was initially a joint venture involving Canada's Co-Steel. Co-Steel sold its 50 percent direct interest to its partner Texas Industries in 1983 but in that transaction became a 25 percent stockholder in Texas Industries.

Table 5.3 shows the growth of the minimill share of the merchant bar and shape markets, and the simultaneous decline of integrated mills' share.

Table 5.3
HOT-ROLLED BAR AND BAR SHAPES:
IMPORTS, MINIMILLS, INTEGRATED MILLS

(Thousands of net tons)

	Domestic Shipments	U.S. Exports	U.S. Imports	Apparent Consumption	Import %	Minimill %	Integrated Mill %
1959	7,602,597	45,037	215,541	7,773,101	2.77	42	55
1969	8,659,045	179,854	1,319,255	9,798,446	13.46	50	47
1979	9,959,000	132,561	837,936	10,664,375	7.86	55	37
1989	7,617,000	104,010	885,357	8,398,347	10.54	56	33
1993	8,798,570	353,288	1,266,919	9,712,201	13.04	68	19

NOTES:
Breakdown of minimill versus integrated mill market shares are authors estimates based on production capability, not actual shipments. Includes both merchant quality and special quality bar but not rebar or cold-finished bar as reported by the AISI.

Integrated companies producing hot rolled bar in 1996 are Bethlehem Steel at Steelton, Pennsylvania; Inland Steel Bar Company and USS–Kobe Steel. LTV Steel's bar division was sold as Republic Engineered Steels in November 1989; this company is classed in the integrated mill column for 1989. Stainless and alloy bar production is classed in the "integrated" column where a producer also had major integrated carbon steel production in the year in question.

MINIMILLS REACH MATURITY: THE 1980s SHAKEOUT

The deep steel recession of the early 1980s coincided with the minimills' reaching a point where their initial markets—re-bar, low-end wire rod, and then merchant bars and light shapes—were saturated. By the early 1980s, the integrated mills had for the most part been driven out of these markets, and imports were driven back. Now minimills were forced to compete with each other, and the capacity additions of the 1970s meant that in a slump, the classic minimill strategy of pricing to fill the mill could no longer guarantee full output. As freight rates fell in the 1980s, minimills tried to sell their products farther afield, but this only increased the competition between minimills to cutthroat levels. Moreover, the rise in interest rates threatened highly leveraged companies, and the slump in the oilfield affected a region of the United States thickly populated with minimills. A shakeout of weaker players was inevitable.

After 1982, when planned mill construction and expansion under way since 1980 was completed, there was no net increase in minimill capacity in the United States for five years. During this time, at least 20 plants changed owners. Six minimills were permanently closed, and others were shuttered temporarily.[7] When new capacity was built after 1982, it would be for products not previously associated with minimills. An indication of the new direction was the first new mill built during the 1980s steel slump, the MacSteel plant of Quanex in Arkansas, an SBQ bar producer, opened in 1985. The minimill industry also grew through the sale of integrated companies' capacity into the minimill sector, such as the Bethlehem Steel mill in Seattle, sold in 1985 as Seattle Steel. In addition, seven major independent EF producers began to describe themselves as minimills and were henceforth generally so classed, during the early 1980s: Copperweld Steel, Keystone Consolidated, Laclede Steel, Lukens Steel, Northwestern Steel and Wire, Oregon Steel, and Phoenix Steel. The last-named, owned by the French group Creusot-Loire, closed in 1987 and was reopened by Chinese investors in 1989 as Citisteel.

Two companies emerged as major beneficiaries of the shake-out, through their ability to acquire minimill assets at distressed prices. North Star Steel has already been mentioned; the second company, Birmingham Steel, was founded only in 1984 and in three years acquired six steel mills. Both North Star, owned by Cargill, and Birmingham Steel, founded by a New York investment group, AEA Investors, Inc., had the financial resources—and the willingness to take a long-term approach to the minimill industry—that allowed them to pursue an aggressive policy of expansion. Overseas investors were also attracted to the prospect of minimill bargains, while others were eager to sell out of investments whose value had declined. As has been mentioned, the Kuwait Investment Office purchased a majority stake in Georgetown Steel; other overseas investors buying and selling minimill assets in the United States and Canada included companies from Austria, Australia, Brazil, Britain, China, France, Germany, Italy, Japan, and Switzerland. For a time in the mid-1980s, it seemed as if every asset in the minimill industry except North Star and Nucor was for sale.

North Star Steel acquired three mills in the mid-1980s. In addition to the Georgetown Texas mill of Korf Industries, whose capacity (rated today at 800,000 tons per year) remained North Star's largest single facility until the late 1990s, the company acquired the bankrupt former Hunt Steel seamless pipe mill in Youngstown, Ohio. It also bought Ohio River Steel in Calvert City, Kentucky (near Paducah), in 1986, a structural mill with no steelmaking hot end. Each acquisition took North Star into a new product range; each mill operates essentially independently (although Calvert City sources most of its billets from other North Star mills). Only one acquisition did not pay off: the purchase of Milton Manufacturing in Milton, Pennsylvania, a historic small independent dating from 1919 that had changed to a minimill configuration in the 1960s, producing re-bar. The mill was acquired in 1988 but closed in 1991. North Star did not undertake new construction of a steel mill between its completion of the Monroe, Michigan, mill in 1979 and the company's commitment to two new mills in 1994—a bar/rod mill in Arizona and a joint-venture flat-rolled mill with BHP Steel of Australia, in Ohio.

Birmingham Steel adopted a somewhat different acquisition strategy, focusing at first on buying and modernizing first-generation rebar minimlls. In 1984, the newly founded company acquired two minimills in Alabama and Illinois operated by the Birmingham Bolt Company. Birmingham Bolt had originally acquired the Birmingham mill to supply its roof bolt business with rebars, but the mills sold predominantly to outside rebar fabricators. Birmingham Steel quickly added additional rebar producers, struggling from overcapacity and low construction activity: Magna Corporation's Mississippi Steel mill in Jackson; Intercoastal Steel in Chesapeake, Virginia; Northwest Steel Rolling Mill in Seattle, Washington; and Judson Steel in the San Francisco Bay area. The Birmingham plant was re-equipped with a larger, modern furnace, and the Kanakee mill equipped with a new caster, giving the combined group a capacity of 1.29 million annual tons in 1988. Birmingham Steel proved to be just as pragmatic about its assets as other minimill investors. The former Intercoastal and Judson mills were closed in the early 1990s, while its other mills were steadily expanded. Birmingham acquired the struggling former Bethlehem mill of Seattle Steel and merged its other Seattle facility into that plant. Birmingham's biggest acquisition was its 1993 purchase of American Steel and Wire, the former rod and wire operations of U.S. Steel that had been sold off in 1984. Partly to supply these operations, in 1995–96 Birmingham built its first greenfield mill, an SBQ rolling mill in Cuyahoga Heights, Ohio, close to the AS & W plant. Of the publicly traded minimill groups, Birmingham Steel reported the second-highest rate of shipments in 1995, with 2.346 million tons shipped compared to Nucor's 6.745 million. North Star—which does not publish such figures—is also believed to have shipped over 2 million tons, as did Canada's Co-Steel, the latter from mills in Canada and the United Kingdom as well as its Co-Steel Raritan wire rod producer in New Jersey.

A varied group of investors acquired minimill interests during the shakeout, but for the most part they were companies with a commitment to and knowledge of the steel business. Other than North Star and Birmingham Steel, other minimill companies acquired additional mills: Structural Metals (Connors Steel in Birmingham, Alabama, 1984); Florida Steel (Knoxville Iron, 1986); NS Group (Kentucky Electric, 1986); and Sheffield Steel of Sand Springs, Oklahoma (Continental Steel, Joliet, Illinois, although only the rolling mills were operated, 1987). Cascade Steel Rolling Mills in McMinnville, Oregon, was acquired by its major scrap steel supplier, the Schnitzer group, in 1984; while Bayou Steel in Louisiana was acquired by a different type of scrap processor, RSR Corporation of Dallas, the largest secondary lead smelting group in the United States. Foreign investment entering the industry in the 1980s included the purchase of 50 percent of Ameron in California by Tokyo Steel and Mitsui U.S.A., the mill being renamed TAMCO; the purchase of Courtice Steel in Ontario by the Brazilian minimill group Gerdau; investments by Imetal of France and Daido of Japan in Copperweld; and the acquisition of half of Georgetown Steel by Kuwait and subsequently of the balance of that company by France's Usinor-Sacilor. With the exception of the RSR and Kuwaiti investments, these were all moves by companies established in different areas of the steel business. Companies that sold their minimill holdings during hard times, conversely, tended to be either conglomerates with no strategic commitment to steel or those in weak financial positions.

The companies that survived the 1980s shakeout intact and with the same owners were largely those with captive downstream markets for some portion of their output, regardless of size. Thus, Nucor and Roanoke Electric with joists and Florida Steel and Owen Steel with rebar were cushioned from the worst effects of the downturn. Other companies simply had strong investors with a long-term commitment to steel, as was the case with the Japanese owners of Auburn Steel in New York and the Swiss owners of New Jersey Steel.

By the time the steel recovery was under way in 1987, the shakeout had left the minimill industry transformed but much stronger than before. Average company size had increased through the wave of acquisitions and closures, and the companies that remained could for the most part be described as *steel companies* rather than investors in steel and other businesses. Of the approximately 25 million tons of minimill capacity in the United States at the end of 1987, the six largest firms accounted for nearly 10 million tons, or 40 percent.[8] The North American minimill industry had attracted international investors as early as Willy Korf in 1969, but although in 1987 one Canadian and six U.S. plants had at least 50 percent non-North American ownership, net foreign ownership actually declined during the shakeout. Four foreign-owned mills (Bayou, Georgetown Texas, Judson, and Knoxville Iron) were sold to U.S. owners; another (Hurricane Industries in Texas) was permanently closed after a brief spell of German ownership. Only Ameron/TAMCO and Copperweld saw an increase in their percentage of overseas ownership.

Perhaps the most important change, though, was the change in minimills' approach to pricing and competition. In the 1970s, the integrated producers' price umbrella gave a degree of protection to the minimills, which benefited from low costs relative to the integrated mills. In the 1980s, the exit of integrated producers from minimill markets and the end of oligopolistic pricing in most of the industry forced minimills to compete on a level playing field against each other and against imports. In a minimill-saturated commodity market with slow growth and excess capacity, continued company growth meant, first, rolling more sizes of existing product ranges and adding value via special quality and alloy products. Second, as these niches approached saturation, it required diversifying into new types of steel products that were still dominated by the integrated mills.

NEW WORLDS TO CONQUER: SPECIAL QUALITY BAR

The emergence of stronger and more committed minimill companies had three immediate effects on the U.S. industry. First, it allowed remarkably little capacity to be lost in the minimill industry, during the period from 1982 to 1987 when integrated mills shed approximately 43 million tons, or just over one-third of their total capacity. The minimills' relative size and share of the total steel market grew considerably even though their own expansion was essentially on hold. Second, the surviving companies were much better poised to take advantage of the upturn when it arrived. Third, product diversification in the minimill sector was encouraged in a number of ways: the arrival of independent producers such as Oregon Steel and Laclede Steel firmly in the minimill camp; the steelmaking focus of the bigger companies, rather than a single product or market focus, made them more willing to try different products; and the obvious distress of the integrated sector was a beckoning invitation to try to enter their markets. In the 1980s, minimills moved steadily ahead in capturing shares of successive markets: special quality bar; structurals, including wide flange beams; plate; and tubular products.

The high-quality bar market, known as SBQ (special bar quality), includes both bars that are subsequently cold-rolled and bars that are used in their hot-rolled form in demanding applications that require high strength, special chemistries, or tight tolerances. A broad definition of SBQ bars would also include leaded (free-machining) bars, spring steel, forging bar stock, and most alloy bar grades other than stainless and high-alloy bars. At the start of the 1980s, five integrated companies dominated the SBQ bar business: U.S. Steel, Bethlehem, Inland, Republic, and Jones & Laughlin (J&L). Electric furnace producers of smaller tonnages included Armco at its Koppel, Kansas City, and Houston mills; Timken; Copperweld; and the new minimills in Michigan, North Star at Monroe, and Quanex Corporation's MacSteel division at Jackson.

Republic and J&L used much of their hot-rolled bar output in their own cold-finishing plants, while the other producers sold part of their output to independent cold-finishers. With the merger of J&L and Republic, the combined LTV Steel held over 36 percent of the U.S. cold-finished bar market; the Antitrust Division of the Department of Justice investigated the merger. Justice decided not to require divestments of any of the company's extensive bar operations—four steelmaking plants, five hot-rolled and fifteen cold-finished bar plants. In the event LTV rapidly shed both bar capacity and market share; in 1989 it sold its remaining bar group assets—one steelmaking facility, three hot-rolled bar mills and five cold-finishing plants—to an ESOP under the name Republic Engineered Steels.

Other integrated hot-rolled bar producers underwent similar, if not as dramatic, retrenchment throughout the 1980s. Armco left the hot-rolled bar business in 1985. Bethlehem Steel struggled to keep afloat its Bar, Rod and Wire division based at Johnstown, but finally closed it in 1993. Inland Steel was more successful in establishing its bar operations as a separate, lower-cost division within the Indiana Harbor plant, with its own electric furnaces and caster. U.S. Steel concentrated its bar operations at the Lorain, Ohio, integrated mill and in 1989 brought in Japan's Kobe Steel as a 50 percent partner in that plant in return for financing extensive modernization.

Unlike most categories of steel products, SBQ shipments are not separately recorded, due to inevitable problems defining "special quality." Estimates of the annual U.S. carbon and alloy SBQ market, including sales to cold-finishers, average close to 4 million tons, out of a total carbon and alloy bar market of a little over 15 million tons. Such shipments are recorded within the overall categories of carbon and alloy hot-rolled bar shipments plus shipments of cold-finishers. It is, therefore, hard to track the decline of the integrated companies' market shares and the rise of the minimills' share. However, Inland and USS-Kobe remain major suppliers of high-quality hot-rolled bar in the 1990s; Bethlehem Steel also produces a small quantity of large-size flat bars from its Steelton plant. Combined, these three "integrateds" appear to ship around 1.25 million tons of bar a year, compared to minimill production, including "specialty" mills such as Timken and Republic Engineered Steels, of around 2.5 million tons.

In the 1980s, two new minimills were dedicated to SBQ: Quanex/MacSteel at Fort Smith, Arkansas, in 1985, and Timken's Faircrest Plant, near Canton, Ohio, in 1987. Two formidable merchant bar producers also sought to enter higher-value bar markets. Chaparral Steel began producing SBQ bar after its mill expansion and upgrade was completed in 1982, and Nucor began operating its own cold-finishing operations. Mills upgraded to target some portion of the SBQ market included Auburn Steel, North Star's St. Paul mill, Atlantic Steel, and Roanoke Electric. NS Group entered the market when it reopened and upgraded its Kentucky Electric Steel mill in 1986, and then added Armco's 22-inch bar mill, closed in 1985, as part of its Koppel plant purchase in 1990. In the 1990s, the pattern continued. Bethlehem's bar operations were split up and sold to J-Pitt Steel in 1993 (the Gautier bar mills at Johnstown) and Bar Technologies in 1995 (the balance, including the electric furnace steelmaking operation). Construction of a new SBQ mill in Indiana was begun in 1996 by the start-up company Qualitech Steel, and with capacity expansions at other mills a market glut appeared likely.

NEW WORLDS TO CONQUER: HEAVY STRUCTURALS

The minimill sector also came to dominate the wide flange beam market in the 1980s. The United States uses between 5 and 6 million tons of all structural sections over 3 inches each year, including beams, channels, heavy angles, and piling rolled on structurals mills. In 1980, Northwestern Steel and Wire was the only nonintegrated producer of heavy structurals, rolling beam sizes up to 18 inches at its large mill in Sterling, Illinois. Chaparral became an important producer of smaller sizes with its expansion in 1980 to 1982, while the heavier end of the beam market was challenged for the first time when Nucor announced plans for a new mill to produce beams up to 24 inches. The new mill, in which structurals producer Yamato Kogyo of Japan held a 50 percent interest, opened in 1988. In 1989, Northwestern bought and reopened Armco's shuttered Houston wide flange beam mill, allowing it to expand its size range up to 24 inches, and Chaparral added a new near-net-shape beam caster to expand its capability of rolling up to 24 inches. The addition of 2 million tons of new capacity in a wide flange beam market that rarely exceeds 4 million tons per year, coinciding with a downturn in the construction market in 1988-89, had a dramatic effect. Inland Steel and U.S. Steel left the beam market; and imports were effectively driven out in sizes up to 24 inches. Bethlehem, which could produce beams up to 36 inches in size and a number of unique sheet piling sections, was the only firm from the integrated sector remaining in the market in the mid-1990s.

Until the 1980s, the beam market operated in two tiers. Structural steel fabricators could go to a mill such as Bethlehem and get quotes on the entire steel requirements for a job's bill of materials, usually cut to length and possibly including not only beams but angles, flat bars, plate, and other steel products. The mill would quote a price based on modifying the list price by obscure formulas to assess the size of the job and of the fabricator, the fabricator's loyalty to the mill, the likely competition, and so on, but in practice the price was gauged to maintain the market price umbrella and the regional market positions of the major mills. In the 1970s, increasing imports were channeled through service centers, which the integrated mills also supplied with beams in standard sizes but at prices that "protected" their ability to supply the major fabricators directly. In the 1980s, as the integrated mills retreated from parts of the product range, their ability to supply a full bill of materials decreased, while the service centers' ability to offer a range of products and services increased, based on both imported and minimill steel. Beams came to be priced on a commodity basis, with transparent pricing announced by mills such as Nucor-Yamato and marketed through service centers that performed cutting and sometimes other operations for the fabricators.

Bethlehem tried to maintain its bill-of-materials marketing strategy from its Structurals Products Division in Bethlehem, Pennsylvania, into the 1990s. The historic hometown structurals mills were supplied by a high-cost, ingot-practice integrated hot end at a site lacking both raw materials and water transportation. Nevertheless, the company found it emotionally difficult to sell or close its hometown structurals business. Therefore, in the late 1980s and early 1990s, it sought a partner to modernize the mills, talking at length with British Steel about investing in new electric furnaces and casters in exchange for half the business unit and minimill-like manning practices. The Steelworkers' refusal to grant the work-rule concessions British Steel sought caused the talks to terminate. Bethlehem then decided to proceed alone, and actually did expand the mill's size capabilities up to 40 inches. However, the expansion of the Nucor-Yamato mill in 1992–93 to roll up to 40 inches proved fatal to Bethlehem's plans. In 1993, it announced the cancellation of plans to build electric furnaces at Bethlehem and the closure of the older and larger of the two rolling mills, the 48-inch mill. The company would exit the market for sizes over 24 inches and supply its smaller combination mill with billets from the company's Steelton electric furnace mill. The future of even this limited operation, in a market dominated by low-cost minimill producers, seemed in doubt. With the end of BOF steelmaking at Bethlehem in November 1995, the USS-Kobe joint venture at Lorain and the U.S. Steel seamless rounds caster at Fairfield are the last U.S. mills producing long products by the integrated steelmaking route.

PLATE: A SUBTLE SHIFT

Plate, the heaviest group of steel mill products, would appear to be suitable for straightforward, large-scale tonnage production, implying an advantage for integrated production. The reality is actually more complicated. Plate products include a sometimes bewildering array of grades, ranging from commodity grades through high-strength, abrasion-resisting, free-machining, and a range of specifications for shipbuilding and cold-weather applications, through a range of higher alloys to high-cost, sophisticated products such as armor plate and rolled bimetallic or clad plates. Plate sizes range in thickness from 3/16 inch (less than this is considered a sheet size) up to 12 inches or heavier. Heavy plates—over 4 inches—are usually burned to size and then machined to make large parts such as valve bodies, for which they can compete with cast or forged parts; large length and width dimensions

Table 5.4
PLATE: IMPORTS, MINIMILLS, INTEGRATED MILLS

(Thousands of net tons)

	Domestic Shipments	U.S. Exports	U.S. Imports	Apparent Consumption	Import %	Minimill %	Integrated Mill %
1959	7,028,572	65,585	291,360	7,254,347	4.02	13	83
1969	8,238,172	221,347	1,201,276	9,218,101	13.03	15	72
1979	9,035,000	207,860	1,819,812	10,646,952	17.09	14	69
1989	7,384,000	630,695	1,437,123	8,190,428	17.56	22	60
1994	9,087,927	288,922	2,460,907	11,259,912	21.86	28	50

NOTES:
Breakdown of minimill versus integrated mill market shares are author's estimates based on production capability, not actual shipments.

Lukens Steel, Oregon Steel (formerly Gilmore Steel), and Citisteel (formerly Phoenix Steel) are classed as minimills throughout, as are specialty plate producers such as Eastern Stainless Steel and Ingersoll Johnson Steel (now both part of Avesta Sheffield).

are therefore not usually needed. In smaller thicknesses, large surface areas—up to 120 inches width or wider—are desirable, whether to minimize the amount of welding needed in tanks and ships' hulls, for example, or to minimize the setup time and scrap losses in production processing operations. As shown in table 5.4, integrated mills retain a strong position in plate, but the market has seen both minimills and imports increase in importance.

Plates can be produced in one of two principal ways: rolled on a conventional, reversing plate mill, producing discrete "flat" or "plate mill" plates cut to length; or rolled on a continuous mill producing plate in coil form, such as a Steckel mill or a continuous hot-strip mill. Until 1987, industry statistics did not record separately the small amounts of plate-thickness coils produced; the tonnage was included under hot-rolled sheet and strip. Since the mid-1980s coiled plate has grown to take over a third of the plate market, or perhaps 60 percent of the market in plate of up to 1/2-inch thickness, the practical limit of coiled plate at present due to the market's lack of heavier leveling capabilities. A small tonnage of a narrow plate product known as universal mill or UM plate, which is rolled in widths up to 12 inches on bar-type mills, is also produced.

Because of the heterogeneous nature of plate markets in the United States, a strong independent sector targeting niche markets has always existed alongside the major integrated producers. In the 1970s, Lukens Steel and Phoenix Steel near Philadelphia, and Gilmore Steel in Oregon, were independent electric furnace plate mills. All had started as open-hearth integrated producers, which Alan Wood Steel, also near Philadelphia, still was. Major integrated plate producers included U.S. Steel with five plate mills, at Baytown, Gary, Geneva, Homestead, and South Works; Bethlehem at its Burns Harbor (two plate mills) and Sparrows Point plants; Inland Steel; Armco at Houston; Kaiser Steel; and Republic Steel at Gadsden, Alabama. The last of four boom years for plate was in 1981, when plate was in demand for capital goods in general but especially in the oilfield, for the construction of drilling rigs, tanks, and similar equipment, and also for conversion into pipe. In each year from 1978 to 1981, the U.S. plate market (including continuous mill plate) exceeded 10 million tons, plus as much as a million tons converted into large-diameter line pipe. With the energy slump in 1982, the plate market collapsed to a little over 5 million tons and remained at that level until 1987. From 1988, a slow recovery in capital spending allowed plate consumption to approach the 10-million-ton mark again in 1990 and remain close to that level into the late-1990s, but the mid-1980s recession changed the face of the plate sector.

Between 1980 and 1987, six of the twelve integrated plants producing plate were closed, as was Phoenix Steel, from the electric furnace sector.[9] Two more, Geneva and Gadsden, were sold and became part of newly independent integrated mills. The 50 percent drop in demand had led rapidly and directly to a cut of almost 50 percent of capacity. However, one new minimill-type plate producer was built at Tuscaloosa, Alabama, in 1984-85. Tuscaloosa Steel used purchased slabs to roll coiled plate on a Steckel mill, a compact reversing flat-rolled mill with a coil box heating furnace on either side of the rolling stand. Employing just 125 people and selling either coil plate or plate cut to length on its leveling line, Tuscaloosa introduced true minimill practice to the plate industry. Initially majority owned by Tippins Inc., the Pittsburgh steel mill engineering group, with 20 percent of its equity held by three other partners including British Steel, which supplied much of the slab requirements, Tuscaloosa became wholly owned by British Steel in 1989. British Steel committed in 1994 to add a new 1-million-ton melt shop and DRI plant to supply an expanded Tuscaloosa operation.

Other independent mills moved over into the minimill camp during the 1980s. Oregon Steel, the former Gilmore Steel, adopted minimill practices vigorously, as did Citisteel, the new owner of the former Phoenix Steel in Delaware. Lukens Steel, often classed as a specialty steel mill because of its production of armor plate and other sophisticated alloys and its business toll-rolling stainless plate, remained a much more sophisticated and therefore higher-cost company, focusing on higher-value rather than commodity plates, but it too came to call itself a minimill by the end of the 1980s. Lukens acquired the former Alan Wood rolling mill at nearby Conshohocken, Pennsylvania, in 1983, and expanded at that location in 1995 by adding a Steckel mill. Oregon Steel similarly added a Steckel mill in 1995 as the popularity of coiled plate increased.

The growth of coiled plate consumption at the expense of discrete plates reflected a change in the steel marketplace that tied in to the growth of minimills. In 1982, one-third of domestic plate shipments were reported as going to the end-use categories of steel service centers and "non-classified," the latter usually meaning some form of distributor. In 1993, that percentage had risen to 55 percent, while shipments "for converting and processing" at outside companies had grown from almost nothing to nearly 12 percent, representing both shipments to pipe producers and to other specialized plate processors. As with structural shapes, plate had become much more of a commodity or merchant product, with the distribution sector growing not only in size but in processing capabilities (especially coil-processing). Fewer manufacturers and fabricators found it economic to buy flat plates directly from mills and perform intermediate processing operations themselves. The move to outsourcing of plate processing benefited service centers; the growth of service centers benefited minimills; and the growth of service centers' processing capabilities drove the market away from discrete plates toward coils.

PIPE AND TUBING: AFTER THE FALL

The slump in the oilfield beginning in 1982 and described in chapter 4 saw the rapid exit from the oil-country tubular goods market of all but one integrated producer, U.S. Steel. At the end of the decade, U.S. Steel at Fairfield and Lorain (the USS-Kobe joint venture) produced a full range of seamless products from 2 inches to 26 inches outside diameter (OD), and supplied about a third of the seamless market. Imports supplied another third, while the balance was divided among minimills and pipe finishers without their own steelmaking facilities. These included NS Group's Koppel Steel near Pittsburgh; Quanex at its Michigan Seamless Tube division; North Star at Youngstown, Ohio; and CF

& I Steel in Pueblo, Colorado, which produced with electric furnaces only after 1982. Independent pipe finishers included Plymouth Tube in Winamac, Indiana; the Sawhill Tubular Division of Armco, Inc., in Sharon, PA (formerly part of specialty steelmaker Cyclops, acquired by Armco in 1992); and the Shelby Division of Copperweld Corporation, in Shelby, Ohio (separate from the steelmaker CSC Industries' Copperweld Steel Corporation since 1986). Unlike U.S. Steel, each of these producers supplies a limited part of the size range, and some—such as Copperweld and Quanex—specialize in small-diameter pressure tubing rather than OCTG.

In the early 1990s, a significant consolidation in the minimill pipe sector occurred when Oregon Steel acquired CF & I in 1993. Oregon Steel thus joined NS Group and Quanex in producing both seamless and welded pipe. However, the diversity of pipe sizes and markets is such that there is effectively no overlap among most of their production ranges. Quanex produces small sizes of pressure and mechanical tubing, up to 4.25 inches in seamless and 2.375 inches in welded sizes. NS Group's Newport Steel and Koppel Steel mills specialize in larger welded and seamless pipe for the oilfield and standard pipe markets, up to 13.375 inches. Oregon's CF & I produces seamless sizes from 2.375 inches to 9.625 inches, mostly for the oilfield, while Oregon's Napa, California, pipe mill produces large-diameter line pipe for oil and gas transmission pipelines from the company's plate, ranging up to 48 inches in diameter.

Despite these examples, relatively few minimill companies have ventured into welded pipe markets. The simple reason is that most minimill companies have not produced the flat-rolled steel that is the necessary feedstock for producing welded pipe and tubing. Surveying welded markets, in the 1990s, major integrated mills are no longer dominant producers, but the markets are fragmented between imports and domestic minimills, integrated mills and independent pipe makers.

In the North American electric-resistance-welded (ERW) large-diameter line pipe market,[10] in the United States there is one minimill (Oregon), one integrated mill (Bethlehem at Steelton), one independent pipe-former (French-owned Berg Steel Pipe in Panama City, Florida) and Canadian producers Stelpipe (integrated) and IPSCO (minimill).

Smaller ERW welded standard pipe and oil country markets see competition between integrated producers U.S. Steel, LTV, Stelco's Stelpipe division, and Geneva Steel; minimills Newport Steel and Lone Star Steel, plus Canadian minimills Sidbec-Dosco in Quebec and IPSCO with pipe plants in Comanche, Iowa, Regina, and Calgary; and a host of independent pipe producers, such as Northwest Pipe and Casing in Portland, Oregon, and Atchinson, Kansas.

In the square and rectangular tubing market, for structural applications, only Laclede Steel represents the minimill industry as a North American producer. The industry is dominated by independent U.S. and Canadian tubemakers, although an interesting move is the construction by Maverick Tube of a new structural tubing plant at Hickman, Arkansas, in 1993 to take advantage of coils from the next-door Nucor mill.

Except for Quanex, the minimill companies just listed that produce welded pipe and tubing do so from their own steel. Therein lies the probable direction of the pipe industry in the future. As more minimill companies operate flat-rolled mills, either Steckel mills or continuous hot-strip mills, the greater will be the temptation to add value to a portion of the mill's output by converting it to pipe and tubing. In the past, pipe and tube production was a way for small strip mills to survive without having to compete with the major integrated companies in the sheet market. Thus independents such as Newport, Laclede, Lone Star, Ipsco, and Sidbec-Dosco maintained small-scale flat-rolled facilities while they evolved as companies into minimills. In the next decade, the far greater availability of low-cost minimill flat-rolled steel is likely to lead either to independent pipe producers teaming up with minimills, as Maverick has at Hickman, or history will repeat itself as minimills move downstream into pipe production.

MINIMILLS IN THE 1990s: THE THIRD WAVE

Beginning in the late 1980s with Nucor's pioneering construction of flat-rolled mills at Crawfordsville, Indiana, and Hickman, Arkansas, industry and public attention has focused on the move of minimills into flat-rolled steel. The impending battle for market share, as at least seven additional flat-rolled mills enter the market in the 1990s, is so critical as to warrant separate discussion in the next chapter. The move into flat-rolled steel is, however, only part of the story of the resumption of minimill company growth in the 1990s.

Long products markets that were not saturated with minimill capacity during the first two waves of minimill construction, or whose expansion appeared to allow an extra player, came in for close scrutiny in the 1990s. Three have received significant new investment: Western bar and wire rod markets, in which imports and eastern producers still held a major share; the special quality bar market, especially in the Midwest; and the rail market.

To serve the growing demand for wire rod in the western half of the United States, major investments were undertaken in the mid-1990s at five minimills: the former Armco mill in Kansas City, sold to GS Technologies in 1993; Oregon Steel's CF & I division; Cascade Steel Rolling Mills in McMinnville, Oregon; a new North Star rod and bar mill opened at Kingman, Arizona, in 1996; and a new Mexican bar/rod producer, Cia. Siderurgica de California, built in Mexicali, Baja California, in 1993. Birmingham Steel withdrew plans to build another mill in Arizona when it appeared there might be a glut of new capacity. The North Star and Siderurgica de California mills each added 500,000 annual tons of capacity to the market, while expansions at Cascade, GST, and CF & I each added at least 100,000 tons of capacity in mill upgrades that also gave improved costs and quality.

The SBQ market, notably for automotive applications in the Midwest, is served by a mix of minimill and integrated mill production and imports. In 1994, Co-Steel announced that it was planning to build a 1-million-ton-per-year bar and rod mill in the Midwest, but abandoned the idea in favor of expansion at its Raritan division in New Jersey. Meanwhile, a group of industry executives led by Gordon Geiger, a former President of North Star, began to raise money for a 500,000-ton-per-year SBQ mill to be known as Qualitech. This mill would be supplied with iron carbide, from a plant also to be built by the company. Other incremental SBQ capacity additions were made at Quanex's two mills.[11] The new capacity suggests that, to stay profitable, other participants in the market must cut their costs dramatically. One longtime SBQ supplier, Copperweld Steel, did just that in 1995 through a Chapter 11 bankruptcy reorganization.

The rail market, a small niche in North America, has since the 1970s proved able to support only two U.S. and two Canadian producers. American apparent consumption of rail has averaged 700,000 tons per year since 1960 and Canadian consumption less than 200,000 tons. Canada is a net exporter of rails to markets outside North America. Until recently rail appeared to be an exclusively integrated mill market. Rail mills, all of which are at least forty years old but have been extensively modernized and upgraded, are at Bethlehem Steel's Steelton mill; Oregon Steel's CF & I division; Algoma Steel in Sault Ste. Marie, Ontario; and Sydney Steel in Sydney, Nova Scotia. U.S. Steel left the rail business in 1983, while Wheeling-Pittsburgh built a new rail mill at its Monessen, Pennsylvania, plant that operated only from 1983 to 1986.

Both the CF & I and Sydney Steel mills are former integrated operations that converted to electric furnace operation in the 1980s; in the 1990s, both passed into the ownership of companies with minimill holdings. The provincial government of Nova Scotia sold Sydney Steel in 1993 to the Chinese group CITIC, owner of Citisteel in Delaware, which has proceeded to implement the kind of low-cost operations it achieved at Citisteel. Oregon Steel bought CF & I out of Chapter 11 in 1993. Oregon Steel has invested heavily in the CF & I rail mill, to produce the very long, head-hardened rails now demanded by railroads for heavy traffic loads. Both Sydney Steel and Oregon Steel may be expected to increase their market share.

The remaining niches in long products not dominated by minimills are, of course, small compared with the opportunities that flat-rolled steel offers. Sheet and strip, including coated products, accounted in 1993 for about 57 percent of apparent consumption of all steel products and for over 60 percent of steel mill product imports (excluding semi-finished imports) but only 41 percent of exports. The minimill companies investing in the 1990s in flat-rolled mills are betting that the history of minimill domination of long products can be repeated. That process, of targeting low-price and low-quality applications first, then moving steadily up to higher-value products as technology improves and low-end markets are saturated, appears in principle to be applicable to flat-rolled products. The outstanding questions may be more of timing and tactics than of fundamentals—how to secure high-quality metallics feed, and whether the dollar exchange rate will permit large scale exporting. If no unforeseen economic developments occur, the next decade will see the third wave of minimills trigger further fundamental changes in the North American steel industry.

6

WHITE KNIGHTS OR VULTURES? FOREIGN INVESTMENT IN THE U.S. STEEL INDUSTRY

FROM AUTARKY TO OPEN MARKET

The growth of U.S. steel imports in the 1960s put an end to sixty years of autarky for the nation's steel industry. The nineteenth century had seen generally unrestricted trade in iron and steel, with the United States importing large tonnages of steel mainly from Great Britain. The principal import products reflected the major growth areas of demand: rails until the 1880s, then tinplate until the end of the 1890s. The rapid growth of the domestic industry from the 1870s to the end of the century tended to drive out imports as exploitation of domestic ores and coal drove U.S. prices below the landed costs of British imports. The United States became a net exporter of steel in 1893, and to quote Father Hogan, ". . . by 1900 imports . . . had ceased to be of any consequence to the domestic industry."[1]

Prior to World War II, the pattern of U.S. steel trade was reasonably stable. An average of 5 percent of U.S. production was exported; around 2 percent of the domestic market was supplied by imports. Exports were primarily to Canada, Latin America, and the Far East, while imports were primarily from Europe. Exceptional years, such as

1921, when exports accounted for 10 percent of U.S. shipments, were caused by differences in national economic cycles: that year the United States was still in a deep recession while the rest of the world was recovering from the postwar slump. The 1930s saw a dramatic decline in steel trade due to the damaging effects of protective tariffs erected worldwide in response to the recession; in the United States, the Smoot-Hawley Tariff increased duties on steel products to between 20 and 25 percent. The only growth in trade in this period was in scrap exports, as Japan and other countries came to see scrap U.S. automobiles as a valuable resource.

After World War II, there was a brief surge in U.S. steel exports to rebuild Europe, but the booming U.S. economy could absorb all the output of U.S. mills, and fears of domestic capacity shortages caused companies to devote all their energy and investment to the home market. Similar domestic needs and opportunities preoccupied both European and Japanese producers through the 1960s, as postwar rebuilding and then the development of local automobile, shipbuilding, and appliance industries created new levels of demand for steel. Global steel trade in 1960 represented only 10 percent of total steel shipments, including sales between the west European countries of the European Coal and Steel Community. Given that only 39 countries produced steel in 1960, this low level of steel trade reflects the level of concentration of steel-consuming industries as much as it does the high cost of ocean freight relative to the cost of steel.

By 1992, over 25 percent of all world steel production was traded internationally, with 78 countries producing steel and wide disparities between regional steel production and consumption patterns. As described in chapter 2, national steel industry capacities were expanded, in many cases deliberately ahead of the expected ability of local markets to absorb their products, as an instrument of national economic development policies. In addition, the gradual global decline of both tariff and non-tariff barriers under GATT, and the decline in the 1960s and 1970s of ocean freight rates while steel prices were still increasing, all tended to drive up the volume of steel traded.

International steel industry investment has tended to follow international steel trade, with a lag of one or more decades. In 1960, the only significant transnational investments in steelmaking facilities, as opposed to iron ore mining, were relics of past wars and empires: French investment in the neighboring German Saarland and residual British interests in South Africa and India. No U.S. mill was owned, even partly, by a non-U.S. company. The only U.S. steel company investments overseas, other than in raw materials, were Armco's Latin American fabricating operations.

THE 1960s: THE FIRST FOREIGN INVESTMENTS

The decade of the 1960s saw not only a dramatic rise in U.S. steel imports but the first moves by foreign investors into U.S. steel production and by U.S. companies into overseas steel production. The investments by U.S. companies, although short-lived, are interesting for revealing what "might have been" if priorities and the timing of commercial pressures had been different. Three companies—Armco, Bethlehem, and U.S. Steel—had historically been the only U.S. carbon steelmakers to sell their products systematically in export markets. Among specialty steelmakers, Allegheny Ludlum, Cyclops, and Crucible Steel were active exporters.

In the 1960s, Bethlehem Steel was committed to the new Burns Harbor integrated mill on the shore of Lake Michigan, plus long-term plans for expansion on the West Coast, and had little interest in further expansion overseas. Armco, however, built a wire rod minimill in Mexico City to supply its wire operations in that country, and continued to add grinding ball and other fabrication units in Latin America; uniquely among U.S. steelmakers, its sales from international operations remained close to 20 percent of company revenues until it began asset sales in the early 1980s. U.S. Steel, however, made the moves in the 1960s that came closest to establishing a genuinely international, American-based steel company.

U.S. Steel's market perspective was inevitably unique. It had long taken responsibility for being the pricing leader and the labor contract negotiator for the oligopolistic group of integrated mills. Alone among U.S. steelmakers, it had a truly national, as opposed to regional, market position, including southern and West Coast mills as well as eastern and midwestern operations. Again uniquely, it maintained its corporate headquarters (until the 1970s) in New York City, close to Wall Street, rather than in a midwestern steelmaking city (or, worse, in a "company town" such as Middletown or Bethlehem). This distance of executives from individual company operations, and the perspective offered by New York's emphasis on trade and finance rather than manufacturing, may have contributed to the company's willingness to look at steelmaking outside the United States.

In the 1960s, U.S. Steel looked at the European steel market, then growing at a much faster rate than North American markets, and recognized that southern Europe, especially Spain and Italy, offered major opportunities. Although these countries lagged economically behind northern Europe, they were likely to catch up quickly, while they did not have the powerful established steel groups (and excess capacity) that northern Europe had. In 1961, U.S. Steel joined with the Italian specialty steel group Terni to establish a 50/50 joint venture, Terninoss Acciai Inossidabili, producing flat-rolled stainless steel. Further Italian joint ventures were established in 1962 in wire drawing and structural steel fabrication. In 1964, U.S. Steel entered into an arrangement with Spanish integrated producer Altos Hornos de Vizcaya, under which U.S. Steel took a 25 percent equity holding in the company. In 1976 this relationship was extended when the companies entered a joint venture to build a new cold-rolling mill at Altos Hornos' Sagunto mill near Valencia.

Although the European investments were for the most part profitable (the structural fabricator was not and was sold in 1967), events in the United States overtook the strategy. As the steel market deteriorated after 1974 and the corporation's relations with the union became critical for cooperation in improving labor costs, it became politically impossible to justify investments overseas while U.S. Steel was laying off steelworkers at home. In the early 1980s, when a decision was made to diversify out of steel and into energy, the Italian and Spanish assets were sold to help finance the new strategy.

Two other investments were made in Europe, both by specialty steelmakers, in the 1960s. Crucible Steel took a stake in a new stainless bar mill, while Allegheny Ludlum joined with the Luxembourg-based Arbed group to build a major new stainless steel coil and plate mill, ALZ, in Genk, Belgium. Both U.S. companies sold their interests during the 1970s.

That these first moves toward overseas investment came to nothing was not a reflection on the soundness of the investments or the strategy. It was a reflection on how, when a company's core businesses are threatened, noncore assets have to be jettisoned. There was simply not enough time for the overseas strategies to bear fruit before the forced restructuring of the U.S. industry required their liquidation. Many foreign companies did not face the same pressure for survival, and therefore were able to pursue a longer-term strategy of international investment.

FIRST MOVES: FOREIGN INVESTMENT IN THE 1970s

In the 1970s, the first international investments in U.S. steelmaking capacity took place. Although a seemingly large number of transactions took place, the total capacity with partial or complete foreign ownership amounted to only 3 percent of U.S. capacity in 1979. Two different trends were evident. First, a number of small and struggling U.S. steelmakers were acquired, in whole or in part, by Canadian or European companies, usually quite cheaply, at prices close to the book value of the assets. Second, new mills, part of the "second wave" of minimills, were built by Canadian and overseas companies. Although some of these moves triggered a great deal of discussion and even resistance in industry journals and from the Steelworkers union, the net effect was to add jobs and capacity—both in the new mills and in mills that foreign ownership may have saved from closure. This influx of new competitors was not, of course, welcomed by the major mills. Table 6.1 shows the U.S. companies that attracted foreign investment in this first wave.

It is notable that three foreign electric furnace steelmakers, Co-Steel, Kyoei, and Korf, all experienced in building new mills in their home countries, invested in new mills in the United States. Each of these mills was a technical and commercial success, even if the Korf mills had to be sold in the 1980s to pay off debt. The other newly built mill, Bayou Steel, was built by the state-owned Austrian integrated steelmaker Voest-Alpine, in part as a prototype and demonstration plant for the technology of its engineering subsidiary, a leading manufacturer of casters and other steel mill equipment. As a result, no expense was spared in its construction, and its construction cost, reportedly in excess of $300 million, far exceeded any other minimill built to that date. Unfortunately, it opened just as the Gulf Coast economy ended the oil boom, and the mill lost $153 million in its first three years of operation. It was sold for just $76 million, after bringing down the head of Voest Alpine in Austria and causing a political crisis in that country. The new owner, Dallas-based RSR Corporation, made the mill profitable by a novel strategy, since widely emulated, of shipping its products by barge up the inland waterways to "mill depots" in cities such as Pittsburgh and

TABLE 6.1
FOREIGN INVESTMENT IN U.S. STEELMAKING, 1967–1979

Company	Date	%	Investor	Nationality	Notes
Alan Wood	1974	15	Creusot-Loire	France	Sold 1976; closed 1980
Atlantic Steel	1979	100	Ivaco	Canada	
Auburn Steel	1975	100	Kyoei Steel, Ataka Trading	Japan	Ataka's 50% share sold to Sumitomo in 1984
Azcon Corp. (Knoxville Iron)	1975	85	Consolidated Gold Fields	U.K.	Management buy-out 1985; mill sold to Florida Steel 1986
Bayou Steel [a]	1979	100	Voest-Alpine	Austria	Sold to RSR Corp., 1985
Chaparral Steel	1975	50	Co-Steel	Canada	Stake sold to partner Texas Industries, 1985 [b]
Copperweld Corporation	1975	67	Imetal	France	Steelmaking spun off to shareholders (as CSC) 1982, and finally sold in 1995
Georgetown South Carolina	1969	100	Korf Industries (built new)	Germany	Sold 51% to Kuwait Investment Office, 1983
Georgetown Texas	1976	100	Korf Industries (built new)	Germany	Sold 1982 to North Star Steel
Hawaiian Western Steel	1974	100	Western Canada Steel Ltd.	Canada	Subsidiary of Cominco, sold to IPSCO in 1988
Laclede Steel	1973	18	Ivaco	Canada	Raised to 49.8% in 1980s
Judson Steel	1978	100	Peko-Wallsend	Australia	Mill closed 1985, sold to Birmingham Steel 1987
North Star (St. Paul, MN)	1967	25	Co-Steel	Canada	Stake sold to partner Cargill in 1974
Phoenix Steel	1976	100	Creusot-Loire	France	Closed 1986

NOTES:
a Bayou Steel did not commence operations until early 1982.
b Co-Steel took 25% of the equity of Texas Industries as a result of this transaction.

Co-Steels shares of Texas Industries were finally sold in 1994 and 1995.

Chicago, thus bringing minimill pricing of merchant bar products into the heart of the integrated mills' market.

Other Canadian minimill groups had different strategies for investment in the United States. Western Canada Steel was a subsidiary of mining giant Cominco, with minimills in Vancouver and Calgary. It acquired the small ingot-practice rebar mill Hawaiian Western Steel during the post–Vietnam War recession in that state's construction market, but invested little in a clearly "nonstrategic" business. Cominco chose to leave the steel business in 1988, selling all three mills to Canadian pipe minimill IPSCO. Ivaco, the holding company for the Ivanier family of Montréal, had interests that included a minimill at L'Orignal, Ontario, and a number of steel fabricating companies. Ivaco's investments in Atlantic and Laclede, long-established independent mills, were to play an important role in modernizing both of those mills and introducing minimill practice to them. Ivaco's acquisitions, however, helped set a trend of foreign investors acquiring and turning around low-priced assets in the U.S. industry.

Investments by three international mining companies were perhaps best described as portfolio investments by metals conglomerates having no special strategic commitment to steelmaking. Consolidated Gold Fields, which at the time was the world's second-largest gold mining company; Peko-Wallsend, a diversified Australian mining company; and Imetal, a company holding many of the metals and mining interests of the French branch of the Rothschild family, all bought existing U.S. mills at low prices. Imetal's acquisition of a majority of shares of Copperweld, a public company, was bitterly opposed by management and by the Steelworkers union; the takeover battle featured worker demonstrations, posturing by Ohio politicians, and a court appearance by Guy de Rothschild.[2]

The largest and the only integrated mill acquisition of the "cheap assets" investments was by Creusot-Loire, a large French specialty steelmaker. After briefly holding a small stake in competitor Alan Wood Steel, Creusot-Loire bought Phoenix Steel in 1976. The troubled company had only had one profitable year since 1967—in 1974, at the height of the steel shortage; it suffered from obsolete equipment, a problematical new caster, and a troubled labor relations history. Creusot-Loire, the largest specialty steel producer in France, with six electric furnace plants and one integrated mill, had great hopes for Phoenix Steel. It quickly closed the 60-year-old structurals mill, leaving the company with open-hearth furnaces at Phoenixville, Pennsylvania, feeding a seamless pipe mill, and a mill at Claymont, Delaware, with electric furnaces and a slab caster (new in 1968) feeding a plate mill. The problems with the caster were eventually solved, but the slump in the mill's markets—the oilfield and (for plate) similar capital goods markets—combined with financial problems of the parent company in France to doom the company. The Phoenixville open hearths were closed in 1983 after the end of the seamless boom, and the seamless mill itself was closed in 1985. Closure of the plate mill followed a year later; two years later the company was reborn under Chinese ownership as Citisteel.

If a lesson is to be learned from the fate of the early foreign investments in the 1970s, it is the same as that of American steel investments overseas at that time: businesses not considered part of the core interests of the owner are liable to sale or closure if the parent's needs change. Nonstrategic investments are often short-term investments. Ivaco is clearly committed to a North America–wide, long-term strategy of operating minimills and downstream businesses, and both Laclede and Atlantic Steel have been core elements in that strategy—although Atlantic's unprofitability in the 1990s casts a shadow over its future. But strategy is not everything: Korf Industries' Georgetown mills were also key parts of Willy Korf's strategy, but they fell foul of double-digit interest rates in the early 1980s.

THE 1980s: THE FIRE SALE

The wave of international investment in U.S. steelmaking that began in 1984 can be divided into three parts. First was the acquisition of interests in existing integrated steelmaking assets, either through joint ventures or direct acquisition of assets or equity. Second was the wave of new construction of sheet finishing facilities in the mid-1980s, most notably in the form of new galvanizing capacity but also including new cold-strip mills. Much of this expansion was financed by inviting overseas steelmakers to enter joint ventures to build and operate the new lines. A third wave of investment by major overseas steelmakers, beginning in 1986 with the announcement of the Nucor-Yamato structural minimill, has focused on the U.S. minimill sector, including both start-ups of new flat-rolled minimills and the acquisition of existing mills.

A "fire sale" of integrated mill assets occurred as the early 1980s steel slump lasted into mid-decade. In the 1980s, the carbon steelmaking assets of three companies, Kaiser, National, and Armco, were acquired by overseas investors, and two more major steelmakers, Inland and Wheeling Pittsburgh, sought Japanese investment. Two U.S. Steel mills, in Lorain, Ohio, and Pittsburg, California, became joint venture operations with 50 percent held by a foreign partner, while two other joint venture proposals—for U.S. Steel's Fairless Hills mill and Bethlehem Steel's Bethlehem mill—came to nothing. Although the details of the transactions were different, the motivations of the foreign investors were broadly similar. Each had a long-term commitment to integrated steelmaking; each saw their home markets saturated and growing slowly; each sought to grow by expanding internationally; and each saw the opportunity to acquire market share cheaply by buying low-priced existing assets.

The first major integrated steelmaker known to be for sale and talking to foreign prospective buyers was Kaiser Steel. Kaiser's integrated mill at Fontana, east of Los Angeles, had been extensively modernized in the 1970s but operated in a market increasingly dominated by imported steel, both from the Pacific Rim and from western Europe. The West Coast market was too far in terms of transport costs from most U.S. mills, but the Fontana operation was handicapped by high-cost raw materials and by a location away from water transport options. The mill also required extensive additional investment in pollution control facilities at its coke ovens and blast furnaces, to meet both EPA and California's strict state standards. In 1979, Kaiser held discussions with Japan's second-largest steelmaker, NKK, about the purchase of the mill, and in 1980, the company talked with LTV Corporation, owner of Jones & Laughlin. With no sale agreed, and continuing losses from the operation, Kaiser announced the closure of the mill's hot end in 1983, eliminating 3 million annual tons of U.S. capacity. During 1983 and 1984, Kaiser sought to maintain rolling operations on a reduced scale with purchased slabs but finally closed the plant entirely in 1984.

In 1985, terms for the sale of the hot-strip mill and finishing facilities were concluded with a group formed by a locally resident English businessman, Michael Wilkinson, but backed primarily by Japan's Kawasaki Steel and Brazil's state-owned iron ore giant, CVRD. Kawasaki and CVRD owned the Tubarão mill in Brazil, which had a surplus of slabs for export to feed the Fontana mill. Under the name California Steel Industries, the mill resumed production from Brazilian slabs in 1985, with dramatically reduced crew sizes and lower wage rates. The following year Wilkinson and Associates sold their 50 percent interest to the Kawasaki/CVRD consortium, making California Steel Industries the first fully foreign-owned flat-rolled producer in the United States. In 1994, the partners studied the possibility of building an electric furnace hot end to supply the mill, but no decision was made.

Nisshin Steel made the first equity investment by a foreign company in an operating U.S. integrated steelmaker in Wheeling-Pittsburgh in February 1984. Nisshin, Japan's sixth-largest and smallest integrated steelmaker, agreed to buy 10 percent of the common stock of Wheeling-Pittsburgh, the eighth-largest U.S. steelmaker. Wheeling reciprocally bought $5.3 million of Nisshin stock, or less than 1 percent of that company's equity. Nisshin also agreed to enter a joint venture with Wheeling in constructing a new hot-dip galvanizing and aluminizing line, of which Nisshin would own 67 percent.

The two steelmakers were of similar size, but Nisshin was by far the stronger company financially. Because Wheeling was viewed as a marginal company at best by industry analysts, it could not raise the capital it needed to modernize and expand. One option for Wheeling was merger with a larger U.S. company, but in the winter of 1983-84 the U.S. Department of Justice announced its opposition to two announced mergers, those proposed between LTV (Jones & Laughlin) and Republic and between U.S. Steel and National Steel. An equity investment by a foreign partner would not need antitrust approval.

The Wheeling-Nisshin joint venture galvanizing line at Follansbee, West Virginia, was to become the successful model for a number of similar partnerships. The investment in Wheeling equity, however, could not save the company from bankruptcy in 1985. Wheeling would reorganize successfully under bankruptcy protection, but in so doing it sold its stake in Nisshin and Nisshin's stake in W-P was diluted. Nevertheless, the two companies have retained a strong working partnership, including construction of a second galvanizing line at Follansbee. In 1994, Wheeling also sought Asian partners to construct a second joint venture coating operation, a new tin mill products coating line at Yorkville, Ohio. Wheeling's partners in this venture are Dong Yang Tinplate of Korea and Nittetsu Shoji of Japan, a trading company. The mill began shipments in late 1996.

Shortly after the Wheeling-Nisshin announcement, a second and larger Japanese investment was announced. National Steel was the sixth largest U.S. steelmaker after the LTV-Republic merger. It had undergone significant changes between 1981 and 1984, including the elimination of 2.5 million tons of capacity at its Granite City, Illinois, mill and the sale of the Weirton mill to employees. The company had diversified into aluminum and the savings-and-loan industry in the 1970s, and set up its coal mines as a stand-alone profit center. Reflecting these changes, a new holding company was established in 1983 called National Intergroup, Inc. (NII). This new parent sought to sell its steel subsidiary, still called National Steel, to U.S. Steel in January 1984, four months after the announcement of the proposed LTV-Republic merger. When the Justice Department announced its antitrust objection to the sale, NKK approached NII. NKK had studied acquisitions in the U.S. industry at least since 1979, when it looked at Kaiser Steel, and was prepared to move quickly. The U.S. Steel–National Steel merger was announced on February 1, blocked on March 8 by the Justice Department, and a sale of 50 percent of National Steel to NKK was announced on April 24.[3]

NII earned $300 million from the sale and reinvested the proceeds in pharmaceuticals distribution and oil operations, which proved far more profitable than integrated steelmaking. With NII eager to get out of the steel business entirely, NKK quickly assumed direction of the joint venture. One of its first moves was to leave the integrated companies' joint labor negotiating group in July, marking the beginning of the end for that aspect of the traditional steel oligopoly. In 1986, an NKK executive, Kokichi Hagiwara, became president of National Steel; he was the first Japanese executive to become head of a major U.S. steelmaker, and during his four years in the post, NKK supplied the greater part of the capital needed for a $800 million investment in upgrading the company's two integrated mills. The company also adopted many Japanese management practices, including a no-layoff policy, adopted in exchange for union concessions in the 1986 contract. NKK increased its stake in National Steel to 70 percent in 1988, and a further 10 percent of the company's equity was sold off in a public offering. When NII sold its remaining stake in 1990, NKK owned 76 percent of the company.

Despite the solid financial commitment of NKK and the access that its parent gave National Steel to Japanese transplant automakers, National Steel's history under NKK has not been entirely happy. In the early 1990s, the company lagged behind other integrated steelmakers in financial recovery, and faced persistent reports of quality problems as well as labor and operations difficulties. In 1991, the company announced that it would consider filing for Chapter 11 bankruptcy protection if it did not achieve labor cost savings, which were in fact accomplished in a new contract. Its headquarters were slimmed down and moved to a suburban office park in Mishawaka, Indiana. A joint venture hot-dipped galvanizing line in Hamilton, Ontario, built by National, NKK, and Canada's Dofasco, was hit with antidumping duties in 1994. Also in that year, NKK fired its (American) president and chief financial officer, replacing them with executives hired from U.S. Steel's Gary mill. In 1995, the company seemed to be returned to a more even course, with a further stock issue raising $105 million; part of the proceeds were earmarked for a new galvanizing line at the Granite City mill. After the 1995 stock offering, NKK held 69 percent of the company's equity.[4]

A company whose recent history bears comparison to that of National Steel is Armco. The fifth-largest U.S. steelmaker after the LTV-Republic merger, Armco, Inc., had diversified away from steel into titanium, insurance, and oilfield services in the 1970s and early 1980s. Like National Steel, it closed significant amounts of capacity, notably its Houston mill in 1983 and its seamless pipe operations in 1986. Its steel operations were divided into three divisions. The Eastern Steel division, with integrated carbon flat-rolled mills at Ashland, Kentucky, and the company's hometown of Middletown, Ohio, operated the bulk of the company's steelmaking capacity. In addition, there was an electric furnace wire products mill in Kansas City operated as the Midwestern Steel division, and a specialty steel division including stainless mills in Butler, Pennsylvania, and Baltimore, Maryland.

Armco's most consistently profitable unit was its specialty steel division, which in the 1980s produced the widest product range of any stainless steel producer, including flat-rolled, bar, and pipe products. While other integrated steel companies involved in the stainless business, such as U.S. Steel and LTV, had divested themselves of their stainless operations, Armco chose the opposite route. In 1988, it began to implement a strategy of focusing on the stainless steel business while divesting itself of other assets.

Armco did not have to look far to find a partner to buy into its carbon steel operations. It had a long-standing relationship with Kawasaki, the third-largest Japanese steelmaker, which supplied Armco with technical assistance, while Kawasaki already had a presence in the U.S. market through its share in California Steel industries. In November 1988, Armco sold 40 percent of its Eastern Steel division, with about 5 million tons of capacity, to Kawasaki Steel for $350 million. Kawasaki also assumed a 40 percent share of the plants' pension liability and debt, worth about another $250 million, and had the right—quickly taken up—to expand its equity share up to 50 percent by financing new facilities, including a second electro-galvanizing line, at Armco.[5]

The Armco-Kawasaki joint venture, like National Steel, did not find partial Japanese ownership to be a panacea, even if it opened some doors among Japanese manufacturers in the United States. The company was heavily dependent on the automotive market, in which quality was of ever-increasing importance. The company was handicapped by a poor quality rejection rate and also by high cost iron ore and coal commitments, a location at Middletown without water access, and poor labor productivity. In 1992, a new management team headed by former U.S. Steel president Tom Graham was installed, with a ruthless focus on cost cutting. Again paralleling National Steel, the partners agreed in 1994 on a public stock offering, which would both finance further modernization and allow the U.S. partner to pull away from the joint venture. The new management team also raised the capital market's confidence in the company enough to allow the pension fund to be financed by a $325 million long-term debt issue.

The public stock offering, under the name AK Steel, was completed in April 1994, after which Kawasaki's share was diluted to 20.4 percent, while Armco sold the majority of its stock, reducing its holding to just 4 percent, and later selling even this. AK Steel's share of the stock sale exceeded $220 million, while in 1995 it was also able to sell $200 million of preferred stock. The refinancing of AK left the company with a fully funded pension fund and a solid balance sheet, while the combined effects of Tom Graham and high automotive demand for steel allowed the company's net profits in its first year after the public stock sale to exceed 12 percent of sales.

Another Japanese investment made in the 1988–89 period marked a further pairing off between previously uncommitted U.S. and Japanese integrated companies. Inland Steel, the fourth-largest U.S. steelmaker, and Nippon Steel, the largest Japanese steel company, announced an agreement reminiscent in structure of that between Wheeling-Pittsburgh and Nisshin in 1983. To supplement and safeguard their agreement to build the joint ventures in cold-rolling and coating known as I/N Tek and I/N Kote, Nippon and Inland each purchased 1 percent of the other's common stock. In 1989, this was supplemented by Nippon's effectively loaning Inland $185 million, by the purchase of a special class of preferred stock redeemable in between seven and ten years' time. The stock effectively gave Nippon another 13 percent of Inland's equity, but was accompanied by an agreement not to increase its holding or to sell its stock without Inland's approval.

So far three types of foreign investment have been described. In one, small shareholdings have been exchanged by U.S. and Japanese partners, conveying the appearance of equality in a relationship, while the major investment is undertaken in newly built joint venture facilities. In the second type of investment, National Steel and AK Steel have seen a Japanese partner effectively take control of a major integrated steelmaker through purchase of a major equity stake from the former U.S. parent company. In the third model, exemplified by California Steel Industries, two partners maintain a private joint venture company, with equal shares in and direct, joint control of a single plant. This third model was the preferred vehicle for U.S. Steel, in two major joint venture investments.

In 1985, U.S. Steel announced its sale of half the Pittsburg, California, mill to Pohang Iron and Steel, or POSCO, the largest Korean integrated steelmaker. The industry was surprised at the identity of the partner, but not at an announcement that pointed to major restructuring of U.S. Steel's operations in the west. U.S. Steel's Western Division operated the integrated, open-hearth mill at Geneva, Utah, rolling plates and hot bands; and shipped much of the hot band to a second mill near San Francisco, on the Sacramento River estuary at Pittsburg. There a cold-rolling mill reduced the hot bands to feed galvanizing and tinplate lines, supplying California's construction and vegetable canning industries. The Geneva mill required extensive modernization, at a cost U.S. Steel estimated at up to $1 billion, including coke ovens, a modern steelmaking shop, caster, and improvements to the hot-strip mill. The Pittsburg mill also needed its obsolete cold-rolling mill replaced. There was no chance that U.S. Steel could justify, or afford, such a huge investment. The company determined, therefore, to close the Geneva mill and find a partner to help finance the modernization of Pittsburg. In POSCO, it found a partner eager to enter the U.S. market, one that also could supply hot bands to the mill by sea from Korea, once the VRA limitations expired.

USS-POSCO, as the new joint venture company became known, committed to spending $400 million to update the plant, divided equally between the partners, on top of the $90 million POSCO paid U.S. Steel for its share of the plant. The expenditure included $300 million for a new six-high cold reduction mill, the first new-generation cold-rolling mill in the United States to have four backup rolls for each work roll, giving superior flatness and gauge consistency. Work had barely started on upgrading the mill when, in August 1986, it was idled by the six-month U.S. Steel strike. U.S. Steel used the opportunity to close and later sell the Geneva mill, so that when production resumed in 1987, hot bands were sourced largely from U.S. Steel's Fairless Hills plant on the Delaware River, shipped via the Panama Canal. As soon as the VRA renegotiation in 1989 permitted, the majority of coils were sourced more cheaply from Korea, with POSCO supplying almost a million tons per year of hot band and an additional half-million tons coming from U.S. Steel facilities, primarily the Gary, Indiana, mill after 1989. In 1995, the decline of the dollar allowed USS-POSCO to increase Gary's share of its coil supply to 50 percent.[6]

A second U.S. Steel mill saved through a joint venture was the Lorain, Ohio, long products mill. The mid-1980s saw the closure of much integrated capacity dedicated to long products, and the 90-year-old Lorain mill looked set to follow. The plant, with a capacity of a little over 2 million annual tons, produced special quality bar products, seamless tube rounds, and both seamless and welded pipe. The plant also supplied wire rod to the former U.S. Steel wire operations at Cuyahoga, Ohio, and Joliet, Illinois, spun off as American Steel and Wire in early 1986. The mill sourced its coke and strip for welded pipe production from other U.S. Steel plants in the Mon Valley. At the start of the 1986–87 strike, U.S. Steel threatened to halt steelmaking at Lorain. Industry analysts frequently predicted that no part of the mill would be reopened after a settlement, although eventually all the corporations mills except Geneva and Baytown did come back on line.[7]

In 1989, the mill had all of U.S. Steel's remaining bar and rod capacity. The corporation's seamless pipe range was divided between Lorain and the Fairfield, Alabama, mill, Fairfield producing sizes between 3.5 and 9.625 inches, and Lorain producing both larger and smaller sizes. Welded pipe, similarly, was split between Lorain and Fairless Hills. By 1989, it was one of only two remaining integrated mills in the United States dedicated exclusively to long products production, the other being Bethlehem Steel's Bethlehem structurals mill. Like the Pittsburg, California, mill, Lorain needed major capital investments to secure its future, especially to improve the efficiency of ironmaking, to add a second caster to allow 100 percent continuous casting, and to improve the quality of the bar products.

Kobe Steel, Japans fifth-largest integrated steelmaker, is the oldest and second-largest bar and rod producer in Japan, although it had no experience in seamless pipe products. The company's original Kobe Works, its second largest mill, is an all–long products integrated mill similar in size to Lorain. Like other Japanese producers, Kobe had changed its strategy in the U.S. market in response to VRAs and to the declining value of the dollar. It had all but ceased selling to distributors and "spot" sales, but had long-term commitments to the expanding group of Japanese-owned manufacturing plants in the United States. To continue to grow in the U.S. market, Kobe needed its own local capacity, but due to its integrated steelmaking expertise, it was not inclined to construct new minimill capacity. The Lorain joint venture offered Kobe the opportunity to expand its presence in U.S. bar markets and also to acquire expertise in seamless pipe.

Kobe Steel invested over $300 million in the plant over the next five years, in addition to $200 million from U.S. Steel. Improvements included relines and installation of pulverized coal injection equipment at the two active blast furnaces, a new bar/rod mill for small sizes, and the purchase in 1994 of a second continuous caster from the idle Wheeling-Pittsburgh mill at Monessen, Pennsylvania. Quality appears to be as good as any product on the market, evidenced by quality awards from General Motors and Ford. The pipe facilities, which were upgraded by U.S. Steel in the early 1980s in response to the short-lived OCTG boom, have not required major expenditures. The mill is reported to have been profitable in every year since the joint venture was set up, including during the 1990–91 automotive recession. However, in the mid-1990s, the mill faces further challenges to improve its labor productivity, which were estimated to be around 3.5 man-hours per ton before the installation of the second caster. Its minimill competitors had man-hour per ton levels half that number.[8]

THREE THAT GOT AWAY

U.S. Steel's successful joint ventures at Pittsburg and Lorain followed an earlier, unsuccessful attempt to structure a joint venture for its mill at Fairless Hills, Pennsylvania, near Trenton, New Jersey. Built new in 1950 to 1952 on the Delaware River to take advantage of imported ore, the Fairless Plant was one of the last facilities built with open-hearth furnaces, which in the mid-1980s were increasingly high-cost and obsolete. The plant had an 80-inch hot-strip mill and was an efficient finisher of flat-rolled steel with relatively modern cold reducing and annealing facilities, galvanizing and tinplate lines, and welded pipe facilities. The plant's facilities were a mirror image of the British Steel flat-rolled mill at Ravenscraig, near Glasgow, Scotland. Ravenscraig had modern ironmaking and steelmaking facilities, including a slab caster, but obsolete hot-strip and finishing mills. British Steel's chairman in the early 1980s was an American citizen, Ian MacGregor; MacGregor, the former chairman of Amax, the largest molybdenum mining company in the world, was a well-known figure in the American steel industry. Discussions between U.S. Steel and British Steel over plans to supply Fairless Hills with slabs from Ravenscraig—both mills having ocean shipping terminals—seemed to indicate great benefits to both sides. The venture foundered on politics rather than economics. In 1983 no major international joint venture had as yet been concluded in the United States; and the dramatic capacity cuts at U.S. Steel and other producers had barely begun. Word of the discussions became public due to an ill-timed remark to the press by Britain's Secretary of State for Scotland, George Younger, in March 1983. It seems unlikely that Mr. Younger understood the implications of his disclosure that British Steel was discussing buying a steel plant in the United States "so that British Steel could export more steel [from Ravenscraig] than it was currently allowed"; but at a time when the fate of both Fairless Hills and Ravenscraig was known to be in doubt, the industry quickly recognized what was being proposed. The potential for job losses at both plants was immediately obvious to both companies' unions, and a major outcry ensued on both sides of the Atlantic.[9]

The U.S. Steel–British Steel talks dragged on until December 1983, but were ultimately broken off. U.S. Steel was forced by pressure from the union and Congressional Steel Caucus politicians to say that it would entertain other offers and options for the Fairless Hills mill, while British Steel faced a battle against regional interests trying to save Scotland's last steel mill. Two or three years later, with both countries' unions chastened by massive industry closures, the deal might easily have been struck. As it was, the January 1987 settlement of the 1986–87 U.S. Steel strike included the commitment to build a new caster at the Edgar Thompson Works. On its completion in 1991, the closure of the Fairless Hills hot end and welded pipe mills were announced. Fairless Hills remains open as a finishing mill, configured like USS-POSCO with a cold reducing mill, galvanizing line, and tinplate line, and without its hot-strip mill that would have remained open under the proposed joint venture. The Ravenscraig mill of British Steel was also closed in 1991.

British Steel's interest in East Coast assets continued, and five years later the company showed interest in Bethlehem Steel's aging Bethlehem structurals mill. British Steel is, with Luxembourg's Arbed, one of the two major producers of wide flange beams in Europe, while Bethlehem Steel was, until the early 1990s, the leading U.S. producer of wide flange beams. In the 1980s, the Bethlehem mill became increasingly threatened both by imports and by the new minimill structural capacity built by Nucor-Yamato, Chaparral, and Northwestern Steel and Wire. Lacking a continuous caster, the Bethlehem hot end's BOF shop was sized for optimal production levels approaching 2 million tons per year, while the Bethlehem mill's output of beams and piling might approach 1 million tons in a good year. Looking forward into the 1990s, the mill could be expected to have a hard time shipping 600,000 tons per year, while its cost position without major investment would continue to deteriorate. In 1985,

Bethlehem's management first proposed abandoning the plant's hot end, substituting slabs from Sparrows Point that would have to be cut into bloom-like shapes to feed the structurals mills. This plan was aborted when the union local agreed to a plan to cut 550 jobs, but the savings were not enough to guarantee the plant's future.

In 1988, Bethlehem and British Steel announced a tentative agreement to create a joint venture of the Bethlehem mill, whereby British Steel would finance the construction of a new electric furnace steelmaking facility to supply "near-net-shape" beam blanks to the structurals mills. The venture was contingent on the successful conclusion of negotiations with the Steelworker's local to allow manning arrangements similar to those of competing minimills, where labor inputs approaching one man-hour per ton were the norm, rather than the Bethlehem plant's five or more man-hours. Failure to conclude such an agreement after nearly a year of negotiations led to the joint venture being canceled in November 1989.[10]

The Bethlehem facility was to see further uncertainty in the 1990s. A 1993 plan for Bethlehem Steel to build its own electric furnace shop and a beam-blank caster was canceled in 1994, when a write-down of $350 million was taken on the Structural Products division and on an abandoned coke oven battery. Currently billets are supplied from the electric furnace mill at Steelton, Pennsylvania, to a single structurals mill at Bethlehem. The 1995 closure of the hot end, a full decade after it was first suggested, seemed long overdue. While it is possible that the remaining Steelton and Bethlehem long products operations of Bethlehem Steel will be the subject of a future sale or joint venture, the company's shrinking share of the structurals business suggests that the moment for foreign investment in the business has passed.

Like British Steel's failure to conclude either of its proposed joint ventures, France's Usinor-Sacilor announced but did not conclude an investment in LTV Steel. Operating under Chapter 11 bankruptcy protection between July 1986 and June 1993, LTV was approached in 1990 by the state-owned French steelmaker. Formed by the merger of France's state-controlled steelmakers in 1988, Usinor-Sacilor pursued a strategy of large-scale investments in the United States. Different divisions of Usinor-Sacilor had already acquired Berg Steel Pipe, the large-diameter welded pipe mill in Florida, and half of wire minimill Georgetown Steel. After the combined company was formed, it added Edgcomb Metals, a large carbon and stainless steel service center chain headquartered in Philadelphia; and in 1989, it bought the former LTV stainless steel operations, which had been sold to management as J&L Specialty Steel in 1986.

Usinor-Sacilor wished to acquire 50 percent of LTV Steel, on terms that would include financing of major investments to upgrade capacity at LTV's major Cleveland and Indiana Harbor mills. With over 20 million tons of capacity in France and 5 million tons at its SaarStahl and Dillinger Hutte mills in Germany, Usinor-Sacilor was second in size only to Nippon Steel on its formation in 1988. Control of an additional 10 million tons of capacity at LTV would have made the group the undisputed world leader. The proposed acquisition would also have been the largest foreign investment to date in the U.S. steel industry. The plan was, however, contingent on one important decision that was outside the two parties' control: the assumption of LTV's pension obligations by the Pension Benefits Guarantee Corporation (PBGC). In 1990, LTV had more than three retired employees owed pension and health care benefits for every active worker, a burden that Usinor-Sacilor, not surprisingly, did not wish to shoulder. The fight among LTV, its creditors, and the PBGC is detailed in chapter 7, but the refusal (and indeed financial inability) of the PBGC to allow LTV to unload its pension obligations led LTV to withdraw its offer.

The Usinor-Sacilor proposal appeared to offer LTV Steel's parent LTV Corporation an opportunity to do what National Intergroup and Armco, Inc., were doing: unload the parent's carbon steel operations, to allow concentrating on other assets—which for LTV were oilfield equipment and aerospace manufacturing divisions. The withdrawal of the offer, and the recovery of the steel market in the 1990s, led LTV to adopt the opposite course. In 1993–94 it sold the aerospace divisions, and in 1995 it began to "explore options" for the sale of Continental Emsco, its oilfield services company.

Table 6.2 lists the actual and proposed investments in U.S. integrated steelmaking. This wave of joint ventures in existing capacity between 1983 and 1990 gave Japanese and Korean companies a stake in seven integrated plants of five U.S. companies, including the small stakes in Inland and Wheeling-Pittsburgh. These plus the Fontana and Pittsburg, California, flat-rolled finishing mills account for a total of about 23 million tons of shipping capacity. Excluding the USS-Kobe long products mill, this accounted for around 40 percent of U.S. sheet capacity in 1990. The capacity offered to European partners for joint ventures that were not concluded amounted to another 15 million tons of shipping capacity, 13 million in flat-rolled products. In one way the

TABLE 6.2
U.S. INTEGRATED CAPACITY:
INTERNATIONAL JOINT VENTURES AND PROPOSALS

Company	Initial Date	Partner	Max. Equity %	Description
AK Steel	1988	Kawasaki	50	Purchase from former parent Armco; diluted by public offering to 21%
Bethlehem Steel	1988	British Steel	N/A	Bethlehem mill; not completed
California Steel Industries	1983	Kawasaki and CVRD	50 50	Former Kaiser Steel mill, Fontana, CA; steelmaking not restarted
Inland Steel	1988	Nippon Steel	14	Stake supporting joint ventures in finishing capacity
LTV Steel	1990	Usinor Sacilor	N/A	Major stake in company, contingent on pension settlement; not completed
National Steel	1984	NKK Steel	76	Purchase from former parent NII; diluted by public offering to 67%
U.S. Steel	1984	British Steel	N/A	Fairless Works, PA; not completed
U.S. Steel	1985	POSCO	50	Pittsburg, CA, mill (no steelmaking)
U.S. Steel	1988	Kobe Steel	50	Lorain, OH, mill (long products)
Wheeling-Pittsburgh Steel	1984	Nisshin Steel	10	Equity stake plus joint venture galvanizing lines

NOTES:
N/A: Not applicable as the proposed investment was not implemented.

investments were bargains. The overseas investors acquired equity in production capacity that would cost billions to build new, for an average of a quarter of the replacement price. For sums similar to those being invested in minimills or in new flat-rolled facilities with a fraction of the capacity, Japanese mills were able to become the largest shareholders of National Steel and Armco/AK Steel, the fifth- and sixth-largest U.S. steelmakers. In these two cases, the Japanese owners probably ensured the independent survival of both U.S. partners, during a period when sale, merger, or extensive reorganization in bankruptcy would otherwise have been likely.

On the other hand, it is harder to see what benefits these shareholdings actually conferred on the shareholders. In the ten years after NKK bought its initial 50 percent of National Steel in 1984, National Steel made money in only three years, and its common equity dropped from $1 billion in 1983 to $200 million in 1994. Kawasaki had either better timing or judgment in its investment in Armco; after suffering losses in the 1990-91 steel recession, AK Steel has been turned around into the most profitable integrated mill on a per-ton basis. Control of large but struggling companies, with very different management and labor cultures, has had to be exercised—if at all—through local partners and managers. The decisions of both NKK and Kawasaki to float their affiliates on U.S. stock exchanges and dilute their equity (although NKK retains two-thirds of National) may reveal their disillusionment with their investments. This is not to say that the companies did not make money, especially AK Steel in the mid-1990s; rather, the hoped-for strategic benefits of a major presence in the U.S. market were elusive.

The smaller-scale investments, by Nisshin in Wheeling-Pittsburgh and by Nippon Steel in Inland, do not appear to have brought either Japanese company any immediate return but have provided a means for them to exercise greater control over their joint venture sheet processing facilities and (negatively) to prevent the U.S. companies merging or seeking other partners. Perhaps the most successful joint ventures have been those in which the partners had clear objectives and direct, equal control of a single plant: USS-Kobe, USS-POSCO, and California Steel Industries. At least in those cases, the fact that the three ventures were private companies that did not release their financial statements allowed the partners to claim complete success!

THE JOINT VENTURE GALVANIZING BOOM

In the mid-1980s, the one steel product that defied the downward trend of the industry was galvanized flat-rolled steel. North American automakers seeking to upgrade their product quality demanded electrogalvanized steel, while hot-dipped galvanized steel was being specified for an increasing range of construction products that earlier were produced from painted hot- or cold-rolled steel. Just when U.S. integrated mills were trying to stem their financial losses and close excess capacity, they had an opportunity to expand their sales of a high-margin, value-added product—if they could afford the capital investment.

With VRAs capping the permitted import tonnage, but with dramatic growth in Japanese automotive, appliance, and electronics manufacturers' operations in the United States, Japanese companies needed a way to participate in the U.S. market for galvanized and other

TABLE 6.3
JOINT VENTURE FLAT-ROLLED PROCESSING CAPACITY BUILT IN NORTH AMERICA, 1983–1995

Plant and Location	Domestic Partner and Equity %	Foreign Partner and Equity %	Operation	Date	Capacity (tons/year)
DNN Galvanizing, Windsor, Ontario	Dofasco, 33.3	National Steel, 33.3 and NKK Steel, 33.3	HD zinc	1993	400,000
I/N Kote, New Carlisle, IN	Inland Steel, 50	Nippon Steel, 50	EG zinc or zinc alloy	1991	450,000
I/N Kote, New Carlisle, IN	Inland Steel, 50	Nippon Steel, 50	HD zinc	1993	450,000
I/N Tek, New Carlisle, IN	Inland Steel, 50	Nippon Steel, 50	Cold reduction mill	1989	1,440,000
L-S E, Cleveland, OH	LTV, 50	Sumitomo, 50	EG zinc	1986	400,000
L-S II, Columbus, OH	LTV, 50	Sumitomo, 50	EG zinc or zinc-nickel	1991	360,000
Pro-Tec Coating, Leipsic, OH	U.S.Steel, 50	Kobe Steel, 50	HD zinc	1993	600,000
Stelco "Z line", Hamilton, Ont.	Stelco, 60	Mitsubishi, 40	HD zinc & galvannealed	1993	350,000
USS-POSCO, Pittsburg, CA [a]	U.S. Steel, 50	Pohang Iron & Steel, 50	Cold reduction mill	1988	1,500,000
Wheeling-Nisshin, Follansbee, WV	Wheeling-Pittsburgh, 33	Nisshin Steel, 67	HD zinc & aluminized	1984	360,000
Wheeling-Nisshin, Follansbee, WV	Wheeling-Pittsburgh, 40	Nisshin Steel, 60	HD zinc & Galvalume®	1991	240,000
Wheeling-Pittsburgh Yorkville, OH	Wheeling-Pittsburgh [b]	Dong Yang and Nittetsu Shoji [b]	Tinplate	1996	250,000

NOTES:

a The entry for USS-POSCO shows only the new capacity (the six-high cold reduction mill) added by the joint venture, not the two galvanizing lines (combined capacity 405,000 tons per year) and two tinplate lines (460,000 tons per year) taken over by the joint venture on its formation in 1985.

b The Wheeling/Dong Yang/Nittetsu Shoji tin line was announced in June 1994, the first new tinplate line in the United States for thirty years. Wheeling-Pittsburgh and Koreas Dong Yang each hold 50 percent of the equity; Nittetsu Shoji America, a subsidiary of Nittetsu Shoji Co. of Japan, holds a preferred stock interest in the company. First shipments were expected in late 1996.

light sheet products. The combination of Japanese and U.S. needs led to a wave of new sheet finishing capacity financed and operated as joint U.S.–Japanese ventures. Some of these ventures were put together by companies that were already partners in broader join ventures, such as U.S. Steel and Kobe Steel, or were explicitly tied to broader relationships between companies, such as the Wheeling-Nisshin relationship. More often, though, they were put together as straightforward new entities of defined scope. Reflecting the transborder nature of the auto industries, the new investments crossed the U.S.-Canadian border in pursuit of automotive purchases.

Table 6.3 lists the major joint ventures in new flat-rolled processing capacity in North America. The nine galvanizing lines built with Japanese companies added 3.6 million tons of annual steel coating capacity. To this total might be added two more categories of overseas investment. First, counting capacity built by National Steel and Armco/AK Steel since those companies became partly owned by Japanese companies adds a further 540,000 tons per year of electrogalvanized capacity, plus a joint venture hot-dip line of National Steel and Bethlehem at Jackson, Mississippi, with 260,000 tons capacity. Second, coating capacity existing at USS-POSCO, National Steel, and Armco when those mills were bought into by their foreign shareholders accounts for an additional 1.5 million tons per year at AK Steel, 1.1 million at National, and 865,000 at USS-POSCO. By this reckoning, around 7.8 million tons of U.S. and Canadian galvanizing capacity belongs to joint ventures with Japanese and Korean companies, not counting the small equity holdings in Wheeling-Pittsburgh and Inland. This accounts for about 40 percent of North American capacity, but for over 70 percent of the capacity built new since 1983.

Total consumption of galvanized steel, including related coatings such as galvannealed and Galvalume®, doubled in the United States and Canada between 1984 and 1994, increasing by nearly 8 million tons. Of the increase, a little over 50 percent comes from increased use in automotive applications, with the balance going to construction-related applications via service centers. The new joint ventures were certainly helped by their Japanese partners in terms of opening doors at Japanese-owned companies, but the "transplants" account for only around 1 million tons of galvanized use per year. No joint venture could live off its sales to transplants. Instead, galvanized steel—both hot-dip and electrogalvanized—has been cleverly marketed, as a low life-cycle-cost, corrosion-resisting material, and its price has fallen against competing materials. It has therefore gained market share and has proved to be a successful investment for the companies that invested in it—despite the fears of many in the 1980s who predicted an overcapacity of galvanizing capacity when so many new investments were announced.

THE NEW MINIMILL JOINT VENTURES

The most recent wave of international investment in the U.S. steel industry has been targeted at the new wave of minimills under construction since the late 1980s. Of the ten U.S. flat-rolled minimills for which ground had broken by mid-1995, five had non-U.S. owners or partners. However, unlike the 1980s wave of investment from Japan in integrated steelmaking and coating capacity, interest in flat-rolled minimills has come primarily from the English-speaking world: Canada, the United Kingdom, and Australia. The investors in flat-rolled capacity have often been companies with an integrated steelmaking background, such as Dofasco, British Steel, and BHP Steel.

In addition to investment in the flat-rolled sector, there has been continued investment in minimill long products, although at a lower rate than in the 1970s. The shakeout of minimill capacity in the early to mid-1980s has meant that there are few opportunities for low-cost acquisitions by foreign investors, and the number of acquisitions has declined as the price of entry has risen. Nevertheless, there have been some notable purchases, including that of Ameristeel (formerly Florida Steel), the fourth-largest minimill group, by Kyoei Steel in 1992. Other foreign-owned minimills have changed hands or been offered for sale, although not always successfully; New Jersey Steel, for example, was offered for sale by its majority owner, Von Roll Corporation of Switzerland, in both 1983–84 and from 1993 to 1995. Table 6.4 lists recent foreign investments in long products and plate minimills.

In the United States, the largest foreign investment in existing minimill capacity was the acquisition of Florida Steel in 1992. Although it had been quietly offered for sale for at least ten years, it took the combination of an extended construction recession and operational problems, especially from a new DC electric arc furnace at the company's Tampa mill, to get Florida Steel's majority owners to agree to a price. Kyoei Steel, one of Japan's five major minimill groups, was itself put together by combining a number of different companies owned or influenced by the Sumitomo group. The Florida Steel investment brings to four the number of Japanese minimill groups with partnerships or subsidiaries in the United States, including Yamato with Nucor, Tokyo Steel with Tamco, and Daido with Copperweld Steel. Only NKK's electric furnace subsidiary, Toshi, has no investment in the United States. Of the four investors, Kyoei is by far the biggest in the United States, although it is only number three in Japan. Kyoei, along with other Sumitomo group companies, owns not only of Florida Steel but also Auburn Steel, Austeel Lemont (the former Thomas Steel), and Arkansas Steel Associates. The combined raw steel capacity of these mills in 1995 was 2.45 million tons, which would make the group the third-largest U.S. minimill company if combined.

TABLE 6.4
FOREIGN INVESTMENT IN U.S.
MINIMILLS, 1980–1995: LONG PRODUCTS AND PLATE

Company	Date	%	Investor	Nationality	Notes
Arkansas Steel Associates	1991	100	Kyoei and Sumitomo	Japan	Former Razorback Steel tie plate minimill
Austeel Lemont -	1994	100	Kyoei and Sumitomo	Japan	Former Thomas Steel, Lemont, IL
Citisteel	1988	100	CITIC	China	Reopened former Phoenix Steel mill, Claymont, DE
Co-Steel Raritan	1981	100	Co-Steel Industries	Canada	New wire rod mill
Copperweld Steel (later CSC, Ltd.)[a]	1989	33	Daido Steel	Japan	Purchased from Imetal, which retained 23%
Florida Steel (later Ameristeel)	1992	100	Kyoei Steel	Japan	Affiliate of Sumitomo. 5 minimills, rebar shops
Georgetown Steel Technologies [b]	1983; 1986	51 49	Kuwait; Usinor.	Kuwait; France	Purchased from German-owned Korf Industries
New Jersey Steel	1981	100	Von Roll	Switzerland	Stake reduced to 60.4% via public offering
Nucor-Yamato Steel	1986	50	Yamato Kogyo Co.	Japan	New joint venture structurals mill
Oregon Steel-CF&I division, Pueblo, CO [c]	1993; 1995	10 3	Nippon Steel, Nissho-Iwai	Japan	Equity in exchange for assistance on rail mill and export sales
Tuscaloosa Steel	1984	100	British Steel	U.K.	Plate rolling mill; BSC bought out partners 1987

NOTES:

a Copperweld Steel Corporation was spun off to shareholders by former parent Copperweld Corporation in 1982. Imetal originally owned 67 percent of the mill, as it did of Copperweld Corporation. Imetal's holding was steadily reduced to 23 percent by sales to Japanese investors, first to minimill group Daido Steel and later smaller stakes to trading companies Marubeni, Okaya, and Itochu. In 1993, the company filed for Chapter 11 bankruptcy protection. In 1995, the steel mill assets were sold to the Reserve Group of Akron, Ohio, and the French and Japanese investments were written off. The mill adopted the name CSC Ltd. in 1996.

b The Kuwaiti stake in Georgetown Steel was an investment of the Kuwait government's asset management organization, the Kuwait Investment Office. Georgetown's owners sold the company in 1995 to Boston-based Bain Capital in the course of the merger of Georgetown with GS Technologies Corp., Kansas City, Missouri.

c Ownership of CF & I in late 1995 was shared between New CF & I L.P. (95.2 percent) and the Pension Benefits Guarantee Corporation, a creditor of the bankrupt former CF & I.

It is noticeable that foreign investment in long products and plate capacity in the 1980s continued to be predominantly in existing, lower-priced assets, even in newly-built mills. New Jersey Steel was originally financed by Italian investors, who sold out to Von Roll before the mill opened. Likewise, Tuscaloosa Steel was originally 80

TABLE 6.5
FOREIGN INVESTMENT IN U.S.
MINIMILLS, 1980–1996: FLAT-ROLLED PRODUCTS

Mill	Date [a]	%	Investor	Nationality	Notes
Beta Steel, Portage, IN	1991	100	Alpha Steel	U.K.	Hot-strip mill only in phase 1; hot end to open late 1996.
Caparo Steel, Sharon, PA	1995	100	Caparo Group PLC	U.K.	Acquisition of former Sharon Steel EFs and hot-strip mill
Gallatin Steel, Warsaw, KY	1995	50 50	Dofasco, Co-Steel	Canada, Canada	New mill, start-up April 1995
Ipsco, Montpelier, IA	1996	100	Ipsco	Canada	New mill, start-up early 1996; coiled plate and HR sheet
North Star BHP, Delta, OH	1996	50	BHP Steel	Australia	New mill, start-up late 1996
Steel Dynamics, Butler, IN	1995	20	Preussag	Germany	Sale of equity to Preussag to finance new cold rolling mill
Trico Steel, Decatur, AL	1997	33 33	Sumitomo, British Steel	Japan, U.K.	3-way joint venture with LTV; start-up 1997
Tuscaloosa Steel Tuscaloosa, AL	1996	100	British Steel	U.K.	Addition of hot end and expansion of coil plate mill

NOTES:
a Date is start-up date for shipments, actual or target for construction contract.

percent owned by Tippins, Inc., of Pittsburgh, with British Steel being only one of three minority shareholders; it bought out the others after three years. British Steel committed in 1994 to construction of a hot end for Tuscaloosa and rolling mill improvements that would, in effect, convert the mill to a true flat-rolled minimill. Co-Steel's Raritan mill and the Nucor-Yamato joint venture beam mill at Blytheville, Arkansas, represent exceptions—new long products mills constructed by investors who remained long-term owners.

Foreign investments in flat-rolled minimills are shown in table 6.5. Long-term patterns in this sector cannot be determined yet. However, the companies investing in such capacity are for the most part financially strong groups with a major commitment to steel. Most of the integrated producers among the investors are also experienced in electric furnace steelmaking in their home markets: British Steel through its United Engineering Steels subsidiary and Avesta Sheffield affiliate; BHP at its Sydney minimill; Sumitomo through its affiliate Kyoei Steel. Even Dofasco committed in 1995 to build a new "minimill" EF/thin-slab casting shop alongside its integrated capacity at Hamilton, Ontario.

Some of the projects listed in Table 6.5 are not, strictly speaking, greenfield or new mills, although they all represent additions to U.S. steelmaking capacity. Beta Steel operates a 60-inch hot-strip mill formerly operated in Wales by British minimill Alpha Steel, which was rebuilt in Portage, Indiana, in 1991. The mill is capable of rolling around 800,000 tons per year. The company installed a new EF shop and caster in 1996. The California Steel Industries joint venture at Fontana, California, also studied adding a hot end to include thin-slab casting, although in 1994 this was deferred in favor of upgrading its finishing facilities. Both these companies suffered in the 1990s from rising world prices of slab as global steel demand has grown, although the Fontana mill is somewhat protected by the partial ownership of its principal slab supplier, Tubarao of Brazil, by California Steel Industries and its parent joint venture partners.

Tuscaloosa Steel also depended until 1996 on imported slabs. Founded in part to develop the Steckel mill technology of Tippins, Inc., the mill employs a reversing hot-strip mill to produce coiled plate. However British Steel's expansion of the mill, announced in 1994, includes a 1-million-ton-per-year hot end and caster, giving the mill steelmaking capacity in excess of its 600,000-ton-per-year rolling capacity.

The Caparo Steel mill, the former Sharon Steel plant purchased in 1994 by the Caparo Group of Anglo-Indian businessman Swaraj Paul, reopened in 1995 using the mill's electric furnaces, augmented by purchased slabs, to supply the hot-strip mill. The hot-strip mill has a rolling capacity of around 1.3 million tons, while the EF shop can produce a maximum of 800,000 tons. Eventual plans included a new hot end with more of a "minimill" configuration to bring the steelmaking and rolling capacities into line. Caparo is the only company among the new investors in U.S. flat-rolled steelmaking that has no other steelmaking capacity, although it includes a number of downstream tube, wire, and fastener producers in the United Kingdom and United States, including Bull Moose Tube, a major U.S. producer of mechanical and structural tubing.

The three greenfield flat-rolled minimills with foreign investment add at least 4.2 million tons of hot-rolling capacity, with more eventually likely. Like Nucor's mills, Gallatin Steel, for example, is planned to be built in two stages, stage I with 1 million tons capacity having been commissioned in April 1995 and a stage II expansion to around 2 million tons likely in 1997–98. The combined capacity of the foreign investments listed here, at around 7 million tons, account for nearly 40 percent of the total new flat-rolled capacity announced and built since Nucor entered the flat-rolled business.

The 40 percent of capacity mark, that is, around 40 percent of effective capacity having *some* international ownership, applies also to the level of foreign investment in U.S. integrated steelmaking, and to U.S. coated sheet capacity. Minimill long products, even with Kyoei's acquisition of Florida Steel, seem to be a little lower, but the number is still close to one-third. Similarly in specialty steels, around a third of U.S. stainless steel rolling capacity is owned by five Canadian, European and Korean companies.[11] These numbers can be misleading; certainly they do not represent either the percentage of equity ownership overall or any measure of control. Executives of a U.S. company such as Inland Steel would resent the suggestion that it is a foreign company in any sense, although they may be very grateful to have a supportive major shareholder with as much to offer in both technical and financial terms as Nippon Steel. Nevertheless, the high percentages of foreign participation in each major sector of the industry—integrated steelmaking, coil processing, minimill production of both long and flat products, and specialty steel—indicate how far the United States has come from the autarkic steel industry of 1960.

Canada and Mexico have also attracted their share of international investment in recent years. Canada has seen mills acquired by groups from Brazil, Korea, China, and Indonesia, in the latter two cases when provincially owned mills—Sidbec-Dosco in Quebec and Sydney Steel in Nova Scotia—were privatized.[12] Mexico's privatization of its state-owned steel companies saw the integrated Lazaro Cardenas mill, formerly part of Sicartsa, sold in 1991 to the Ispat Group of Indonesia. Ispat thereby acquired 2.5 million tons of integrated steelmaking capacity, becoming overnight the third-largest steelmaker in Mexico, and went on to add two more formerly state-owned companies in the wider North American market—the Trinidad and Tobago minimill of Iscott in 1992 and Québec's Sidbec-Dosco in 1994.

In all this wave of international investment, it is remarkable how little outward investment has been done by U.S. companies. Perhaps most astonishing, in the light of the dominance of U.S. investment in many sectors of the Canadian and Mexican economies, is the absolute lack of U.S. steelmaking investment in either country. Even though U.S. steelmakers own major portions of Canada's iron ore industry and U.S. service centers operate in Canada (and vice-versa), there have been no investments in steelmaking.[13] Similarly, although Armco operated a short-lived minimill in Mexico in the 1970s and early 1980s, no U.S. company has attempted to take advantage of the liberalization of Mexico's investment climate, its sale of state assets, and its entry into the North American Free Trade Agreement.

Among the reasons for this startling omission, of course, are cultural factors as well as hard economic facts. U.S. steelmakers have traditionally come largely from the most insular region of the country, the Midwest, and from an industry that developed a remarkably insular, almost xenophobic, culture. While many U.S. industries are subject to criticism as inward-looking, the contrast between the steel industry and other U.S. metals industries, with global operations in aluminum, copper, molybdenum, and so on, is remarkable. Much of steel's insularity has broken down over the last ten years as the industry has internationalized and a new generation has taken over the helm of steel companies, but there is still a defensiveness born of a generation of steel restructuring to overcome. In the early 1990s, however, there were portents of changing attitudes in investments: Nucor's iron carbide plant in Trinidad and Tobago; Inland Steel's service center chain Ryerson established operations in Mexico and China; and stainless bar maker CarTech invested in a rod mill in Taiwan.

In the rest of the 1990s, there may well be additional foreign investments in North American steelmaking and more cross-border investments within North America in both new and existing capacity. It is probable, however, that the availability of "bargains"—low-priced capacity available from distressed companies—has for the medium term dried up. The price of entry may be to build new capacity. Regarding U.S. firms, moreover, it is probable that the stronger U.S. steelmakers will look more closely at international expansion—driven, as always in the steel industry, initially by exports to overseas markets. As the dollar declines, and the United States enjoys an increasing edge in steelmaking costs in real (exchange-rate adjusted) terms, a U.S. steel industry that is a net exporter will likely follow other major exporters and become an investor in its overseas markets.

7

IN THE FIERY FURNACE: THE "BORN AGAIN" MILLS

STEEL SURVIVAL STRATEGIES

The category of "born again" or reconstituted mills was first identified in the late 1980s by Peter Marcus of Paine Webber, long the best-known steel analyst in the U.S. financial community. Since 1986 Marcus has been host of an annual meeting sponsored by Paine Webber and the *American Metal Market* newspaper entitled "Steel Survival Strategies." In the turmoil of the industry in the 1980s, survival strategies for integrated mills included some dramatic transformations of companies, voluntary and involuntary. "Born again" mills are steel plants that, in the religious language beloved of the American interior, have cast away their sins—the high costs and poor strategies of the past—and been transformed into low-cost, aggressive examples of corporate virtue. Such rebirth in the face of the meltdown of the old integrated steel industry might indeed suggest miraculous happenings, or at least alchemy. In practice, the transformation of a large part of U.S. integrated capacity has been achieved not by divine intervention but by a combination of new management and old entrepreneurial spirit, hard-headed costing of assets and products, and the aggressive use of bankruptcy and labor law. Miracles in industry generally can be attributed to good public relations, but such publicity may be a necessary part of a company's strategy when it needs to raise money in competition with minimills.

In the 1980s and early 1990s, almost a third of U.S. integrated capacity restructured itself in ways that represented a sharp break with the companies former costs and strategies. The greatest publicity was given to companies' that transformed themselves in bankruptcy, notably LTV Corporation because of its size and the public policy issues concerning its pension obligations. Four integrated steelmakers filed for Chapter 11 in the 1980s; one, Sharon Steel, eventually was liquidated, while LTV, Wheeling-Pittsburgh, and McLouth reorganized and emerged with dramatically lower costs. A second category of reconstituted companies includes those mills sold by their former parents to new U.S. owners not formerly in the steelmaking industry. Geneva Steel and Weirton Steel are the best known of the five "spun-off" integrated mills that have transformed themselves under new ownership without bankruptcy. Other spun-off nonintegrated capacity, such as Republic Engineered Steels, and possibly joint ventures, such as USS-Kobe, might also be considered in this category. A third category would include independent mills that have de-integrated: companies that have moved from integrated steelmaking practice to electric furnace steelmaking and minimill practices. This category, including a number of smaller mills, overlaps the first two because such changes have often involved bankruptcy protection, changes in ownership, or both. Only Lone Star Technologies has managed to accomplish the transformation and maintain its independence. Table 7.1 shows twelve integrated companies that have undergone extensive restructuring amounting to "rebirth".

BARRIERS TO EXIT

At times when the steel industry and the steel market are downsizing, closure of capacity would seem to be a more rational business response than the sale or restructuring of capacity, especially if it leads to the creation of new, more aggressive competitors. Closure of capacity may, however, be difficult, for cost or for psychological reasons.

Psychology poses two obstacles to capacity closure decisions. One is that executives do not like to put themselves out of a job, even if their companies' shareholders would be best served by a closure decision. Integrated steel executives, like union steelworkers, tend to have few alternative career opportunities that offer comparable finan-

TABLE 7.1
INTEGRATED MILLS RESTRUCTURED AS LOW-COST PRODUCERS, 1980–1995

Restructuring	Company	Capacity in 1980 (million tons per year)	Capacity in 1995 (million tons per year)	Notes
Bankruptcy reorganization	LTV Steel	25.117 [a]	10.500	Chapter 11, 1986–92
	Wheeling-Pittsburgh	4.400	2.400	Chapter 11, 1985–89
	McLouth	2.400	1.700 [b]	Chapter 11, 1981-82 and 1995-96; bought by Hamlin Holdings, 1996
Integrated mills spun off by former owners	Geneva Steel	2.650	2.700	Closed and sold by U.S. Steel in 1986-87
	Gulf States Steel (Gadsden)	1.320 [a]	1.400	Sold by LTV under antitrust agreement, 1987
	Rouge Steel	3.500	3.028 [c]	Sold by Ford Motor Co., 1989
	Warren Consolidated	1.700 [a]	1.700	Sold by LTV, 1988
	Weirton Steel	3.400	3.000	Sold by National Steel to ESOP, 1984
Companies "de-integrated"	CF & I	1.870	1.000	BOFs shut 1982; Chapter 11, 1990; bought by Oregon Steel, 1993
	Lone Star Technologies	1.280	0.450	BOFs closed 1985 [d]
	Phoenix Steel	0.650	0.250	OHs closed 1983, EFs 1986; EFs reopened 1988 as Citisteel
	Sharon Steel	1.310	0.540	BOFs closed 1989, EFs 1992; EFs reopened 1995 by Caparo

NOTES:
a In 1980, what is now LTV Steel included both Gulf States and Warren Consolidated.
b The McLouth mill has a BOF shop/continuous caster steelmaking capacity of 1.2 million tons; additional electric furnace capacity of 500,000 tons has been used intermittently. In 1982, 65 percent of the companys stock was bought by Cyrus Tang in a bankruptcy reorganization plan sponsored by the Steelworker's union. Tang invested enough to keep the company alive in the mid-1980s; he sold his shareholding to an ESOP formed by management and the union in 1987. The company entered bankruptcy again in 1995 and was closed in March 1996. The mill assets were then purchased by Hamlin Holdings for reopening in late 1996.
c Rouge Steel has a BOF shop steelmaking capacity of 3.028 million tons per year, and an idled EF shop with a capacity of an additional 850,000 tons per year. Given a hot-strip mill capacity of 2.95 million tons per year, it is unlikely that the EF shop will resume operations.
d Lone Star Steel has purchased significant quantities of slabs since the closure of its open hearth steelmaking shop in 1985. In 1995, it negotiated to buy the former U.S. Steel electric arc shop at Baytown, Texas, closed in 1986, which had a rated capacity of 1.14 million tons per year.

cial rewards. This fact is particularly influential in companies with a single mill or production facility; it seems easier to close a plant if the company can continue in business at other operations. Thus in the U.S. steel industry there has been a disproportionate rate of survival of capacity at smaller, single-plant companies that might, if owned by a U.S. Steel or an LTV, have been closed.

A second psychological barrier to exit is ignorance or prejudice about alternative investments. Executives who have spent a lifetime in the steel industry may not be able to evaluate steel versus non-steel investment opportunities objectively. Two companies, Armco and National Intergroup, did indeed exit their original basic steelmaking business in favor of businesses offering a higher return, and both U.S. Steel (oil) and Inland Steel (steel distribution) have acquired and grown non-steelmaking businesses that now far exceed in revenue the size of their steel operations. However, for each of these examples, there are others of companies that have sold off more profitable non-steel businesses to keep their carbon steelmaking afloat—these include LTV, Bethlehem, and Lone Star.

Costs of capacity closure may appear to be readily and objectively measurable. Some may indeed be quickly identified—write-offs on U.S. company balance sheets due to steel capacity closure amounted to over $15 billion between 1980 and 1994. Nevertheless, such costs are hard to gauge accurately, and many—such as liability for pensions or for environmental cleanups—may be spread over many years. To justify closure of a plant in the short term, the costs of closure—immediate cash costs plus the much greater reserve that must be taken for future obligations—must be greater than the present value of the expected stream of continuing losses from the plant, plus foreseen necessary capital expenditures.[1]

If the high costs of closure of capacity can be significantly reduced by sale of a plant, that may be an attractive alternative. If the new owner will assume some portion of a plant's debt, pension and health care obligations to retirees, or liability for environmental cleanup costs, then the seller's advantage may be far greater in monetary terms than a cash payment. In most cases when existing operations are sold, the new owners have assumed environmental liability (Ford's sale of Rouge Steel is a partial exception); in a number of cases, existing long-term purchase and sale agreements have been honored; but in few cases labor agreements have been carried over to the new owners. In the case of Weirton Steel, where an ESOP sponsored by the plant's independent union bought the mill, the new company did assume the retiree pension and health care benefits, although even in this case a new labor contract was agreed for active employees.

Another major factor in a decision to sell a plant may be the need for additional capital investment. Steel mills require continuous inputs of capital for modernization and maintenance; just to re-line a blast furnace every ten to fifteen years costs up to $100 million. Capital sums of up to $10 per ton of capacity are typically spent on existing steelmaking plants each year just to prevent their decline into an unsafe or inoperable condition. These continuing expenditures make sale of capacity an attractive alternative to either continued operation or closure. In the 1980s, mandatory investment in pollution-control equipment, often amounting to tens of millions of dollars per plant, was added to other necessary capital expenditures to maintain excess capacity. The desire to avoid environmental expenditures, as well as other needed capital investments, was cited in the sale of the Geneva, Warren, and Weirton mills.

Taking the Weirton sale as an example, the mill, which was valued on National Steel's books at $314 million, was sold to the employee ESOP for $75 million cash and $119 million in notes. National Steel made loss provisions for the sale on its balance sheet that finally totaled $286 million after National retained all liabilities and the costs of the sale. The plant was relatively modern at the time of sale, although, to quote the company, ". . . its capital requirements during the next few years will be substantial, and . . . it is not economically feasible for National Steel to commit such large amounts of capital at Weirton since funds would have to be diverted from other projects [with a] substantially higher return . . . ."[2] The new company did indeed spend $90 million on maintenance-type capital projects in 1985–86, then $550 million on upgrades in the period from 1988 to 1992. National Intergroup—soon to sell out the steel operation to NKK—certainly did not have such funds to invest, and its steel group's focus was on opportunities in the automotive galvanized market rather than in tin mill products, which are the Weirton mill's largest product. The new company assumed most employee-related obligations of National Steel for the division, but as part of the terms of the buyout it agreed to a new labor contract that cut labor costs—salaried and union—by 32 percent and froze pay for six years. In exchange, the new employee-owners would receive 50 percent of the company's profits. The new company took control of the mill—more than 18 months after negotiations began—on January 11, 1984, and has been profitable in most subsequent years. The company was taken public in 1989, to help finance its modernization, and the ESOP's share of profits was reduced to 35 percent. Weirton was the first major spin-off, and perhaps because of that the mill's purchase price seems high in retrospect, compared with other subsequent acquisitions. The union involvement, however, meant a strongly motivated and captive buyer existed, while National Steel was negotiating hard to minimize its exit costs.

BARRIERS TO ENTRY

The availability of surplus capacity for sale—operating and closed—has meant a low cost of entry into the steelmaking industry since the early 1980s, compared with very high historic costs of entry by building new capacity. In choosing between operating and closed facilities, a potential buyer must balance the need to avoid taking on existing high-cost legal and contractual obligations by taking over an operating plant against the costs of restarting a shuttered operation and acquiring a position in the market as a new entrant. Both routes have been tried successfully, with mills such as Fontana, Geneva, and Sharon being restarted under new ownership after periods of closure, while others such as Weirton, Warren, and Gadsden were taken over as operating plants.

The restructuring of the steel industry since 1980 has seen the entry of over a dozen new companies into flat-rolled steelmaking in the United States, compared to just one—McLouth Steel—in the period from 1945 to 1980. The initial cost of entry has ranged from $26 million for Caparo to buy Sharon Steel's assets in a Chapter 7 bankruptcy liquidation, to around $400 million for the minimills currently under construction. At the low end of the range, acquisitions such as Geneva Steel ($44.1 million), Gulf States ($57 million), and Caparo/Sharon have been inevitably followed by subsequent necessary capital investments that bring the total costs into the low hundreds of millions. The total cost of entry to integrated steelmaking—purchase price plus subsequent essential modernization—appears to be similar to the cost of equivalent new minimill capacity, or in excess of $200 per annual ton of capacity. Nevertheless, these sums are dramatically lower than the theoretical cost of new "greenfield" integrated capacity, which might range from five to ten times higher. The reduction in entry barriers at the same time that exit barriers remained high has led, in a stable market, to both an increase in the numbers of participants in the industry and a shrinking of average company size (and market share).

No new firms would have entered the industry, however, if an adequate return on the investment did not seem possible. The key to such returns, stated most simply, has been to operate at costs significantly lower than the costs of existing suppliers. Cost cutting has been the key to the survival (or otherwise) of the reconstituted mills, which almost invariably are facilities formerly at the high end of the industry's cost range. Costs have been reduced through selective investment; through changed product/market strategies; by altering the sources and supply terms of energy, raw materials and freight; but above all by cutting out labor inputs—salaried and hourly. Along with access to capital, then, the other hurdle faced by new entrants to the industry has been to have a credible operating plan (and management in place) to drive down costs.

The strategies of firms attempting to reconstitute themselves as "born-again" steelmakers may be best illustrated by examining case studies in detail. Three companies are studied in the balance of this chapter, representing different types of strategic challenge and outcome. CF & I, Geneva Steel, and LTV vary greatly in their respective sizes, product mixes, strategies, and outcomes. Each, however, is a company whose restructuring has been cost-driven, and each was radically transformed in the decade between 1985 and 1995.

CF & I: FROM INTEGRATED MILL TO MINIMILL

CF & I Steel, formerly the Colorado Fuel and Iron Company, has a long and glorious history beginning in the late nineteenth century. As the western frontier became settled, CF & I developed coal, iron ore, and limestone mines in Colorado, Wyoming, Utah, and New Mexico, feeding a sprawling integrated steel mill in Pueblo, Colorado, which produced products necessary to the development of the frontier: barbed wire and similar products for fencing in the formerly open range; structural steel; and rails for the ever-growing network of railroads. CF & I and its largest supplier and customer, the Denver and Rio Grande Western Railroad, vied with each other to be the largest employer in Colorado (and by extension all of the Mountain West) for 100 years until the 1960s.[3]

In the two decades after World War II, CF & I underwent a dramatic period of expansion under the ownership of New York financier Charles Allen. Allen focused the company's attention in the Northeast in an attempt to break out of its role as an essentially regional steel company. CF & I bought and operated blast furnaces, open hearths, and wire operations in Massachusetts, New York, New Jersey, and Pennsylvania;

iron ore mines in New Jersey; and between 1951 and 1960, it owned the Claymont, Delaware, open hearth plate producer that is today the electric furnace minimill Citisteel. These ventures were ill-fated: in most cases, high-cost producers were bought cheaply, and during the 1960s, they were closed or sold. In the West, however, operations continued profitably, and major expansions included the addition of a seamless pipe mill in 1953 to supply the West's growing oil industry; in 1961 the open hearths were supplemented by two 150-ton BOFs. In June 1969, the company was bought by Crane Corporation, an engineering-based conglomerate, which moved CF & I's headquarters from Denver to the mill at Pueblo.

The company that became a division of Crane in 1969 was a profitable integrated steel mill with nearly 2 million tons of capacity, the third-largest steelmaker in the West (after U.S. Steel at Geneva and Kaiser Steel at Fontana). Although not a major mill in terms of overall size, its product range was among the broadest of any steel company; it made a wide range of bars, wire, rail, pipe, and beams, plus fabricated products for western industries such as fence posts, grader blades, rail spikes, grinding balls, and mine bolts. All its raw materials except fluorspar were produced on the company's properties. Crane obviously believed the company had a rosy future, for it financed a major modernization. The last open hearths were replaced by electric furnaces; a new sinter plant, two coke batteries, blast furnace upgrades, a billet caster, a new bar mill were all added between 1970 and 1975. In the late 1970s, however, the company felt the same sharp downturn in steel markets that the eastern companies suffered. Two of four blast furnaces were idled, and the company focused on the more specialized products of which it was the only western producer—the rail mill was upgraded and a new caster and seamless pipe mill planned. The oil country boom in 1980-81 brought a brief respite, but when the oil market collapsed, CF & I faced a major crisis. With production at only a quarter of the plant's capacity and no prospect of a rapid recovery, Crane closed the company's integrated steelmaking facilities in 1982. Mines, coke ovens, blast furnaces, and both BOFs were closed and written off at the end of the following year, as were the blooming, structural, and bar mills and much of the company's fabricating shops. The new seamless pipe mill project, half completed, was halted, although the rounds caster was completed. With no long-term interest in steelmaking, Crane put the division's remaining operations up for sale. CF & I's timber, agricultural, and minerals lands were quickly sold off, but Crane scoured the world for a buyer for the mill without success.

The operation that Crane offered for sale from 1983 to 1985 was a hybrid between a traditional steel company and a minimill. Although now using electric furnace steelmaking exclusively, with around 700,000-tons-per-year capacity, CF & I was encumbered by overhead staff, land and buildings, and labor contracts and practices appropriate for a 1.9-million-ton-capacity integrated steelmaker. Its configuration was now two electric furnaces (supplied in part by the company's own scrap subsidiary); billet and rounds casters (rails were still produced from ingots via a blooming mill); and rail, bar, rod, and seamless pipe mills. Rails accounted for over half of the company's total tonnage. In addition to these core operations, the company also still had its own foundry and maintenance shops with a wide range of capabilities; and much of its rod and bar products were used internally in a variety of wire drawing and fabricating operations, for fencing products and rebar fabricating shops. The company employed 2,200 people at Pueblo in mid-1984, down from 6,500, but still far in excess of a minimill-type operation, in part because of the large number of downstream operations. Although the Steelworkers had taken CF & I off the basic steel-pattern contract and agreed to a $5-an-hour wage cut in 1982, benefits and labor practices were still reminiscent of integrated steelmaking. Two profitable quarters in 1984 encouraged the company, but no buyers could be found. No steelmaker wanted to add capacity in CF & I's key products; there was massive overcapacity in seamless pipe, the rail market was threatened by the imminent entry of Wheeling-Pittsburgh's new mill, and imports and aggressive minimills were fighting over the wire market.[4]

In May 1985, Crane abandoned the search for a buyer and spun off CF & I to its own shareholders, on the basis of 0.4 shares in CF & I for every share of Crane. In this way, Crane was neatly rid of the obligations and liabilities of the company, but CF & I now had no deep-pocket support. Just when CF & I was forced to stand on its own feet again, the oilfield went through a second collapse, with oil prices dropping in 1985–86 from $26 a barrel to $12. The company was forced to idle its seamless mill. The union, recognizing the possibility of the company's complete closure, agreed to further reductions in wages and benefits in 1986 in exchange for the establishment of an ESOP and an agreement to distribute 20 percent of any profits (after interest) to the employees. By the end of 1988, the ESOP controlled 38 percent of the company's shares.

The last years of the 1980s saw CF & I essentially adrift, despite management's heroic efforts. The company was unable to finance the capital expenditure needed to take advantage of slowly recovering steel markets or to increase its productivity, and it was saddled with massive pension liabilities. While workforce levels continued to decline, to around 1,400 by 1990, the overhang of 8,000 retirees from the company's closed mining and steelmaking operations presented liabilities the company could not meet. In November 1990, it filed for Chapter 11 bankruptcy protection.

The bankruptcy court eventually liquidated the old CF & I corporation, and responsibility for the pension liability was passed to the Pension Benefits Guarantee Board (PBGC). However, as the largest creditor, the PBGC benefited from the sale of the company's steelmaking assets. The facilities were bought by a new entity, CF & I Steel Inc. Limited Partnership (LP), 95.2 percent of which was owned by Oregon Steel through a subsidiary, New CF & I Inc. Oregon Steel paid $100 million for control of the plant; non-PBGC creditors and previous shareholders received the token 4.8 percent balance of the limited partnership. The new venture, essentially a subsidiary of Oregon Steel, took the plant out of bankruptcy in March 1993.

The reorganization accomplished three things. It shed the liabilities associated with the plant's history; it supplied a new parent company with the financial ability and desire to invest in upgrading the plant; and it finally put in place real minimill management and culture. Oregon Steel had itself been successfully transformed in the 1980s from a traditional "independent" mill to a plate minimill. Its advantage over CF & I was that it was originally a much smaller, single-product producer with no encumbrances of mines, fabricating operations, and associated retiree overhangs. It had extensively upgraded its facilities and slashed its labor force; decertified the Steelworkers and reduced its hourly labor costs 25 percent; transferred majority ownership of the company to an ESOP; and moved its sales effort away from its traditional base of the Pacific Northwest's shipbuilding, lumber, and railcar manufacturing industries. While targeting service centers as its new primary market, Oregon Steel also acquired Kaiser Steel's former plate rolling mill in Fontana, California, and its large-diameter line pipe mill in Napa, California. The pipe operations increased the steelmaking throughput at the company's Portland mill and diversified its market. In the 1990s, it was ready to expand its product range, and studied opportunities for entering the minimill flat-rolled sector as well as the long products markets.

Oregon Steel was prepared to invest $180 million in upgrading the CF & I mill, on top of the $100 million it spent to buy the facility. A new bar and rod mill was built from 1993 to 1995, reflecting the need to defend CF & I's dominant position in the western market for low-end wire products against new minimill entrants.[5] Next, Oregon Steel sought help in modernizing the rail operation from Nippon Steel, the world's largest rail producer. Oregon sold Nippon a 10 percent stake in New CF & I Inc., and Nippon licensed CF & I to use its proprietary deep head-hardening technology for producing advanced, hard-wearing rails. The rounds caster was modified to produce continuously cast blooms for the rail mill, eliminating ingot practice, and the melt shop and billet caster were upgraded to supply more steel to the bar/rod mill. Completion of the full modernization program will give the mill the ability to produce close to 1 million tons of long products, at a capital cost (purchase price plus subsequent modernization) of $280 per annual ton.

CF & I is thus a mill that, in a little over a decade, has seen in microcosm the transformation of the U.S. long products steel industry. It has changed from a traditional steelmaker, integrated from mine through fabrication operations, to become part of a minimill group. A Japanese investor, Nippon Steel, participates in the company. It has narrowed its product range, although with four main product areas it is still much less specialized than most single-location minimills. It operates with less than a fifth of its 1980 workforce, for a similar tonnage of product shipments. One major difference from many minimills is determined by the nature of its rail, wire, and seamless products: CF & I sells a very low percentage of its output to distributors. Nevertheless it appears to be pursuing aggressive minimill marketing strategies. It is locked in battle for market shares with integrated competitors, Bethlehem Steel in rails and U.S. Steel in seamless pipe, and with other minimills in bar and wire, while imports are steadily retreating from all its product markets. Most important, CF & I has become a financial success, after fifteen years of almost continuous losses. While it has lost its independence, it has found a future.

GENEVA STEEL: THE INTEGRATED MILL AS MINIMILL

Four hundred miles west of CF & I's Pueblo, Colorado, mill is the largest steelmaker in the western United States, Geneva Steel. While CF & I was a historic, "home-grown" western producer, Geneva was essentially an overnight, wartime emergency creation of the federal government.

Ironmaking from Utah's rich reserves of iron ore, coal, and limestone was begun in 1924 by the Columbia Steel Company, absorbed into U.S. Steel in 1930. However, the blast furnaces at Ironton, near Provo, sent their pig iron to Columbia's open-hearth mills at Torrance and Pittsburg, California, where flat-rolled, tube, and wire mills supplied the growing California market. In May 1941, the imminent threat of U.S. entry into World War II led the Defense Plant Corporation to seek additional western steelmaking capacity to supply the West Coast shipbuilding industry that was gearing up to supply naval and merchant ships to the U.S. and its allies. Besides funding the creation of Kaiser Steel at Fontana, California, the government contracted with U.S. Steel's Columbia Steel division to build and manage a major new mill at Vineyard, Utah, between Salt Lake City and Provo, and close to its Ironton plant. Opened in 1944, the new Geneva mill had 2 million tons of plate and sheet capacity, using blast furnaces and ten large open-hearth furnaces to feed a unique combination wide-plate and sheet reversing mill, capable of producing 132-inch-wide plates or 80-inch hot-rolled coils.

U.S. Steel bought the mill from the Defense Plant Corporation in 1945 to feed hot bands to the Pittsburg, California, mill in place of that plant's former open hearths and hot-strip mill. The Geneva Works also sold plate to U.S. Steel's western customers, taking care not to ship east to compete with the corporation's Chicago-area plate mills. Welded pipe operations and blooming and structural mills for light beams and other shapes completed the plant. At first, natural ore from southern Utah was used exclusively, but in 1962, U.S. Steel opened a taconite pellet plant at Atlantic City, Wyoming, to supply the mill with higher-grade feed.

In the early 1980s, the forty-year-old mill had seen very little investment since its construction. Along with U.S. Steel's Fairless Hills mill in the East, it had been last on the corporation's list for the replacement of open hearths with BOFs because its open hearths were relatively large and efficient. However, the need for a modern hot end, including continuous casting, was increasingly evident as product prices fell and costs continued to rise in the 1980s. In 1983–84, U.S. Steel reviewed the investment needs of the Western Steel Division, including Geneva and Pittsburg, and concluded that over $1 billion would have to be spent to make the mills competitive—a sum not beyond the corporation's means, but simply not in the cards at a time when the corporation was committed to acquiring oil assets, not saving low-return steelmaking assets. In 1983, the Wyoming ore mines were closed and Geneva started to source its ore pellets from U.S. Steel's Minntac plant in Minnesota, which in the steel slump was operating at only 25 percent of capacity. The elimination of excess ore capacity made sense to U.S. Steel in the short run, but the 1,600-mile rail haul costs put one more nail in Geneva's coffin. In 1985, U.S. Steel found a way to save the Pittsburg mill, when the USS–Posco Industries joint venture was formed to take over and modernize the California finishing mill. The joint venture included provision for Korean hot band to supply the waterfront Pittsburg mill beginning in 1989, thus removing the customer for over a million tons of Geneva's output—nearly two-thirds of its 1985 shipments. While this seemed to set a deadline for the Geneva mill's closure, it actually came even sooner. When the USWA struck U.S. Steel in July 1986, the corporation announced that the Geneva mill would not be reopened after the strike.

Perhaps people with no steel industry background were needed to take on a mill that had been generally written off within the industry. Two Salt Lake City attorneys from prominent local families, Joseph Cannon and Robert Grow, decided to buy and run the mill, based on its historic record of profitability (even though those profits had been derived from internal sales to Pittsburg) and on a shrewd belief that the mill's modernization could be accomplished for a fraction of U.S. Steel's estimates. U.S. Steel sold the closed mill on an assets-only basis, retaining unfunded pension and post-retirement liability costs and agreeing to indemnify the new Geneva Steel for environmental liabilities over $10 million. U.S. Steel refused to consider sourcing part of UPI's hot-band needs from an independent Geneva, but the prospect of shipping steel east into markets historically served from other U.S. Steel mills did exist.

As the mill's survival was the only prospect for continued high-earnings employment for most of its union and salaried employees, union, local, and state support was solidly behind any attempt to rescue it. Most of the $44.1 million purchase price was raised within the state, and the new owners took over the mill—by then shuttered for over a year—on August 31, 1987. The low purchase price reflected the fact that the mill was shut down—there were no product inventories or receivables to be paid for—and the assessment that its obsolete equipment posed little commercial threat to U.S. Steel, whose nearest mill was now at Gary, 1,000 miles further east. With both the Geneva and Baytown, Texas, mills closed in 1986, U.S. Steel was in effect willing to abandon the plate and hot-rolled coil markets west of the Mississippi.[6]

The mill resumed shipping in late 1987, with a new Steelworkers contract cutting about $7 an hour from the previous U.S. Steel wage and benefit rates and with new, reduced-price contracts for electric power, rail freight, and iron ore. The company took over U.S. Steel's western mining properties, producing some of its own raw materials, but it has continued to buy taconite pellets from Minntac as well as use smaller quantities of natural ore from the southern Utah mines. The company also supplements local coal with imported coke landed at Richmond, California. The company pursued aggressive purchasing and out-sourcing of work formerly done in-house by U.S. Steel, although Geneva did reopen the mill's foundry, finding it cheaper to produce its own ingot molds and other castings. Geneva Steel also restarted the mill's welded pipe mills, producing standard and line pipe sizes over 6 inches for distributor markets.

To reenter the plate and sheet market after a year's closure, and to replace much of the throughput lost from the Pittsburg hot-band shipments, the new company aggressively pushed its plate and coils into midwestern and southern markets via service centers. A mill that had historically not shipped east of Denver now sold to distributors as far afield as Pittsburgh, Pennsylvania, and Birmingham, Alabama, at railcar-load prices that were competitive with imports—but significantly undercut the major mills' pricing structure. The company today ships more than 60 percent of its steel east of Colorado, and ships 80 percent to distributors. The use of "minimill-type" pricing caused resentment among some market participants and helped to drive down overall transaction prices in 1988, but it was successful in quickly building the mill's order books to a point where it was shipping at close to 70 percent of capacity, or around 1.4 million tons per year—enough to bring it to the break-even point within a year of its reopening. The mill's success also brought disagreements among the company's participants, however, especially in the Cannon family, as to whether it should be used as a "cash cow" or whether significant capital should be invested in it for the long term. The "operators," as they were styled, led by chairman Joseph Cannon, won and the mill committed to a modernization program that was to cost nearly $400 million from 1989 to 1995—dramatically less than the U.S. Steel estimates, but enough to bring the mill up to the rule of thumb of over $200 of capital cost for every ton of modern annual capacity.

The mill's modernization from 1991 to 1994 included replacing the open hearths with two bottom-blown, 235-ton basic oxygen furnaces bought secondhand from LTV's closed South Chicago mill; a new ladle metallurgy furnace; and a continuous slab caster, at 126 inches the world's widest, in line with the existing combination plate/coil mill. This new hot end configuration increased the mill's raw steel capability from 1.9 to 2.5 million annual tons and eliminated costly ingot practice. The rolling mill has also been upgraded, with a coilbox—also said to be the world's largest—designed to handle wide plate coils of up to 60,000 pounds. The wide slabs eliminate the previous need to cross-roll slabs at a broadside mill stand to achieve the broader plate widths, thus improving surface quality and yield. During the most intensive period of the modernization program, from 1992 to 1994, production was disrupted and the company was forced out of the plate market for seven months; those years saw losses for the company, but Geneva Steel subsequently returned to profitability in late 1994 and saw record shipments, though not consistent profits, in 1995 and 1996.

In many ways, Geneva Steel has behaved like a classic minimill. The company acts as a price-taker in its markets, selling at prices it perceives as necessary to beat out imports and other low-priced suppliers, rather than seeking to support any given pricing structure. The mill is known for a policy of stressing commodity sizes—its lead times and price extras for nonstandard thicknesses and coil widths are generally higher than at other flat-rolled mills. It sells largely to service centers, although—like many minimills—it has also attracted independent coil processors: in 1995, Western Flat Rolled Steel and Processing installed a cold-rolling mill next door to the Geneva mill to augment its existing pickling, slitting, and tube-making facilities. Its investment program has walked a careful line between being frugal—for instance, in buying used equipment when available—and going for state of the art technology when new equipment was necessary. Labor productivity is reported to be the best of any U.S. integrated mill, although a Performance Dividend Plan for productivity bonuses has been the subject of tough bargaining with the USWA. The mill takes about 1.4 man-hours per ton of steel from the BOF shop forward, compared to Nucor's minimill standard of just under 1 man-hour. The overall cost of production of finished steel products in 1995 was around 30 percent lower, in current dollars, than under U.S. Steel in 1985—but then, average selling prices were also 20 percent lower.

Geneva Steel is certainly a mill that has been brought back from the dead, transformed by a combination of new investment and new management strategies. To claim, as its management has done on occasion, that Geneva Steel is a minimill is to distort the term beyond usefulness, but as a textbook case of a successful "born-again," reconstituted mill, Geneva Steel looks able to compete on costs with true minimills. No new minimill in the 1990s is likely to challenge its regional position in the western flat-rolled market. In the plate markets, two developments will challenge Geneva in its targeted service center markets. Oregon Steel's Steckel mill, started up in 1996, will increase the capacity of its Portland mill by about 750,000 tons per year. Further east, Ipsco's new plate and sheet minimill in Iowa, also brought on line in 1996 with 1 million tons of capacity, challenges Geneva's position in the midwestern market, although neither the Ipsco mill nor Oregon Steel have Geneva's wide and heavy plate capabilities.

For Geneva Steel even to consider competing with new minimills is a remarkable achievement. To guarantee its competitiveness in the next century, the company is now experimenting with ways of making iron units to feed its BOF shop more cheaply. The company built a small plasma-fired cupola furnace in 1995, supplementing the ironmaking capabilities of its three blast furnaces. It is also studying a 1 million-ton-per-year Corex direct reduction plant, to produce iron without the use of coke. This could be built by 1999, with financial support as a technology demonstration project from the U.S. Department of Energy. Such a facility would replace about half the mill's current blast furnace output, while permitting greater use of cheaper, low-quality local ore and coal feeds than at present. Now metallurgical (coking) coal must be brought by rail from the east or coke must be imported via California ports. Like the efforts of Nucor, Oregon Steel, Tuscaloosa, and others to develop new sources of iron units, the Corex project is likely to further blur the definitions of minimill and integrated mill that Geneva Steel, by its strategy, costs, and culture, has already challenged.

LTV STEEL: THE USES OF BANKRUPTCY

On its formation in 1984 by the merger of LTV Corporation's Jones & Laughlin Steel division with Republic Steel corporation, LTV became the second largest steelmaker in the United States, beating out Bethlehem Steel for second place behind U.S. Steel. The combined company was the largest U.S. producer of bar products and of pipe and tubing and the second-largest producer of stainless steel and of flat-rolled carbon steel. Although each company had closed capacity between 1977 and 1983, and LTV was forced by the Justice Department as a condition of approval of the merger to spin off its Gadsden, Alabama, integrated mill and its Massillon, Ohio, stainless cold-rolling mill, the company still had some 35 steelmaking plants, ranging from six fully integrated mills to small cold-finished bar and welded pipe operations. The company's raw steelmaking capacity including Gadsden was approximately 24.6 million tons.

Less than ten years later, the LTV Steel that emerged in June 1993 from seven years of bankruptcy protection was a very different company. With just 9.8 million tons of steelmaking capacity at two integrated mills, plus two separate cold-rolling mills, LTV is almost exclusively a producer of flat-rolled carbon steel. Five welded pipe operations, using the company's flat-rolled steel, remained, but all seamless pipemaking had ceased. The stainless flat-rolled operations, the specialty carbon and stainless bar operations, and the Warren integrated flat-rolled mill were all sold. On the other hand, the company participated with Sumitomo of Japan in two new joint venture galvanizing lines. It was also studying a joint venture flat-rolled minimill project, Trico Steel, launched in 1994 with both Sumitomo and British Steel participation.

The J&L-Republic merger, announced in September 1983 and finally completed in June 1984, after lengthy negotiations with the Antitrust Division of the Justice Department, combined the fourth- and fifth-largest U.S. steelmakers. Both J & L and Republic were based in the Midwest, with their principal operations (after the sale of Republic's Gadsden plant) concentrated in the Pittsburgh, northern Ohio, and Chicago regions. Each company had mills in Cleveland; in the Mahoning Valley; and in the Chicago–northern Indiana region. Both companies had much obsolete and excess capacity—1984 raw steel production of 10 million tons represented just 40 percent of rated capacity—and both were losing money heavily. However, each company had spent large sums on upgrading certain facilities; for example, both J & L and Republic had invested heavily in seamless pipe facilities at Aliquippa, Pennsylvania, and Youngstown, Ohio; Republic's bar operations had an impressive electric furnace steelmaking plant, the Canton Alloy Shops; and J & L's Indiana Harbor and Republic's Cleveland flat-rolled mills were equipped with modern casters. In theory, the combination would allow the parent company, conglomerate LTV Corporation, to prune excess capacity and, avoiding new capital expenditure, combine the best facilities of each into a successful major steel company. LTV spent $714 million to acquire Republic, a sum that could be justified by the firm's stated intention of saving the combined operations between $300 and $400 million a year by eliminating duplicate facilities and overhead.

In practice, the continuing steel recession between 1984 and 1986 made a mockery of the optimistic predictions. Prices of all steel products continued to fall, while LTV's market share—which had been as high as 38 percent in hot-rolled and cold-finished bars at the time of the merger—fell in products where J & L and Republic had previously been direct competitors, as customers sought to maintain a diverse supply base. The seamless business, into which both companies had poured money, was effectively dead as oil drilling dried up. The carbon flat-rolled business remained stable but unprofitable, while the stainless operations were the only bright spot, growing their sales, margins, and profits. Numerous small bar and tubing facilities were closed, the two companies' adjacent Cleveland plants were combined under one management, and the headquarters staffs were combined (with generous relocation allowances) in the former Republic offices in Cleveland. However, the savings realized by 1986 amounted to less than half the target and were more than offset by declines in margins.[7]

By mid-1986, the company was desperately seeking to keep afloat. The stainless operations were sold off to management for $150 million, and the parent LTV Corporation was draining its profitable aerospace and defense divisions of cash to pay LTV Steel's huge debt. From 1987 to 1989, the company faced payments of $1.7 billion just for debt service, for borrowings incurred not only by the purchase of Republic but by both companies' borrowing for capital expenditures and to offset cash drains from losing operations. LTV's continued financing ability was seriously diminished by the downgrading of its debt ratings, and rumors of possible bankruptcy began to erode the company's steel sales as well as increase pressure from its banks. Further drastic closures and cost cuts were needed, but LTV faced a problem that seems to have been little analyzed at the time of the merger. The pension plan liabilities from retired (and terminated) workers continued regardless of the downsizing of the active workforce, and in 1986, the 66,000 retirees exceeded the 56,000 active employees for the first time. In 1986, the company's four major pension plans (former J&L and Republic plans for each of salaried and union employees) were underfunded by around $1.7 billion, and LTV's cash payments to the plans were running at around $125 million a year. Plant closures would simply increase these obligations as employees with vested pension and health care benefits were terminated.

In July 1986, LTV Corporation and its subsidiaries filed for Chapter 11 bankruptcy protection. The company immediately terminated its pension plans, thus throwing onto the federal Pension Benefits

Guarantee Corporation the obligation to continue paying pensions at the level insured by law—that is, at a lower pension level for most retirees. The company also quickly closed a number of marginal facilities, including its seamless pipe facilities; most operations at the mills at Pittsburgh, Aliquippa, Youngstown, and South Chicago; and a number of obsolete facilities at other plants.[8] In August 1987, the company settled a new labor contract with the USWA in which it agreed, among other provisions, to pay its retirees' amounts that would approximate the difference between their PBGC payments and their former company pensions, thus returning the retirees' pensions to their former level but at a fraction of the cost to the company. The PBGC immediately attempted to restore the original pension plans, claiming that the labor agreement demonstrated LTV's ability and willingness to continue to fund the pensions. The PBGC itself was by now struggling to keep afloat, as LTV's bankruptcy had approximately doubled its own rate of payments on terminated plans; and subsequent bankruptcy filings in 1986–87 had stretched its resources to the point where it faced the possibility of having to ask for a congressional bailout. The total sum at stake, the balance needed to fund the pension plans at their original level, was around $2.2 billion.

The pension dispute was the subject of national attention and of tens of millions of dollars of legal fees throughout 1987 and 1988. Meanwhile, LTV still had to honor retiree health and life insurance benefits. In 1988, the company took a charge of $2.26 billion as a reserve to recognize its total estimated nonpension obligations to retirees. It also took a further $1.34 billion charge for the write-down of assets and to cover reorganization costs. On top of a $510 million write-down for closures in 1986 and the company's accumulated losses, LTV had a balance sheet with a negative net worth of $5.3 billion at the end of 1988. Moreover, it still faced the threat of having to reassume the pension plans and reimburse the PBGC for as much as $1.7 billion in payments and interest for the period since bankruptcy.

Set against this bleak picture were a number of signs that LTV was not entirely hopeless, however. The recovery of steel markets, especially in flat-rolled products, in 1987–88 restored operating profits to LTV Steel's remaining core operations for those two years. The company spent little on capital equipment but benefited from concentrating output at its two most modern plants, Indiana Harbor and the combined Cleveland Works. The Warren, Ohio, integrated mill, which needed modernization, was sold in 1988 to investors, who renamed the operation

Warren Consolidated Industries, later WCI Steel. LTV also agreed to sell the ailing bar operations, now based largely on the Canton and Massillon plants, to a management group; that spin-off, as Republic Engineered Steels, was completed in November 1989. Surplus coal and iron ore properties were sold, as were surplus real estate and fabricating shops. The combination of bankruptcy protection, operating profits, the cash surplus from new investment not meeting depreciation, and asset sales quickly built up a cash hoard that exceeded $1 billion in 1989.

During the lengthy bankruptcy proceedings, the PBGC's attitude seemed to change at least twice. In 1986 and early 1987, it appeared that LTV might not survive, and the PBGC seemed resigned to accepting liability for the pensions. By mid-1987, however, the recovery of the steel market and the deal between LTV and the Steelworkers, combined with political and financial pressure on the agency, caused the PBGC to become strongly hostile to the company, leading to bitter litigation. From around the end of 1988, it appeared to both sides that neither could afford the risk of an all-or-nothing outcome of litigation, and hostility was replaced with negotiation through which the PBGC became in effect a partner of LTV in managing the continuing business. When, in 1990, the Supreme Court finally ruled that the PBGC was within its authority to restore the LTV pension plans, the issue came down to how much of LTV's cash would be paid to the PBGC as a contribution to the restored plans versus how much would be spent on revitalizing the company.

LTV's successful reorganization depended not only on a resolution of the pension issue but also on decisions on modernization that could not be postponed indefinitely. In 1989, LTV and the PBGC began to negotiate a settlement, but agreement on a plan of reorganization was complicated by the intervention of Usinor-Sacilor, whose 1990 offer to buy half of LTV was contingent on the PBGC's retaining the pension obligations. The Supreme Court ruling led the state-owned French steelmaker to withdraw, and LTV and the PBGC began to draw up a reorganization plan that was filed in court in May 1991. It would give the PBGC nearly $1 billion cash and an equity position of approximately 3.3 percent in the reorganized company. The company, the PBGC and its other creditors also agreed to authorize major capital investments in upgrading the company's coke ovens and blast furnaces, and the construction of a Direct Hot-Charge Complex' (DHCC) at the former J&L (west) side of the Cleveland Works.

The 1991 reorganization plan was further contested, primarily between the PBGC and other creditors who felt the federal agency was getting too much at their expense. In 1992, the aerospace and defense operations were sold to Martin Marietta and Loral, and the proceeds distributed among the creditors. LTV was left as a steel company with an oilfield equipment group, Continental Emsco. LTV finally emerged from bankruptcy in June 1993 after the largest, longest, and most costly bankruptcy case in history. The write-down of the company's pre-bankruptcy debt in the reorganization allowed LTV to take an extraordinary credit of $3.96 billion in the second quarter of 1993, thus restoring its balance sheet to something approaching respectability. In the healthy steel market of the mid-1990s, the company was able to issue new equity in 1994, part of the proceeds of which was contributed to the still-underfunded but continuing pension funds, and the PBGC was able to sell off its LTV equity.

While the debates over the final shape of the reorganization plan continued, the company had been able to proceed with its cost-cutting and modernization investments. To quote one industry analyst, Charles Bradford of UBS Securities in New York, "I think you can make a case that when a lot of the major steel companies spent a lot of money, it was wasted. But, in this instance, you probably have a much better record on spending properly because the investments were reviewed in great detail by the company's creditors."[9] Among the major expenditures from 1990 to 1993, the Direct Hot-Charge Complex stands out. The DHCC took advantage of the fortuitous layout of the Cleveland West plant: there was just enough space between the BOF shop and the hot-strip mill to build an in-line continuous caster. In addition, the BOF shop was upgraded, a ladle furnace added, and the hot-strip mill and chemistry lab upgraded. The USW agreed on a radically new contract involving minimill-style manning practices for the plant, eliminating 500 jobs. On its completion in late 1993, the DHCC represented one approach to an integrated minimill. It was the first plant of one of the traditional integrated companies to get below 2 man-hours per ton, surpassed in the integrated sector only by Geneva Steel. Although capable of producing high-quality steel, the DHCC is used by LTV primarily for high-volume production of commodity hot bands and coiled light plate, plus feeding cold reduction mills at Cleveland and elsewhere. LTV's automotive steel, including coils for galvanizing, is primarily produced on Cleveland's east side and at the Indiana Harbor plant, where costs per ton are higher but care is taken to guarantee surface finish.

LTV by late 1993 had 100 percent continuous casting, three efficient steelmaking facilities (two combined in the Cleveland Works), and a good reputation for quality and service. In the last years of Chapter 11, the company had done more than renew its flat-rolled steelmaking. It had rationalized and updated its ore operations (LTV Steel Mining Co.); had updated its coke operations and brought them into environmental compliance; introduced integrated computer controls and power cogeneration throughout its major plants; and added automation to many of its maintenance functions.

Among the six major integrated flat-rolled producers, LTV appeared in 1995 to hold its own. Steel operating profits ran well over 5 percent of sales in 1994–95, or between $25 and $40 per ton in each quarter, around $10 a ton below the integrated industry average. LTV appeared to be behind U.S. Steel and AK Steel in total costs per ton but ahead of such producers as Bethlehem Steel (back in the number-two producer slot) and Wheeling-Pittsburgh. Further incremental improvements might be possible at Cleveland, Indiana Harbor, and the company's finishing operations, but LTV seemed in 1995 set to move toward true minimill operations. LTV announced in December 1994 that it would build a greenfield flat-rolled minimill with 2.2 million tons capacity, in partnership with Sumitomo and British Steel. The mill, to be known as Trico Steel, would be co-owned by LTV (50 percent) and by the two other partners (25 percent each). To be built in the Southeast, the new mill would compete directly with Nucor's new Charleston, South Carolina, minimill and with, among others, the integrated Gulf States Steel mill at Gadsden that LTV was forced to sell off in 1985.

Unlike similar new mills such as that of Nucor, the planned Trico mill faced unusual public hostility from both sides of the integrated steel industry. The USWA asked that the money be spent instead on financing the pension funds. Regional integrated producers, such as Gulf States and U.S. Steel's Fairfield mill, complained about the incentives offered by Alabama to bring the plant there and claimed the plant would imbalance the scrap market. The protests revealed the fears of each. The USWA evidently did not believe it could organize a flat-rolled minimill managed by LTV. U.S. Steel, which had studied and rejected building such a minimill itself in the early 1990s, may have feared it had made the wrong decision as much as it feared another competitor. Both sides seemed to regard LTV's behavior quite differently from other minimill investors—as that of a betrayal. A last vestige of the old oligopoly mentality and a sure sign of defensiveness and fear.[10]

Before Geneva Steel signed up for it, LTV studied the Corex cokeless direct reduction process and was the first company to consider building the Department of Energy's 1-million-ton-per-year demonstration plant. Building it at Cleveland, however, offered lower prospective savings than at a location like Geneva, far from readily available coking coal. Ohio also mandates lower prices for the cogenerated electricity that the plant would generate, while Utah's Public Utilities Commission sets a more attractive purchase rate for the excess electricity.[11] The decision not to proceed with the Corex plant did not reflect on LTV's openness to new technology, which was seen by the Trico announcement in the same year; indeed, it is likely that Trico will use some directly reduced iron feed, sourced from the British Steel Midrex units relocated to Mobile, Alabama. The company's active interest in new processes (with technology purchased, not developed in-house) is significant, especially because the lakefront Cleveland and Indiana Harbor mills are located as optimally as possible for traditional integrated production in North America and because LTV has invested heavily in securing low-cost raw materials production. It is one more aspect of the minimill culture that LTV's management has adopted.

LTV presents an extreme case of the restructuring of the integrated steel industry. Strictly speaking, five reconstituted steelmakers have emerged from the LTV Steel of 1984-85. In addition to the surviving LTV Steel, two integrated mills (Gulf States and WCI Steel), one stainless company (J&L Specialty Steel), and one specialty barmaker (Republic Engineered Steels) were all carved out of the old LTV. An additional company, J & L Structural, acquired the 14-inch structural rolling mill at the shuttered Aliquippa, Pennsylvania, plant, which produces a unique range of light beams and shapes for mobile home and trailer builders and other special end-use applications. This company's plans to build a new minimill melt shop adjacent to the Aliquippa rolling mill, rather than rely on purchased billets, would create a sixth steelmaker out of the pieces of the old LTV. The only "spin-off" failure was that of the Massillon stainless cold-rolling mill, sold under antitrust order in 1985 as Enduro Stainless; Enduro failed within two years, and the mill passed to Mercury Stainless and thence to Washington Steel before its final closure.

A FORMULA FOR REINCARNATION?

LTV's transformation certainly exceeded that of any other major integrated company, with the possible exception of that of Armco/AK Steel.

In both the size of the company involved and the radical scope of the transformation, LTV's rebirth seems a heroic achievement. The simultaneous financial, operational, and legal battles fought during the seven years of bankruptcy ultimately resulted in a profitable, independent company, able to support its original pension plans—something no observer of the industry would have bet upon in 1986. Even the ultimate failure to get the PBGC to assume the pension obligations may have been beneficial in the long run, by keeping LTV independent and out of the control of Usinor-Sacilor, the West's last major state-owned steel giant. Among the headline-grabbing political and human aspects of the LTV restructuring, though, certain underlying principles can be identified that LTV has in common with Geneva Steel, CF & I under its new management, and other reborn mills. These mills also have much in common with their competitors the minimills.

The underlying operational strategies pursued successfully by a variety of mills include:

- Focusing intensely on controlling the costs of labor, raw materials, energy, and freight inputs, usually including abandoning or renegotiating contracts and practices long taken for granted.
- Having labor productivity far in excess of traditional industry practices, not just by eliminating traditional union craft divisions and work rules but also through the use of incentive pay, profit-sharing or employee ownership plans, education, and pushing responsibility down to the lowest level.
- Cutting out marginal product lines and facilities, focusing on core strengths and products.
- Acting as a price-taker in the market, pricing products to meet market competition (whether domestic or imported) and minimizing "special deals" and differential pricing.
- Using service centers and more specialized processor/distributors rather than seeking to maintain value-added operations in-house and sell directly to end users.
- Attempting to maximize mill throughput at all times via price flexibility and by pushing into geographically distant markets when necessary to keep output up.
- Outsourcing services wherever possible, including finishing operations, maintenance, mill services, and sometimes sales and marketing representation.

- Embracing new technology, to the point of taking technical risks, especially if it can be bought from outside equipment and engineering firms rather than developed in house—but only if it can be justified financially.
- Taking an international view of the steel industry and its markets, including exporting, technical exchanges, and purchases from foreign companies, using international capital markets (including foreign equity investment in the U.S. companies), and assuming that steel trade will continue inevitably to grow.
- Viewing steel as an investment to be compared with other potential investments rather than a vocation or a national public utility.

At the core of this view of the steel business and its place in the world is acceptance of the reality of the market setting prices; the steel company's job, therefore, is to produce at costs sufficiently below the market to be able to earn returns as good as those of other investments of comparable risk. This does not sound like a radical theory. What is astonishing is that it was not the view prevailing in the U.S. steel industry for more than three generations.

8

A WHOLE NEW BALL GAME: THE FLAT-ROLLED MINIMILLS

THE FIELD OF DREAMS

The integrated mills have tremendous capacity for producing sheets and it is unthinkable that the semi-integrated, electric-furnace operators would move into this area.

—The Reverend William T. Hogan
in *World Steel in the 1980s,* 1983

In 1986, the "unthinkable" happened. Nucor broke ground on a new, electric furnace sheet mill in a cornfield outside Crawfordsville, Indiana, in what quickly became the closest-watched and best-publicized venture in the steel industry in this century. The Crawfordsville mill was widely publicized both because of the openness of Nucor and its chairman, Ken Iverson, to reporters and industry visitors and because it represented hope for a fresh start after two decades of plant closings and gloom in steel and in U.S. industry in general.

Politicians and pundits used the story of Crawfordsville's construction and start-up as a symbol of something much greater than the construction of a new type of steel plant; it became an icon of American ingenuity and entrepreneurship. A writer encouraged by Ken Iverson to

TABLE 8.1
NORTH AMERICAN "GREENFIELD"
FLAT-ROLLED MINIMILLS, 1989–1997

Mill	Date	Steelmaking Capacity (million tons per year)	Rolling Capacity (million tons per year)	Process Vendor	Notes
Gallatin Steel, Warsaw, KY	1995 (1998)	1.2 (2.0)	2.0	SMS	Phase II, including second caster, may commence 1997
Ipsco, Montpelier, IA	1996	1.0	1.0	Mannesmann Demag	Steckel mill, 96 inches wide; coiled plate and HR sheet
North Star BHP, Delta, OH	1996	1.5	1.5	Sumitomo	
Nucor, Crawfordsville,IN	1989	1.8	1.8	SMS	July 1989 start-up was first commercial thin-slab caster
Nucor, Hickman, AR	1992	2.2	2.2	SMS	
Nucor, Charleston, SC	1997	1.8	1.8	SMS	
Steel Dynamics, Butler, IN	1996 (1999)	0.9 (2.0)	2.0	SMS	Phase II, including second caster, deferred until 1998
Trico Steel, Decatur, AL	1997	2.2	2.2	Sumitomo	LTV/Sumitomo/British Steel joint venture

NOTES:
Numbers in parentheses are eventual capacities, assuming completion of expansion plans. Other projects, not listed, have been studied by U.S. Steel and Worthington Industries' (joint venture project; decision not to proceed); Nucor and Oregon Steel (joint venture for West Coast; on indefinite hold); Chaparral Steel; and Birmingham Steel, among others. World Class Steel, a minimill project of Pittsburgh steel processor World Class Processing, Inc., was canceled in late 1995, but in early 1996 financing was being sought for the project to proceed under new ownership by the Mesco Group of New Delhi, India.

follow the start-up, Richard Preston, wrote a best-selling book of the story, *American Steel,* which was serialized in *The New Yorker* magazine.[1] The media attention goaded the Steelworkers union, faced with the prospect of a non-union mill in its Midwest heartland, to level allegations of unsafe practice against Nucor, but the cost to the company of defending the subsequent investigations was undoubtedly offset by the effect the publicity had on Nucor's stock price.

Crawfordsville started up in July 1989 and a year later was turning a profit. With such a public success, steel became, for the first time in decades, a darling of Wall Street. For the next five years, steel mills became easy to finance as investors bought into the attractive story of how Nucor and its prospective competitors were going to transform the steel industry. By 1995, seven entirely new, greenfield mills were built or under construction in the United States. At least ten more North American mills were being transformed by the addition of new technology, becoming "minimill" sheet or

TABLE 8.2
NORTH AMERICAN "BROWNFIELD"
FLAT-ROLLED MINIMILLS, 1989–1997

Mill	Date	Additional Tons per Year: Steelmaking	Rolling	Configuration
Acme Metals, Chicago, IL	1997	270,000 (phase 1) 900,000 (phase 2)	2,000,000	Existing BOF hot end. Phase 1, a new SMS caster/HS mill, adds 270,000 tons of capacity. Phase 2 would add EFs, a second caster, and ladle metallurgy to fully use rolling capacity.
Algoma Steel, Sault Ste. Marie, Ontario	1997	0	2,000,000 (estimated)	Existing BOF hot end, new thin-strip caster and hot-strip mill under construction. Small net capacity increase.
Armco, Mansfield, OH	1995	0	0	New Voest-Alpine medium-slab caster; existing EF shop and hot-strip mill. Stainless and carbon. Negligible net capacity increase.
Beta Steel, Portage, IN	1992	0 (900,000)	400,000 (900,000)	Used HS mill reassembled at new site in 1992. New EF/caster and second HS mill in 1996-97.
Caparo Steel, Sharon, PA	1995	260,000	0	Restart of former Sharon Steel mill. EFs upgraded for restart (capacity increased from 540,000); thin slab caster studied (1997/98?).
Dofasco, Hamilton, Ontario	1996	1,350,000	450,000	New EF shop and caster to feed additional slabs to upgraded existing HS mill; supplements existing BOF shop.
Hylsa, Monterrey, Mexico	1994	0	830,000	New SMS caster with existing DRI/EF hot end and hot-strip mill.
Lukens, Inc., Conshohocken, PA	1995	0	500,000	New 102-inch Steckel mill supplied from existing 110-inch roughing mill. Plate only.
Oregon Steel, Portland, OR	1996	0	700,000	New 120-inch Steckel mill; will replace existing plate mill at Fontana, CA, with small net reduction of capacity. Plate only.
Tuscaloosa Steel, Tuscaloosa, AL	1997	1,000,000	0	New EF hot end and caster; upgrade to existing 112-inch Steckel mill. Plate only.

coil plate producers. (See tables 8.1 and 8.2.) Others were planned or under study. The 20 million tons of minimill flat-rolled capacity to be commissioned by 1998 represents a 30-percent increase on the U.S. hot-strip mill capacity in existence prior to the Crawfordsville startup.

The revolution in the steel industry represented by the new entrants raises a number of obvious questions. Will the supply of quality scrap support the new entrants, or must scrap substitutes be used widely? Are the economics really so attractive that so many new projects can be justified, or is the steel industry once again exhibiting the herd mentality that led to so many idle new seamless pipe mills? Can the new mills produce to quality levels that will allow them to enter automotive and even tinplate markets, or will they all compete for the low end of the commodity sheet market? Finally, if the answer to each of the three previous questions is yes, who will be driven out of business to make way for the new capacity?

SCRAP: PLENTIFUL OR SCARCE?

The first challenge to any new minimill, whether it produces flat-rolled or long products, is to secure a reliable supply of iron feedstock, usually in the form of scrap. The U.S. price of benchmark grades of scrap fluctuates over a wide range during a business cycle, with the peak prices approaching double the inflation-adjusted (real) prices of each trough. In recent years, this has meant nominal prices ranging, for example, from $84 per gross ton in November 1992 to $142 in January 1995 for the benchmark grade of Number 1 heavy melting scrap[2]. Scrap prices not only vary with time, but also show major differences regionally and by grade of scrap. Premium grades, such as cut structurals and plate, or railroad scrap, such as rail crops and wheels, command a premium of up to 25 percent over Number 1 heavy melting scrap, increasing as the maximum size of the sheared or burned pieces declines. Conversely, inferior grades—those requiring further cutting or sorting, or needing further operations to remove zinc, tin, or other metal residuals—receive lower prices.

The quality of steel produced by the electric furnace method depends on the quality of the scrap charged into the furnace. Metallic elements other than iron that are contained in the scrap charge become residual alloy elements in the finished steel. Even high-quality grades of scrap, such as Number 1 heavy melting scrap, contain residual elements that exceed the permitted limits for higher grades of flat-rolled steel. An electric-furnace, flat-rolled steel mill must, therefore, find ways to improve its iron sources—diluting the impurities in its purchased scrap with virgin iron—or it must limit its production to lower-quality grades of sheets. While sheets produced from scrap alone may be acceptable for most merchant uses, it cannot be employed for automotive or appliance uses or for other applications requiring high strength and formability, such as tinplate.

The highest-quality scrap is by definition low-residual scrap, with known, consistent chemical and metallurgical properties, usually generated from a single source. The ideal source is, of course, home scrap—scrap generated internally within a steel mill. Next to home scrap, prompt industrial scrap or factory bundles represent the next best source of metallics—consistent quality steel returned from stamping plants, for example. After this comes the great majority of scrap tonnage: obsolete scrap, generated from the recycling of metal products at the end of their useful lives—whether cans, cars, appliances, machinery, or buildings. Home and prompt industrial scrap generation is not affected by the price of scrap. It is essentially all recycled and varies only with levels of production in the economic cycle. The supply of obsolete scrap, on the other hand, is sensitive to the price it commands, expanding (especially in lower-quality grades) when scrap prices increase.

Over the last twenty years, a number of trends have changed the nature of the scrap market. Several of these trends have led to a tightening in the market:

- Increased continuous casting and the use of outside processors has diminished home scrap generation.
- Improved quality steel shipments (fewer rejections) and more efficient processing methods (higher yields) have led to declining prompt industrial scrap generation.
- Reduced velocity of circulation of steel as products become more durable (longer life cycle) has threatened obsolete scrap generation.
- Demand has increased from electric furnaces and from increased scrap use in BOFs.
- Costs of scrap processors have increased, notably from environmental regulation.
- There has been greater use of galvanized and other coated steels, which require more expensive processing techniques.

Offsetting these market-tightening trends have been a number of opposite ones:

- Industrial production has increased, partly offsetting the decline in prompt industrial scrap generation.
- The recyclability of many products has improved, due to auto and appliance dismantling standards, among others.
- Scrap sorting techniques have improved, so that less metal is lost in municipal landfills.
- Scrap collection networks have expanded, increasing the proportion of used steel actually recovered.
- Demand from open-hearth furnaces has been eliminated, and demand from foundries has declined.

The deceptive net result of these trends has been the appearance of remarkable stability in the scrap market seen from a tonnage viewpoint.

Domestic U.S. scrap consumption has varied over the economic cycle by only 10 to 15 percent from peak to trough, while cyclical peaks have slowly risen at a trend rate of around 2 percent per annum. Scrap consumption in the 1980s ranged from a low of 48 million tons in 1983 to a high of 58 million tons in 1989, while an additional 10 to 12 million tons were exported throughout the decade. In the 1990s nearly 60 million tons of scrap have been consumed in the peak years of 1990 and 1994, while the cyclical low was 53.8 million tons in 1991.[3] In 1994, of the 60 million tons of scrap used, 55 million tons were purchased scrap, of which 53 million tons was generated domestically and 2 million imported. On the other hand, 10 million tons were exported, so that the domestic scrap processing industry generated 63 million tons. In theory, the exported tonnage could be diverted to meet domestic requirements, and the scrap industry does not appear to be near its capacity limit to collect and process high-residual grades of scrap. The recovery of 63 million tons compares with the absorption into the economy that year of over 110 million tons of steel products (domestically produced and imported), so that a high percentage of steel goods are still not returned to the scrap stream at the end of their useful lives. Taking a longer time perspective, scrap recovery has averaged only 40 percent of steel absorption in the economy 15 years previously (the typical life of a steel product), according to the leading U.S. scrap analyst, Stephen Wulff of the David J. Joseph Company.[4] The prospects for increased recovery appear strong, both from potentially increased scrap prices and from social and political trends toward increased recycling. While the average real costs of scrap feed may have increased as home scrap and other captive supplies have diminished, the average prices of traded scrap at cyclical peaks and valleys have remained similar in real terms across the last three business cycles.

Against this optimistic global picture must be set the reality of a highly fragmented scrap market. The relatively low market value of scrap means that freight costs are a high proportion of any mill's delivered scrap costs, ranging from 10 to 30 percent of total cost. This effectively limits scrap markets to the radius of around 300 land miles from the point of origin, although the availability of rivers and seaports dramatically changes the nature of the transportation equation. The scrap market has become much more homogeneous in the last two decades, as most minimills have lost control of "their" semicaptive local scrap generators and been forced to search farther afield for scrap, dislocating other local markets. Even mills with their own networks of scrap processors have not been protected, as scrap sellers have become more sophisticated about seeking the best price for their material.

Scrap availability was one constraint in the site selection of the 1980s second generation of minimill projects, which require from 300,000 to 600,000 tons a year of purchased scrap; other factors included power rates and local markets. A 1990s flat-rolled minimill with two to three times the annual scrap requirement faces a much greater challenge; the quality demands of flat-rolled steelmaking for low-residual metallic inputs compounds the problem. The site selection equation is now heavily weighted toward the logistics of supplying scrap or scrap substitutes, with proximity to water transport and multiple rail lines being desirable. Of the nine sites chosen for greenfield flat-rolled minimills through late 1995, seven have water transport adjacent. Only Nucor's original Crawfordsville, Indiana, location and Steel Dynamics' Delta, Ohio, site (west of Toledo) are remote from water transport options, although both are in the heart of the rich manufacturing and scrap-generating belt of Chicago–Detroit–northern Ohio. Nucor's third flat-rolled mill location, north of Charleston, South Carolina, is the first true flat-rolled minimill on an ocean site, where it will be able to use the company's iron carbide source in Trinidad as well as scrap brought by ocean barge from the Northeast and overseas.

Table 8.3 shows the current and possible future balances of metallics supplies, showing the 1993 to 1995 peak of one steel cycle and assuming that the year 2000 will be close to the top of the next demand cycle. The impact of the addition of 15 million tons of electric furnace steelmaking capacity depends very largely on the future patterns of U.S. trade in steel. Significant tonnages of blast furnace/BOF steelmaking will be displaced if the pattern of U.S. steel imports and exports remains largely unchanged. There will be less idle integrated capacity, however, if 1995 exchange rates prevail throughout the balance of the decade, as U.S. exports and import substitution allow a significant increase in domestic product shipments.

The possible outcomes shown as Cases A and B in the table imply that integrated capacity—the higher-cost producers—will be the marginal or "swing" capacity whose operation will depend on the increase of overall shipments. Scrap demand, then, is relatively similar in both cases, as electric furnace production is maintained at a high level even under less favorable industry outcomes.

The increased scrap and substitutes demand forecast would be met if the planned domestic and captive offshore DRI/HBI/iron carbide

TABLE 8.3
FORECAST U.S. METALLICS REQUIREMENTS

(millions of net tons)

	1993	1994	1995	2000 Case A	2000 Case B	% Change, 1993 vs. 2000 Case A
Apparent U.S. demand [a]	99.5	102.5	101	102.5	102.5	+2.8
Net U.S. imports [a]	(10.5)	(11)	(10.5)	(10.5)	(3.5)	no change
Steel mill product shipments	89.0	91.5	90.5	92	99	+3.37
Raw steel production	97.9	100.7	99.6	100.2	108	+2.35
[% Electric arc furnace]	[39]	[39]	[40]	[51]	[49]	[+12 points]
Metallics required	113.5	116.7	114.5	115	124	+1.3
Blast furnace hot metal	52.6	54.2	53	41	46	-22.1
Imported pig iron [b]	0.9	1.5	1	1	1	+10
Scrap and substitutes needed	60	61	60.5	73	77	+21.67
Home scrap production	11	11	10	10	10	-9
Prompt scrap production	15	14	14	12	12	-20
Obsolete scrap production	44.5	44.5	44.5	51	52	+14.6
Net scrap exports	(10.5)	(10)	(9.5)	(6)	(4)	-42.85
DRI/HBI/Iron carbide use [c]	1.5	1.5	1.5	6	7	+300

NOTES:
a Excluding slab and other semifinished imports for steel mills
b Excluding ferroalloys
c Domestic production plus imports
Case A: Assumes that a recovery in the value of the dollar against other major currencies prevents U.S. mills achieving significant growth in exports; the net import levels remain unchanged.
Case B: Assumes that the exchange rates prevailing in 1995 allow a major increase in U.S. steel exports to levels in the region of 10 to 12 million tons per annum.
Both cases assume that continuing efficiencies in steelmaking and manufacturing will maintain low growth in steel demand and a continuing slow fall in the generation of home and prompt scrap.

capacity is commissioned, and if the recovery of obsolete scrap grows by around 3 percent a year. Such growth is probable given continued political support for recycling and no major fall in scrap prices. Finally, the forecast assumes a fall in scrap exports, driven by changes in the pattern of U.S. consumption rather than by any reduction in overseas demand. U.S. scrap exports are largely from the Northeast, Houston, and California. These areas still have a scrap surplus that can support exports, given their high concentrations of both population and manufacturing industry and the relatively low local demand from EF steelmaking. The balance in some of these markets will change quickly if, for example, California Steel Industries built a new EF melt shop in the Los Angeles area, or if steelmaking resumed at the Baytown (Houston) melt shop.

In the near term, it appears that there is no shortage of scrap in the United States. Globally, increased scrap generation—notably from the former Soviet Union and Eastern Europe, but also from the mature consumer economies of Japan and Western Europe—is likely to hold down the prices realized from exporting scrap. What is likely in the United States, however, is an increasing spread between the prices of low-residual and high-residual grades as the demand mix changes. The first generation of minimills, producing metallurgically undemanding products such as rebar, could use a high-residual, poor-quality scrap mix. With the diversification of minimills into higher-quality wire and bar products in the late 1970s, scrap quality became a critical issue, and the spread between the prices of different grades of scrap began to widen. The third-generation, flat-rolled minimills are skewing demand toward the high end of scrap quality to an unprecedented degree. Industry analysts are divided as to whether this will have a decisive impact on the economics of the flat-rolled mills. With 15 to 20 million extra annual tons of EF steelmaking capacity likely to come on stream in North America, however, major minimill companies are forced to hedge their bets and invest in scrap substitutes.

SCRAP SUBSTITUTES

The alternatives to EF dependence on fluctuating scrap prices involve the use of virgin iron units produced from iron ore, usually in varying combinations with scrap according to the costs and availability of different scrap grades. Electric furnaces can, in theory, be charged with any mixture of scrap; pig iron from blast furnaces, which is essentially 100 percent pure iron; or directly reduced sponge iron produced in a furnace from ore by a number of processes that result in a product with typically over 90 percent iron content. The remainder of the sponge iron content is a mix of carbon (from the furnace fuel) and gangue (inert earthy residues from the ore), which are lost in gas and slag from the electric furnace; no contaminating metals are present. DRI is often converted to hot briquetted iron (HBI), in which the sponge iron is formed at high temperature into evenly shaped pellets known as briquettes, for greater convenience in transport and charging into steelmaking furnaces. A somewhat purer form of DRI, iron carbide, has a typical iron content of around 92 percent, the balance being carbon. Even purer molten iron can be produced from DRI by the Corex method, a coal-fueled, two-stage technology developed in South Africa that converts the sponge iron into molten iron in a second, higher-temperature reaction similar to that in a blast furnace. Further coal-based processes for the manufacture of iron are under development.

Typical commodity flat-rolled grades of steel call for a "recipe" of electric furnace charge that includes from 25 to 30 percent virgin iron units, based on the prevailing residual levels in common grades of scrap in North America. The actual mix of iron feed materials chosen to supply any electric furnace mill is the outcome of a trade-off between the costs of different feed materials and the quality of steel required. As with different grades of scrap, the cost of different types of scrap substitute (virgin iron) feedstock is roughly proportional to the purity of the iron units supplied, although the limited trade in sponge iron and pig iron means that prices are more negotiable than for scrap. In 1994, about 6.4 million tons of DRI and HBI were traded worldwide, twice the level of two years previously. The lack of a widespread market in established grades of DRI historically made mills hesitant to depend on non-captive suppliers, especially from distant parts of the world, but DRI trade is likely to grow rapidly in the remainder of the 1990s.

DRI production has been developed chiefly in areas where ore and energy are available cheaply and scrap is scarce. In 1994, around 27 million tons of DRI/HBI was produced, or around 5 percent of the worldwide production of blast furnace iron. Nearly 90 percent of the world's DRI production capacity was in developing countries, in Latin America, Southeast Asia, and the Middle East, where natural gas is available cheaply. Some production was also undertaken in India and South Africa from coal-fueled DRI processes. In developed countries, relatively small amounts were produced at a handful of plants in Russia, Canada, and the United States, where cheap, long-term supplies of natural gas could be obtained. In 1994, the United States imported 1 million tons of DRI from Venezuela and Russia, essentially all for consumption in electric furnaces; and about 500,000 tons of DRI was produced domestically, all at Georgetown Steel at Georgetown, South Carolina. Other DRI-based steelmakers in the North American market, are at Hylsa in Monterrey, Mexico; Tamsa, also in Monterrey; and Ispat group mills in Trinidad and Tobago (Iscott), Mexico (Lazaro Cardenas), and Quebec, Canada (Sidbec-Dosco). Other U.S. companies that have operated DRI plants are Oregon Steel, at Portland, Oregon, and the former Armco mill in Houston, Texas.

The economics of DRI hinge on the availability of cheap energy and the price of its competitor, low-residual scrap. DRI plants could not operate profitably in the United States as long as scrap of adequate quality was available at lower prices than the production cost of DRI.

Thus, in the case of the Oregon Steel plant, for example, a rise in the price of natural gas combined with low scrap prices to cause the plant's mothballing in 1984. The production cost per ton of DRI in the United States today is estimated to be in the range of $120 to $130, although the one current producer understandably does not disclose its actual numbers. This is attractive if the price of Number 1 heavy-melting scrap—a qualitatively inferior product—is sustained at close to $130, as has been the case in most U.S. markets since late in 1993. In countries with lower natural gas, iron ore, and labor costs, such as Venezuela, production costs may be as low as $80 per ton, although capital costs and freight to the consuming steel mill must be added.

Although a variety of coal-based DRI processes have been successfully commercialized in India and South Africa—countries that lack plentiful supplies of both natural gas and scrap—to date the two lowest-cost processes in most markets, and therefore the most widespread, are the gas-fueled Midrex and HYL processes. In North America, the Midrex process, developed by the Midland-Ross Corporation in the 1970s and now owned by Japan's Kobe Steel, is used at Georgetown and at Sidbec-Dosco. The Midrex unit at Oregon Steel is not expected to be restarted, but in Canada, Sidbec-Dosco reopen in 1995 an idled, second DRI unit, to increase its DRI-to-scrap mix from 50/50 to 70/30.[5] Mexico's Hylsa developed its own HYL process, which has been adopted at three Mexican steelmakers that, as in Venezuela, benefit from government policies promoting the use of inexpensive natural gas for industrial development. Ispat, the world's largest DRI steelmaker with approximately 6 million annual tons of capacity in four countries, looks set to standardize on the Midrex process it uses in Canada, Trinidad, and Indonesia, and will supplement its Mexican DRI production by adding a Midrex unit to the Lazaro Cardenas mill's existing HYL modules.

IRON PLANTS: THE NEXT BOOM

In late 1996, the United States had five new iron plants—DRI, HBI, or iron carbide—under construction, while three more projects in the Caribbean also aimed at the U.S. market. Each of these developments was triggered by the sustained high price of scrap and a relatively low price for natural gas in North America. With Number 1 heavy-melting scrap trading around its apparent ceiling level of $130 to $140 a ton, natural gas–fueled DRI is now competitive in those parts of North

America where gas is available on long-term contracts priced significantly below spot prices, which range seasonally and regionally from $1 to $1.60 per million British Thermal Units (BTUs).

The first new DRI plant in the United States in fifteen years is expected to open in early 1997 outside Mobile, Alabama. Owned by British Steel, the new plant uses two Midrex modules that had been purchased in the 1980s for use at Hunterston, in Scotland, but were never operated there.[6] The location makes use of the availability of plentiful local natural gas and the proximity of two new flat-rolled minimills that need the plant's output, British Steel's wholly owned Tuscaloosa Steel and 25 percent-owned Trico Steel.

A second new Midrex DRI plant is being built in Louisiana by GS Industries, with participation by Birmingham Steel, with a capacity of 1.2 million tons per year. On its completion in late 1997, the new plant will supplement the existing 500,000 tons that GS produces for its Georgetown Steel mill and in addition supply part of the iron requirements of both GS's Kansas City mill and Birmingham's new Memphis melt shop. Each of these mills produces billets for high-carbon and other high-quality wire rod products, and each has a steelmaking capacity of over 1 million tons; depending on the future production mix at the two mills, they may take all the DRI output available from the new plant.[7]

The pioneer of flat-rolled minimills, Nucor, has moved in a different direction to secure future supplies of virgin iron units. Although using conventional DRI imported from Russia for up to 15 percent of its feedstock mix at both the Crawfordsville and Hickman mills since their start-up, Nucor chose to pioneer the commercialization of iron carbide production. Iron carbide offers a number of cost advantages over conventional DRI, apart from producing a higher-grade product. Iron carbide can use iron ore fines rather than pellets; the product does not need to be briquetted; and it has a lower net energy use, all of which save around $10 per ton. On safety grounds, iron carbide is not flammable in the presence of water, as is conventional DRI, although it must still be kept completely dry throughout its transit to the consuming mill to avoid the hazard of steam explosions in steelmaking furnaces due to any dampness in the furnace charge.

In 1994 Nucor started up the first commercial-scale iron carbide plant on the island of Trinidad, sited geographically between the Venezuelan ore fields—accessible by barge via the Orinoco River—and southern U.S. ports. The republic of Trinidad and Tobago also offered Nucor an English-speaking location within the preferential tariff regime of the

Caribbean Basin Initiative and plentiful, cheap natural gas, which already supports a local DRI-based steel industry. The target production cost of iron carbide in Trinidad was estimated prior to the plant's start-up to be in the region of $79 per ton, including $55 of cash (operating) costs.[8] The initial iron carbide module suffered from mechanical start-up problems that have increased these costs somewhat, but the plant has demonstrated the economic practicality of the product for U.S. electric furnace mills. A delivered cost of little more than $100 a ton appears to be likely at full production levels. Expansion of the plant from one 320,000-tons-per-year module to four was planned for the rest of the 1990s, while Nucor's third flat-rolled minimill was due to be completed in 1997 at a waterside location near Charleston, South Carolina, to which iron carbide could be shipped directly from Trinidad. Based on current plans, iron carbide may provide around 20 percent of the total metallics charge at Nucor flat-rolled mills during the latter part of the decade. The availability of iron carbide by ocean freight from Trinidad will allow Nucor to make flat-rolled steel in areas deficient in high-quality scrap, including not only the southeast U.S. but also potentially on the West Coast.

Other North American electric-furnace steelmakers are likely to become major users of scrap substitutes over the next decade. Birmingham Steel, for example, announced in July 1995 that it expected to use HBI for up to 70 percent of the raw material needs of its new electric furnace meltshop under construction near Memphis, Tennessee. Later that year the company purchased a stake in GS Industries' planned Louisiana DRI plant, but indicated that it would also study options for its own DRI/HBI plant in the southern United States, or for entering a long-term partnership with an existing South American HBI producer.[9] The Memphis mill is designed to produce billets for the company's long products mills, notably to allow the American Steel and Wire division to be a more competitive player in high-quality wire products than is possible when it depends on purchased billets. Although the new Memphis mill reinforces Birmingham Steel's concentration on long products, the company has long expressed interest in the flat-products market, and a captive source of HBI could expand its options for entry into flat products.

BHP Steel of Australia, which is a partner with North Star Steel in a new, 1.5-million-ton-per-year flat-rolled mill at Delta, Ohio, opened in 1996, indicated that it expects the Ohio mill to use up to 30 percent HBI. BHP Steel is constructing a new 2-million-ton-per-year HBI plant in Western Australia, although its distance from inland Delta makes it unlikely that BHP will supply the U.S. mill from that source.[10] BHP is also considering long-range plans to backward-integrate its cold-rolling and coil-coating operations on the U.S. West Coast, where the use of imported HBI would presumably be more practical. BHP was studying a possible DRI plant in Venezuela to supply North American markets, with a decision expected before the end of 1996.

Qualitech Steel, a new company founded in 1994 and led by Gordon Geiger, a pioneer of iron carbide and former executive of North Star Steel, was preparing to build a 660,000-ton-per-year iron carbide plant on the U.S. Gulf Coast, which would supply the same company's planned 500,000-ton-per-year Indiana special quality bar mill as well as sell iron carbide on the open market. Steel Dynamics, the new flat-rolled minimill led by Keith Busse, has purchased a minority position in Qualitech's project and will take part of the output. However Steel Dynamics also plans eventually to build a 500,000-ton-per-year HBI plant near its mill at Butler, Indiana. The flat-rolled minimill is expected to use around 40 percent scrap substitutes in its feed.

Not only are steelmakers entering the DRI boom. In March 1996, Tondu Corporation of Houston, a company that manages power plants and develops industrial projects in oil and gas, announced that it would build a DRI plant on the Mississippi River in Burnside, Louisiana. The plant had a planned initial capacity of 1.5 million tons per year.

Midrex Direct Reduction Corporation, the engineering subsidiary of Japan's Kobe Steel that licenses its proprietary DRI technology to others, was studying construction of a plant on the Gulf Coast. The Kobe-Midrex joint venture, to be known as KM Iron LLC, would produce 900,000 metric tons per year of DRI by Midrex's new Fastmet process.

Oregon Steel, which operated a Midrex DRI module in the 1970s, participated briefly in the Comsigua HBI project in Venezuela, but pulled out in early 1996. That project, led by a consortium of Kobe Steel and Japanese trading companies, will start-up in late 1998 and supply about 1 million tons to export markets. It will supplement another Kobe-managed plant in Venezuela, Opco, which started up in 1990 and produces around 900,000 tons a year, primarily for shipment to the United States.

Finally Cleveland-Cliffs, the iron-ore mining company, was studying a DRI plant in Trinidad and Tobago, as well as options for coal-based DRI to be produced close to its Minnesota mines.

Assuming most of these planned facilities are completed, U.S. consumption of scrap substitutes could increase from 2.5 million tons in 1994 to as much as 10 million tons in 1999. While this level of increase does not approach the level of increased EF capacity in the decade, which is likely to approach 20 million tons between flat-rolled and long products projects, it is likely to offset a potential shortage of low-residual scrap.

In addition to the rising use of new sources of iron, another foreseeable development is increased trade in blast furnace pig iron. Although merchant blast furnaces were numerous in the United States through the 1960s, producing both for independent steelmakers and for iron castings manufacturers, they were extinct by the early 1990s. Electric furnace producers have proved reluctant to depend in any way on their integrated rivals for any portion of their iron supply, so trade in pig iron for steelmaking has dwindled to around 2 million tons per year, largely sales between integrated mills to meet spot shortages. About 1 percent of the total U.S. electric furnace charge in 1995 was of pig iron, including consumption at EFs within integrated steel mills and producers of steel castings. This low number reflects in part the decline of electric furnace steelmaking at integrated companies, for whom pig iron use in electric furnaces was historically much more common; at least one integrated mill, Armco's former Houston, Texas, plant, operated blast furnaces exclusively to supply electric steelmaking (supplemented in the late 1970s by DRI). The pouring, cooling, transport, and reheating of pig iron represents a significant cost penalty compared with its immediate use in steelmaking within the same mill, due in part to the need to make the "pigs," or iron ingots, small enough to be recharged into an electric furnace easily. Nevertheless, the economics of merchant pig iron sales are not radically different from those of semifinished steel sales. With excess blast furnace capacity now apparently available in Eastern Europe, some revival in traded blast furnace pig iron seems likely.

In the production of pig iron, alternatives to blast furnaces are likely to be the next major commercial development in North American steelmaking. The use of coal-based processes such as Corex, already commercialized in South Africa and Korea, is likely to be introduced commercially in the United States in the next few years. As these technologies are most likely to benefit existing integrated steelmakers, they are considered in more detail in the following chapter. Nevertheless, the existence of an increasing range of iron sourcing options is likely to continue to hold down scrap prices and to further blur the distinctions between integrated and nonintegrated producers.

On the whole, it appears that the new generation of electric furnace mills will not face difficulties in sourcing adequate metallics supplies, but that those mills with their own sources of virgin iron units will be in better competitive shape over time. If the current estimates of delivered costs of scrap substitutes hold true—around \$100 to \$120 fully costed at a midwestern mill—then such material will have a significant cost advantage during peak periods of the business cycle, when low-residual scrap commands over \$130 per ton today and may go to higher short-term peaks when faced with increased demand from new EF capacity. Conversely, in periods of weak demand, low residual scrap costs are likely to fall as before below \$100 per ton, and import DRI prices will likely follow suit. It is probable, however, that the next cycle's troughs and peaks will show real increases over past cycles, reflecting the need for higher prices to attract the increased generation of scrap needed to satisfy the additional electric furnace capacity in North America.

THE ECONOMICS OF FLAT-ROLLED MINIMILLS

The comparative costs of minimills and integrated mills may be broadly divided into three categories: raw materials costs, operating costs (variable steelmaking, rolling, and finishing costs), and capital costs.

The scrap prices prevailing in the period from 1993 to 1996 may represent a worst case for raw materials for electric furnace mills. The consistently high demand failed to sustain average Number 1 heavy-melting scrap prices above the \$140-a-ton ceiling, and the average cost of the furnace charge of most carbon EF mills remained well below this level. Even those mills facing demanding quality requirements—producers of flat-rolled products, special bar quality, and high-end wire rod mills—rarely exceeded an average raw material cost of \$130 a ton, taking into account their home and captive sources of scrap, purchased DRI/HBI, and a proportion of lower-cost, higher-residual material diluted in the overall mix. At such top-of-the-cycle costs, electric furnace producers are still competitive with the hot metal costs of integrated producers, whose raw material costs are cyclically more stable given captive sources and long-term contracts. The best U.S. integrated mills had hot-metal iron costs in 1995 in the region of \$130 per ton. After steelmaking (BOF/EF) and casting, these raw materials numbers translate into 1995 slab costs of around \$200 a ton at Nucor-type minimills versus the same \$200 a ton at the lowest-cost integrated mills.[11] Table 8.4 shows the estimated 1995 costs per ton of representative minimills and integrated mills.

TABLE 8.4
ESTIMATED 1995 U.S. OPERATING COSTS PER NET TON, INTEGRATED MILLS VERSUS FLAT-ROLLED MINIMILLS

Production Stage (cumulative costs)	Flat-Rolled Minimill	Lowest-Cost Integrated Mill	Average of Integrated Mills	Minimill Advantage vs. Average
Iron inputs	$ 130	$ 130	$ 135	$ 5
Liquid steel	$ 180	$ 185	$ 200	$ 20
Slab ex-caster	$ 210	$ 215	$ 230	$ 20
Hot-rolled band	$ 250	$ 250	$ 290	$ 40
Cold-rolled coil	$ 300	$ 320	$ 400	$ 100
HD galvanized coil	$ 375	$ 450	$ 485	$ 110

Steelmaking costs in minimills are therefore comparable to those in integrated mills in the worst case, with peak scrap costs; but the integrated mills face progressively worse costs at other times in the economic cycle. As demand falls, scrap prices fall significantly, more than offsetting reduced economies of volume for the minimills. Integrated mills, with their high nonfinancial fixed costs of maintaining mines, lake freighters, coke ovens, and the like, are much more volume sensitive and have increased per-ton costs of iron- and steel-making. In a year of lower volumes and scrap costs, such as 1992, the comparable slab costs were around $185 a ton for Nucor's minimills and $205 for the most efficient integrated mills. During a declining market, then, costs rise per ton in integrated mills while costs fall in minimills. In an average business cycle, integrated mills may be able to compete on operating cost for between a quarter and a third of the time; in other years they face significant cost penalties.

From the hot metal stage to the shipping of finished products, the minimills' advantage over U.S. integrated mills increases progressively. While an extensively modernized, in-line casting/continuous hot-strip mill facility such as LTV's Cleveland Direct Hot Charge Complex has operating costs through hot-band production of as low as $250 per ton, close to Nucor's cost at Hickman and Crawfordsville, more typical Class I integrated mill hot-band costs are in the region of $270 to $280, while Class II (smaller and older) integrated mills go as high as $320 per ton. Nucor's hot-band advantage, under tight scrap market conditions, appears to be in the region of $40 per ton against the average of all U.S. integrated producers and may grow to as much as $70 per ton in weak scrap markets. In downstream processing, the great advantage of minimills in cold-rolling and galvanizing is due to management policies and labor productivity rather than to any technological reason. Significant growth in independent cold-rolling and galvanizing companies has occurred in the 1990s due to the relatively high costs of cold-rolling and galvanizing at integrated mills.

The minimill advantage is not uniform or universal. The lowest-cost integrated producer hot-strip mills, for example, may actually have lower operating costs at high throughput levels, due to the much greater speeds of the Generation II continuous hot-strip mills than the "compact" strip mills installed at minimills. Nevertheless, compared to the average of existing U.S. integrated sheet capacity, the operating cost advantage of 10 percent in hot band, or 30 percent in value-added, products represents a dramatic change in the economics of the industry. The advantage may be expected to increase over time even without the expected improvements in raw materials costs over a business cycle. Minimill flat-rolled production is an essentially new process in which a learning curve effect may be expected to generate cost savings over time as operations are refined. Integrated flat-rolled production is a mature process in which—thanks to the remarkable process of transformation that many integrated mills have undergone—most of the identifiable, "easy" process improvements and cost savings have already been realized. In theory, it should be harder for mature, integrated mills to continue to reap cost improvements over the next decade than for new minimills.

Capital costs represent the other major category of cost advantage for minimill flat-rolled producers. A direct comparison of capital costs between integrated and minimill producers is difficult, because the dates of construction (and therefore the historic costs), the financing methods, and the depreciation schedules used will differ widely between any two steel mills. Moreover, any steel mill requires continuous capital expenditure—whether of a "maintenance" basis such as furnace relines, or to upgrade or replace facilities to meet changing product requirements. Each facility will therefore be unique in the details of its capital costs and balance sheet. Older facilities may appear to have lower capital costs than new ones—U.S. Steel or Bethlehem Steel show lower interest and depreciation charges than Korea's POSCO, for example—but may require larger annual capital spending just to maintain production levels.

The most objective comparison of minimill versus integrated mill capital costs is to identify the per-ton capital costs of new construction of each process, using greenfield sites to eliminate distorting site-specific factors. No new integrated plant has been constructed in North

America since Stelco's Lake Erie mill in the early 1970s. Nevertheless, cost estimates, using the costs of new integrated facilities in Korea and elsewhere applied to U.S. conditions, and using actual costs of recent integrated mill equipment purchases for retrofits, show that the cost quoted for U.S. Steel's canceled Conneault mill project, abandoned in 1979, remains representative. The $3.6 billion price tag for a 3-million-ton mill, complete from sinter plant and coke ovens through to cold-rolling mill, is probably largely unchanged. Cost inflation of factors such as construction labor and permitting may have been offset by price reductions for engineering, equipment, and materials supplies. A similar-size greenfield plant today would cost at least $1,000 per ton of installed annual capacity through the hot-strip mill, while smaller, conventionally configured integrated mills would probably cost up to 20 percent more per ton. The cost of Nucor's first flat-rolled mill, Crawfordsville, was initially $265 million for the 1 million tons of raw steel capacity in its first phase, plus some $75 million in additional start-up costs, including modifications to the hot-strip mill. The cost of the pioneering thin-slab caster itself was reportedly around $70 million, with a money-back guarantee given by the German manufacturer SMS. The economics of Crawfordsville look even better when the capacity expansion of its second phase are included: the additional cost of a second caster and associated equipment to boost capacity to 1.8 million tons of raw steel was only about $40 million. The total cost per installed ton of around $220 (not including cold rolling and galvanizing, added later) was less than a quarter of the cost of the hypothetical integrated mill, and Crawfordsville's costs were presumably inflated to some degree by the start-up and learning costs of being the first commercial user of the technology.[12]

Similar project costs have been announced for minimills under construction in the mid-1990s. Gallatin Steel, which began operations in early 1995, cost a reported $360 million through its hot-strip mill. Like the two Nucor mills, Gallatin's initial capacity of around 1 million tons per year will be increased at low cost by the addition in 1997-98 of a second caster, which should bring down the eventual cost per ton of capacity from $360 to perhaps $210. Steel Dynamics, the Butler, Indiana, minimill, cost $354 million for its 700,000-ton capacity first phase. This gives a much higher initial capital cost, around $500 per capacity ton, but includes a "second-generation" SMS casting/rolling facility to produce much thinner hot-rolled sheets than the Nucor or Gallatin mills, which will be able to substitute for cold-rolled steel in many applications. Steel Dynamics does plan to add cold-rolling and galvanizing later, like Nucor, at an additional cost of up to $180 million, and will probably also add a second caster to at least double its capacity. [13] Other reported capital costs include the Acme Steel project, using the existing BOF hot end, to install a thin-strip caster and hot-strip mill for $372 million (970,000-tons-per-year initial rolling capacity); the Ipsco mill at Montpelier, Iowa, costing $360 million including a Steckel mill (1 million tons per year); and the Dofasco "in-plant" minimill, costing U.S.$142 million for 1.35 million tons per year of slab capacity, with no hot-strip mill.

These representative numbers suggest that a "no-frills" 2-million-ton-per-year flat-rolled minimill can be built for as little as $400 million through the hot-strip mill, or $200 per ton. These numbers must be applied against a depreciation schedule and an estimate of the interest rate charged on the project's debt, to come up with a per-ton capital charge on top of the raw material and operating costs. Some of the 1990s flat-rolled minimills, especially those of start-up companies, have been financed largely from borrowing rather than equity. If 10 percent interest and a 12.5 year depreciation schedule are assumed, a per-ton capital charge of up to $36 per hot-rolled ton can be attributed. The equivalent for a new integrated plant, assuming it could be ever be financed, would be in the region of $170. More realistically, the actual depreciation and interest costs at major integrated companies in 1994, reflecting continuing "brownfield" capital expenditures, came to $60 per ton shipped. A significant proportion of this must be applied to downstream, finishing facilities, so that the actual capital charge per ton of hot-roll band may not be widely different from those for a highly leveraged new minimill.

Over time, the difference in capital costs between a flat-rolled minimill and an integrated plant might be expected to widen as the minimill operation ages and its construction debt is paid down. The major capital expenditures required to maintain stable levels of production at an integrated facility are greater by an order of magnitude than those for electric furnace steelmaking. The life of a battery of coke ovens is approximately twenty years, with expensive midlife rehabilitation necessary after around ten years. Similarly, each blast furnace needs a major reline every ten to fifteen years, with intermediate relines every five years or so. In 1994, for example, Bethlehem Steel spent approximately $300 million—the cost of a new minimill—to maintain the ironmaking capacity at its Burns Harbor plant. The money was spent to rebuild one of the mill's two coke batteries, at a cost of $200 million, and to reline one of its two blast furnaces, at a cost of $100 million. An additional $135 million was spent at Burns Harbor in 1993-94 to add pulverized coal injection (PCI) in the mill's two blast furnaces, to reduce the amount of coke required in ironmaking. Bethlehem will need to spend similar sums, equivalent to the cost of building a greenfield flat-rolled electric furnace mill, every four or five years just to maintain the ironmaking capacity of its two major integrated plants, Burns Harbor and Sparrows Point. Similarly, LTV Steel spent $145 million between 1993 and 1995 on three intermediate blast furnace relines, and $57 million on rehabilitation of two coke batteries. Each of the LTV investments will extend the life of the unit in question by only five years or so.[14] Each integrated steelmaker faces similar regular needs. Such expenditures may lead to small cost improvements—the addition of PCI may gain Bethlehem as much as $5 per ton—but essentially they are maintenance expenditures, necessary to prolong the life of an existing asset or to comply with safety and environmental standards.

Flat-rolled minimills face a fraction of these maintenance costs. Depending on the mix of scrap and purchased or internally sourced virgin iron units, the flat-rolled minimill may have little or no such continuing capital requirements. If a captive source of virgin iron is deemed necessary, the capital cost of new DRI/HBI capacity is a one-time expense of similar proportions to the recurrent needs of integrated ironmaking. Midrex DRI or Nucor's iron carbide capacity can be built at around $100 million for a half-million-ton-per-year capacity plant, appropriate for a typical flat-rolled minimill, or perhaps $360 million for a 2.5-million-ton-capacity unit, roughly equivalent in capacity to the ironmaking facilities on which Bethlehem spent $300 million at Burns Harbor. Once the initial expenditure is made, maintenance requirements of DRI furnaces, on the evidence of units installed in the 1970s, amount to about one-tenth of those of coke oven/blast furnace installations.

The continuing capital needs of in-place minimills are relatively small. Periodic replacements of the electric furnace bottom and shell, caster molds, and rolls are necessary, as they are for BOF/caster configurations in integrated mills. Major capital expenditures at existing long products minimills have focused on process improvement rather than maintenance—the upgrading of electric furnaces to use ultra-high power or conversion to DC furnaces, for instance, and the widespread introduction of ladle metallurgy. As operating experience with flat-rolled mills accumulates, it may be expected that similar incremental capacity and quality improvements will be made. However, by analogy with the older long products minimills, it is likely that the mills currently under construction will be able to operate for perhaps 30 years without the operational need (as opposed to the economic need) for further major capital spending. It is therefore possible to assume, when financing minimill flat-rolled capacity, the permanent reduction of debt from earnings over time, without the need for continuing heavy capital expenditure. This fact has contributed to the eagerness of investors to participate in the new U.S. flat-rolled capacity, and to the relative ease of financing such a proportionally large addition to U.S. capacity.

It would appear, then, that minimills have significant advantages over integrated mills in both operating costs and capital requirements. Initially, the capital cost advantage is minimal if the comparison is between a new minimill facility and an old integrated facility; but as the minimill ages, capital charges (before profits) should decline well below integrated mill levels. Similarly, the cost advantage of minimills in raw materials (iron units) may be negligible in times of high demand but are potentially great when scrap prices are at the low end of the cycle. It is also likely that as technologies such as iron carbide are more widely commercialized, the cost of scrap substitutes will fall. On all current cost indicators, the economics of flat-rolled minimills appear to justify the rush to build them. The remaining open question concerns the impact of the new capacity on prices. It is inevitable that the addition over a decade of between 15 and 20 million tons of additional capacity in a market served by 60 million tons of existing integrated capacity will depress transaction prices. The extent to which it does so depends in part on whether the new capacity will be competing across the full spectrum of flat-rolled products or limited to the low end of the range in terms of quality and value.

THE QUALITY DEBATE

The extent to which minimills will be able to compete with integrated producers at the higher end of the quality spectrum is one of the most intensely debated questions in the steel industry in the 1990s. As with many issues in the industry, this is both a technical and an economic question, and the answer also depends on the time frame concerned. Sheet product quality depends both on the quality of the metallic inputs—the issue of residual contaminants in scrap—and on the ability of the equipment, especially the caster, to roll a product that has both adequate surface quality and internal consistency to allow its use in more demanding applications.

Hot-strip mill products are commonly categorized as high end, midrange, or low end, depending on the product quality criteria they are able to meet. The most common, high end quality requirements are for tinplate—a product that must retain consistency of strength, shape, and surface quality while drawn to very thin gauges—and sheet for use in exposed automotive body applications, usually but not always electrogalvanized. In the middle of the product range are sheets for other automotive and appliance applications, including most coated and uncoated cold-rolled steels. At the low end are the commercial grades, generally heavier gauge, hot-rolled sheets sold through distributors to sheet metal fabricators for use in construction and less critical manufacturing applications. This low end also includes hot-dipped galvanized coils sold to duct manufacturers, coil plate, and most skelp or strip sold for conversion to pipe and tubing. Essentially all U.S. integrated flat-rolled mills are capable of producing midrange and low-end products; most of the major midwestern mills are also capable of producing high-end automotive grades. Of 60 million tons of integrated hot-strip mill capacity, about 40 million tons—usually but not entirely the largest and newest, Generation II hot-strip mills at the bigger companies sometimes known as Class I producers—can compete in the high-end market, but such mills need to sell a full range of grades to keep their order books full. Every flat-rolled producer—some two dozen companies in the United States and Canada—competes at the low end of the market. At the top end, seven U.S. and two Canadian producers compete in the tinplate market, and seven U.S. and two Canadian companies supply essentially all the auto body sheets.[15]

While it is difficult to pinpoint precisely which of the three divisions a given shipment fits into, it is generally accepted that the high-end category includes at least 20 percent of all flat-rolled shipments, including essentially all of the 4 million-plus tons per year of U.S. tinplate shipments and 5 to 6 million tons per year of automotive galvanized and cold-rolled sheets. In a year at the midpoint of recent steel cycles, with 50 million tons of shipments of flat-rolled products (including coiled plate but not including stainless), perhaps 10 million tons could indisputably be considered high end, and another 20 million tons—including most shipments to distributors, coil plate, and tube manufacturers—could indisputably be considered low end. The identity of the remainder could be debated profitlessly, but most probably belongs to the midrange gray area. Most flat-rolled imports, perhaps 5 out of 7 million tons in an average recent year, would belong in the low-end category.

On the basis of these rather arbitrary divisions, the initial minimill offerings from Nucor and from a minimill-type hot-strip mill operation like Beta Steel were clearly aimed at the low end of the market only. Given that the low end, including imports, accounts for nearly half the market, early minimill capacity had plenty of scope to enter the market without a major impact on prices. If on the other hand, by 1999 15 to 20 million tons of minimill capacity are competing for the same 25 million tons of demand with imports, the Class II integrated producers, and Class I mills trying to supplement their high-end business, the low-end market will be a very crowded place.

As the minimill capacity in commission increases and as experience with the process grows, each flat-rolled minimill producer (other than those focused solely on coil plate) intends to move up the quality scale. Nucor began the process almost as soon as it began shipments from Crawfordsville, with the early decisions to commit to cold-rolling and galvanizing facilities. To penetrate even midrange markets successfully, however, requires near-perfect surface quality. Thin-slab casters oscillate gently while operating, to keep the liquid steel flowing smoothly through the mold without sticking. The movement can scar the surface of the metal, resulting in imperfections that will be magnified when rolled into thin sheets. Conventional casters normally are configured to allow surface conditioning, or scarfing, of the slab before it is rolled down; the in-line configuration of the SMS compact strip process does not allow this. Companies are trying various ways of resolving this problem; one promising approach by the integrated company Inland Steel is the use of electromagnetic dams to keep the molten steel suspended away from the caster mold walls.

In the absence of successful commercial-scale demonstrations of such technology, some new minimills have taken what appears to be a step backward, and have settled on medium-slab casters rather than the thin-slab SMS casters. The Trico mill, for example, will use a Sumitomo caster producing slabs around 6 inches thick, rather than the 2 inches or less produced by the SMS casters. Armco-Mansfield has installed a Voest Alpine (VAI-Conroll) caster producing 4-inch-thick slabs for most applications. The medium-thickness slabs require more rolling, thereby adding costs; on the other hand, they potentially offer greater flexibility in terms of grades, gauges and alloys. The medium-slab minimills are clearly targeted at the mid-range applications and may prove able to supply high-end requirements. Steel Dynamics, at Butler, Indiana, will compete for the exposed auto body panel market using an SMS thin-slab caster; the company is convinced that "fine-tuning" the thin-slab technology can produce a high-quality product. Steel Dynamics' changes to the design of previous SMS installations include adding soft-shell reduction rolls at the caster to contain the configuration of the slab as it cools; this prevents the slab from forming small folds and edge cracks as it solidifies, similar to the cracks that appear in a bread loaf as it rises and bakes.[16]

The experience of steel distributors handling Nucor products, whether hot-rolled, cold-rolled, or galvanized, appears to bear out the company's claims that the material is acceptable for 80 percent of all applications—that is, for all but the indisputably high-end uses. A greater constraint than quality may in fact be the limited coil width and gauge range offered by Nucor. The Crawfordsville hot-strip mill can only roll up to 53 inches wide, thus making 48-inch coil the mill's largest-volume product, although the Hickman mill rolls 60-inch coils on a 61-inch hot-strip mill. Higher-end applications increasingly use 72-inch and wider coils; perhaps a quarter of the total carbon sheet demand is for coils wider than the 60-inch effective limit of the nonplate minimill capacity planned to date. In terms of thickness, mills such as Steel Dynamics', which is planned to roll hot strip down to 0.040 inch, or about 18 gauge, will surpass the minimum 14-gauge hot-rolled limit of the Nucor mills. This 18-gauge hot-rolled steel can compete with cold-rolled products when it is passed through a pickle line, temper mill, and stretcher-leveler.

STRATEGIES FOR MARKET ENTRY

Nucor's overall strategy for flat-rolled steel has followed the company's philosophy in long products: concentrate on the highest-volume commodity sizes in the market and price in such a way as to fill the mill's order books. Nucor has not needed to supply automakers or width and gauge niches to be successful; it has profited by supplying 36-, 48-, and 60-inch commodity coils to service centers and processors, the sector of the business that integrated mills find least attractive.

The cost structure of the producer frequently determines marketing strategies. High-cost producers have to realize a high price for their product, so they attempt to sell differentiated products in high-value niches. Low-cost producers can make money simply by increasing their volume throughput of undifferentiated, commodity products. Integrated mills have sought to produce high-value products and sell them directly to end users. With a few outstanding exceptions, such as the relationship between U.S. Steel and processor Worthington Industries, they have historically kept at arm's length from processors and distributors. To the mills, flat-rolled processors are both customers (for commodity products) and competitors (for value-added products). Mill management has sought to maximize the value added in-house to its product, pursuing niche marketing and product differentiation as a response to lower-cost imports, while the Steelworkers union has opposed the transfer of downstream functions to (usually) non-union labor outside the mill.

While integrated mill strategies have focused on making profits by selling the highest-value product possible, minimills have historically focused more on commodity steelmaking, and this philosophy has carried over into the flat-rolled marketplace. A minimill like Nucor tends to seek to maximize the profitability of its steelmaking rather than its downstream operations. It therefore has sought to guarantee throughput on its mills by partnerships with high-tonnage users of commodity sizes, in addition to its own captive users, such as Nucor Building Systems, a (reportedly marginally profitable) maker of prefabricated metal buildings. Located adjacent to the Hickman mill are a structural tube maker, Maverick Tube, and Skyline Steel, a flat-rolled service center; next to the Crawfordsville mill is a pickling line of Heidtman Steel Products; and the new Charleston mill will see a flat-rolled service center of Klockner Namasco Corporation.

Other new mills are seeking to attract such processors, both to guarantee base loads for their mills and to avoid the necessity of their own heavy downstream investment in facilities such as pickling lines. Examples are Gallatin Steel's attracting a pickling facility of processor Steel Technologies, Inc., and the decision by Worthington Industries to build pickling, slitting, and galvanizing facilities adjoining the North Star/BHP mill rather than build its own minimill. Such facilities take on much of the marketing responsibility traditionally retained by the integrated mill. The key minimill pricing decision becomes its hot-rolled, high-volume transfer price per ton to the small number of large downstream processor customers, whether published or privately negotiated; overall market prices to end users are of less importance.

A few new minimill entrants have the benefit of immediate, captive markets for significant tonnages of their steel. Gallatin's co-owner Dofasco has indicated that it could take up to a third of the mill's hot-band output in its first couple of years, to supply its cold-rolling mills in Hamilton, Ontario. In the longer term, however, Dofasco has decided to build an "in-house" minimill at Hamilton to augment the steel supply to its hot-strip mill and thereby to meet its cold mill's needs in-house. Nucor uses about 300,000 tons per year of flat-rolled steel internally at its steel deck and metal buildings operations, or less than 7 percent of the capacity of its first two flat-rolled mills; this represents a much lower share of mill throughput than Nucor uses from its bar mills, for its joist, fastener, and cold-finished bar divisions. Ultimately, neither captive nor partner downstream users will fill the order books of the minimill capacity coming on stream, although they will certainly give a significant boost to the prospects of mills with such relationships.

The alternative to a strategy of finding large-scale, commodity-user partners is to emulate the integrated suppliers, targeting higher value, niche markets, and trust that the minimills' quality and cost structures will allow such competition to be successful. One niche that minimills are pursuing is stainless steel, notably the 400 series grades used for such applications as automotive exhausts and fuel systems. The rebuilt Armco mill at Mansfield has historically divided its production between these grades and carbon steel to supply the company's Dover, Ohio, galvanizing facility; this mill's new thin slab caster configuration is designed to allow it to continue to compete against a player such as Nucor, which began producing Type 409 stainless at Crawfordsville in 1995 after the installation there of an AOD furnace.

The major test of a high-end strategy will be the acceptance of its product by automotive users for exposed applications. To position itself for this market, Steel Dynamics seeks to control much of its own iron supply in the form of captive HBI and iron carbide producers. It has made construction of high-quality finishing facilities a higher priority than expanding the mill's hot end to its optimum size. Ultimately, though, success in penetrating such markets will depend on the ability of the core technology, in this case the SMS thin slab caster, to move up the learning curve toward automotive-standard surface quality. The manufacturer is optimistic that such standards will be reached in the

1990s. In mid-1995 an SMS spokesman stated that there "is no doubt" about the ability of the process to achieve such standards and added that "the real goal is tinplate."[17]

Timing is a problem for the several minimill entrants into the flat-rolled steel market between 1995 and 1998. The weakness in the flat-rolled steel market that appeared in mid-1995 after a boom of almost two years did not herald a general downturn in the U.S. economy, but recessions cannot be postponed indefinitely. In the previous two recessions a shrinking economy caused a cut of between 5 and 6 million tons of flat-rolled steel consumption over a two year period. If this were to occur in 1997 or 1998, while at the same time nearly 10 million tons of new capacity comes on stream, the effect on a flat-rolled sector operating at a shipment rate of 52 to 54 million annual tons at the height of the cycle will be profound. Average capacity utilization would be cut from nearly 90 percent to around two-thirds; at which level prices could be reduced by up to 30 percent, based on past cycles. At such prices and operating rates, most integrated and many minimills will be losing money.

Such a scenario requires closer examination. Effective hot-strip mill capacity in the United States in mid-1995 amounted to approximately 68 million tons, excluding capacity dedicated solely to stainless steel. This number reflects an increase in 1994-95 of nearly 4 million tons, following the expansion of both Nucor's Hickman and Crawfordsville mills, the opening of Gallatin Steel, and the reopening of Caparo Steel's former Sharon mill. Apparent consumption of carbon hot-strip mill products during the peak demand period from late 1993 to early 1995 averaged 66 million tons, including coiled plate and strip converted to pipe and tubing, after deducting over a million annual tons of exports and adding in nearly 10 million tons of imports. Domestic shipments averaged over 57 million tons during the period, including exports, implying a shipping rate of around 84 percent of the industry's strip-mill capacity. This capacity utilization rate is lower than the rate for steelmaking, because of the imbalance between U.S. steelmaking and hot-strip mill capacity. Steelmaking capacity is now as much as 10 million tons less than installed hot-strip mill capacity. Some of this difference can be made up through slab imports, but their availability depends on exchange rates and the level of steel demand elsewhere. U.S. slab imports reached a high of 6.5 million tons in 1994 but quickly dropped again in 1995 to half that rate.

The addition of 10 million tons of flat-rolled capacity (steelmaking capacity, feeding new hot-strip mills) would automatically push down the early-1995 utilization rate to 73 percent, assuming no change in the levels of imports and exports. If a typical, but not severe, steel recession occurs, driven by cutbacks in automotive production and destocking by service centers, the domestic shipment rate could be expected to fall by around 6 million tons, to around 51 million tons. At this rate the capacity utilization rate would be only 65 percent.

Two variables in international trade could offset such a decline. U.S. imports have historically been less volume-sensitive on the down side than might be expected to both domestic demand and to fluctuating exchange rates. This is because both foreign mills and the trading companies and importers that bring in their steel normally choose to continue to serve existing customers in the United States, rather than walk away from the market when their margins are squeezed. Companies are reluctant to abandon their investment in building a position in the U.S. market, especially when conditions might reverse and make the market more attractive again later. This institutional inertia will maintain some significant degree of imports into the United States, although the increasing volume of low-cost domestic capacity will undoubtedly displace some imports. The low exchange rate of the U.S. dollar in 1995 could be expected to recover over time, but in the short run it also adds to the lack of appeal of U.S. markets at a time when Asian and European markets are healthy. It is therefore possible that, by 1997, domestic shipments will displace as much as three million tons of imports. Conversely, the United States is already approaching the point where its domestic costs and prices are low enough by world standards to induce significant increases in exports. Some observers foresee exports doubling from only 4 million tons in 1993 (just over 1 million of which was in carbon flat-rolled products) to around 8 million in 1997, with flat-rolled leading the growth. Mills such as U.S. Steel and Nucor made significant gains in coil shipments overseas in 1995 and 1996. As much as 4 million tons of flat-rolled exports are foreseeable in 1997 if European markets, which are lagging the U.S. business cycle by as much as three years, hold up.

If the optimistic forecasts for reduced imports and increased exports come true, domestic shipments in the next recession could be around 57 million tons; thus, the gains from shifts in trade patterns could offset the fall in domestic demand related to the business cycle. Nevertheless, these gains would come at a price; such business would have to be bought with low selling prices. They would still not push operating rates above around 73 percent, while average revenues would be cut dramatically.

In conditions such as the demand peak of 1993 to 1995, hot-rolled coil prices from U.S. domestic mills were in the range of $360 to $400, excluding spot "shortage" sales to nonregular buyers. Cold-rolled prices typically averaged over $100 more; Nucor's posted prices reached a high of $510 from the Crawfordsville mill. Hot-dip galvanized similarly commands an additional premium, of $30 to $50 over cold-rolled pricing, with peak prices in the range of $550 per ton. These peak price levels compare with cyclical trough pricing around 25 percent lower; around $280 to $300 for hot-rolled coil, with proportional reductions for cold-rolled and coated products. At both the peak and the trough of the cycle, transactions are made outside these ranges, notably (on the low side) for secondary material and for imports from producers without a track record, such as much of the Russian and Ukrainian coil imported to the U.S. in 1993-94; or (usually, but not always, on the high side) contract prices with automakers. Nevertheless, the steel market is sufficiently liquid that perhaps 80 percent of steel transactions take place within a narrow band of plus or minus $15 a ton for a given commodity product. Nucor's posted prices tend to track the center of that band quite well.

Given past behavior and stated minimill operating philosophy, it is reasonable to expect the new flat-rolled market entrants to be willing to price down to their level of marginal cost if necessary to fill their order books. This would suggest a bottom of around $250 a ton for hot-rolled coil in the next cyclical trough, or well below the marginal costs of most if not all integrated mills. At such prices, higher-cost mills have to determine whether they can walk away from low-end tonnage that they have historically used to maintain mill throughput levels. The dilemma for high-end, Class I producers is how much semifixed cost they can cut out if operations are maintained at low operating rates to serve only the premium, high-end markets. The dilemma for Class II producers is how to survive when, on the basis of 1995 costs, they might be losing $50 on every ton shipped.

These numbers suggest a stream of red ink for the flat-rolled segment of the industry during recession periods—hardly surprising given the similar experiences of the 1970s and 1980s. Which capacity is likely to be closed and which will thrive will be determined chiefly by the ability of the integrated mills to adjust, which will be examined in chapter 9. However, an analogous situation might be examined, the case of the market for heavy structural shapes in the United States in the late 1980s and early 1990s.

The market for wide flange beams and piling sections has averaged under 5 million tons a year over the last three business cycles. In 1988, the market contained a little over 5 million tons of domestic capacity, including three major integrated producers—Bethlehem, U.S. Steel, and Inland Steel—and two minimills, Northwestern Steel and Wire and Chaparral Steel. Imports added around 1 million tons a year. In 1988-89, an extra 3 million tons of minimill capacity was added by the existing minimill producers and by the entry of Nucor-Yamato Steel, at the same time that the construction market went into recession, reducing apparent consumption by over 1 million tons. Beam transaction prices fell by over a third. Imports were almost entirely eliminated from the market. U.S. Steel and Inland Steel exited the market, and Bethlehem Steel cut its capacity by half after six futile years of looking for ways to compete profitably in a product it historically dominated. In eight years, the heavy structurals market went from a supply mix of 60 percent integrated mills, 20 percent minimills, and 20 percent imports, to one of 90 percent minimill, 10 percent Bethlehem Steel, and negligible net imports.

Many differences exist between the structural shapes market and the flat-rolled market. Moreover, the proportional impact of the new minimills, in a much smaller market, was far greater than the possible effect of announced minimill flat-rolled capacity. Nevertheless, the example of a significant market sector being invaded by low-cost minimills is instructive. The minimills' domination took just thirteen years, from the 1981 expansion of Chaparral Steel into the wide flange beam market, to the 1994 decision by Bethlehem Steel to downsize its Structural Products division. Partisans of the minimills expect a similar triumph in flat-rolled steel.

9

SADDER BUT WISER: THE INTEGRATED MILLS IN THE 1990s

DEATH THROES OR FIGHTING BACK?

Life is unfair to integrated steel mills. Between 1979 and 1994, the net worth of integrated U.S. steelmakers fell by around 70 percent in constant (inflation-adjusted) dollars. They abandoned half of their capacity. They gave up, with only minor exceptions, every product group except flat-rolled carbon coil and plate. But on their chosen battlefield, in flat-rolled products, they achieved something close to a miracle. In sheet and strip, domestic tons shipped over the course of a business cycle have been essentially unchanged over the last 15 years. However, during this period, the selling prices of flat-rolled products have remained essentially unchanged in nominal dollars, while falling by 50 percent in constant dollars due to inflation.[1] Despite this stark decline in price, in 1994, the North American integrated mills earned just over $30 operating profit per ton shipped, while in 1979 (at a similar point in the business cycle), they earned an average of only $12 nominal ($24 in 1994 dollars) per ton.[2]

The profitability of integrated mills in the strong economy of the mid-1990s rested upon prices averaging $60 a ton higher than those prevailing in 1991-92, in the down side of the cycle. To earn $30 a ton at such prices does not suggest a strong outlook for integrated production on average over a business cycle. Indeed, the integrated mills lost an average of $44 a ton in 1991, and lost $26 a ton in 1992. Nevertheless, their ability to make money since 1993, at real price levels that have dropped one-half, is a remarkable testimony to their resilience. In effect, the integrated mills reinvented themselves over about 15 years to be able to compete with imports in a world awash with cheap steel. They then discovered, with the advent of the flat-rolled minimill, that competition had leapfrogged ahead of them, and now they are being asked to do the same thing again, this time to compete with domestic challengers for their market. This chapter will discuss whether they are likely to achieve this, both by looking back at how much they have achieved and by looking at their future options. The discussion of the born-again mills in chapter 7 showed extreme examples of how large and small mills turned themselves around. In this chapter, discussion of the several strategies used in the first wave of cost cutting is followed by an analysis of possible survivors and losers in a second wave of transformation. The chapter concludes with a more detailed review of flat-rolled markets in an attempt to draw conclusions about the future patterns in this, the largest sector of the steel industry.

THE FIRST TRANSFORMATION: 1979–1994

The surviving integrated companies—regardless of ownership or diversification—found (in some cases by trial and error) that three strategies worked to drive down costs and ensure their survival. First, they simplified their product and process mix by concentrating on the flat-rolled segment of their businesses and largely abandoning product lines where they could not compete on cost grounds. Excess facilities and overhead have been shed and management structures simplified. The historic model of a massive integrated mill producing a range of products from sheet, plate, and pipe to bar, rod, and wire has been replaced with focus on (usually) a single product—flat-rolled coils of various finishes. Second, product mix changes within the flat-rolled product line have enabled mills to sell a higher percentage of their output in higher-value forms such as galvanized steel, thus partly offsetting the decline in real steel selling prices. Third and most important, the cost per ton of making flat-rolled steel has been cut in half, driven by the need to compete with low-priced imports. To cut unit costs, companies have focused on selective capital investment, chiefly in casters and ladle metallurgy; on labor productivity growth through crew size and work rule changes; on lowering costs of material inputs; and on reducing plant and corporate overhead. In 1979, integrated producers made 119 million tons of raw steel, including steel they made in electric furnaces. Integrated mills' capacity of 135 million tons accounted for 87 percent of all U.S. capacity, including approximately 87 million tons of BOF capacity, 30 million tons of open-hearth capacity, and 18 million tons of electric furnace capacity. Integrated mills were the dominant producers of beams, pipe, wire rod, and stainless steel. Even in rebar, the largest producer (and fabricator) was integrated Bethlehem Steel. By 1993, integrated companies' raw steel capacity was limited to 66 million tons from BOFs and 4 million tons from electric furnaces. Of their actual 1993 production of 62 million tons, supplemented by 4 million tons of imported slabs, all but about 3.5 million tons went to feed plate and strip mills. In terms of finished products, integrated companies shipped 47 million tons of sheets and strip, 6 million tons of plates in coil and flat form, and half a million tons of pipe welded from plate and strip. Shipments of all other products included only around a million tons of rail, structural shapes, and piling (Bethlehem Steel); around 2 million tons of bar and rod products (USS-Kobe, Bethlehem, and Inland); and half a million tons of seamless pipe (U.S. Steel and USS-Kobe). Upon the closure of Bethlehem Steel's hot end at Bethlehem, Pennsylvania, in 1995, only four integrated company operations produced steel for long products: U.S. Steel at Fairfield, Alabama, producing seamless tube rounds; USS-Kobe producing seamless tubing and bar; Inland Steel Bar Company, making bar with electric furnaces at Inland's integrated mill; and Bethlehem, casting blooms from electric furnaces at Steelton, PA, for rolling to rail at Steelton and to beams at Bethlehem. Much of the capacity closed was evidently in long products production; at least 20 million tons of steelmaking closed during the period can be attributed to the exit from long products, although the predominant use of ingot casting in 1979 (when only 23 million tons were continuously cast) makes it difficult to say with certainty whether some raw steel capacity could be attributed to flat-rolled or long products within a given plant. Another 6 million tons of electric furnace capacity was spun off or sold by the integrated mills, including all of their stainless steelmaking, and such long-product facilities as LTV's Canton plant (Republic Engineered Steels), and the Seattle plant (now part of Birmingham Steel), and Johnstown plant (BRW Steel) of Bethlehem

Steel. The CF & I mill de-integrated, closing 1 million tons of capacity and transferring half a million tons to the nonintegrated sector.

Capacity closures have by no means been confined to the products in which the integrated mills have given ground to minimills and specialty producers. As shown in table 9.1, plate mills accounting for around 5.5 million tons of capacity have been closed, while around 19 million tons of hot-strip mill capacity has been closed, beginning with Youngstown Sheet & Tube's Campbell Works in 1977. Unlike the wholesale flight from long products, however, the capacity closures in flat products have been selective. In every case but one in table 9.1, the closure of a sheet or plate facility did not take the company concerned out of that product. (The exception was Armco leaving the heavy plate business.) Each closure was of a higher-cost facility from among two or more such facilities operated by a company. Each closure therefore had a double effect on average costs for a company. It eliminated the higher-cost production, but it also—by concentrating shipments onto fewer mills—reduced the average cost at the survivors by spreading their fixed costs over a greater throughput.

In most cases, the Darwinian process of selecting each company's lowest-cost facilities meant the elimination of old and obsolete capacity. However, there were cases where new plants had to go. The Baytown plant, near Houston, was U.S. Steel's newest mill, only 14 years old at the time it was closed. But after the end of the oilfield boom, U.S. Steel's sales of Baytown's product, heavy plate, could be adequately supplied from any one of the corporation's four plate mills. The selected survivor, at Gary, Indiana, benefited from sharing low-cost steelmaking with the corporation's best hot-strip mill. U.S. Steel sacrificed not only Baytown but the historic Homestead and South Works mills to maintain the volume throughput at the efficient Gary plant.

The elimination of excess capacity had other beneficial side effects. Open-hearth steelmaking was eliminated by 1991, and most integrated steelmakers also eliminated electric furnace production. No longer was there a need to engineer and maintain three methods of steelmaking and a wide range of rolling mills (often all within a single plant). The simplicity of a single process flow within a plant, in most cases blast furnace–BOF–hot-strip mill-finishing mills, replaced the complex and expensive historic practices of scheduling and rolling steel for a wide range of finished shapes and (often) transferring steel between plants for different operations. In-process inventories could be reduced and production times shortened. Investment and operational scheduling

Table 9.1
CARBON FLAT-ROLLED CAPACITY CLOSURES IN THE UNITED STATES, 1977–1996 (PLATE AND HOT-STRIP MILLS)

Company and Location	Mill	Year	Capacity (tons per year)
Armco, Ashland, KY	80" HS mill	1988	1,700,000
Armco, Houston, TX	130" plate mill	1983	650,000
Armco, Houston, TX	160" combination slab/plate mill	1983	(if rolling plate: 850,000)
Bethlehem, Sparrows Point, MD	56" HS mill	1985	2,480,000
Bethlehem, Lackawanna, NY	79" HS mill	1983	2,500,000
Inland, East Chicago, IN	44" HS mill	1985	1,700,000
LTV Steel (J&L), Aliquippa, PA	44" HS mill	1981	1,600,000
LTV Steel (J&L), Pittsburgh, PA	96" HS mill	1979	1,500,000
U.S. Steel, Baytown, TX	160" plate mill	1985	1,230,000
U.S. Steel, Fairless Hills, PA	80" HS mill	1992	2,800,000
U.S. Steel, Homestead, PA	160" plate mill	1986	980,000
U.S. Steel, Homestead, PA	100" plate mill	1985	830,000
U.S. Steel, South Works, Chicago, IL	96" plate mill	1982	927,000
U.S. Steel, South Works, Chicago, IL	30" UM plate mill	1982	216,000
U.S. Steel, Youngstown, OH	43" HS mill	1979	1,300,000
Wheeling-Pittsburgh, Allenport, PA	66" HS mill	1985	900,000
Youngstown Sheet & Tube, Campbell, OH	79" HS mill	1977	2,500,000

NOTES:
Sharon Steels 60-inch hot-strip mill was closed in 1993 and reopened in 1995 by Caparo Steel; Alan Woods 110-inch plate mill was closed in 1977 and reopened by Lukens Steel in 1982; and Phoenix Steels 160-inch plate mill, closed in 1986, was reopened as Citisteel in 1988. In each of these cases, a once-integrated facility was reopened as a non-integrated plant. Lone Star Steel also de-integrated" in 1986, transferring its 72-inch hot-strip mill to the non-integrated category.
McLouth Steel closed in April 1996, but was purchased by Hamlin Holdings and was intended to be restarted before the end of 1996. McLouths 60-inch hot-strip mill has a nominal capacity of 2 million tons per year.

could be directed toward closely matching the steelmaking and rolling capacities in a single process flow.

As companies selected their surviving flat-rolled facilities, they focused their capital investment on upgrading these mills. With the losses companies faced in the 1980s, investments had to be relatively small and have fast paybacks. This requirement was met by investments in casters and in ladle metallurgy. Casters lowered production costs immediately by an average of $20 a ton, replacing the two-stage ingot pouring and slabbing mill process by the single stage of the slab caster. Cast slabs also produced better surface quality sheets, once crews learned optimal operating practices. Ladle metallurgy—the use of ladle furnaces to hold liquid steel between the BOF and the caster—had three advantages. First, it allowed greater production flexibility, by linking the batch-type BOF process with the more flow-type caster operation; liquid steel could be held until needed and a steady flow maintained to the caster. Second, it could be used to increase the steelmaking output of a BOF shop, by reducing the time steel needed to be held in the BOF vessel for alloying and temperature equalization. Third, it improved steel quality, by allowing more precise temperature control of the steel poured into the caster and by facilitating more precise degassing and alloying than possible within the BOF. An alternative strategy for investment has been to seek to increase a mill's revenue per ton, by targeting markets for value-added products. Galvanized steel, both hot-dip and electrogalvanized, was the obvious product to pursue in the 1980s. Consumption grew from 8.5 million to 15.7 million tons, largely by displacing uncoated hot- and cold-rolled sheets. Including other metallic coatings, coated sheets grew from 18 to 32 percent of all flat-rolled shipments, a rate of growth exceeded only by coiled plate. Companies that invested heavily in new galvanizing lines were able to add significant increments of margin per ton.

In 1994, at the peak of the steel cycle, North American integrated flat-rolled steelmakers ranged in profitability from over U.S.$50 per ton shipped at AK Steel, Algoma Steel, and Dofasco, to under $20 a ton for Weirton Steel (which suffered a major business interruption due to fire) and laggards Bethlehem and National. While the three Canadian steelmakers averaged $20 a ton better performance than their U.S. counterparts, for a variety of reasons including lower ore costs, labor costs, more modern facilities, and a greater proportion of higher-value products in their mix, more important differences emerge when comparing the performance of North American flat-rolled mills. In the peak period of 1993 to 1995, mills heavily dependent on automakers generally performed well. The leading U.S. mills for profitability per ton, AK Steel and Rouge Steel, had the highest percentage of sales to automakers, while Canadian producers Dofasco and Stelco had similarly high auto sales. AK Steel appears to have increased its automotive market share, in part due to its location as the geographic balance of automotive production in the United States shifted away from the Great Lakes and toward the Ohio and Tennessee valleys. Rouge similarly benefited from its historic ties to, and location next to, Ford in Detroit, and its dedication to the auto market at a time when U.S. and transplant automakers' order books were full. Automotive sales represent high-volume, repeat business of high-value products, but they do not guarantee success. National

Steel, with a mill in Detroit and a high volume of automotive business, trailed all other mills in operating performance in the early 1990s, while the most profitable mill of all on a per-ton basis, Algoma, has no galvanizing facilities and a low level of automotive sales. Investment and product mix could not account for the differences in performance between mills of similar configuration or at a single mill over time. What can and does make the difference is management driving down costs.

COST MANAGEMENT: TWO 1990s CASE STUDIES

In the early 1990s, North America has seen two remarkable success stories in turning around integrated companies threatened with closure. AK Steel, owned in 1991 by a Japanese-American joint venture of Kawasaki (60 percent) and Armco (40 percent), and Algoma Steel, owned in 1991 by fellow Canadian steelmaker Dofasco, were both at the bottom of any index of profitability and productivity, and their owners were under pressure to cut their losses and abandon these subsidiaries. Both were transformed by new management teams into the most profitable integrated mills in their respective countries. At AK Steel, the partners were determined to avoid a bankruptcy proceeding. To stave off what many observers thought was inevitable, they recruited perhaps the best-known cost-cutter in the U.S. steel industry. Thomas C. (Tom) Graham was chief operating officer (COO) of U.S. Steel from 1982 to 1991, and then spent a year turning around loss-making specialty steelmaker Washington Steel. As chief executive officer of AK Steel from 1992 to 1995, his focus was to drive up the productivity of basic steelmaking and rolling functions without heavy capital investment. During his ten years as COO of U.S. Steel, that company closed or sold 14 million tons of steelmaking capacity and moved from an average of 11 man-hours per ton of steel to 4.0. At AK Steel he improved productivity similarly, from 6 to 3.5 man-hours per ton. Given that labor costs have approached $30 an hour at integrated mills since the early 1980s, these savings amounted to nearly $200 per ton over ten years at U.S. Steel—cutting out half the total cost of hot-rolled coil.

Some part of these dramatic improvements can be attributed to facilities rationalization (at U.S. Steel) and to increased throughput at in-place facilities (AK Steel). However, the turnaround of AK Steel in just three years from the worst per-ton financial performance of U.S.

integrated steelmakers to the best such performance cannot be attributed to anything other than aggressive management. The intensive drive for productivity at existing assets was effected largely with labor cooperation at AK Steel, which had the benefit of an independent union at the key Middletown mill, unlike Graham's record of confrontation at U.S. Steel. At a time when integrated companies' managements were often dominated by executives with a legal or accounting background, Graham's operations background and hands-on approach allowed him to approach cost-cutting more directly than others. A key component in Tom Graham's strategy was setting very high operational targets for mill management, in return for high rewards. At AK as at U.S. Steel, complacent or low-performing managers were weeded out ruthlessly, but the surviving, high-achieving managers exhibited great respect and loyalty toward Graham and his small team of key operations managers. At AK Steel, Graham's approach led to world records for production and productivity at elderly facilities. In 1994, a small, 1950s blast furnace at the Middletown mill recorded the world's highest hot-metal output of 13.5 tons per 100 cubic feet of working volume; a cold-rolling mill achieved consistent throughputs approaching 350 tons per hour, where industry best practices had aimed at a target of 300. Adjustments in operating practice, such as high-pressure oxygen injection in the Middletown blast furnace, plus the use of incentives and individual responsibility throughout management in ways previously regarded as the prerogative of minimills allowed gains that other companies attempted only through major investments. Another key emphasis in Graham's approach has been on maintenance programs. Integrated steel is a highly maintenance-intensive business, even excluding major capitalized costs such as blast furnace relines. AK Steel devotes about 40 percent of its workforce to maintenance, spending about $300 million each year in this area. Graham's approach, however, has been to focus on preventive maintenance designed to increase the reliability and extend the campaign life of each major production unit, while eliminating the costly duplicate, backup equipment maintained by many integrated companies.[3]

Canada's Algoma Steel, whose per-ton profits reached a high of U.S.$ 95 per ton in the first quarter of 1995, is a turnaround story that superficially resembles AK Steel. Like AK, Algoma has made great advances in per-ton costs and mill productivity, to move from the poorest to the best-performing integrated mill in its country, but the similarity ends there. Algoma is the last single mill in North America producing five product lines—sheet, plate, beams, rail and seamless tubing—at one location. Just as AK lagged behind other U.S. integrated mills in 1991-92 to the point where its future was threatened, so Algoma in 1991 came close to closure. Dofasco, its owner since 1988, despaired of being able to turn the mill around, and placed the company in bankruptcy protection in February 1991. Dofasco wrote off its investment, and after reorganization Algoma became independent again, now owned 60 percent by its workforce and 40 percent by its former creditors. Its reorganization was facilitated by cooperation from the Steelworkers, which agreed to wage reductions and layoffs in exchange for employee ownership and the mill's remaining in each of its product lines. The extent of labor-management cooperation appears to extend much further than in other ESOPs, such as Weirton Steel. Location may have something to do with this; the lack of alternative employment opportunities in northern Ontario makes a powerful incentive to support the company.

Where AK Steel retains the traditional hierarchy of management and labor, effectively strengthening the role of management by driving responsibility down to the lowest levels of operating management, new management at Algoma sought to accomplish the same thing by co-opting unionized workers into decision making. The symbolic removal of punch-clocks has been accompanied by more substantive measures of worker education, flexible work teams, and measuring employees by tasks completed rather than hours. In both cases the assumption of responsibility for increased production on the mill floor has worked. Algoma has had some additional advantages. Its iron ore costs are the lowest in North America, due in part to the company's captive ore supplies at its Wawa mine and sintering plant, north of Sault Ste. Marie, and its interest in the Tilden mine in northern Michigan. All the mill's iron supply moves less than 200 miles to the plant by rail. The mill was also able to make a major improvement in its configuration by closing in 1993 the older and smaller of its two BOF shops, using a new ladle transfer facility to move hot steel from the number 2 BOF shop to the bloom caster at the older number 1 shop. The change also eliminated ingot casting and allowed the idling of a blast furnace and coke battery. The mill's steelmaking capacity of 2.5 million tons per year now more closely matches its effective product capacity, governed by a 1.9-million-ton-per-year strip mill and plate and long products markets which have typically accounted for between 600,000 and 800,000 tons per year of production.

As at AK Steel, Algoma's success in turning around an ailing mill was aided by the strong steel market from 1993 to 1995. However, Algoma has determined to prepare for the down periods of the steel cycle not by continuing to push beyond perceived limits with existing equipment but by investing in thin-slab casting. In 1995, the company announced the results of a company-wide strategic planning exercise, and its decision was to buy a thin-slab caster and a new 2-million-ton-per-year hot-strip mill. In addition, the company would install a new but mothballed tube rounds caster and update the mill's downstream finishing facilities. To finance this, employee ownership was diluted by a new equity issue, and eliminating one-quarter of the workforce over four years is planned. The investments are likely to drive the cost of the company's sheet products down by around $30 a ton, while the cost of its seamless tubes should fall by up to $60. The job cuts may test the effectiveness of the company's exemplary labor-management cooperation if the mill is no longer seen to be under threat of closure.

In many ways, the turnarounds of AK Steel and Algoma Steel represent opposite examples of steel industry corporate culture. They suggest that while there is more than one way to become successful as an integrated mill, success is measurable first and foremost in low costs per ton. The apparent strategies for the future of the mills are also revealing. Algoma's decision to mix traditional integrated steelmaking with thin-slab casting reflects both its location in an iron-ore-rich, scrap-deficient region and a recognition of the need for technological change. AK Steel's commitment to pushing the envelope with existing technologies—and existing management/labor structures—is equally revealing. It may be unfair to suggest that a management team that originated at U.S. Steel was unlikely to try new options, but it certainly has shown that there is plenty of scope within traditional industry structures for radical improvement. The turnarounds of AK and Algoma, both in serious jeopardy in 1991, meant that there were few casualties of the brief and shallow steel recession of 1990 to 1992. Only one flat-rolled company, Sharon Steel, left the industry, and it had already abandoned its integrated steelmaking to concentrate on electric furnace production. One major mill was closed, the hot end of U.S. Steel's Fairless Hills, Pennsylvania, works, although it continues to cold-roll and finish hot bands sent from the company's Mon Valley Works in Pittsburgh. The capacity lost at Sharon and Fairless Hills was offset by the new Nucor mills coming on line. The next recession may not be so gentle.

THE NEXT BUSINESS CYCLE: A FURTHER SHAKEOUT?

With much more new minimill capacity coming on stream, will there be further major losses of integrated capacity, or can the integrated industry achieve more miracles such as the AK and Algoma turnarounds? Any assessment of the vulnerability of integrated mills must start with certain assumptions about the steel market over a decade or more. Among the "most likely" assumptions, viewed from the mid-1990s, are that there will continue to be business cycles approximately every five to seven years that lead the demand for flat-rolled steel to vary cyclically by about 10 percent in terms of real demand. The single greatest variable in real sheet demand is automobile production, with automotive sheet demand varying by over 3 million tons from top to bottom of the business cycle. Changes in real consumption are magnified by inventory accumulation and destocking, so that apparent demand varies by as much as 20 percent in terms of mill shipments. As a result of this cycle in demand, spot pricing varies by as much as 30 percent per ton over the business cycle. Spot pricing covers the majority of all steel sales but a little less than half of integrated mill flat-rolled shipments. Once the less volatile contract sales are included, mill revenues per ton vary by around 20 percent over a cycle. Another key factor for the balance of the 1990s, although unlikely to hold true for long into the next decade, is that technology breakthroughs in ironmaking or steelmaking will not be commercialized to an extent likely to transform the fundamental economics of the industry. Mills now built, being built, or in an advanced stage of planning, and possibly some clones, will be the principal competitors over the next business cycle; "what you see is what you get."

Another key short-term assumption, although unlikely to remain true over time, is that flat-rolled steel demand will hold to the pattern of slow or zero growth between cycles that has prevailed since the mid-1970s. It is certainly possible that flat-rolled steel will see a return to somewhat higher levels of consumption growth, given changes in the economics of competing materials. The growth of galvanized steel framing in U.S. residential housing is one area likely to prove a permanent boost to steel consumption, while the prospects for the recovery of can markets for tinplate against aluminum, as in several European markets in the 1990s, are reasonably good. It is certainly possible that between exports and import substitution, which will require the continuation of a low valuation for the U.S. dollar, and new markets for steel in construction, U.S. flat-rolled shipments could increase by 5 million tons, or 10 percent, between 1994 and the next cyclical peak—say, around 2000. Equally, however, the possibilities of substitution working against steel in areas such as auto bodies make it unwise to assume such growth. A conservative investor would probably assume stable inter-cyclical demand for flat-rolled steel through the year 2000.

With carbon flat-rolled product demand stable in the 56- to 60-million-ton range at the next peak, and around 75 million tons of flat-rolled capacity including the new minimills, it is hard to envisage average capacity utilization exceeding 75 percent. If the United States is still a net importer of flat-rolled steel, the utilization rate may not exceed 70 percent. Breakeven rates for integrated mills at peak 1994 prices are estimated to be in the 75 to 80 percent range; actual flat-rolled operating rates for 1994 approached 100 percent of steelmaking capacity, with purchased slabs to make up the shortfall in supply. The existence of excess capacity in the next cyclical peak will prevent a recovery of prices from cyclical trough levels to anything near the shortage levels of 1994. It is therefore probable that, because of lower prices, the average breakeven operating rate at the next peak will be in excess of 80 percent, even allowing for further cost savings. The industry is likely to face a situation where at cyclical peaks, the higher-cost producers will not return to profitability. In such circumstances, some players will be forced out.

Integrated steel mills are large community and regional employers. The local consequences of their closure are enormous. It is vital that public policymakers identify individual mills at risk. An attempt to measure the relative costs and strengths of mills is therefore desirable. But any ranking of integrated steel mills at any given time is a poor guide to survival, given the potential for turnaround at any facility—as was demonstrated by AK and Algoma. Costs can be changed dramatically over time by strong management. Survival can also depend on noncost factors—product and customer mix, labor relations, even whether a mill is the sole producing facility of a given company. Mills with the higher costs at any given time may simply prove to be those with the greatest scope for improvement; a company like AK Steel, which has already optimized the usage of its plant, such an argument goes, will find it difficult to achieve further gains.

The ranking shown in table 9.2 is necessarily based on both public information and on some subjective judgments of mill strengths and weaknesses. Mills are understandably reluctant to discuss their costs in detail unless they have a notable success story to tell. Industry analysts do, however, maintain close track of industry costs. Analysts' reports such as the world capacity cost curve regularly updated by Paine Webber indicate mill rankings with a good degree of accuracy. The steel industry is also one of continuous gossip and one in which visits between rival companies' plants are common. The quartiles in the table reflect analysts' and industry opinion of the approximate rankings of cost per flat-rolled ton shipped during an average year of a business cycle.

Rankings based solely on cost per ton do not fully reflect the profitability of a given mill. Acme Metals, for example, is effectively a specialty steel operation rather than a volume producer; until its installation in 1995-96 of a new minimill-type caster and hot-strip mill, it rolled strip no wider than 30 inches in small heats, supplying steel to manufacturers that need precise, nonstandard chemistries and dimensions. The installation of a 60-inch rolling mill and the reduction of costs by eliminating ingot practice will dramatically reduce the company's cost per ton. Acme's future per-ton costs are unknown, but they are still expected to service a much more specialized niche than most producers, at higher cost but also potentially highly profitable. Of the 20 U.S. integrated mills, Acme, Geneva, and USS-Kobe are each distinctive in the geographical or product markets they supply and cannot strictly be rated as competitors of the others.

The seventeen remaining mills compete or potentially compete against each other at least for commercial quality hot- and cold-rolled sheet products, although their dependence on such business may be limited. They are also the mills directly challenged by the new minimill flat-rolled producers. The mills shown as having a high percentage of automotive business and the producers of tin mill products are less likely to be impacted initially by the introduction of minimill capacity, at least until minimill quality consistency makes it economically viable to enter these product areas.

An assessment of the factors determining costs at integrated mills, other than management or operating practices, would have to include the following considerations:

- Size. Economies of scale still count, especially in the operation of blast furnaces and hot-strip mills. Multiple blast furnaces or BOFs allow more flexibility in scheduling and in surviving inevitable outages for relines and other maintenance.

Table 9.2
U.S. INTEGRATED MILLS IN 1995: A COST RANKING BY QUARTILES

Mill (alphabetical within quartile)	Continuous Casting Capacity (million tons per year)	Auto	Ore Dock	Products
First Quartile				
AK Steel, combined plants [a]	4.0	A	L	HR/CR/HD/EG/AL
Bethlehem, Burns Harbor, IN	4.0	A	L	HR/CR/HD/EG/PL
Inland Steel, East Chicago, IN [b]	5.0	A	L	HR/CR/HD/EG/AL/PL
LTV, Cleveland, OH	4.9	A	L	HR/CR/HD/EG
U.S. Steel, Gary, IN	7.0	A	L	HR/CR/HD/EG/TM
Second Quartile				
LTV, Indiana Harbor, IN	3.7	A	L	HR/CR/HD/TM
National Steel, Ecorse, MI	3.0	A	L	HR/CR/EG
Rouge Steel, Dearborn, MI	2.5	A		HR/CR/EG
U.S. Steel, Mon Valley Works, PA	2.7	A		HR/CR/HD
Weirton Steel, Weirton, WV	3.0			HR/CR/HD/TM
Third Quartile				
Bethlehem, Sparrows Point, MD	3.4		O	HR/CR/HD/TM/PL
Geneva Steel, Geneva, UT	2.4			HR/PL/welded pipe
National Steel, Granite City, IL	2.5			HR/CR/HD
U.S. Steel, Fairfield, AL [c]	2.74			HR/CR/HD/seamless pipe
Wheeling-Pittsburgh Steel [d]	2.4			HR/CR/HD/AL/TM
Fourth Quartile				
Acme Steel, Riverdale, IL	1.0		L	HR/CR
Gulf States Steel, Gadsden, AL	1.0			HR/CR/HD/PL
McLouth Steel, Trenton, MI [e]	2.0		L	HR/CR/HD
USS-Kobe Steel, Lorain, OH [f]	1.77		L	Bar/seamless pipe
WCI Steel, Warren, OH	1.95			HR/CR/HD

NOTES:
A = High percentage of shipments directly to major automotive manufacturers.
L = Lake ore dock; O = Ocean ore dock.
HR = Hot-rolled coils; CR = Cold-rolled coils; HD = Hot-dip galvanized; EG = Electrogalvanized;
AL = aluminized; TM = Tin mill products; PL = flat plate.

Product capabilities may include associated or joint-venture facilities supplied primarily from the listed facility—U.S. Steel's Fairless Hills, Pennsylvania, mill from the Mon Valley Works, or I/N Tek and I/N Kote from Inland Steel.

a AK Steel's Ashland, Kentucky, and Middletown, Ohio, mills are assumed to continue to operate as one, supplying the Middletown hot-strip mill.

b Does not include Inland Steel Bar Company, electric furnace producer co-located at East Chicago.

c U.S. Steel Fairfield operates a slab caster rated at 1.9 million tons and a bloom caster, supplying the mills seamless pipe operations, rated at 840,000 tons.

d Wheeling-Pittsburgh's combined Steubenville/Mingo Junction, Ohio, and Follansbee, West Virginia, plants.

e McLouth Steel closed in April 1996, but was purchased by Hamlin Holdings and was intended to be re-started before the end of 1996.

- External logistics. A lake or ocean location for ore transportation reduces cost by more than a river- or rail-dependent location. Access to multiple rail lines gives greater negotiating power on in- and outbound freight.
- Internal logistics, or plant layout. An in-line layout maximizes throughput speed, saves energy (especially in reheating steel for different processes), and cuts in-process inventory. In addition, significant freight may be incurred between locations if multiple plants have been combined to utilize the best individual facilities of separate locations, as with the AK Steel Ashland/Middletown combination.
- Age. The average age of facilities is an important determinant of maintenance costs, down time, and quality.
- Quality. Steel quality matters if it allows tinplate- and automotive-quality production without a high rejection rate.
- Strip mill width. The market for 60-inch and 72-inch coils, and wider, is steadily growing.
- Value added. Investment in electrogalvanizing and tinplate lines permits adding the most value to steel.

If automotive and tinplate suppliers have some measure of temporary protection against minimill challenges to their products, it may be worth looking closer at those integrated mills that have no such protection. The table shows five mills that are competitors in the mainstream hot-rolled, cold-rolled, and hot-dip galvanized markets but which do not supply tin mill products or significant tonnages of automotive sheets. One of these, McLouth, was forced to close in early 1996 but the mill was purchased with a view to its restart. The other four—U.S. Steel's Fairfield, Alabama, mill; National Steel at Granite City, Illinois, near St. Louis; Gulf States Steel at Gadsden; and WCI Steel at Warren, Ohio—also give cause for concern on a number of grounds among the cost factors just listed. Each of the five mills is in the low end of the size range of U.S. integrated mills (and is very small by contemporary international standards). Four of the five lack deep-water access for ore, requiring either costly transshipment or all-rail freight. None of the five has a high proportion of automotive sales, due to either location or quality or both. Each is a relatively old mill, and in two cases—Gulf States and McLouth—there has been no significant investment in new facilities other than continuous casters since the introduction of BOFs in the 1960s. Three of the mills—the two Alabama mills and the Granite City mill, outside St. Louis—are in regions which could be considered the core regional markets of new flat-rolled minimills in Alabama and both north and south of St. Louis in Arkansas and Iowa. Of the five, only Granite City has a Generation II continuous hot-strip mill capable of rolling 72-inch-wide sheets; Fairfield and McLouth can roll 60-inch sheets, but WCI and Gulf States are limited to standard commercial widths no greater than 48 inches.

The 1996 closure and sale of McLouth highlighted the inherent structural weaknesses of some of the independent mills. McLouth underwent a series of financial restructurings between 1982 and 1992, leading ultimately to full employee ownership under the aegis of the Steelworkers union. McLouth had a labor cost advantage of at least $5 per hour over other integrated steelmakers, although it dissipated much of this advantage in poor tonnage productivity per hour worked. It made profits in 1993 and 1994 for the first time in a decade, but not at a level that would support significant capital investment. The mill has no value-added coating lines and is increasingly limited in its customer base by quality constraints. The softening of steel prices in late 1995 saw the mill begin to lose money again, and in early 1996 a strike at General Motors led many of McLouth's auto part manufacturer customers to cancel or postpone orders. Out of cash, the mill closed in March 1996, and was purchased from the bankruptcy court three months later by Hamlin Holdings. Hamlin's head, Michael Wilkinson, had put together the consortium that re-started the shuttered Kaiser Steel mill ten years earlier. He faces a major challenge. In the frank words of McLouth's former CEO, Joseph Corso, "the equipment has been harvested"; significant capital investment is needed to renew the mill to face the minimill challenge.[4]

The future of the Fairfield and Granite City plants, parts of larger steel companies, will be determined in part by broader considerations (and by greater financial strength) than at single-mill companies. In the early 1990s, Granite City appeared to have suffered for years from its parent's neglect in favor of the larger Ecorse, Michigan, mill. National Steel's heavy losses in 1993-94 led stock analysts to suggest that Granite City might have to be closed. The increasingly public criticism of National Steel's management in 1993-94 led NKK of Japan, which at the time controlled 76 percent of the company's stock, to terminate National's two top managers in June 1994. They were immediately replaced with senior managers from U.S. Steel's Gary Works. Both the public firing and the poaching of a total of seven senior U.S. Steel managers, which led to legal action, were unprecedented in recent times in an industry that usually emphasizes continuity and courtesy in executive changes. In addition to introducing a strong dose of Tom Graham–style cost management at National, the new management team benefited from the strong steel market in 1993-95 and from the company's ability to raise new equity on the stock market in 1994. Part of the resulting cash inflow has been invested at Granite City. The mill began a major modernization program in 1994 on the 80-inch hot strip mill, to improve its gauge and shape controls for higher-quality markets, and in 1995 a new galvanizing line was announced for the plant. The new line's production was aimed at the same construction industry markets targeted by much of the new minimill capacity—pre-engineered metal buildings and residential roofing, siding, and framing. The new expenditures, combined with National Steel's overall return to profitability under new management, appear to augur well for Granite City's survival. However, the ultimate decision continues to rest with parent NKK, which retained approximately 69 percent of National's stock after the 1994 share issue. NKK can be expected to be supportive but not sentimental; if long-term profitability cannot be assured under National, Granite City could be a candidate for either closure or spin-off.[5]

U.S. Steel's Fairfield mill is similarly both cushioned and threatened by being part of a larger enterprise. It is cushioned because U.S. Steel can afford investment not possible at independent mills, but threatened by exposure to internal comparisons with mills offering greater returns. During the lengthy 1986 strike against U.S. Steel, the Fairfield mill was repeatedly identified as a facility unlikely to be reopened afterward. Investment at the mill in the early 1980s had been focused on a "world class" modern seamless pipe mill and continuous rounds caster, an expenditure authorized during the oilfield boom but that showed no signs of generating profits once the seamless oil country market evaporated. The flat-rolled side of the mill suffered from ingot casting and an older, narrow hot-strip mill. However, as part of the strike settlement in January 1987, U.S. Steel agreed to install continuous slab casters at both the Fairfield and Mon Valley works and to upgrade those plants' hot-strip mills to higher speeds and closer tolerances. The Fairfield Works, like National Steel's Granite City mill, has added a new coating line in 1996, an investment geared to serving construction markets. The first coating line at the Fairfield plant, the new line is aimed at supplying the growing market for galvanized framing for residential housing in the South and is a direct competitor for such markets with the flat-rolled minimills. With the new galvanizing line open, Fairfield will supply a diverse range of markets including supplying much of U.S. Steel's export tonnage. While the mill has made relatively small inroads into the growing number of automakers in the south-central United States, it does have a solid base of appliance and other manufacturing customers whose loyalty to U.S. Steel comes, in part, from the mill's location; its southern customers might not be as well served from Gary or from Pennsylvania mills. The seamless pipe mill is now thought to be profitable, reflecting the strengthened pricing in seamless pipe. Although it competes with low-cost minimill producers such as North Star, it supplies a key portion of U.S. Steel's seamless range, between the 4- and 9-inch pipe sizes. Smaller and larger sizes are supplied from USS-Kobe at Lorain, giving the company the unique ability among North American mills to supply a complete size range of seamless pipe, a significant advantage when dealing with pipe distributors. On balance, it appears that Fairfield looks set to weather the next economic cycle and is likely to remain a competitor in markets increasingly dominated by minimills as long as U.S. Steel's corporate strategy supports such competition.

The two other mills facing cost challenges have many superficial similarities but have pursued very different strategies. Both Warren and Gadsden were similar-sized, former Republic Steel mills spun off by LTV Corporation, although in slightly different circumstances: Gadsden was sold in 1986 as a condition of antitrust approval for the LTV-Republic merger, while the Warren mill was sold cheaply to a New York investment firm in 1988 as an alternative to its closure and a larger write-down on LTV's books. Gadsden and Warren both have old, narrow hot-strip mills that exclude them from the market for 60- and 72-inch coils. The two mills have pursued very different marketing strategies: Gulf States has supplied largely the distributor and fabricator markets, helped by its wide plate mill, and sought to gain economies by long production runs and pricing to fill the mill in minimill fashion. Warren, on the other hand, has targeted smaller OEM customers, being willing to accommodate small customer orders with (expensive) continuous adjustments at its furnaces, caster, and mills.

Gulf States' owner from 1986 to 1995, steel fabricator Brenlin Group of Akron, Ohio, spent over $100 million on plant renovations in the late 1980s, including increasing the plant's steelmaking and rolling capacity by the installation of ladle metallurgy, a slab caster, and a coil box on the hot-strip mill. Although Brenlin did not publish accounts for

Gulf States, the mill was reportedly profitable for much of the late 1980s and in the mid-1990s, in contrast to its record under Republic Steel and LTV ownership. Losses in the early-1990s down market brought spending to a halt, however, and the need for a further $150 million or more in capital expenditure caused Brenlin to place the mill on the market. It was hoped that its purchase in 1995 by a Boston-managed private equity group would lead to renewed capital spending. Major needs include an upgrade to the aging hot-strip mill and possibly a second continuous caster, to allow better utilization of the plant's steelmaking potential. Given its size and configuration, the Gadsden mill could be a potential candidate for an Acme Steel–type installation of a thin-slab caster and in-line hot-strip mill. Without major expenditure, however, the mill will be severely handicapped in competing against the new Trico minimill in Decatur, Alabama; one sign of this has been the bitterness of Gulf States' legal and political challenges to the State of Alabama's actions granting Trico tax rebates and other start-up assistance.[6]

The Warren mill of WCI has been one of the "reconstituted" mill success stories since its purchase in August 1988 by Renco Group, a vehicle for its chairman, investor Ira Rennert. As at Gulf States, Warren's new owner invested in a ladle metallurgy facility and slab caster in 1991, but Warren had a better track record of earnings than the industry average through the 1990s. WCI's management used the mill's relatively small size to advantage in pursuing niche markets in a manner somewhat akin to Acme Steel. In addition to commodity sizes and grades, Warren produces a high proportion of special width or alloy orders, plus silicon electrical steels and nickel- and terne-coated products. Markets include auto parts stampers; appliance, office, and electrical equipment manufacturers; and cold-rolled strip producers. This formula allowed the mill to earn money during the early 1990s recession and helped the mill secure significant refinancing though debt issues in 1993 and debt and equity in 1994. In 1995, part of the proceeds of these transactions was used to upgrade the hot-strip mill and reline the company's blast furnace. However, this formula is likely to be adopted by a number of the new minimill market entrants, at least three of which are within 300 miles of Warren, Ohio.[7]

It is not likely that any of the integrated steelmakers will roll over and die, quietly exiting the market as a result of losses in the late 1990s. Even the closure of the weakest companies, such as McLouth and Sharon Steel, does not remove their mill's capacity from the market—they are simply reopened by another new entrant. Many of the mills most directly threatened by low-cost minimills, including the five just examined, may well still be around to enjoy future steel "shortages" akin to that of 1994. Plate mill closures, however, may be more final. Inland Steel, for example, finally closed its 95-year-old, 100-inch plate mill at East Chicago at the end of 1995, taking Inland out of the heavy plate business. Bethlehem Steel also has a marginally economic, older plate mill, the 110-inch mill at Burns Harbor. Neither mill is critical to the survival of the major integrated plant at which it is based, and neither could, as a practical matter, be separated from the rest of the plant and sold. Inland's decision to exit the market reflects the prospect that increasing amounts of the market for plates up to 1 inch thick—more than half the total plate tonnage—will be supplied in the future by coiled plates. The entry into a plate market totaling 7 to 8 million tons a year of a net additional one million tons of Steckel mill plate capacity at Ipsco, Tuscaloosa, Oregon Steel, and Lukens may displace additional traditional capacity but will still leave room for a number of integrated plate producers to offer heavy and wide sections of flat plate. Mills that can convert plate to large-diameter line pipe, such as Geneva and Bethlehem (which supplies its Steelton pipe mill with plate from Sparrows Point), also have a competitive advantage. Plate is ultimately a sideshow in the battle for integrated mill survival. While it is an important niche product for a number of mills, it has (since the end of the oilfield boom in 1981) been a low-margin product used more to absorb incremental output than as the core of any integrated mill's strategy. High-value products such as armor plate and high-alloy plate for offshore rigs will continue to be the focus of competition among, chiefly, Lukens, Bethlehem, and U.S. Steel, but they are small markets with high associated costs. Plate is, however, likely to reflect the larger pattern of flat-rolled steel: both integrated and electric furnace producers will compete for survival by a combination of cost-driven commodity production and competition on service and quality for the loyalty of niche markets.

FLAT-ROLLED MARKETS: "NICHES" vs. COMMODITIES

The term "niche markets" is widely used in steel as in other industries, with little consensus of what it actually means. Like "world class," "market mill," and "customer-driven," it is beloved of the writers of annual reports and press releases but means little. In this chapter, it refers to those users of flat-rolled steel who, for whatever reason, choose not to buy generic steel coils of common commercial grades and sizes from a variety of steel processors and distributors. The reasons for choosing to buy directly from one or another mill rather than on the broader distributor or "spot" market may include simple ignorance, prejudice, or friendship. Usually, however, the user determines that distributor benefits (delivery reliability and speed, inventory holding, preprocessing, and usually price for small purchase quantities) are outweighed by mill benefits (quality reliability, specific chemistries or tolerances, and usually price if contracted for large quantities).

In 1995, mill sales of U.S.-produced flat-rolled carbon steel amounted to about $30 billion, while the total market for final sales of flat-rolled carbon steel to end users amounted to over $40 billion. Just over half of all mill sales of flat-rolled carbon steel (by tonnage) were at contract prices, meaning negotiated prices fixed for a period of between a quarter and a year. These sales amounted to about $20 billion and included a high proportion of the value-added sales—including, for example, most electrogalvanized and most tinplate production. The balance was sold at spot prices fixed at the moment of sale based on posted prices, formal and informal customer discount schedules, and the judgment of a mill's commercial staff as to the mill's need to sell the tons forecast in its rolling schedule and the price the market could bear at any moment. Most imports, most secondary products, and most mill shipments to service centers and converters are sold at spot prices. In addition, most service centers and processors that resell sheet use spot pricing. The spot market therefore contains a large number of players: U.S. mills, trading companies and importers, and large and small service centers and processors. The spot market is far from a perfect commodity market in an economic sense—as yet there is no commodity exchange with a fixed contract in flat-rolled carbon steel, and identical transactions can have widely different prices. Nevertheless, it is a market that operates in a relatively narrow price band for any given quantity and type of steel, and it is one that has become more liquid with the growth of both distributors and imports.

The volatility shown by spot pricing is a major factor in the cycles of the steel industry, both because of its direct revenue effect and because of its indirect inventory effects. Companies seek to hedge against future spot price rises in strong markets by purchasing excessive amounts of steel and accumulating inventory. Once the steel market perceives that an over inventory situation has occurred, usually but not necessarily when the economy starts to slow, destocking will cause steel orders to slump much faster than they otherwise would, creating a glut of steel and rapidly falling prices as mills seek to sell their production. The only way for a mill to avoid such boom-and-bust conditions is to maximize its contract business and minimize its spot sales.

Most niche tonnage sold to end users of steel is sold at contracted prices because nonstandard products require advance planning by the mill to melt, roll, cut and ship. To achieve such lead times, commercial departments of mills attempt to secure advance tonnage commitments in exchange for fixing prices for the tonnage committed. A typical commercial department will attempt to sell as much as possible of the mill's production capacity in advance to contract buyers while offering the balance of production to distributors or for export at spot prices. This strategy assumes that, on average, contract end-user sales generate higher margins and the risk of losing revenues in a rising market is more than offset by the measure of protection afforded by guaranteed income in a falling market.

The bulk of flat-rolled steel that is not sold to service centers and distributors is shipped to one of five major direct-purchase markets. Automotive, containers, appliances and office equipment, construction products, and manufacturers of welded pipe and tubing account in total for well over half of the shipments of domestic flat-rolled mills, especially when indirect shipments via service centers are included. These markets will be reviewed briefly, but data on consumption are flawed by lack of reliable statistics on the final destinations of imports, secondary shipments, and service center shipments. Estimates of total use by sector therefore vary among industry observers.

AUTOMOTIVE MARKETS

In an average year of recent business cycles, about 11 million tons of flat-rolled steel, or 20 percent or more of flat-rolled shipments, are made directly to the automakers and parts manufacturers. These shipments include the largest annually negotiated steel contracts, and many non-automotive contract prices follow the general direction of prevailing automotive prices. Until the mid-1970s, contract negotiations between the major steel companies and the three major Detroit automakers were reasonably amicable affairs, conducted with the knowledge that Detroit, like Big Steel, was operating on the assumption that it could pass along cost increases to the customer.

The impact of import competition in the U.S. auto market was similar to that in the steel market. Forced to drive down costs and raise quality to compete in a global market, U.S. automakers have very successfully restored their competitive position, but have done so in part by placing increasing demands on their suppliers, including the U.S. and Canadian steelmakers. Two major changes have taken place that give automakers far greater leverage in price negotiations with flat-rolled steel suppliers. First is the encroachment of competing materials—aluminum and plastics—into traditionally steel auto body parts. Second, automakers have cut certain steel mills out altogether and from time to time move significant tonnages away from one mill to another, instead of the historic pattern of sharing out the tonnage among mills so that every company was reasonably assured of keeping a stable share of the auto business. Price negotiations have also become much keener as mills genuinely compete with each other on price, instead of acting as a collusive oligopoly. On the other hand some things have shifted in favor of certain steel companies. As car weights have been reduced to improve energy efficiency, steel has responded with greater strength from thinner sheets, while surface quality from the leading mills has improved dramatically. The increasing use of two-sided galvanized, especially electrogalvanized steel with very thin molecular zinc coatings, led to a shortage of galvanized capacity in the 1980s, with the result that the price premium for galvanized steel widened.

The nine U.S. and Canadian steelmakers that have maintained a position as major automotive industry suppliers have had to undertake major investments, both in coating lines and in strip-mill gauge controls. Generally these investments have paid off, both because of the increased revenue from higher-value coated products and due to the market growth in North American vehicle manufacturing, including the phenomenon of Japanese- and European-owned "transplants." The automakers are likely to welcome the increased negotiating strength that the addition of flat-rolled minimill capacity will bring them, but are equally likely to be initially reluctant to entrust significant tonnages to new, unproven suppliers. The most likely path for minimill tonnage to make inroads to automotive markets is via parts suppliers and shipments to service centers and processors that have long-term partnerships with automakers, rather than through direct sales. The integrated mills' position with the automakers cannot be taken for granted, but it is at least a highly defensible position from which they will not be easily dislodged.

STEEL CONTAINERS

The market for tin mill products is similarly likely to remain a bastion of integrated steelmaking at least over the next cycle. A steady 4 million tons of tin mill products are consumed annually in the United States, or over 7 percent of flat-rolled product shipments. Six integrated companies dominate the market, led by U.S. Steel (including its USS-POSCO joint venture in the important California food canning market) and Weirton Steel. The canning market is in turn dominated by a handful of major can companies that buy tinplate and aluminum can stock and operate canning lines for food and beverage producers. Essentially all of this material is bought on a contract pricing basis. Aluminum drove steel cans out of the important beverage can market in the 1960s and 1970s, a market that, at over 100 billion cans a year in 1994, was equivalent to almost another 4 million tons of steel. In numerous developed countries, including Canada, steel has been able to retain a proportion of this market, although the pattern varies greatly with national boundaries even within the European Union. Major U.S. container producers have considered reintroducing steel beverage cans in the mid-1990s as aluminum prices have risen, leading to an apparent price advantage for steel of over 5 percent in 1995. However, North American tinplate capacity is operating at close to full capacity supplying the food container industry, and at least one major beverage executive has publicly questioned whether steel companies are really willing to make the capacity, technical, and pricing commitments necessary before can-line conversions will occur.[8] In 1995–96, construction of the first new tin line in the United States for thirty years was undertaken: the Yorkville, Ohio, plant of Ohio Coatings, a joint venture between Wheeling-Pittsburgh and Japanese and Korean partners. The new line, with a capacity of only 250,000 tons per year, replaces one of two existing lines operated by Wheeling-Pittsburgh. If, however, it triggers competitive moves by other producers, it could mark the start of a more eager pursuit of the beverage can market by integrated mills. Equally likely, as thin-strip quality improves with time, is the entry of minimills into this area in the next decade. Based on Canadian and European experience with similar competitive economics, it is possible that around a million tons of steel beverage cans could be produced annually by the year 2000, representing an attractive niche for any mill that can produce steel of acceptable quality.

Apart from steel "tin" cans, the container market also includes about a million annual tons of steel used in drums, pails, paint cans, strapping, and other containers and packaging materials that do not use tinplate. These markets usually require uncoated cold-rolled steel of heavier gauges than are rolled for tinplate, as the products require greater strength but have less hygienic need for corrosion resistance. Unlike the major can manufacturers, these other container markets are highly fragmented and have lower quality requirements. Their "commodity" steel requirements often are supplied by service centers and by imports, and they are likely to be natural targets for flat-rolled minimills.

APPLIANCES AND OFFICE EQUIPMENT

About 3.5 million annual tons of flat-rolled steel are consumed in the broad category of home and office equipment. The largest component of this group and the third largest end-user market for integrated mills (after automakers and canning companies) are the manufacturers of major household appliances. This segment is generally held to include air conditioners, refrigerators and freezers, dishwashers, washers/dryers, and kitchen ranges and ovens. In an average year, about 1.5 million tons of steel—primarily cold-rolled sheet and hot-dip galvanized—are used in major appliances, often being slit and prepainted or coated with enamel or plastic materials at a steel service center before being delivered to the appliance maker. Major appliances are manufactured, as are cars and cans, by a small number of major steel buyers, in this case primarily the Big Five of Whirlpool, Maytag, GE, Frigidaire, and Raytheon. To a greater degree even than in auto bodies or food and beverage cans, carbon steel competes intensely with alternative materials, primarily plastics and aluminum but also in some applications with stainless steel. At least another million tons of flat-rolled steel is consumed annually in smaller appliances, including consumer electronics such as television sets and videocassette recorders; electric housewares such as irons, vacuum cleaners, and toasters; outdoor appliances such as barbecue grills and lawnmowers; and microwave ovens. In these markets, too, steel competes intensely with aluminum and plastics, both of which have made major inroads over the past forty years. Cost, rather than quality, is critical, and while steel may be less expensive than competing materials on a per-pound basis, it is often at a disadvantage in terms of final assembled cost. A single plastic mold, for example, can often replace multiple metal stamping operations. Because these markets are much more fragmented than major appliances, they are much more likely than major appliance makers to use intermediary processors and distributors, although they are still likely to have either formal or informal contract pricing arrangements. Steel is also used in kitchen and bathroom applications such as tubs, sinks, countertops, and related devices such as in-sink disposal units and spa units, plus their related plumbing. This area uses predominantly stainless rather than carbon steel, although some enameled carbon steel is used in residential applications. Much more steel is used in residential kitchen and bathrooms in continental Europe than in the United States, where porcelain dominates; any growth in steel use in these areas in the United States is likely to benefit stainless rather than carbon producers.[9]

The other large component of the broader appliance/office equipment market is computers and other information technology-related equipment, including copiers, telephones, and fax machines. Driven by the massive growth in home use of personal computers beginning in the late 1980s, the traditional boundaries between "home" and "office" equipment have become blurred. Steel use in such equipment, which amounts to around a further 1 million tons, has grown along with the demand for such products, a demand that is a long way from reaching the saturation point. However, steel is primarily used in the bases and frames of such equipment and has lost out to plastics for most external body casing. As such machines become smaller and lighter, steel use is not likely to increase despite the greater penetration of such equipment into home markets.

Appliance and office equipment applications generally place less demands on steel for corrosion resistance and weight-to-strength ratios, and thicker paint (or enamel) coatings reduce surface quality requirements. Even major appliance steel is often purchased through or in partnership with a steel processor or service center, although the price of material shipped directly or indirectly to the Big Five tends to be set by annual negotiations. Most appliance steel is bought under contract pricing, but this reflects the pattern of long production runs requiring uniform steel, rather than special product characteristics. Because appliance steel is more of a commodity than automotive steel, new entrants in the carbon flat-rolled market will probably make rapid inroads into these sectors.

CONSTRUCTION PRODUCTS

A fourth large sector of flat-rolled steel usage is that often described as construction and contractors' products. About 4 million tons of flat-rolled steel (including coil plate) are reported shipped directly from mills to this sector in an average year. This figure probably grossly understates the use of flat-rolled steel in construction, given that many important construction sectors depend on service centers to supply their steel. Major construction markets for directly shipped flat-rolled steel include manufacturers of roof and floor decking; prefabricated metal buildings; heating and air-conditioning ducts; and building studs, joists, and trusses. Steel siding and corrugated roofing, large markets historically, have been displaced by lighter aluminum and vinyl products, but the new and quickly growing market for framing residential housing, displacing wood, is offsetting this trend. Most companies making steel components for construction are relatively small, and as spot buyers of commodity grades of steel have materials costs that are at the mercy of the spot price of steel.

A strategy likely to return to popularity in the late 1990s is for flat-rolled mills to acquire captive construction products manufacturers. The costs of such acquisitions are relatively low—the industry is relatively fragmented and is not capital-intensive—and the benefits to both sides appear large, given fair intracompany transfer pricing. The downstream fabricator is protected from spot price fluctuations, and the upstream steel company adds value to, and gains a guaranteed outlet for, its galvanized steel production. While Nucor has long been a major fabricator of metal buildings and contractors' products, integrated mills mostly liquidated their holdings in this area in the 1980s to generate cash. One integrated mill has taken the opposite course, however. Wheeling-Pittsburgh has long been the largest fabricator of corrugated galvanized steel, which is roll-formed and used in such varied applications as roof decking, highway culverts, and farm buildings. In 1994, Wheeling-Pittsburgh acquired Armco's subsidiary Bowman Metal Deck Products, a major roof, floor, and bridge deck maker, and followed it in 1995 by buying companies in the steel framing and in the roofing and siding businesses. These downstream subsidiaries account for over half of Wheeling-Pittsburgh's total hot-dip galvanized production. Such a strategy guarantees that Wheeling-Pittsburgh will be partly insulated from minimill competition in the key market of low-end galvanized steel.

The low quality requirements of most construction uses for flat-rolled steel make it a logical target for minimills, and indeed much of the output of Nucor's first two mills has gone to construction markets, either directly or via service centers. It is likely that much of this tonnage, including possible future growth in residential framing, will go to those minimills that have their own galvanizing capacity or a strong partnership with independent galvanizers. Nevertheless, the continued construction of new hot-dip galvanizing capacity in the late 1990s by integrated mills such as U.S. Steel and National Steel suggests that this sector will see one of the hardest fights for market share.

INDEPENDENT CONVERTERS I: PIPE AND TUBE MILLS

Intermediate between the market categories of end-users and distributors are the buyers of flat-rolled steel who convert it into other forms of steel mill product. The term "steel mill product" is necessarily arbitrary but is generally accepted as referring to semifinished forms of steel product traditionally rolled by steel mills and not subsequently fabricated into specific components or structures. Independent converters, then, usually are understood to include pipe and tube producers, cold rollers and coaters of sheet and strip, and cold-finished bar makers. Until the 1980s, a majority of welded pipe and tubing and much cold-rolled strip was produced in-house by integrated mills from their own flat-rolled product, although there have always been strong independent producers in the United States in these areas. In the 1990s, although a handful of flat-rolled producers still produce welded pipe, these "steel mill products" are now almost entirely produced by independent companies.[10] U.S. pipe and tube makers buy about 4 million tons per year of carbon flat-rolled steel, including some plate for large-diameter line pipe; and cold-strip mills buy more than half a million tons of domestic carbon hot-rolled steel for conversion. The great majority of such purchases are made at spot prices and include a proportion of imported steel.

Welded pipe and tubing products and markets are highly fragmented, ranging from high-volume commodity products such as standard pipe and piling pipe that sell in the range of $500 to $600 a ton, to pressure pipe and oil country goods that compete with seamless pipe and command twice the price. Of average annual U.S. pipe and tubing consumption in the 1990s of nearly 6 million tons, about 4 million tons represents domestic production of welded products. Welded pipe producers have suffered from serious overcapacity, a persistent problem in the industry at least since the early 1980s oil slump, and from cheap imports. These factors have meant that producer margins have been squeezed badly whenever flat-rolled steel prices increase, as between 1993 and 1995, because they are not able to pass on increases in their material costs by raising their own prices. Only structural (square and rectangular) tubing has seen consistent growth among major carbon steel pipe markets, although this sector has been constrained by competition for end-use applications with the new, low-cost capacity in wide flange beam production. Beams command about 80 percent of structural steel frame applications versus tubing's 20 percent, but tubing is expected to continue to slowly grow its share in the United States toward the much higher levels of penetration in Canada and certain other national markets.

Historically it has been rare for independent pipe and tubing producers to form long-term partnerships with supplying hot strip-mills. With the exit of most flat-rolled producers from the pipe business, however, the relationships appear to be evolving toward closer partnerships. An example of the possible future direction of the pipe and tube industry is the construction by Maverick Tube, previously a manufacturer of welded oil country tubulars, of a new structural tubing plant at Hickman, Arkansas, adjacent to Nucor's mill, which supplies it with coil. On the other hand, Caparo Steel and Ipsco's Iowa mill suggest an alternative strategy: the start-up of a hot-strip mill in part to supply a parent company's existing tubular operation, possibly leading to a recombining of the flat-rolled and tubular sectors of the industry. For the foreseeable future, the United States will have excess capacity at both hot-strip mills and welded tubular producers; it would therefore seem to be in the interest of flat-rolled producers to build partnerships with tubular mills as outlets for their hot-rolled coil. Conversely, however, the pipe and tube mills may now wish to maintain their independence to pursue bargains in a falling market for flat-rolled steel. The only secure prediction is for the volatility of the pipe and tube markets seen over the past decade to continue.

INDEPENDENT CONVERTERS II: COLD-ROLLED AND COATED SHEET AND STRIP

Cold-rolled strip, as produced by a number of independent, specialist strip producers in New England and the Great Lakes areas, is a highly specialized steel product with annual shipments ranging over the business cycle between 800,000 and 1 million tons, of which over a third are stainless steel.

Cold-rolled strip—defined as coils less than 24 inches wide and under 1/4 inch thick—is often known from its largest application as spring steel, although its uses are far broader than flat spring manufacture. It is used in strapping and cutting tools (including cutlery, chain saws, and knife blades) and by producers of automotive and appliance stampings.

The tonnages reported annually for cold-rolled strip production are generally shipments of what is known as specialty strip rather than simply of cold-rolled sheets slit to narrow widths. Specialty strip is rolled and finished to much closer dimensional tolerances than the high-volume cold-rolled sheet products of major mills, with gauge and width tolerances in the thousandths of an inch. Producers can impart special physical characteristics by rolling and heat treating, such as formability, heat and wear resistance, and "springiness." Special surface finishes can similarly be imparted, by pickling, heat treating, and polishing. Finally, the product is often edge-conditioned to produce a uniform rounded or squared edge, eliminating the jaggedness of slit edges. Nevertheless, such specialty products inevitably compete with strip slit from standard cold-rolled sheet coils, which offer a much cheaper alternative if the special qualities of cold-rolled strip are not needed. In the long run, the distinct status of the specialty strip mills is threatened by the improved quality of cold-rolled sheet products and the increased capabilities in cold-rolling, pickling, annealing, and slitting of flat-rolled processors and distributors. The formerly distinct industry segments of flat-rolled processors and cold-strip mills are likely to converge, especially as the growth of flat-rolled minimills encourages major capital investments in cold-rolling and heat treating by downstream processors.

Cold strip mills have traditionally preferred to buy hot-rolled coils from domestic mills at agreed, contract pricing but have not been sufficiently large buyers to get a significant cushion from spot pricing fluctuations. Their business level is often unpredictable, and as a group they buy significant tonnages—perhaps a quarter of their total purchases—from service centers, just as they rely on distributors for a large proportion of their sales. Cold strip mills are likely to buy significant tonnages from carbon flat-rolled minimills, as their own processing capabilities allow them to set only basic quality requirements for their hot-rolled band feedstock. On the other hand, as they face increased competition from processors, partnerships with mills (including integrated producers) will become more essential.

Cold-rolled sheets are produced from hot bands by flat-rolled steel mills both at locations adjoining their hot-strip mills and at captive cold-rolled mills located at geographically remote locations. Examples of non-integrated cold-rolling mills include National Steel's Midwest Division in Portage, Indiana, serving the Chicago market, supplied with hot band from the company's Detroit- and St. Louis–area mills; the USS-POSCO joint venture at Pittsburg, California, supplied largely from Gary, Indiana; U.S. Steel's Fairless Hills mill, which, since the closure of its hot end and hot-strip mill in 1991, has been supplied from the Mon Valley Works in the Pittsburgh area; the I/N Tek-I/N Kote joint venture complex of Inland Steel and Nippon Steel at New Carlisle, Indiana; and two plants of LTV Steel: the Hennepin Works in northern Illinois and the Aliquippa, Pennsylvania, plant, the latter having been an integrated mill into the 1980s.

Each of these mills supports coating lines—tinplate, galvanizing or both—and ships cold-rolled sheets. Although some facilities were either integrated mills or were planned eventually to be integrated, they operate today as stand-alone profit centers whose cold-rolled, as opposed to coated, products are shipped largely to regional markets. Other than the scale of the facilities, these are not different in principle from independent cold-rolling mills that similarly convert hot band into cold-rolled coils for regional markets. Independent, continuous cold-rolled sheet mills, as distinct from specialty cold strip mills, are a relatively recent phenomenon in the United States, although small hand-rolling mills for custom rolling individual pieces of sheet or plate have long been a feature of the periphery of the steel industry. In the 1980s, processor Worthington Industries acquired National Rolling Mills, in Malvern, Pennsylvania, a manufacturer of acoustical suspension systems with its own cold-rolling mill and pickling, electrogalvanizing, and nickel plating lines. In the 1990s, a number of coil processors, including Huntco, Schaeffer Industries, and Steel Technologies, Inc., have added cold-rolling mills as a logical extension to their existing pickling, slitting, and leveling or coating capabilities. Each of these three companies operates locations adjacent to a flat-rolled mill, respectively Nucor (Hickman, Arkansas), Geneva Steel, and Gallatin Steel. In addition, Chicago Cold Rolling, a company formed in 1995 with part ownership by Bethlehem Steel, began operations in Portage, Indiana, in 1996, while at the same time BHP Steel of Australia was building a cold-rolling mill in Oregon to supply that company's West Coast coil-coating operations.

Independent coil-coating operations are also making inroads into markets once dominated by integrated mills. In 1985, only one independent company operated a sheet-width coil-galvanizing line in the United States. Ten years later the number of independent lines has grown to eight. In addition, one Canadian and eight U.S. joint ventures between integrated mills operate galvanizing lines away from the supplying parent companies' mills.[11] Mill-owned joint venture lines tend to be integrated into their parents' sales and marketing operations, although they are operated as separate profit centers. Independent coaters, however, represent new competitors in a segment of the business formerly controlled by the integrated mills. The cost of a large-scale galvanizing line remains high—recent mill-owned facilities have approached $100 million—but barriers to entry are falling as independent processors emulate minimills and build or acquire existing lines for much less.

The significance of converters can be seen by the fact that in 1994, "Further Conversion" surpassed steel service centers as the largest reported market for U.S. Steel's sheet product shipments, taking 24 percent of that company's flat-rolled shipments (compared to 23 percent for service centers and 21 percent for transportation, including automotive). This figure includes shipments to nonconsolidated joint ventures such as USS-POSCO, ProTec, and Double Eagle, but not to the cold-rolling mill at Fairless Hills. It also includes shipments to Worthington Industries, long a close partner of U.S. Steel and operator (among other facilities) of a joint venture blanking line in Michigan, Worthington Specialty Processing, 50 percent owned by U.S. Steel. Such processing ventures reflect the increasing intermingling of mill downstream operations with processing and distribution activities.

The proliferation of stand-alone cold-rolling and coating capacity is a logical response to the changing economics of flat-rolled steel. The internationalization of steel markets, reduced capital costs, the decline of integrated mills' market power, and the excess of U.S. hot-rolling capacity makes it possible for independent companies to invest in downstream operations with confidence that supplies of hot band or cold-rolled coil can be secured. Equally, the increased service demands of end-use customers; the changing balance between freight, labor and materials costs; and the geographic dispersal of manufacturing point to the need for producing mills to invest in new and dispersed downstream facilities. These trends, plus the rise of flat-rolled minimills both with and without their own downstream operations, all suggest a continued rise in the number of producing locations and market competitors. They are likely to grow in importance as markets for long-term contract-type sales by both minimills and integrated mills, despite the inevitable competitive conflicts that will occur.

LESSONS FOR THE INTEGRATED MILLS

Three arguments can be made from this survey of flat-rolled producers and markets. First, barriers to entry are falling. Not only can a minimill be built for a fraction of the cost of an integrated mill, but it is not even necessary to own or operate a complete steel mill. Strategies for entering the business include operating a hot strip mill with purchased slabs (Beta Steel and California Steel Industries); building a cold-rolling mill; operating a pickling line, a coating line, or simply a leveling line. All are in some way competitors in the flat-rolled business.

Second, and related to the first point, the traditional segmentation of the industry—integrated and minimill producers, converters, and distributors—has irretrievably broken down. As flat-rolled minimills "integrate" in search of scrap supplements, integrated producers adopt minimill technology and practices, and as a host of new intermediate processors and converters emerges, a range of different business configurations have become economically viable as ways to make money in flat-rolled steel. As a consequence, the formerly clear-cut distinction between producers and consumers has been replaced with a series of value-adding operations, sometimes combined under one corporate umbrella, sometimes not.

Third, contrary to business school teachings, to the efforts of marketing staffs, and perhaps to intuition, flat-rolled carbon steel is becoming more, not less, of a commodity. More players, improved producer and distributor capabilities, and increased industry-wide quality standards make fewer producer-customer relationships "defensible" on quality grounds. A market niche that might have been supplied by no more than a handful of producers a decade ago might be pursued by twenty or more today. Ladle metallurgy, improved rolling mill tolerances, more (and more capable) downstream processors, and greater international integration all increase the flexibility of suppliers and the range of options in the supply channel.

All these trends point in the direction of continued fragmentation of a flat-rolled steel industry able, only a generation ago, to function as a closed oligopoly. The fragmentation suggests a future of a large number of industry participants; of greater separation of steelmaking, rolling, coating, processing, and distributing functions; of continuing technological ferment; and of aggressive competition in all market segments. These suggest that some key elements in the continued survival of integrated mills, beyond the next steel cycle, include:

- Finding new technological solutions to lowering the cost of ore-based steelmaking, both through adopting new ironmaking technologies and pursuing commercial-scale direct steelmaking. This also suggests not putting all a company's eggs in one basket—especially investments in an expensive, potentially obsolete, intermediate-product technology such as coke ovens or blast furnaces.
- Changing the mix of raw materials and the low-cost sources of each raw material input over time as costs and technology evolve. There is no great advantage in controlling raw materials when they face oversupply. Mill-owned coal and ore mines are likely to be underperforming assets. Flexibility in sourcing raw materials—coal, coke, scrap, scrap substitutes, ore, and semi-finished steel—requires water access for inbound raw materials, or at least access to two or more competing railroads (in a rapidly consolidating rail industry).
- Lowering freight costs. Freight is an ever-increasing factor in steel's economics, as steel's cost per ton falls in real terms. Dispersed locations of, for example, cold-rolling and coating lines may be critical to servicing regional markets, but they must be accessible from the steelmaking location by inexpensive bulk freight routes. Alternately, steelmaking must be done closer to the customer; "close" in terms of freight cost may mean export (ocean freight) markets thousands of miles away, rather than a truck-haul destination a hundred miles away.
- Recognizing that "small is beautiful," meaning that there is no need to be able to do everything for oneself or to be able to supply all a customer's needs. Low costs and high service are far more important to customers, suggesting that the use of processing partners and of locations close to the end user are keys to success. "Partnerships" no longer means steelmaker-customer relationships, but complex arrangements involving steelmaking, processing, warehousing and finally, yes, just-in-time delivery.
- Providing high quality. High quality is not a "value-added", niche-securing, product differentiator. Everybody has it, soon will, or claims to. It is the price of admission.
- Achieving low costs. Achieving costs comparable to the best minimills means achieving one man-hour per ton, not three. Cutting out two-thirds of the hourly workforce of an integrated

> mill will require massive investment in automation and process flow improvement. That investment is the price of survival.

Real costs of carbon flat-rolled steelmaking at integrated U.S. mills have declined by around $10 a ton, in 1995 dollars, every year since 1980. It is likely that the same rate of cost improvement will have to continue over the next ten years to guarantee the survival of something resembling the current integrated steelmaking sector. The track record of these steelmakers in the 1990s suggests that this can be achieved.

10

STEEL, THE GLOBAL ECONOMY, AND THE TWENTY-FIRST CENTURY

EMPLOYMENT, THE ENVIRONMENT, AND PRODUCTIVITY

Few of the changes that have overtaken the U.S. steel industry in the last two decades can be laid at the door of technological change in the industry. The basic elements of a modern steel mill—electric furnaces, ladle metallurgy, even continuous casting—were developed more than forty years ago. Direct reduction of iron ore was commercialized thirty years ago. Even thin-slab casting, at best an incremental gain in technology, was first experimented with more than twenty years ago. The dissemination of such technologies through the U.S. steel industry has proceeded at a slow pace, with periodic bursts of progress generally driven by the external pressures of foreign competition and innovation by new entrants. Compared to other major manufacturing industries, and even to some materials industries such as plastics and composite materials, the rate of change has been glacial. In the time taken to adopt a steelmaking process innovation such as continuous casting on an industry-wide basis, say twenty-five years, two or more life cycles of both product and production process have passed in such industries as electronics, transportation equipment, and information technology.

The difference between steel and these other industries is, of course, that the basic product—carbon steel mill products—has changed little. In addition, much of the capital stock of a steel mill has a very long productive life, even though it requires continuous, heavy maintenance–type expenditures to maintain safety and productivity. However, it also reflects the fact that an existing technology has been adapted to generate very large increases in productivity without major process change. Most of the investment in steelmaking since the late 1970s, whether by new or old mills, has been geared to driving down costs. An industry with less-than-average returns on historic investment has had to limit new investments to projects with fast payback periods. Incremental improvement in existing facilities is favored rather than risky innovation. Even pioneering companies such as Nucor have tended to be conservative in their engineering, using processes well proven on a pilot plant scale. Most of all, the size of the overall market has not increased; all producers have been painfully aware that they are competing to re-slice the pie to their advantage, not to enlarge it. The beneficiary of this intense focus on cost improvement has been the steel consumer. The loser has been the steelworker.

From a postwar high of an average 583,851 employees in 1965, steel industry employment as measured by the American Iron and Steel Institute declined at a rate of less than 2 percent a year through the 1970s to a 1979 level of 453,181. In the 1980s and early 1990s, by contrast, employment shrunk at a rate of over 5 percent a year, eliminating 72 percent of the 1979 jobs. Productivity, measured in terms of output per labor-hour, increased dramatically over this time, the rate of 5.2 percent mirroring the decline of employment. Table 10.1 shows the scale of this improvement.

During the last fifteen years, total employment cost per hour continued to rise slowly in real terms, although at less than 2 percent a year, or a fraction of the rate of productivity increase. However, the rising hourly employment cost conceals a disturbing underlying trend. During the 1980s, the real value of employee wages declined in real terms, although the decline was offset in terms of total employment costs by a dramatic real rise in the cost of nonpayroll benefits—chiefly pensions and medical insurance. In 1979, nonpayroll costs accounted for 21.2 percent of employment costs. In 1993, these had risen to 35.4 percent, or $11.29 for every hour worked. Meanwhile, the actual hourly

Table 10.1
EMPLOYMENT AND PRODUCTIVITY

	1965	1979	1993
Employees	583,851	453,181	127,191
Total hours worked ('000s)	1,158,208	894,078	273,708
Total cost per hour (current dollars)	$4.47	$12.84	$32.30
Total cost per hour (1993 dollars)	$20.60	$25.58	$32.30
Hours per ton shipped	12.46	8.92	3.07
Employment cost per ton	$55.70	$114.53	$99.16
Employment cost per ton (1993 dollars)	$256.68	$228.17	$ 99.16

SOURCE: AISI Yearbooks, various years; U.S. Department of Labor, Bureau of Labor Statistics (price deflator).

wage for nonsalaried employees rose in current dollars from $11.02 in 1979 to $18.10 in 1993, a rise of over 4 percent a year in current dollars but a fall of over 1 percent a year in constant dollars. For workers to have maintained constant purchasing power, their average hourly wage would have had to be around $22 in 1993.

The decline in real incomes but rise in total employment costs in steel in the 1980s reflected similar changes throughout the U.S. economy. The decade saw broad shifts in national income and expenditure away from manufacturing and toward certain fast-growing service industries—insurance, pensions and financial services, medical care, environmental protection, and the professions handling the increased levels of litigation and regulation in U.S. society. The pressure of such macroeconomic shifts penalized the international productivity of the U.S. steel industry in the short term, but the longer-term effects may not have been so damaging. It is possible to argue that the pressure of these changes in society actually increased the international competitiveness of U.S. manufacturing industry, by forcing firms to improve the productivity of all their inputs, labor as well as energy and raw materials.

The steel industry is more hostile to environmental regulation than to any other subject except steel imports. Much of the industry views environmental expenditures as unproductive or as a form of taxation, yet such expenditures have contributed indirectly to productivity by forcing companies to rethink their entire materials throughput flow and to avoid "waste" by more efficient use and re-use of material inputs. Ways of dealing with environmental issues range from a position of minimum compliance and the payment of fines as a cost of doing business, to enthusiastic embrace of company-wide environmental programs at Acme Steel in Chicago, winner of national and local awards for reduction of emissions.[1] The major challenge to U.S. integrated steel mills in the early 1990s was compliance with the so-called 33/50 provisions of the 1990 amendments to the Clean Air Act. These set targets for the "voluntary" reduction of emissions of numerous gases of 33 percent by 1992 and 50 percent by 1995, with the incentive that companies meeting these targets would be exempted until the year 2020 from the progressive implementation of stricter compulsory standards. Most industry facilities appear to be in compliance with the 1995 targets, although about a third of coke oven capacity may not meet the new standards.

Reported operating expenses for environmental compliance ran between 3 and 5 percent of the cost of goods sold for most U.S. steel companies in 1994. This number appears low in comparison to the high political profile of such expenditures, but it may actually be exaggerated given the offsetting economic gains from the recovery of "waste" materials. The use of off-gases and slag for heating and cement manufacturing, respectively, has long been economically feasible but has only recently become universal. In the late 1990s, with increased disposal costs of toxic wastes, even seemingly barren dregs of the steelmaking process such as coke breeze, furnace dust, and rolling mill sludges will be the inputs to new commercial processes aimed at recovering the metals and fuels contained in them. The industry is still along way from being a closed-cycle technology, generating zero pollution or wastes. Such a state is no longer unthinkable, however, and will arise not through punitive regulation but through the economic viability of a range of recycling technologies.[2]

By the mid-1990s, the effects of fifteen years of obsessive focus on costs were visible in terms of the productivity of all steel industry inputs. The U.S. steel industry's costs, admittedly helped by the weakness of the dollar, were at the low end of the developed world, and could match those of much capacity in the developing and ex-Communist economies. Further dramatic gains in the utilization of energy and materials inputs appeared unlikely given existing technology. The reduction of man-hours per ton shipped, to below an industry average of 3 in 1994, suggests that limits will soon be found to labor productivity improvements. Much specialty steelmaking will continue to require inherently higher levels of expensive manpower inputs, while in long products, the patterns of order sizes, rolling cycles, and shipments suggest that improvement below 2 man-hours per ton may not be possible. Even if the more optimistic carbon flat-rolled minimills increasingly reverse the productivity unit of measure and talk in terms of tons per hour, the fact remains that at existing levels of labor productivity, personnel costs have been reduced to levels that are competitively insignificant. Other inputs—not just raw materials but also electricity and freight—have greater weight in the equation.

THE END OF UNION STEELWORKERS?

The total labor cost per ton of most U.S. minimills is now lower than the freight cost per ton of bringing steel from Korea. At such levels, U.S. companies are indifferent to comparative international wage rates, because distance effectively insulates them from their effects. Logic would suggest that employee bargaining power would be increased in such circumstances and that hourly wages could rise again in real terms. However, the geographical spread of the industry into rural areas has enabled companies to hold down labor costs at new mills while offering significantly higher wage rates than those traditionally offered in these regions and also at older mills by threatening job losses to the new mills. The corollary of such employment shifts has been the decline of unionization and changed patterns of management-labor relations.

At the beginning of 1979, the United Steelworkers of America had 1.2 million dues-paying members, of whom a quarter, approximately 300,000, were in U.S. Basic Steel locals organized at integrated and most electric furnace steel mills; another 50,000 belonged to Canadian steelmaking locals. A further 300,000 were in U.S. and Canadian iron ore or other raw materials operations, or at downstream steel fabricating plants. The rest of the union's active membership included workers in aluminum and other nonferrous metals industries and a range of manufacturing plants. Only three major North American steel mills were not organized by the USWA: Ford's Rouge Steel was organized by the United Auto Workers, while Weirton and Middletown had independent unions. The first non-union minimills were in operation in the United States, including two Nucor plants, but non-union workers produced only 1 percent of the country's raw steel.

At the beginning of 1995, the USWA's dues-paying membership was only 413,000 in the United States and 152,000 in Canada. About 100,000 members in both countries worked in steelmaking and about

50,000 in iron ore or steel fabricating operations. Almost 15 percent of U.S. raw steel was produced by non-union workers, although in Canada the union retained almost 100 percent coverage. In both union and non-union plants, a wide range of bonus and incentive plans, participative teams for decision making, and the "empowerment" of production workers blurred the traditional lines of demarcation between management and "men". Many traditional union functions appeared to be obsolete; for example, the Occupational Safety and Health Administration (OSHA) had replaced union with government monitoring of safety standards, while the educational levels required to run much computer-controlled equipment made seniority alone an insufficient basis for holding down many skilled positions. Start-up mills in the mid-1990s, such as Gallatin Steel, employed a high percentage of recent college graduates in hourly positions. The combination of small, close-knit workforces and high levels of education and individual responsibility make union organization of such mills highly unlikely. By the 1990s, it appeared that only management folly could make union organization at a steel mill possible. In such an environment, the Steelworkers union groped for a new role and sought to survive by merging with other major industrial unions. In 1995, the USWA merged with the 50,000-member United Rubber Workers, then announced a plan for its eventual merger into a giant combination with the United Auto Workers and the International Association of Machinists. The goal of the resulting 2-million-member union is to restore some of labor's former political and organizational clout in manufacturing industry, but it would eliminate the proud identity and industry focus of the Steelworkers. It would also not answer the fundamental question of what a union is for in a modern steel mill.

The dilemma faced by the USWA, and more generally by unions in North America, was revealingly shown when in January 1993 the union's basic steel industry locals adopted a statement of bargaining principles called the New Directions Bargaining Program. Rather than focusing on terms of employment such as wages and benefits, or on the protection of seniority and dispute procedures, the document sounds in part like a fashionable business guru's manifesto for productivity with happy workers. Key elements include worker participation in decision making (including at board level), increased education and training, and "restructuring the way work is done to reduce costs and make the work place less authoritarian, safer, more fair and more rewarding in terms of worker skills and involvement in the solution of operating problems."

Concerns about continued restructuring are reflected in appeals for no-layoff programs and for "corporate successorship guarantees," the legal and contractual protection of workers in the event of corporate sale or reorganization. On a more cooperative theme, the union proposed such measures as joint, multicompany negotiation of lower health insurance costs. The union committed to work jointly with the steel companies for industry public-policy goals such as health care and retirement cost reforms. It also made significant concessions in the area of contracting-out jobs once automatically done by union steelworkers, claiming in effect only the right to retain maintenance and processing jobs directly related to core production operations. The program referred ambivalently to the union's desire to "eliminate all significant remaining contracting-out problems."

In the 1990s, the USWA was still capable of conducting aggressive "corporate campaigns" such as that against Bayou Steel, the Louisiana minimill that continued operations with replacement workers after a USWA local struck in March 1993. Bayou's disregard of collective bargaining led to a three-year campaign against it in the courts, the use of allegations of safety and environmental violations to incur regulatory inspections (and fines), and political pressure against financial aid for Bayou's restart of a second minimill in Tennessee. Nevertheless, the campaign's lack of success pointed out the fundamental weakness of the union against tough management in a southern, rural environment traditionally hostile to unions.

The steel workplace of the next decade is likely to be patterned after two alternative models. One is a high-tech plant producing flat-rolled or specialty steel, with a small but highly skilled workforce participating in both the decision making and the rewards of their plant's success. Algoma Steel among older mills, and Gallatin Steel among new, are examples suggesting the broad applicability of this model. The second and more traditional model, especially viable for less technically sophisticated products, is of a well-paid, often small-town workforce closely managed by take-charge front-line managers, but who are not themselves required to take responsibility or to think beyond an allotted task at which they can earn significant productivity bonuses. Successful examples of the second model appear to include AK Steel and Bayou Steel. Both models appear applicable in either union or non-union workplaces, with union organization a variable leading to little perceptible difference in employee earnings or satisfaction at comparable companies. Most companies, including industry leaders such as Nucor and the employee-owned companies, have either attempted to find middle ways between these two models or to cling to older patterns of workplace structure. The common elements to all successful companies, however, have included the elimination of much traditional middle management, the driving down of decision making to the plant floor, and the use of monetary incentives (and job-security disincentives) to undermine the union's role as an intermediary and an alternate source of authority in the workplace.

The traditional integrated steel industry of the 1950s self-consciously emulated military models of structure and discipline. In the 1980s and 1990s, the U.S. military found that tactical success required a revolution in its doctrine. Technology, education, and empowerment—reliance on individual and small-team initiative—became the model for military success. The management strategies of the high-tech, participative steel companies suggest that the steel industry may once again be converging with a (very different) military model of organizational success. In such a model, it can be argued that unions can survive only by being co-opted into management.

TECHNOLOGY AND ECONOMICS I: DIRECT STRIP CASTING

The term "high-tech steel mill" still seems to be an oxymoron. Steelmaking, even in the newest minimill, relies on large, bulky, and noisy equipment built for robustness but still prone to breakdown. A time-traveling nineteenth-century engineer would immediately understand the basic technology. A steel mill may contain many microchips, but they are still used primarily to control the operations of a process that has evolved only slowly from the steam age. This is unlikely to change in the near future, although the pace of change in the industry appears to be increasing.

Much of the cost of steelmaking results from the need to operate (and coordinate) several capital-intensive, large-scale processes in sequence, from raw materials preparation through to cold-rolling and coating. The principal advances in steel technology in recent decades have been those that simplify the process and eliminate the need for certain operations—for example, continuous casting and then thin-slab casting eliminated the ingot casting/slabbing and the roughing stages respectively. Two areas of current research give hope for similar developments that might transform the industry's economics in the next century.

Thin-strip casting is the next logical step after thin-slab casting in the steady evolution of casting technology. The solid shapes into which molten steel is poured from the furnace have evolved from boxy ingots, through thick continuously cast slabs, to the thin slabs and near-net-shape casters of modern minimills. The Holy Grail of casting technology is to be able to pour a finished solid shape out of liquid steel, without a separate hot-rolling process. This is, of course, how the foundry industry produces small batches of special shapes; however, foundry molds cannot continuously produce lengthy, rolled products such as steel coils. Instead, engineers have long tried to combine continuous casting of ever-thinner slabs with built-in hot-rolling to produce a strip-thickness product. Direct strip casting would eliminate the hot-strip mill from the production process, in the same way that the continuous slab caster eliminated the slabbing or breakdown mill and the thin slab caster eliminated the need for roughing stands in the hot-rolling process. The simplification of the production process through direct thin-strip casting offers the potential of significant savings in producing hot-rolled band.

In 1995, thin-strip casting had been at the pilot-plant stage of development for over a decade at a number of locations worldwide. Only one plant, the Cremona mill of Italy's Arvedi Group, was in commercial operation. It entered service in 1992, producing directly cast stainless coil as thin as 1.5 mm (0.1 inch). After a protracted start-up period, in 1994, the Cremona mill produced a range of grades of steel at a rate of 500,000 tons per year, reportedly at a profit. The most advanced project in North America appeared to be that conducted jointly by stainless steelmaker Allegheny-Ludlum and the Austrian engineering and steel giant Voest-Alpine. At Allegheny-Ludlum's Lockport, New York, plant near Buffalo, a prototype commercial-scale caster was installed in 1992, capable of producing stainless steel coils 48 inches wide and 0.012 inches (3 mm) thick, using a 15-ton heat from Lockport's small electric furnaces. Stainless steel is easier to direct cast than carbon steel, as it requires lower casting temperatures at which the molten metal is less corrosive to the caster and easier to control.

Other pilot projects or development programs were under way by a consortium of Canadian steelmakers at Boucherville, Quebec; and in Australia (BHP with IHI of Japan), France (Ugine/Usinor/Thyssen), Japan (Nippon Steel and Mitsubishi), and Korea (Posco with Davy International). Other companies have made major contributions to specific problems, such as Inland Steel's development of electromagnetic dam technology for edge containment of liquid steel at the sides of the caster, where rolls cannot retain the metal. A promising carbon steel project of Armco, Inc., with U.S. federal government support, was terminated in 1994 when Armco cut back its interests in carbon steel with the end of its participation in AK Steel. This left the Canadian program, known as Projêt Bessemer and conducted at the Canadian government's Industrial Materials Institute (IMI), as the principal North American contender for carbon steel strip casing. In this as in other areas of competitive technological development, secrecy reigns about the actual progress of production quantities and quality. It appears, however, that a number of these projects, most likely the stainless-oriented processes of Allegheny Ludlum/Voest-Alpine, BHP, and the Posco/Davy team, will be offered commercially before the end of the 1990s.

The slow speed in developing reliable direct strip casting reflects, in part, the fact that the casting of metals is still as much an art as a science; increasing difficulties arise in consistently achieving high surface quality as the cast product becomes thinner. In the absence of complete theoretical knowledge or computer models of the behavior of molten steel as it solidifies, engineers have been forced to develop processes partly by extensive trial and error.

The other factor slowing the pace of development of direct strip casting is the fact that thin-slab casting, as commercialized by Nucor and others, offers much of the potential economic benefits of direct strip casting without the technical risk. It may be possible to produce hot bands by direct strip casting for only one-half a man-hour per ton. If, however, "conventional" thin-slab casting and rolling can produce steel with less than one man-hour per ton, as at Nucor's plants, the cost saving is very small—perhaps $10 an hour in labor costs. Further savings would be chiefly in the area of capital costs; elimination of the need for a hot-strip mill could cut the capital cost of a flat-rolled minimill by one-third. However, the pioneers of such a process would almost certainly face significant additional start-up costs that would offset such savings.

Direct strip casting offers the future prospect of sheet production at smaller minimill plants than are economical with current technology. It is possible that profitable carbon flat-rolled steel units as small as 500,000 tons per year could be operated in North America, thus increasing the geographical spread of the industry. BHP Steel's new cold-rolling mill on the Columbia River in Oregon, for example, has a capacity of 300,000 tons per year; this would become an ideal base load for a small direct-strip steelmaking plant. As the real price per ton of steel declines, true "market mills" for sheet products would become economical for regions that are increasingly remote in freight cost terms, such as the Pacific Northwest. The introduction of such mills would increase the downward pressure on overall pricing in North America.

Strip casting is likely to be commercialized in North America before the end of the 1990s, at least for specialty steel. Failure to introduce it for carbon steel by the turn of the century could reflect probable downward pressure on prices and overcapacity in the flat-rolled market during the next recession, combined with pressure by financial markets on steel companies to show returns on their earlier investments in capacity expansion. Probably, however, one or more companies will take the plunge into carbon-direct strip casting. Likely candidates include companies that own existing downstream processing facilities and wish to secure captive hot-band supplies but that cannot afford or support the volume of a thin-slab plant. They also include existing steelmakers (including integrated companies) that have chosen to ride out the current wave of investment in thin-slab casting and that are looking to "leap-frog" a generation of technology.[3]

TECHNOLOGY AND ECONOMICS II: DIRECT STEELMAKING

Direct steelmaking is likely to be commercialized somewhat later than strip casting. As the direct reduction of iron by various processes becomes more widely adopted in North America, more attention is being focused on the next logical development: combining the operations of direct iron reduction and steel refining into a one-stage continuous process of direct steelmaking. Unlike strip casting, however, such a step would be much more than an evolution of existing technologies. Steel refining—whether in electric or basic oxygen furnaces—is a batch process in which a specific quantity of iron is refined to steel in a closed vessel, then cast before the process is repeated. Ironmaking in the blast furnace, on the other hand, is a continuous process; an economical single-stage process must make steelmaking continuous. A number of major technical challenges are involved. One is to develop refractories that can handle the corrosive by-product liquids reduced from coal, at the very high temperatures involved in a one-stage process. Another is to make the process energy-efficient, using fuels that can not only reduce iron but superheat the product to refine it to steel. A third is to make the whole process environmentally friendly; the same problems that occur today with coke ovens, blast furnaces, and steelmaking processes would be concentrated in one complex, toxic reaction. Whatever process solves all these problems must also be fast, reliable, and cheap enough to justify commercialization.

A number of pilot-scale projects have attempted to resolve these problems, with mixed success to date. Most research has tended to be based on the Corex and similar processes, which use coal as fuel for direct ironmaking but which do not incorporate the final process of steel refining. One such effort, by a consortium of integrated steel companies funded by the U.S. Department of Energy, was abandoned in 1994 after five years' work; it developed technology that worked but produced inconsistent grades of steel and took too long to be applicable on a commercial scale.

A direct steelmaking project that has raised considerable interest in the steel industry brings together the unlikely partners Nucor and U.S. Steel, together with Praxair, a major supplier of industrial gases. The two steel companies have made very different public statements about their reasons for interest in the project—in almost a parody of their respective public images, Nucor cites the potential for cost savings while U.S. Steel has stressed relief from regulatory control of pollution—but both have an intense common desire to be in the forefront of a potential transformation of the industry.[4] The partners' research is focused on adding to Nucor's gas-fueled iron carbide technology rather than the coal-fueled processes that have attracted most research effort to date. The iron carbide process, still in the early stages of its commercial use by Nucor in Trinidad, introduces methane gas to heated iron ore fines, producing water from the combination of hydrogen from the gas with oxygen from the ore, and produces iron carbide from the combination of the gas's carbon with the iron. There should be enough carbon present to act as a fuel in smelting the iron carbide to liquid iron. The key to the second stage, generating additional heat to refine the iron to steel, lies in capturing the heat of the reaction whereby carbon monoxide, released from the iron carbide, is converted to carbon dioxide as oxygen is introduced in the refining vessel.

This experimental sequence is still in many ways a three-stage process: iron carbide production, iron smelting, steel refining. The project seeks, initially, to combine the smelting and refining stages in a two-chamber, closed pneumatic vessel, using imported iron carbide; but it could ultimately lead to an enclosed, continuous, three-stage process. Among the factors likely to govern the timing of developments on this front are the speed at which iron carbide itself becomes reliably and cheaply available. Nucor encountered frustrating start-up problems and delays at its Trinidad plant in 1994–95, although these appeared to be caused as much by equipment malfunctions as by a need to fine-tune the process itself. A second important player in the iron carbide area emerged in 1995 with the establishment of Qualitech Steel by Gordon Geiger, the engineer who developed much of the technology for iron carbide first as Vice President of Technology for North Star Steel, then as a consultant to U.S. Steel on the direct steelmaking project. His decision to establish his own company, with a new SBQ minimill fed by what will become the second commercial iron carbide plant, suggests the prospect of another early entrant into the competition to develop carbide-based direct steelmaking.

Nucor has spoken publicly about the possibility of a pilot plant being built at one of its Arkansas properties within the next few years. However, whether iron carbide-based or coal-based processes eventually prove viable, it is unlikely that a commercial-scale direct steelmaking plant will be attempted before early years of the next decade. Once the technology is proven, however, it potentially represents the kind of economic breakthrough on the primary steelmaking or hot end side of the industry that has taken place with the development of net shape casting downstream. Forecast savings of around $50 a ton in steelmaking costs may prove optimistic, but they must be seen in the context of total steelmaking costs of only around $120 through the caster (on top of raw materials) at U.S. electric furnace mills.

TECHNOLOGY AND ECONOMICS III: CONTINUED EVOLUTION

The steady reduction in steelmaking costs over the last twenty years owes more to the refinement of existing processes and practices than to new processes, despite the importance of casting and ladle refining developments. The steady progress of improving raw materials production, steelmaking, rolling, and finishing operations continues in the late

1990s, and suggests that further cost reductions will be achieved without process breakthroughs.

Steel's competitive need to drive down costs has made the business school panacea of continuous process improvement a reality. To single out particular developments in such an environment is difficult. However, among the more significant developments likely to be widely adopted in the next two decades are direct-current (DC) electric arc furnaces, continuous cold-rolling, and the replacement of acid pickling by saltwater treatment.

Electric arc furnaces have grown in size and power as they have captured market share from other furnaces. Engineering firms are currently promoting a number of EF configurations, while intense debate rages as to which confers the greatest energy savings. After a development period that included major problems at one pioneering installation, Florida Steel's Tampa EF shop (now closed), DC furnaces have become widely accepted. A DC furnace costs at least 30 percent more than a similar-sized AC model, although the reduced capital costs of associated electric power supply equipment can offset this. DC furnaces typically use a single electrode (instead of three for most AC designs) and use less total power, while being able to use higher voltages with less "flicker" and strain on the supplying power grid. Electrode consumption, which accounts for between $10 and $15 per ton in a conventional AC furnace, is cut by about half. Difficulties in developing furnace bottoms and refractories to deal with the higher temperatures offset part of these savings.

In DC furnaces as in so many other innovations, it was Nucor that successfully pioneered their use in the United States. After Nucor introduced a small DC furnace at Darlington, South Carolina, in 1985, Nucor selected the technology for its new Hickman, Arkansas, flat-rolled mill and for a second large DC furnace at Darlington. At least seven other U.S. installations were on line or under construction by 1995.[5]

Meanwhile, the AC furnace has itself developed in ways that generate major cost savings. The use of scrap preheating reduces overall melt times and electrode consumption. The use of twin furnace shells sharing a common set of electrodes allows the second vessel to be charged with scrap while the first is using the electrodes to melt the charge, thus cutting down time. Reactor-type furnace vessels allow the use of higher voltages and long arcs in the melting process. These developments have allowed a number of new EF installations, such as Steel Dynamics' new mill at Butler, Indiana, to use AC furnaces with costs similar to DC installations; one decisive element appears to be the need for very large, premium-priced electrodes—30 inches in diameter or more—in DC furnaces above about 125 tons capacity. From recent furnace selection decisions, it appears that below this capacity level, DC technology has a cost advantage, while above this level, AC furnaces are still competitive. Developments in Europe in EF technology, such as the Fuchs shaft furnace and the Danieli "saturable" reactor furnace, focus on the efficient distribution of energy within the furnace, maximizing melt speed while minimizing power inputs and the thermodynamic stress and excess refractory use from hot spots in the furnace.[6]

As with the solidification of steel in casters, today the reactions involved in steel melting are becoming better understood and more closely controllable. Science is slowly replacing art, although each new advance in the steelmaking process requires much fine-tuning of prototypes. The level of process knowledge and control that allows Boeing, using computer modeling and design, to build a new aircraft design to production standard without prototyping is still a generation away from being applicable in the steel industry.

Developments in cold-rolling focus on well-understood technology but seek to convert a number of discrete batch operations into one continuous process. About half of all hot-rolled coils are subsequently cold-rolled, and the percentage is likely to grow; but as now conducted at most integrated mills, it is a very high-cost, labor-intensive operation. To produce cold-rolled coils from hot-rolled ones, the hot bands—master coils about half a mile long and typically 1/8 inch thick—are first pickled in acid to clean the surface of oxide scales formed as the hot-rolled coil cooled. The coil is then cold-rolled, which increases the coil's length by perhaps four times in proportion to the reduction in its thickness. As cold-rolling reduces steel's formability for drawing and shaping, the metal must then be reheated in an annealing furnace to restore its original malleability or to impart other strength and hardness characteristics. Finally it must be pickled again, to reduce the oxide formed again by the annealing stage, before shipment. In a traditional batch process, the steel is uncoiled and recoiled at each stage, four times in all.

Linking these four procedures in a continuous process generates savings in a number of ways. Continuous processing gives greater uniformity and higher overall quality, faster processing time, and lower labor costs. It reduces the costs and potential for damage of repeated handling, often including the freight cost between sites when operations are not co-located. If the process is coordinated correctly, it eliminates down time that results when batch processing is dependent on the speed of the slowest operation in the sequence. Continuity of flow is achieved by automatically joining coils by flash butt-welding as they are fed into the initial pickling operation, and the entire process is monitored and controlled by computer.

A few continuous lines have been built in North America in the last decade, including the USS-Posco and I/N Tek joint ventures and Dofasco's mill at Hamilton. Other mills, such as LTV at Cleveland and Bethlehem at Burns Harbor, have upgraded and linked existing facilities to attempt similar savings. Costs—in the region of $500 million for an all-new complex—and market size limit the number of such installations. Throughput of at least a million tons a year is necessary to generate a return on an investment of that size. Nevertheless, these mills show reported operating cost savings of up to $10 a ton over the previous generation of purpose-built, full-scale cold-finishing mills such as LTV's Hennepin Works, in north-central Illinois, and National Steel's Portage mill. The savings compared to older facilities must be far greater.

Modern continuous cold-rolling lines are one way for integrated mills to fight minimill entrants into the flat-rolled business. On the other hand, equipment vendors are rushing to offer minimill companies designs for smaller, low-capital-cost but noncontinuous cold-rolling "market mills," whose competitiveness would depend on minimill operating practices to achieve high productivity. The entry of stand-alone cold-rolling mills, independent of supplying hot-strip mills, also suggests a growing market for small-scale cold-rolling plants. Over the next decade, cold-rolling looks certain to attract as much attention and investment at both ends of the size spectrum as any other aspect of the steel industry.

One aspect of cold rolling—of many wire and bar products as well as sheet—that has long been taken for granted is the use of acid to pickle the surface of steel after hot processing. Pickling is usually done in either hydrochloric or sulfuric acid, at high levels of concentration. This process is highly toxic, and recycling the acid is difficult and expensive; the alternative, dumping it in hazardous waste sites, is no more appealing. In the mid-1990s, a number of companies were experimenting with alternative ways of cleaning steel to replace the use of acid.

The most promising process uses salt water as the cleaning agent. Although salt water is not strong enough to dissolve surface oxide coatings itself, a salt bath can be combined with electrolysis to loosen the scale. In a process being commercialized for wire production by a Canadian company, Dynamotive, the scale is then peeled off using ultrasound pulses, leaving the oxide suspended in the salt water rather than dissolved as in acid pickling. In this process, oxide can be filtered out easily for its return to the steel furnace or for sale as magnetite in applications such as magnetic tapes. This reduces not only the costs of iron recovery and acid disposal but also the corrosion of equipment in the plant (and the safety hazards) from the acid and its fumes. It could also reduce the proportion of pickled steel that is lightly coated with oil before shipment to retard rust, as saltwater corrodes steel less rapidly than does acid.[7]

In 1995, the first commercial-scale saltwater cleaning systems were coming on-line for wire and rod at U.S. and Canadian plants. No flat-rolled steel producer had committed to install such a process, but the level of interest was great; it is probable that before the end of the decade this process, or a variant of it, will be introduced in the (much larger) flat-rolled steel sector.

The greenfield steel mill of the early twenty-first century could well include a range of new technologies, from direct steelmaking, through direct-strip casting, to acid-free cleaning, all in a continuous, computer-controlled operation. Yet for the next twenty years or more, however, most steel will be produced using a combination of old and new technologies, and the greatest part of North American production will be from capacity installed or under construction by 1996.

Finally, not only will most steel be made in the same way, at the same mills, in twenty years' time; most will still be made to the same specifications as at present. Based on public information about materials research in steel and in competing products, it appears unlikely that any new material or radical change in the economics of steel or a competitor will change the availability and attractiveness of the major industrial materials. One possible exception to this stable pattern is wood, although the areas of competition between wood and steel are limited, as will be discussed further. There will be continued slow movement in the steel market toward value-added products—higher alloy grades, including steady growth in stainless steel and coated carbon steels. Nevertheless, although steel may on average be cleaner, more consistent, and more precisely shaped, it will be of the same grades and chemistries now manufactured. The steel industry thinks it is undergoing a revolution. By manufacturing industry standards, it is not. The real drama was the end of oligopoly in the industry, a process largely completed by the mid-1980s. But by comparison with other raw materials, steel is certainly evolving at a fast and increasing pace.

As the rate of technological change of increases, so will the competitive pressures on all participants in the industry. In a competitive, commodity market, incremental additions to capacity (and the incremental changes in technology they embody) will have decisive effects on the pricing and profitability structure of the industry. As technology and competition drive down costs, North American steel has the opportunity to resume a higher growth path. Before looking at the prospects in North America, however, it is necessary to look briefly at the global picture.

STEEL IN THE WORLD ECONOMY

In 1996, the United States, Canada, and Mexico account for around 15 percent of global steel production, and—reflecting the higher proportion of scrap-based steelmaking in North America—just under 12 percent of blast furnace pig iron production. Although the North American Free Trade Agreement will evolve only slowly toward becoming a homogeneous trading block, and is far behind both the European Union (EU) and the Commonwealth of Independent States (CIS) in terms of integration, for steel purposes—especially when looking toward the future—it may nevertheless be considered as one market. As a region, North America's 124 million tons of raw steel production in 1993 compared with nearly 159 million tons from the 15-state European Union; 104 million from the five steel-producing ex-Soviet states that adhered to the CIS; and from the giants of East Asia, Japan and China, 110 million and 98 million tons respectively. Four smaller regions contributed most of the balance of world production—Eastern Europe between the EU and the CIS; India; South America (dominated by Brazil); and the "tigers," the booming smaller economies of East Asia, led by South Korea and Taiwan. Of 81 steel-producing countries, the five national and organizational giants—North America, the EU, the CIS, China, and Japan—accounted for 73 percent of world production. The next five—South Korea, Brazil, India, Taiwan and Poland—add another 13 percent. The industry is thus very highly concentrated, reflecting the limited global distribution of metal-based manufacturing industry. Steel is unique among major metals industries in that historically it has located close to its markets. In contrast to most other mining and smelting industries, it was able to do so because its raw materials were very widely available.

In the 1970s and 1980s, the emergence of major steel industries in rapidly developing economies such as Korea and Brazil suggested two new developments in world steel. One was the emergence in Brazil and Venezuela (and elsewhere, in the 1990s) of production of both DRI and steel close to the iron source. As a way of promoting development by adding value to primary resources, of course, this represented a classic development strategy, pursued by companies and countries in industries from copper to petroleum. For the steel industry, it represented a novel development, one that contributed significantly to the rise in global trade of semifinished steel products. The second development was the creation of major steel industries based from the start entirely on imported raw materials, as in Korea and Taiwan. These countries followed the models of Japan and, more recently, most of Western Europe, where national steel industries quickly exhausted limited local resources, leading ultimately to complete import dependence. In both cases, the diffusion of steelmaking technology moved in step with the global decline in freight costs and increase in trade.

In the long term, more of the long-discussed projects for adding value near the mine are likely to come to fruition. In the late 1990s, projects under construction to produce slabs at Saldanha Bay, South Africa, and DRI in Western Australia, plus the growth in exports of semifinished steel from Russia and the Ukraine, suggest further separation of "upstream" and "downstream" steelmaking operations globally over time.

Global patterns of steel consumption in the 1990s appear to show similarities across widely different regions in terms of the long-term relationship between steel consumption and economic development over time. China and India showed dramatic growth in steel consumption rates in the 1990s, exceeding their gross national product (GNP) growth rates (of around 9 and 8 percent per annum, respectively, in the first half of the decade). In so doing they followed the historical examples of the United States and Russia, focusing on domestic demand and infrastructure development, instead of Korea or nineteenth-century England, where export-oriented industrialization led overall economic development. The effect is the same, however: growth in metals consumption exceeding GNP growth until markets are saturated, followed by relative growth in services and decline in manufacturing. In both China and India, steel production lagged behind demand, while in export-driven economies such as Korea, steel production increased ahead of domestic demand.

Globally, steel demand in the first half of the 1990s has been stable; growth areas such as China and India were offset by marked absolute declines in the Eastern European economies forced to make the rapid, difficult transition from Communist to capitalist economics. After 1989, steel production in the former Comecon states declined by 195 million tons of annual production in just five years, equivalent to the loss of 22 percent of world production. By 1995, this decline was offset by expansion in all other regions outside Europe, and in 1995 Eastern European and Russian production appeared to have stabilized and be poised for a slow, partial recovery. In the balance of the decade, world production and apparent consumption looked set to grow at perhaps 2 percent a year, still led by the growing economies of Asia and to a lesser extent Latin America, with only Europe (east and west) still struggling with "overcapacity," meaning capacity in the wrong place or with globally uncompetitive costs.

STEEL IN THE NORTH AMERICAN ECONOMY

In North America, the patterns of steel use, like steel technology, have changed slowly throughout the twentieth century. The key long-term determinants of steel consumption have been the overall growth rate of the economy, the growth rates of manufacturing and construction within the overall economy, and the competitiveness of steel with substitute materials for manufacturing and construction applications. The last major change in the long-term pattern of steel demand in the United States and Canada, which occurred in the 1970s, reflected major changes in the economy as a result of several major shifts:

- The overall economic growth rate slowed as a result of the cumulative effects of the oil shocks, the end of the system of fixed exchange rates, budget and trade deficits, and the effects of both inflation and the consequent disinflationary monetary policy used by the Federal Reserve Bank to counter it.
- Within the economy, manufacturing declined relative to other sectors. The relative growth of both true service industries (such as banking) and of non-materials-based production (such as of movies or software programs) enabled North American econo-

mies to grow without the concomitant growth of materials-intensive manufacturing.
- Growth in international trade of manufactured (especially metal) goods increased indirect steel imports and reduced North American steel demand. This long-term change was driven by the diffusion of manufacturing technology and investment, the declining real costs of ocean freight, and the fact that productivity growth in advanced countries such as the United States lagged behind real wage growth.
- In the medium term, increased real costs of energy led to both economic shifts and governmental and societal rethinking of materials usage, increased recycling, and the drive for energy efficiency.

Interestingly, although the 1970s economic changes moved the long-term growth curve of steel consumption downward so that it became almost level (and is declining quite sharply as a percentage of the overall economy), steel has not fared badly in relation to other materials. Its chief competitors, aluminum and plastics in manufacturing and wood and concrete in construction, have all suffered from higher energy costs and environmental regulation, although the timing of the impact of these on individual materials has varied. Steel has declined slightly as a percentage of the material content of automobiles and lost the remainder of the beverage can market during the 1980s, but otherwise has held its own in the balance of competing materials.

Any attempt to forecast changes in pattern of steel use in the medium-term future—say, over the next two business cycles, or into the latter part of the next decade—must first make assumptions as to whether broad, underlying forces of economic change such as those at work in the 1970s will affect North American steel production and trade. Moreover, the reality of the elimination of tariffs on steel within North America over this decade, and the decline of economic nationalism in both Canada and Mexico, makes forecasting more than ever a North American, rather than a national, exercise.

Much of the economic growth of the United States from the 1960s to the 1980s was generated by the integration of the South and Southwest of the country fully into the national economy. The end of a regional, textile- and agriculture-dominated economy in the South reflected a number of broader changes in American society. Some of these were nationwide political and demographic changes, such as civil rights and the demographic shift toward the Sunbelt. Others were economic shifts that impacted directly on the steel industry: the growth of transportation options (such as Interstate highways and passenger jet aircraft); the diffusion of manufacturing in search of lower labor and land costs; and the growth of southern cities and suburbs, with an infrastructure, from sewers to mass transit, put in place some two to three generations later than their northern or midwestern equivalents. A combination of social and economic trends, reinforced by massive federal government transfers (for example, highway, military, and space program expenditures), caused the South to boom, as most southern states came to approach or even exceed the U.S. national average income.

If the South was playing "catch-up" during this period, could comparable regional shifts impact steel over the foreseeable future? With the exception of Canada's Maritime Provinces, regional income disparities in the United States and Canada are more equal than at any time in the past. The addition of Mexico into an integrated North American economy, however, may have an impact greater than that of the South over the previous thirty years. If Mexico maintains the political, monetary, and social stability necessary to take advantage of the opportunity, its membership in NAFTA seems likely to have far-reaching effects on the pattern of steel use. Canada's more mature economy, already well-integrated with that of the United States, is less likely to create new patterns of steel consumption. The Canadian and U.S. steel industries have long been tied by common raw materials interests, common automotive and other customers, and historic understandings about not treading on each other's turf. Canada's minimill companies, on the other hand, have long ignored the national boundary, as companies such as Co-Steel, Ipsco, and Ivaco invest and sell across the United States. Both countries deserve special examination within the context of a rapidly integrating North America.

MEXICO

Mexico has a steel industry that, despite particular national characteristics, in many ways mirrors that of the United States on a smaller scale. It has long included both large, unprofitable integrated producers sheltering behind the protection of both tariffs and government ownership and a vigorous and technically advanced independent sector, based in part on the use of DRI. Mexican use of DRI has far exceeded that of the United States or Canada, based both on cheap Mexican gas and on the technical pioneering of the process by the Monterrey steelmaker Hylsa, part of conglomerate Grupo Alfa. Hylsa was also the second company in the world (after Nucor) to open a thin-slab caster-based, flat-rolled minimill. In addition to five flat-rolled producers, Mexico has a thriving minimill long products sector, a world-class stainless sheet producer, and both integrated and independent pipe and tube producers.

In the early 1990s, Mexican steel production grew at a rate of over 5 percent a year. Capacity reached 12 million short tons in 1994, and 14 million tons in 1996. Capacity utilization ran at a high rate, except briefly in early 1995 when the economy was adjusting to the sharp peso devaluation. The three state-owned steelmakers were denationalized, including the largest producer, Altos Hornos de Mexico S.A. (Ahmsa). International investment was welcomed, although little was made by U.S. or Canadian firms outside the distribution sector. The largest foreign investment was by London-based Ispat, which bought the state-owned Siderurgica de Balsas in 1991 to become the country's third-largest producer (after Ahmsa and Hylsa).

In the 1990s, Mexico's steel industry has sought to expand its capacity ahead of the rate of growth of domestic demand, exporting the surplus north of the Rio Grande and to world markets. Investment decisions were not historically based on export potential, however, with the exception of the stainless and pipe sectors. A sign of changed attitudes, however, may be the construction between 1992 and 1994 of Siderurgica de California, a 450,000-ton-per-year minimill in Mexicali, Baja California. Owned by minimill group Siderurgica de Guadalajara, the new mill is designed to ship wire rod and bar products to nearby U.S. as well as northern Mexico markets and is fed largely by scrap from the Los Angeles area. As steel tariffs between the United States and Mexico end, trade has increased dramatically across the U.S.-Mexico border. Mexican exports to the United States doubled in 1993, doubled again in 1994 to 1.75 million tons, and reached 2.5 million tons in 1995. Shipments to the United States were heavily weighted toward lower-value products, including large shipments of slabs for finishing at U.S. hot-strip mills. Some of this tonnage was taking advantage of the short-term market shortage conditions in the United States. Other arrangements were likely to be long-term commitments, such as an agreement for Ispat Mexicana to supply slabs to Wheeling-Pittsburgh to supplement that steelmaker's inadequate melting capacity, or the agreement by Chaparral Steel and Ahmsa to sell each other's complementary wide flange beam sizes.[8]

If the financial, structural, and political reforms Mexico was undertaking in the mid-1990s succeed, its steel consumption could double from 1994's 8 million tons to 16 million within ten years. Whether Mexican capacity keeps up with this increase remains to be seen, but the fact that in 1995-96 some 2.2 million additional annual tons of capacity were already under construction or planned suggests that it is very likely. Much of the increased demand is likely to come from construction, but a significant additional element will be continued growth of U.S.-owned manufacturing plants, both of the *Maquiladora* type for export into the United States, and for local markets. These companies are likely to wish to maintain relationships with existing metals suppliers, which suggests the possibility of cross-border investments and joint ventures by U.S. companies in Mexico.

CANADA

With 29 million people in 1995 compared to Mexico's 90 million, but four times Mexico's GNP per capita, Canada is a mature steel market of around 13 million net tons at the peak of the steel cycle, as in 1994. The integration of the U.S. and Canadian economies suggests that Canadian steel consumption growth rates will closely track U.S. patterns. Until the early 1980s, Canada was a net steel importer, with capacity additions being kept somewhat behind the growth of Canadian consumption. The decline in steel growth from the 1970s, the addition of new integrated and minimill capacity in the early 1980s, and the prolonged recession in Canada's resource-based industries then combined to make Canada a net exporter, primarily to the United States. Average Canadian costs were historically somewhat lower than in the United States for a range of reasons, including more modern facilities and somewhat lower employment, energy, and iron ore costs.

In 1995, Canadian raw steel capacity was approximately 16 million net tons, down from 21 million in 1987. In the last decade, Canada's production facilities have seen downsizing at each of the three major integrated companies, including the closure of Stelco's open-hearth furnaces, ingot-casting operations at Dofasco, and one of Algoma's two BOF shops. Two minimills in the Ipsco group, in Vancouver (in 1989) and Calgary (in 1994), have also been closed. However, Canadian capacity looks set to resume growth in the late 1990s, as the country's steel companies embrace thin-slab casting for flat-rolled steel. National capacity will be augmented by the opening of a new 1.35-million-net-tons-per-year electric furnace shop and thin-slab caster at Dofasco's Hamilton mill in late 1996. Algoma Steel is also building a new thin-slab caster and hot-strip mill, which will be fed by the company's existing BOF capacity. Minimill groups Ipsco and Co-Steel, on the other hand, have both built new thin-slab casting plants in the United States, the latter jointly with Dofasco as Gallatin Steel in Kentucky.

Canadian steel investment in the United States is extensive, although little investment has been undertaken in the opposite direction except in iron ore. Rather surprisingly, most foreign owners of Canadian steel capacity come from developing countries. Foreign investors acquired three mills, amounting to 15 percent of Canada's raw steel capacity, in 1994 and 1995. In 1994, the Québec government sold the large DRI-based electric furnace mill of Sidbec-Dosco, near Montréal, to Indian-owned (but London-based) Ispat, through its Mexican subsidiary, Ispat Mexicana. Sidbec-Dosco was reported to have absorbed C$1.5 billion in provincial funding during its thirty generally loss-making years of government ownership. A second loss-making mill, Sydney Steel in Nova Scotia, was also long supported by its provincial government as an instrument of economic and social policy in the poor Cape Breton area. The slab and rail producer was sold in 1995 to Minmetals, a Chinese government metals trading firm that also oversees China's investment in Citisteel in the United States, after having lost the province C$2 billion since 1967. Finally, Brazil's Gerdau long products minimill group, with operations in Brazil, Uruguay, and Chile, followed its purchase of Courtice Steel in Ontario in 1989 with the acquisition of Manitoba Rolling Mills in 1995.

Looking to the future, eastern Canada and especially Quebec would appear to have much in its favor as a location for electric furnace capacity, just as it has become a great center of aluminum production. It has abundant low-cost electric power and iron ore and is near the large markets of the North American East Coast and Great Lakes. If natural gas supplies can be secured via pipelines from western Canada, DRI-based steelmaking should, in theory, be highly attractive. Investors appear to have held back, though, in part due to political uncertainty about Quebec's future and in part due to either perceptions or the reality of the labor, language, and regulatory climate in that province.

Table 10.2
NORTH AMERICAN RAW STEEL

(Millions of net tons)

	Output, 1989	Output, 1994	Capacity, 1994	Capacity, 1998	Capacity, 2004
Canada	16.9	15.8	16.1	17.4	17–20
Mexico	8.7	11.1	12.0	14.2	16–19
U.S.A.	97.9	99.9	107.8	118.0	120–124
TOTAL	123.5	126.8	135.9	149.6	153–163

Canada's economy, with its proportionally high dependence on natural resources and agriculture, grew at a faster rate than that of the United States in the 1970s but has subsequently lagged behind as commodity prices have fallen. Growth is expected to increase with the expansion of intra–North American trade, but it is unlikely to keep pace with the United States over the next decade. Unlike Mexico, then, Canada does not appear likely to have a significant impact on the overall pattern of the North American steel market. Table 10.2 shows the relative raw steel output and capacity for Canada, Mexico and the United States.

U.S. GROWTH I: CHANGING PATTERNS OF TRADE

The United States will see a net addition of over ten million tons of capacity between 1995 and 1998, assuming the completion of projects currently under construction and the restart of closed mills. Only one mill closure, at Bethlehem, Pennsylvania, is included in that calculation. If the next steel cycle is not to see significant offsetting closures of higher-cost capacity, either the balance of U.S. steel trade must shift radically or steel consumption growth in the country must rise. Given the success of U.S. steelmakers in driving down costs, it is quite possible to be optimistic about the prospects for some combination of these two factors to lead to renewed growth in the U.S. steel industry.

The upside of the trade component of U.S. steel prospects hinges in large part on the value of the U.S. dollar relative to the major European and Japanese currencies. In 1995–96, after a decade of decline against both the yen and the deutsche mark, the U.S. dollar rallied, rising 20 percent from its low point against the yen back to a level around 115¥ = $1. It is not clear whether the long-term trend line of the yen's appreciation, from a level of 360¥ = $1 in 1970, has halted, but a rise of 10 percent in the value of the dollar against a broader basket of currencies might eliminate the current cost advantage in international trade enjoyed by U.S. mills. At average 1995 exchange rates, however, U.S. mills still have a significant cost advantage over European and Japanese mills.

It is likely that the growth of U.S. steel exports in the next economic recession could follow the example of the period from 1988 to 1991. At that time, the combination of a weak dollar, the decline of real steel consumption as the economy entered a recession, and de-stocking by steel mills and distributors in the United States led to a rise of 5 million tons in exports—from just 1.1 million tons in 1987 to 6.3 million in 1991. In the late 1990s, it is likely that the economic cycles of other industrial nations will continue to lag somewhat behind that of North America, thus leaving demand stronger internationally when U.S. demand falls. This, combined with the effect of low-cost new capacity and the same fundamentals as from 1988 to 1991, could see U.S. exports grow from around 4 million tons seen in the period from 1992 to 1994, to around 8 to 10 million tons. Some portion of these exports probably will be within North America, notably Mexico, but as Mexican capacity grows, net U.S. trade with Mexico is likely to remain stable—in deficit. Exports are more likely to change the pattern of steel trade with high-cost producing areas, such as Japan and the European Union, with which the terms of trade increasingly favor the United States.

U.S. imports have been stable or in decline since the mid-1980s, although they vary over the U.S. economic cycle. This reflects the fact that the U.S. market price of steel is now broadly in line with world export prices and that U.S. mill costs are now competitive with foreign competitors. The 1987–89 cyclical peak saw imports of finished steel mill products in the 18-million-ton range; the peak from 1993 to 1995 saw them in the 15-million-ton range. Imports of semifinished steel, notably slabs for U.S. flat-rolled producers, have grown dramatically, offsetting the fall in imports of mill products. These imports first became significant in the mid-1980s, as U.S. mills such as Tuscaloosa Steel and California Steel Industries were founded expressly to use imported slabs. By the 1990s, slab purchases became an accepted part of the strategy of a number of integrated mills.

Slab purchases are now commonly undertaken when either raw steelmaking capacity is reduced (for example, during a blast furnace reline) or when demand exceeds in-house slab capacity. In the past, companies generally maintained additional, high-cost capacity, usually older open-hearth furnaces and ingot casting shops, to be started up only as demand warranted. With the elimination of such excess capacity, it is now the declared strategy of mills such as Inland Steel and Wheeling-Pittsburgh Steel to use imported slabs to supply peak demands. Doing so allows them to avoid the costs of maintaining idle capacity and to keep the mill's low-cost base capacity utilized at a high rate throughout the steel cycle. Although the cost of purchased slabs is higher than the *average* cost of in-house production, these purchases cost less than the *marginal* costs of steel made from the incremental capacity formerly maintained for use at peak times. Such a policy also allows mills to maintain more stability in the level of their workforce over a cycle, which is essential to companies such as National Steel that have union contracts or policies committing them to job security for their hourly employees. In the 1994-95 period, even companies publicly hostile to steel imports resorted to purchasing imported slabs, such as Bethlehem Steel for conversion at its Burns Harbor mill.

One likely result of the introduction of significant new capacity in the United States will be the reduction of slab imports over the next cycle. Nearly 5 million tons of slabs were imported in each of 1993 and 1994. This figure could be expected to fall back to the previous 2 million tons or so at the bottom of a steel cycle; in future the number will be further reduced to the extent that Tuscaloosa Steel's slab requirements will now be produced in-house. The new flat-rolled capacity could all but eliminate slab imports if steel-deficit companies are willing to purchase from their domestic competitors; but semifinished imports may continue to be attractive to companies with long-term supply arrangements, such as Wheeling-Pittsburgh and California Steel Industries. Billet imports for long products mills may also continue if billet prices from producers in Russia and the Ukraine remain below U.S. costs, as was the case in 1994–95, although a fall in scrap costs would be likely to eliminate this differential.

A realistic expectation is that the new U.S. capacity could displace as much as 3 million tons of semifinished imports at the peak of the cycle and 1 million tons in the cyclical trough. Displacement of imported finished steel depends on a greater number of variables but is also likely to be significant. The 8 million tons of flat-rolled carbon steel imports in the period from 1993 to 1995 are likely to be significantly eroded, especially in lower-value hot-rolled and plate products. It is likely that at least half of these imports will be displaced by domestic production.

The changing international balance of capacity and costs, then, offers the U.S. industry the opportunity to increase its output by between 6 and 12 million tons of raw steel annually, depending on the economic cycle and assuming the continuation of key 1995 fundamentals such as scrap prices and exchange rates. These fundamentals will change, but they are at least as likely to move in favor of the United States as against. Certainly the period from 1993 to 1995 represents a least-favorable period for U.S. steel trade, with surging domestic demand, tight capacity, and high costs of materials such as scrap. Any revival in the value of the U.S. dollar is likely to be offset by declines in the cost of U.S.-made steel in international markets.

U.S. GROWTH II: INCREASED STEEL CONSUMPTION

In chapter 8, tables 8.1 and 8.2 listed some 13 million tons per year of new flat-rolled steelmaking capacity likely to be completed between 1995 and 1998. To this can be added at least 3 million annual tons of long products capacity, led by the new mills of Birmingham, North Star, and Qualitech, plus expansions at a number of other facilities. The new additions in this four-year period, net of announced capacity closures, represent a 12 percent increase in U.S. capacity. The displacement of imports and the growth of U.S. exports, if the assumptions just given prove valid, represents an opportunity for the U.S. steel industry to use, on average, about half of this new capacity. To maintain the same level of capacity utilization over the next economic cycle, then, requires that U.S. consumption also rises, by at least 6 million tons a year.

Table 10.3 suggests that U.S. consumption could, in fact, rise by as much as 9 million tons between cyclical peaks of steel consumption. Taking 1994–95 as the peak of one cycle, the next cyclical peak might be in any year from 1999 onward—the average time for steel consumption cycles to run their course has averaged a little over five years since World War II. The question then becomes whether U.S. steel consumption can rise by approximately 1 percent a year, or a little over a million tons a year. The table shows a rise of 9 million tons between 1994 and

Table 10.3
NORTH AMERICAN STEEL MILL PRODUCTS DEMAND

(Millions of net tons of apparent consumption, excluding imports of semifinished steel)

	1989 actual	1994 actual	1995 (estimate)	1998-2004: cyclical low	1998-2004: cyclical peak
Canada	13.5	12.8	13.5	11.0	14.5
Mexico	6.6	8.0	7.8	9.5	16.0
U.S.A.	96.8	108.5	107.5	102.0	117.5
TOTAL	116.9	129.3	128.8	122.5	148.0

the next peak, or (say) 1.5 percent per year, as the "most likely" or midpoint scenario. Actual increases could range from as low as 6 to as much as 12 million tons, depending on the timing and strength of the cyclical movements.

Predicting 1.5 percent annual growth does not appear aggressive compared to annual GNP growth of 2.5 percent or more. Nevertheless, steel consumption in the United States actually declined sharply between each of the cyclical peaks of 1973, 1978, and 1984. Subsequent highs in 1988 and 1994 have shown positive market growth, but at a level of only 1 percent per annum. The 1994-95 peak is still less than 90 percent of the level of 1973. It is likely, however, that the annual rate of increase will rise not to levels tracking or exceeding GNP growth (as was the norm in the first three quarters of this century) but at better than the 1 percent of the last decade.

Cautious optimism about renewed growth in steel depends on the industry's ability to capture markets away from competing materials. During the period from 1984 to 1995, steel's overall share among industrial materials changed very little in key markets, compared to the earlier period 1973 to 1984. During this earlier period, not only did the overall production of metal goods decline in the United States, but steel was displaced in key markets: in containers (by aluminum), pipe (by concrete and plastics), nonresidential construction (with concrete and rebar replacing steel frames), and vehicles (by aluminum, plastics, and, most important, lighter gauges of steel). The period after 1984 saw relatively little substitution of materials, even though there were some significant declines in steel-intensive sectors such as high-rise construction. This stability was rooted, of course, in the decline in costs and prices, allowing steel to defend its existing markets. It suggested that, for this limited period, the "natural" rate of growth of steel consumption (given no substitution) was about half the growth rate of GNP. This slow growth pattern also reflects renewed growth in U.S. manufacturing during the post-1984 period, but at a much slower rate than the services-driven growth of GNP.

In the late 1990s, the relative decline of steel costs has continued at a rate that will now allow steel to displace competing materials. The areas of greatest growth potential are in residential construction and in beverage cans. Hot-dipped galvanized use in house framing appears likely to grow from almost nothing in 1992, to 1.25 million tons in 1997, and to as much as 3 million tons by 2002. Such numbers assume steel could be used in 15 percent of all housing starts in 1997—say, 200,000 homes at just over 6 tons of steel per unit. The 3-million-ton level would require steel use in just one-third of all new housing. Displacement of aluminum from a quarter of the beverage can market could add a million annual tons of steel consumption.

In addition to these new or recaptured markets, steel consumption is likely to benefit from changes within the U.S. economy that favor the renewed importance of both manufacturing and construction. The growth of the "transplant" phenomena reflects the renewed competitiveness of the United States as a manufacturing location and suggests a continued growth in U.S. manufactured exports (and import substitution). Commercial nonresidential construction, which barely participated in the growth period of 1992 to 1995 due to the overhang of excess buildings from the 1980s boom, looked set for a continued recovery in the late 1990s. Despite the ideology of cutbacks in Washington, government spending on steel looked safe for the balance of the decade, given the Republican Party's susceptibility to defense and highway lobbying; only small areas such as mass transit looks likely to decline. Even the energy industry, since 1981 the basket case of steel markets, looked likely to see a slow upturn worldwide as the decline of existing producing fields brings the industry's global overcapacity back toward balance. The net effects of these changes suggest increased steel consumption growth, beyond that of the two cycles of the period from 1984 to 1994. Such a rise in the growth rate will generate returns on the increased capacity of the U.S. industry and justify investors' faith in new and reopened capacity in the mid-1990s.

Table 10.4 summarizes expected peak-to-peak changes in the U.S. market. Peak-to-peak comparisons of steel demand only tell part of the story, of course. The steel recessions of 1986 and 1991 still saw U.S. apparent demand sink to levels of 85 to 90 percent of the

Table 10.4
INTERCYCLICAL GROWTH OF
U.S. RAW STEEL PRODUCTION

Millions of additional net tons forecast between 1994-95 and an assumed cyclical peak in 2000-1.

Source of Increased Shipments	Optimistic Forecast	Pessimistic Forecast
Decreased semi-finished imports	4.0	2.0
Increased U.S. exports [a]	3.0	1.0
Decreased U.S. imports [a]	6.0	2.0
Steel "natural" growth, at 50% of overall economic growth (6 yrs at 2% optimistic, 1.5% per annum pessimistic case)	6.0	4.5
Steel "additional" growth, from relative growth of manufacturing within economy:	2.0	1.0
Materials substitution: Housing	2.0	1.0
Containers	1.0	0.5
Other	1.0	(1.0)
TOTAL	25.0	11.0

a Note that exports will normally be higher, and imports lower, during recessions than at cyclical peaks. Other categories of steel demand growth will be maximized at cyclical peaks.

preceding peak. The impact of the next U.S. recession is likely to be similar, with demand for steel mill products declining by at least 10 million tons and probably by closer to 15 million. During such a cyclical trough, U.S. mills will, on average, operate at below the 80 percent of capacity level, unless the predicted rise in exports helps maintain mill throughput. Steel will remain a highly cyclical business, and in the troughs of economic cycles, financial losses will continue to drive out high-cost capacity. This is desirable from a long-term standpoint, to prevent overcapacity from damaging the health of more efficient producers and to improve the returns on new investment. In the short term, however, as steel's markets continue to dictate the elimination of jobs at surviving as well as at closed plants, thousands of cases of individual hardship will result in families and communities that staked their future on a volatile commodity industry.

In the next decade, the U.S. steel industry should be cautiously optimistic about improved average consumption, increased domestic shipments, and its ability to maintain or improve capacity utilization despite the impact of new capacity. The U.S. steel market can probably absorb the foreseeable capacity increases. Nevertheless, the industry shows no signs of returning to the halcyon days before the 1970s. A steady, profitable oligopoly cannot return, because steel is so highly competitive with competing materials; because the cost of entry is low and getting lower; and because the entrepreneurial culture of the minimill companies, now spread throughout the industry, will not tolerate it. Steel will remain a highly competitive environment in which high-cost companies will lose money and ultimately be forced out of the industry.

STEEL, THE SURPRISING SUCCESS

The upheavals in the steel industry during the past twenty years often appear more shocking to people within the industry than to outside observers. The pace of change in steel can seem glacial to a person from the computer industry, for example. Yet the steel industry became used to a pattern of stable growth that dated from the creation of U.S. Steel in 1901 and the subsequent consolidation of the industry into a handful of major companies with stable market shares and control of pricing. For the first three-quarters of the twentieth century, steel functioned as an oligopoly, or trust, and was powerful and smart enough to avoid the political and legal consequences of such behavior. It was not, however, smart enough to prevent market forces ultimately catching up with it.

The meltdown of the integrated steel companies that began in the late 1970s can be compared to the bursting of a dam that had held back the growing waters of competition, investment, technological innovation, and social accountability for three-quarters of a century. A flood of pent-up problems hit the industry simultaneously: the collapse of pricing toward world market levels; the obsolescence of much of the industry's plant and equipment; the power of (and the obligations to) the Steelworkers union; and the environmental and safety issues companies had long ignored. Most important, three new competitive elements entered the U.S. steel market: imported steel, domestic minimills, and the independent distributors upon whom the first two depended. These factors undermined the long-established system of mutually understood pricing and market shares. The established companies, protected for so long, were not only poorly equipped to compete but often did not wish to do so. The recurrent pleas for government protection against imports highlighted the integrated companies' lack of other competitive strategies. The focus on one part of the problem, imports, showed up the companies' inability to deal with the greater domestic challenge, from the minimills and service centers.

The triumph of minimills in such an environment does not seem surprising. They have seemingly every advantage that fashion or public relations could confer to attract investors: they are (or were, or have been portrayed as) small-sized, small-town, independent, innovative, entrepreneurial, all-American Davids fighting the Goliaths of the bad old steel industry. What may be more surprising is that many of the Goliaths are still around. U.S. Steel, Bethlehem Steel, LTV Steel, and others are still making profits for their shareholders at real prices that would have seemed disastrous twenty years ago. It is generally harder to change an existing business than to create a new one, but radical change has been effected in the integrated steel industry. Today integrated mills in the United States have significantly lower costs than their competitors in Japan or the European Union, and at present are able to compete with the flat-rolled minimill industry. They have thus defied both their friends, who in the 1970s pleaded for the construction of ever-larger, "world-scale" mills to maintain competitiveness; and their detractors, who believed that only government intervention and enforced restructuring, on the European model, could salvage the industry. While the minimills may have become heroes of Wall Street and business schools, it is no disrespect to them to say that self-renewal of the integrated mills is at least as important a story.

By now, the term "steel industry" itself may be obsolete. The industry is, on one hand, part of a broader metals or even materials industry, because its companies operate in a market of competing materials, not because of conglomerate ownership—essentially all U.S. steel capacity except the U.S. Steel Corporation is owned by companies that exclusively make steel. On the other hand, the industry is seeing vertical de-integration as the historic links among raw materials, steelmaking, rolling, processing, and distributing become unraveled. Independent firms at each layer of the industry may become more closely identified with their function and less with steel—if steel distributors can and do handle multiple metals and even plastics, why cannot other tiers of the industry?

The term "steel industry" with its historic baggage also fails to reflect the extent to which steel is now part of the recycling industry. Although minimills are pressing forward with new sources of virgin iron units, as the electric furnace industry continues to expand so will the proportion of steel recycled from scrap materials. This percentage, already over 45 percent in 1995 when scrap inputs to integrated mill furnaces are included, will exceed 50 percent before the end of the decade. Combined with compliance with the tighter emissions controls, steel could then truly claim to be the environmentally friendly industry it has long aspired to be. The steel industry would be well advised to publicize this landmark when it occurs. It will be a fitting observance of a significant industrial success story.

NOTES

Chapter 1

1. Among the problems of terminology in the steel industry, some carbon steels exist in a gray area of definition between "carbon" and "alloy." These include high-strength, low-alloy steels, which are used in more demanding construction applications and in welded tubes for pressure purposes. These are carbon-manganese steels with manganese contents up to 1.5 percent; statistically they are often counted as alloy steels, although as they are becoming commonly specified for structural uses and are produced by carbon steel mills, I shall continue to refer to them as carbon steels. In addition, silico-manganese steels used for making springs—that is, carbon steels with a substantially increased silicon content at between 0.6 and 2.3 percent manganese—often are referred to as "specialty steels" along with alloy steels and stainless steels.
2. If the metal contains less than 9 percent chromium, it is known as an alloy steel but not a stainless steel; stainless being strictly a subset of alloy steels. If the metal contains less than 50 percent iron, it takes its name from the next most common metal component: thus a metal containing 48 percent iron, 26 percent nickel, 20 percent chrome, and 6 percent other elements is considered a nickel alloy.
3. The best recent brief description of the production processes of the steel industry is in Peter Fish, *The International Steel Trade,* Cambridge, England, 1995, chapter 3. Details of the historical evolution of the processes and their commercialization in the United States can be found throughout the five volumes of the Rev. William T. Hogan, *Economic History of the Iron and Steel Industry of the United States,* Lexington, MA, 1971.
4. Almost all continuous casters produce a single type of semifinished shape, usually in a limited range of sizes. Just two North American companies operate combined slab/bloom casters, which have both capital and operating cost penalties.
5. Exceptions are six steel mills that still sell both flat and long products produced at the same location. These are Algoma Steel in Sault Ste. Marie, Ontario; Inland Steel in East Chicago, Indiana; Laclede Steel at Alton, Illinois; Sidbec-Dosco at Contrecoeur, Québec, Stelco at Hamilton, Ontario; and U.S. Steel's mill at Fairfield, Alabama. There are also a small number of flat-rolled mills that convert flat-rolled steel into welded pipe, strictly speaking a long product.

6. The 74-inch hot-strip mill of California Steel Industries, Fontana, California. Originally part of the defunct integrated Kaiser Steel Corporation, which closed in 1983, this mill has operated as an independent finishing facility since 1984 using slab imported from, among other sources, its Japanese and Brazilian co-owners. Another independent hot-strip mill, Beta Steel in Portage, Indiana, is located in the middle of the largest concentration of steelmaking in North America. However, it chose to add its own electric-furnace steelmaking in 1996.
7. Important exceptions to this statement are a group of long-established electric furnace steel companies including CF & I Steel, Laclede Steel, Keystone Steel and Wire, Northwestern Steel and Wire, and Sidbec-Dosco. Integrated steel mills have entirely left this business, while the newer minimills tend to produce only wire rod, not wire (even though they may be affiliated with wire producers; see chapter 5).
8. The Canadian mills in the Hamilton, Ontario area (on Lake Ontario) have to use smaller vessels to transit the Welland canal or transship upper lakes ore at Nanticoke, Ontario, on Lake Erie, some 30 miles south of Hamilton. Stelco built an integrated mill at Nanticoke to avoid the transshipment problem. The Hamilton mills also bring ore from Labrador in smaller vessels through the St. Lawrence River.
9. An interesting article that graphically reveals the costs and complexity of rail freight arrangements for ore over long distances is in *Trains* magazine, Mar., 1995, pp. 36-47, entitled "Taconite West, Coal East: How Wisconsin Central and Southern Pacific Snared the Big Geneva Steel Ore Haul."
10. Steelmaking data is from the American Iron and Steel Institute's *Annual Statistical Report,* 1993, and various earlier years.
11. The oldest existing steel service center, the Congdon and Carpenter Company of Seekonk, Massachusetts (now a division of Levinson Steel), was founded in Providence, Rhode Island in 1790, and in its early days sold such products as horseshoe stock and similar forge supplies.
12. For 1994, apparent supply of steel mill products can be calculated in net tons as follows:

    Domestic net shipments 95,084,000
    Less exports (3,826,000)
    Plus imports 30,066,000
    Less imports of semifinished to domestic mills (7,937,000)
    Total apparent supply (before changes in stocks) 113,387,000

13. The two major independent U.S. iron ore mining companies have historically cooperated with their customers, the integrated steel companies, in jointly developing and operating a number of mines.

Chapter 2

1. The three-year average calculations are from Donald F. Barnett and Louis Schorsch, *Steel: Upheaval in a Basic Industry,* Cambridge, MA, 1983, pp. 23-24. The six founding members of the European Coal and Steel Community, the predecessor of the European Economic Community and European Union, were Belgium, France, the Federal Republic of Germany, Luxembourg, and the Netherlands.
2. For steel industry financing and returns on investment in the 1950s, see Paul A. Tiffany, *American Steel: How Management, Labor and Government Went Wrong,* Oxford, 1988. This account, unfortunately, ends in 1960.
3. The Erie Mining plant was owned by Bethlehem Steel, 45 percent; Youngstown Sheet and Tube, 35 percent; Interlake Steel, 10 percent; and Steel Company of Canada (Stelco), 10 percent. It had a capacity of 10.3 million tons per year of pellets. The first major pellet plant, that of the Reserve Mining Company, was completed in 1955 with a capacity of 5 million tons. Reserve was initially owned 50 percent by Armco Steel and 50 percent by Republic Steel. Its capacity was later increased to 10.7 million tons, the largest unit in North America. See the Rev. William T. Hogan, *Economic History of the Iron and Steel Industry in the United States,* vol. 4, 1971, pp. 1486-1494.
4. The four companies are:

    1. Iron Ore Company of Canada, with mines in the Schefferville, Québec, and Labrador City, Labrador, areas, originally owned by Armco Steel, Hanna Mining, National Steel, Republic Steel, Wheeling Steel, Youngstown Sheet and Tube, Bethlehem Steel, Hollinger Argus Ltd., and Labrador Mining and Exploration Ltd.; shipments began in 1954.

    2. Wabush Mines, in the Wabush, Labrador, area, formed by Jones & Laughlin, Inland Steel, Wheeling Steel, Stelco, and Interlake, Inc.; shipments began in 1956.

    3. Québec-Cartier Mines, formed as a wholly-owned subsidiary of U.S. Steel in 1957, with mines in the Gagnon, Québec, area, was sold by U.S. Steel to Dofasco in 1989; its current ownership is Dofasco, 50 percent, Mitsui, 25 percent, and CAEMI of Brazil, 25 percent.

    4. Sidbec Normines, with mines in the Fire Lake, Québec, area, was established in 1976 by Sidbec-Dosco, British Steel, and U.S. Steel. In addition, iron- and titanium-bearing ore

(titaniferous magnetite) is mined near Havre St.-Pierre, Québec, by QIT-Fer et Titane, Inc. (the former Quebec Iron and Titanium Co.), which is unique in producing both semifinished steel and titanium products at its blast furnace/BOF operation in Sorel, Québec.

5. In the early 1940s, the wartime Defense Plant Corporation built three major integrated plants in the South and West of the United States: the U.S. Steel mill at Geneva, Utah; the Kaiser Steel mill at Fontana, California; and the Armco Steel mill at Houston, Texas. These were sold after 1945 to their wartime lessor/operators. It also built blast furnaces north of Longview, Texas, that later became incorporated in the integrated Lone Star Steel.
6. Tiffany, *American Steel,* p. 66.
7. Hogan, *Economic History,* vol. 4, pp. 1550-1555.
8. The four pre-1960 continuous hot-strip mills were: (1) a 69-inch mill at Bethlehem Steel, Sparrows Point, Maryland, built 1948, with a capacity of 3.1 million net tons per year; (2) an 86-inch mill at Kaiser Steel, Fontana, California, built 1950, 1.7 million tons; (3) an 80-inch mill at Armco Steel, Ashland, Kentucky, built 1953, 1.7 million tons; and (4) an 80-inch mill at U.S. Steel, Fairless Hills, Pennsylvania, built 1953, with 2.8 million tons capacity.
9. Barnett and Schorsch, *Steel: Upheaval in a Basic Industry,* pp. 17-19.
10. The best description of both the contract negotiations and their impact on human lives is found in John P. Hoerr, *And the Wolf Finally Came,* Pittsburgh, PA, 1988.
11. Barnett and Schorsch, *Steel: Upheaval in a Basic Industry,* pp. 66-71.
12. This story is best recounted in John Strohmeyer, *Crisis in Bethlehem: Big Steel's Struggle to Survive,* Bethesda, MD, 1986, pp. 78-82.
13. Michael K. Drapkin, "Steel Industry Money Woes Boost Pressure on Firms to Reach Accord Without Strike," *Wall Street Journal,* July 21, 1971.
14. Hoerr, *And the Wolf Finally Came,* pp. 112-114
15. A.I.S.I., *Annual Statistical Report,* 1982, Table 6, "Total Employment Cost per Hour Worked—Wage Employees," pp. 18-19. The figures given are straight time pay for hours worked; average hourly earnings, which include shift differentials and premiums for Sunday, overtime, and holiday work, averaged 8 percent higher.
16. Barnett and Schorsch, *Steel: Upheaval in a Basic Industry,* p. 70.
17. Hogan, *Economic History,* vol. 5, p. 2038.
18. Tsutomu Kawasaki, *Japan's Steel Industry,* Tokyo, 1985, pp. 511-518, gives the Japanese view and strategy of exports to the United States in the 1960s.
19. James N. Johndrow, "The Effects of Trade Restrictions on Imports of Steel," in U.S. Department of Labor, Bureau of International Labor Affairs, *The Impact of International Trade and Investment on Employment,* Washington, DC, 1978.
20. Robert W. Crandall, *The Steel Industry in Recurrent Crisis: Policy Options in a Competitive World,* Washington, DC, 1981.

21. Hans G. Mueller, "The Steel Industry," in *Annals of the American Academy of Political Science,* 460, Mar. 1982, pp. 73-82.
22. Barnett and Schorsch, *Upheaval in a Basic Industry,* p. 55; Hogan, *Economic History,* vol. 4, p. 1544.
23. Mark Reutter, *Sparrows Point: Making Steel—The Rise and Ruin of American Industrial Might,* New York, 1989, p. 424.
24. These are described and analyzed in T. J. Ess, *The Hot Strip Mill Generation II,* Pittsburgh, Pennsylvania, 1970 (published by the Association of Iron and Steel Engineers). The eleven mills, all fully continuous unless stated, are: Republic Steel, Warren, Ohio (now WCI Steel), 1961 (a semi-continuous mill); National Steel at Ecorse, Michigan, 1961; Jones and Laughlin at Cleveland, Ohio, 1964 (semi-continuous); Wheeling-Pittsburgh Steel, Steubenville, Ohio, 1965; Inland Steel, East Chicago, Indiana, 1965; Bethlehem Steel, Burns Harbor, 1966; Granite City Steel, Granite City, Illinois (near St. Louis; later acquired by National Steel), 1967; U.S. Steel at Gary, Indiana, 1967; Armco Steel, Middletown, Ohio, 1968; Youngstown Sheet and Tube, Indiana Harbor, Indiana (later acquired by Jones and Laughlin, then LTV), 1968; and Republic Steel at Cleveland, Ohio, 1970.
25. Barnett and Schorsch, *Steel: Upheaval in a Basic Industry,* pp. 22-25.
26. Only Bethlehem Steel had actually made a start on its planned West Coast mill, building a galvanizing line at Pinole Point in the late 1960s—but its long-term intentions had been clear ever since it built a 15-story tower in downtown San Francisco in 1960 to house its regional office.

Chapter 3

1. This does not include cold-metal (scrap-charged) open-hearth plants.
2. AISI, *Annual Statistical Report,* various years. Employment figures published by the AISI are for the companies that report such data to it—the integrated mills, certain "traditional" electric furnace companies, and most specialty steel companies.
3. A good brief description of the 1970s economic changes is in Robert J. Gordon, "Postwar Macroeconomics: the Evolution of Events and Ideas," in Martin Feldstein, ed., *The American Economy in Transition,* Chicago, 1980, pp. 101-162, especially pp. 142-152.
4. Reviews of planned capital investments are published periodically in the industry journal *Iron Age*; see, for example, Mar. 29, 1976, p. MP-3.
5. The Rev. William T. Hogan, speech in Toronto, Ontario, reported in *New York Times,* February 9, 1974, p. 39.
6. Edgar Speer's remarks are in *New York Times,* Jan. 1, 1974, p. 27; AISI general counsel Seymour Grabaud's comments are in *New York Times,* Dec. 11, 1974, p. 76.

7. Charles B. Baker quoted in *New York Times,* interview, Dec. 25, 1974, p. 35. Stewart Cort quoted in *New York Times,* May 23, 1975, p. 59.
8. That is, excluding mining and nonsteel operations. The figures are published in each year's AISI *Annual Statistical Report.*
9. Donald F. Barnett and Louis Schorsch, *Steel: Upheaval in a Basic Industry,* Cambridge, MA, 1983, pp.68-69.
10. In 1973, the AISI's reporting companies (i.e., excluding some non-union minimills) employed 392,851 hourly workers; in 1982, the same companies employed 198,477, barely half the 1973 number. The average hourly payroll cost was $6.31 in 1973 and $16.81 in 1982. AISI, *Annual Statistical Report,* 1982, p. 20.
11. *Iron Age,* Apr. 25, 1977, pp. 25-27.
12. John P. Hoerr, *And The Wolf Finally Came,* Pittsburgh, Pa., 1988, pp. 120-122.
13. Interview with Stephen H. Axilrod, July 25, 1985, in William Greider, *Secrets of the Temple: How the Federal Reserve Runs the Country,* New York, 1988, p. 565.
14. The shutdowns and layoff announcements of 1982 are painfully recorded in that year's newspapers and trade media, notably in the steel industry's publications of record, the daily *American Metal Market* and biweekly *Iron Age.* The Pittsburgh area cutbacks are admirably covered in Hoerr, *And The Wolf Finally Came,* pp. 134-154, 215-223; Bethlehem Steel's cutbacks in John Strohmeyer, *Crisis in Bethlehem: Big Steel's Struggle to Survive,* Bethesda, Maryland, 1986, pp.185-204; and many of the cutbacks are listed in the Rev. William T. Hogan, *Steel in the United States: Restructuring to Compete,* New York, 1984.
15. This section owes much to Hoerr, *And The Wolf Finally Came,* pp. 62-70, 206-214.
16. *New York Times,* Nov. 2, 1981, p. 16.
17. *New York Times,* Nov. 15, 1982, p. 12.
18. The plants covered by the CCSC/BSIC agreement were divided between List One, which included all carbon steelmaking and rolling mills; List Two, the iron ore mines; and List Three, which included essentially everything else operated by the steel companies and organized by the USWA—fabricating operations, forges, limestone quarries, steel service centers, and so on.
19. Hoerr, *And The Wolf Finally Came,* p. 361.
20. Examples are U.S. Steel's mills at South Works, Chicago, where a new rail mill was canceled and all operations except an electric furnace shop and structural mill were closed at the end of 1983 when the union refused concessions (*New York Times,* Nov.11, IV, p. 4 and Dec. 28, I, p. 1); and at Johnstown, Pennsylvania, where negotiated concessions were rejected by a vote of the employees, leading to the foundry and fabricating operation being closed, then sold to Johnstown Corporation in 1984 (*New York Times,* Apr. 21, 1984, I, p. 6 and July 7, I, p. 33).
21. "Steel Panel's Future Clouded," *American Metal Market,* Aug 14, 1984, p.1.
22. Kennedy later admitted the telephone tapping and tax auditing, a clear abuse of power, to the *Washington Post*'s Ben Bradlee: Benjamin Bradlee, *Conversations with Kennedy,* New York, 1975, pp. 111-12.

23. The 1965 intervention by President Johnson is entertainingly described in Strohmeyer, *Crisis in Bethlehem,* pp.74-75; the subsequent price increase saga, with much criticism of U.S. Steel's "failure to lead," can be traced in *Iron Age* during the months June to October 1965.
24. For the 1968 price rise, see *New York Times,* Aug. 1, 1968, p.1, and John Kenneth Galbraith, *The New Industrial State,* Boston, 1971, p. 262; the 1971 price rise, *New York Times,* Jan. 13, 1971, p. 1; Jan. 14, p. 1; Jan. 17, p.1; and Jan. 19, p. 1.
25. *New York Times,* Mar. 22, 1971, p. 49.
26. *New York Times,* Nov. 5, p. 67, and subsequent issues; also the issues of *Iron Age* for November 1968–January 1969 are revealing.
27. See Robert W. Crandall, *The Steel Industry in Recurrent Crisis: Policy Options in a Competitive World,* Washington, DC, 1981, p. 49, for an estimate of the price effects of the VRA. The effects were uneven, depending on the strength of different product markets; the gap in structural beam prices between domestic and foreign steel, for example, did not close until the 1973 period of steel shortage and "allocations."
28. *Iron Age,* Dec. 13, 1976, p. 34.
29. *New York Times,* Oct.7, 1977, IV, p. 8; Oct. 8, p. 29.
30. Crandall, *The Steel Industry in Recurrent Crisis,* pp. 110-117.
31. The most widely followed price indices for the industry are complied by Paine Webber's World Steel Dynamics (WSD) group, from whose publications all price references are taken. These numbers are discussed in WSD *Steel Strategist,* no. 14, Dec. 10, 1987, p. 7.
32. A somewhat different case of published, high base prices and general discounting occurs in specialty steels, where the pricing pattern more closely resembles that of carbon steel between 1975 and 1981. Stainless transaction prices have grown steadily in nominal terms and base prices have been exceeded during periods of shortage and raw materials surcharges in 1988-89 and 1994-95. However, the 1980s and 1990s saw the effective separation of the carbon and stainless steel industries: U.S. Steel and LTV Steel exited the stainless market, while Armco largely exited the carbon steel market, leaving an industry with high import penetration that behaves in a highly price-competitive way even if true supplier price-taking does not yet exist.
33. Clifford Russell and William Vaughan, *Steel Production: Processes, Products and Residuals,* Baltimore, 1976, p. 6; Walter Goldberg, ed., *Ailing Steel, The Transoceanic Quarrel,* pp.221-223.
34. AISI, *Annual Statistical Report,* various years.
35. Goldberg, *Ailing Steel,* p. 223.
36. Hogan, *Minimills and Integrated Mills,* p. 30. *New York Times,* Feb. 14, 1979, p. 3.
37. Strohmeyer, *Crisis in Bethlehem,* pp. 194-202.
38. *Iron Age,* July 12, 1976; *New York Times,* June 17, 1976, p. 18.
39. *New York Times,* Apr. 5, 1976, p. 51. The six mills were Youngstown Sheet and Tube's Campbell and Brier Hill Works (steelmaking ended 1977 and 1979 respectively); U.S. Steel's Ohio and McDonald plants (1979 and 1980); and

Republic Steel's Youngstown Plant (closed 1982) and Warren Plant, the latter operated since 1988 by Warren Consolidated Industries, Inc. (WCI Steel).

40. *New York Times,* Nov. 28, 1977, p. 49. The integrated Alan Wood plant had a plate mill fed by open-hearth steelmaking. The plate mill was eventually bought and restarted by nearby Lukens Steel, a modern electric furnace plate producer.
41. The first approved "bubble plan" in the United States was for Armco Steel's Middletown, Ohio, mill, approved on Mar. 31, 1981. *New York Times,* April 1, 1981, IV, p. 14.
42. Coke production and consumption figures, though not capacity, are published in the AISI *Annual Statistical Report* series.
43. "Problems of Steel in the New Decade," preface to the 1960 AISI *Yearbook* by Benjamin F. Fairless, president of the American Iron and Steel Institute.
44. *New York Times,* Sept. 24, 1976, IV, p. 3. The mill, at Sagunto, near Valencia, is now known as SIDMED (Siderurgica del Mediterraneo, S.A.).
45. Lone Star Steel closed its blast furnace and open-hearth shop in 1986, after being spun off to shareholders by its parent since 1966, Northwest Industries. In 1995, it negotiated to buy the U.S. Steel Baytown EF shop, also closed in 1986 during the Texas oilfield slump. C F & I closed its open hearths in 1982 and filed for Chapter 11 bankruptcy protection in 1990 due to massive pension liabilities. It was bought out of bankruptcy by Oregon Steel in 1993 and subsequently heavily modernized.
46. Armco's Kansas City long products mill, operating at a reduced scale based on its 1976 EF shop, was sold in 1993 to management (backed by Bain Capital group) as GST Steel, which in turn merged in 1995 with Georgetown Steel as GS Industries, Inc. Republic's Canton Alloy Shops, perhaps the most sophisticated of all integrated companies' EF shops when built, was sold by LTV to employees in 1988 through an ESOP, along with that company's stainless and cold-finished bar operations, as Republic Engineered Steels. Bethlehem's Johnstown mill was bought by BRW Steel in 1994; operations were scheduled to resume, as Bar Technologies, Inc., in 1996 after installation of a caster. British-owned Caparo Steel bought Sharon Steel's EF shop and hot-strip mill in 1994 and reopened them in 1995.
47. The Geneva and Fairless Hills mills were two of the three last open-hearth shops operated in the United States. In 1991, steelmaking at Fairless Hills was terminated; the same year the Geneva mill, now independent as Geneva Steel, finally installed a BOF shop (and caster) using furnaces bought from the closed J & L mill at Aliquippa, Pennsylvania. Bethlehem Steel's Sparrows Point mill operated its Number 4 open-hearth shop, the last such unit constructed in the United States (in 1958), intermittently until 1991. The shop was still carried on Bethlehem's books as late as 1994, as shown in that year's *Directory of Iron and Steel Plants* published by the Association of Iron and Steel Engineers, Pittsburgh, Pennsylvania.
48. U.S. Steel's South Works, at which integrated operations and the plate mill were idled in 1982 and closed permanently in 1984, maintained limited operations until 1989 using a 1950s-vintage EF shop to supply a wide flange beam mill.
49. *Iron Age,* Mar. 29, 1976, page MP-10.

50. The only mills not to commit to casters by 1990 were the two companies that specialized in small-tonnage rollings for special applications, Acme Steel and Sharon Steel. Only after Sharon's liquidation in 1993 was Acme able to generate enough profitability to commit in 1994 to building a new thin-slab caster.
51. Sources include a presentation by Charles Perkins of Pipe Logix, Inc., at the 1991 World Steel Dynamics annual conference entitled "Steel Survival Strategies VI"; "Drill Boom Seen Needed to Gauge Tube Capacity," *American Metal Market,* Dec.16, 1985, p. 22; and investment and closure announcements in *Iron Age* and *Preston Pipe Report,* various dates.
52. The three lines operating in 1984 were at Sharon Steel, National Steel at Weirton, West Virginia (from 1986, Weirton Steel), and U.S. Steel in Gary, Indiana. The 1986 new lines were added by National Steel at Ecorse, Michigan; Armco at Middletown, Ohio; and by three joint ventures: Double Eagle Coating in Detroit, between U.S. Steel and Ford's Rouge Steel division; L-S Electrogalvanizing in Cleveland, between LTV Corporation and Sumitomo; and Walbridge Coatings, Walbridge, Ohio, between Bethlehem Steel and Inland Steel. L-S II, a second LTV—Sumitomo venture; a wholly owned line of LTV in Cleveland; and I/N Kote II, a venture of Inland Steel and Nippon Steel, were added in 1992. (I/N Kote I is a hot-dip galvanizing line.) See Appendix: Flat Products (4).

Chapter 4

1. A good review of the strategies of developing nations is in Lloyd G. Reynolds, "The Spread of Economic Growth to the Third World," *Journal of Economic Literature,* 21, no. 3, Sept. 1983, pp. 941-980.
2. For example, S. Padmanabhan, *"Employment and Welfare Effects of Quantitative Restrictions on Steel Imports into the U.S., 1983–87"*, Ph.D. diss., University of Maryland–Baltimore County, 1990.
3. A good brief description of the bureaucratic process of trade investigations is in Wendy Hansen, "The ITC and the Politics of Protectionism," *American Political Science Review,* 84, no.1, Mar. 1990, pp. 22-46.
4. Until 1970, this function was performed by the Treasury Department.
5. ITC decisions on escape clauses are subject to presidential veto and can be overturned by a majority vote of each house of Congress. Such a joint resolution of Congress, overturning an ITC ruling, is also subject to presidential veto, although this can be overturned in turn by a two-thirds vote of each chamber.
6. The applicability of tariff relief to steel imports is discussed in John J. Coleman and David B. Yoffie, "Institutional Incentives for Protection: The American Use of Voluntary Export Restraints" in *Proceedings of the Academy of Political Science,* 37, no. 4, 1990, *International Trade: The Changing Role of the United States,* pp. 137-150.
7. Coleman and Yoffie, "Institutional Incentives for Protection", pp.138-141.

8. *New York Times,* Jan. 19, 1968, p. 21.
9. The early cases are fully covered in Robert R. Miller, "United States Antidumping Policy and the Steel Industry Experience", Ph.D. diss., Stanford University, 1967.
10. AISI president Roche admitted that the industry "does not yet have support in Congress for import controls" in an interview in the *New York Times,* Feb. 20, 1968, p. 63. Hearings in the House of Representatives are in *New York Times,* June 19, 1968, p. 63.
11. See the entertaining account of Johnson's intervention in the 1965 steel contract negotiations in John Strohmeyer, *Crisis in Bethlehem: Big Steel's Struggle to Survive,* Bethesda, Maryland, 1986, pp. 74-75.
12. *New York Times,* Mar. 23, 1968, p. 41.
13. *New York Times,* Oct. 10, 1968, p. 1; Oct. 30, p. 63.
14. *New York Times,* Nov. 18, 1970.
15. The U.S. Department of Labor estimate is by James N. Johndrow, "Effects of Trade Restrictions on Imports of Steel" in U.S. Department of Labor, Bureau of International Labor Affairs, *The Impact of International Trade and Investment on Employment,* Washington DC, 1978, pp. 11-25. Robert Crandall's more plausible estimate is in his *The Steel Industry in Recurrent Crisis: Policy Options in a Competitive World,* Washington, DC, 1981, pp. 105-106. For press criticism of the integrated companies, see, for example, *New York Times* editorial, Sept. 21, 1970, and reply by Bethlehem Steel's Chairman Martin, *New York Times,* Oct. 9, 1970, p. 36.
16. W. Adams and H.G. Mueller, "The Steel Industry," in W. Adams, ed., *The Structure of American Industry,* New York, 1982.
17. J. B. Dirlam and H. G. Mueller, *Import Restraints and Reindustrialization: The Case of the U.S. Steel Industry,* Middle Tennessee State University Conference Paper series, 67, Murfreesboro, 1981, p. 18.
18. *New York Times,* May 21, 1975, p. 61 (first-quarter profits); Aug. 4, p. 29 (second-quarter profits).
19. *New York Times,* Jan. 9, 1975, p. 57; Sept. 19, p. 49; Oct. 18, p. 39; Oct. 24, p. 53.
20. *New York Times,* Jan. 17, 1976, p. 1.
21. *New York Times,* Mar. 17, p. 1; Apr. 7, p. 61; May 19, p. 59; June 8, p. 1; June 12, p. 29.
22. *Iron Age,* July 19, 1976, "How and Why Specialty Steel Producers Won Their Fight to Get Import Quotas," pp. 21-22.
23. *New York Times,* Oct. 7, 1976, p. 4; Nov. 23, p. 56; Nov. 28, III, p.1.
24. The Japanese VRA request is in *New York Times,* May 25, 1977, p. 8; the Rev. William T. Hogan, *World Steel in the 1980s,* p. 202, describes the Japanese-EC contacts. The AISI report, prepared by Putnam Hayes and Bartlett, Inc., and published as *Economics of International Steel Trade,* was reviewed in the *New York Times* on May 26, IV, p. 1. The Gilmore Steel case: filed on Mar. 29, *New York Times,* Mar. 30, IV, p. 7; was quickly investigated by the ITC, *New York Times,* May 25, IV, p. 1; and led to a finding that dumping had occurred and a

32 percent antidumping duty being levied, *New York Times,* Oct. 4, p. 1. This was the first "dumping" ruling for any product against Japan.

25. "A Comprehensive Program for the Steel Industry: Report to the President Submitted by Anthony M. Solomon, Chairman, Task Force, December 6, 1977," in *Administration's Comprehensive Program for the Steel Industry: Hearings Before the Subcommittee on Trade of the Committee on Ways and Means, House of Representatives,* Washington, DC, 1978.
26. *New York Times,* Dec. 7, 1977, p. 1.
27. The TPM, its assumptions and problems, are discussed in the Government Accounting office's report, *Administration of the Steel Trigger Price Mechanism,* Washington, DC, 1980.
28. Imports and domestic shipments data from AISI *Annual Statistical Yearbook,* various years.
29. Import data and comments from 1978 are in *New York Times,* Jan. 17, 1979, IV, p. 1 and Jan. 31, IV, p. 6; reports of the AISI meeting in *New York Times,* May 23, 1979, IV, p. 1. First suggestions that the TPM might be abandoned reported in *New York Times,* Mar. 29, 1979, IV, p. 4. Lukens's withdrawal of the plate suit, *New York Times,* June 25, IV, p. 8.
30. *New York Times,* Nov. 29, 1979, IV, p. 1 and Dec. 2, IV, p. 3.
31. *New York Times,* Apr. 18, 1980, IV, p. 1; Apr. 19, IV, p. 9; May 2, IV, p. 1.
32. The Davignon warning of a trade war is reported in *New York Times,* Mar. 10, 1980, IV, p. 2; visits Washington, Mar. 13, IV, p. 3; Carter's letter to Jenkins, Mar. 27, IV, p. 2.
33. Roderick speech, *New York Times,* June 25, 1980, IV, p. 1; Venice summit, June 30, IV, p. 2; negotiations, Aug. 25, IV, p. 1.
34. The Mitsui case was reported in the *New York Times,* Mar. 25, 1981, IV, p. 15; July 1, IV, p. 18; circumvention is discussed in Hogan, *World Steel in the 1980s,* pp. 236-237.
35. Japan was demonized by the more irresponsible midwestern politicians, with barely concealed racism. In 1982 a senior Democratic congressman, John Dingell of Michigan, attacked the "little yellow people" for destroying the Michigan steel and auto industries, while otherwise moderate Republican congressman Lyle Williams from the Mahoning Valley in Ohio called for "economic war" against Japan. Quoted by Delia B. Conti, "President Reagan's Trade Rhetoric: Lessons for the 1990s," *Presidential Studies Quarterly* 25, no. 1, Winter 1995, p. 102.
36. *New York Times,* June 12, 1982, I, p.1 and p.45; June 19, I, p.34; June 23, IV, p. 3.
37. *New York Times,* July 7, IV, p.8; July 10, I, p. 41; July 23, IV, p. 3; July 26, IV, p. 2.
38. *New York Times,* Aug. 11, 1982, IV, p. 1; Aug. 25, IV, p. 6; Oct. 7, IV, p. 11; Oct. 11, IV, p. 9.
39. *The Economist,* July 14, 1984, p.66.
40. *American Metal Market,* Apr. 3, 1985, p. 1.
41. *New York Times,* Apr. 9, 1984, IV, p. 2; May 3, IV, p. 22.

42. Comments of Lynn Williams and David Roderick to the House Subcommittee on Commerce, Consumer and Monetary Affairs, *New York Times,* Apr. 7, 1986, IV, p. 5.
43. Hans G. Mueller, *Annals of the American Association of Political and Social Science* 460, Mar. 1982, pp. 75-77.
44. This paragraph is based on the discussion in William E. Hudson, "The Feasibility of a Comprehensive U.S. Industrial Policy," *Political Science Quarterly,* vol. 100, no.3, Fall 1985, pp.461-478.

Chapter 5

1. Alan M. Kantrow, "Wide-Open Management at Chaparral Steel," interview with Gordon E. Forward, president of Chaparral Steel, *Harvard Business Review,* May-June 1986, pp. 96-102.
2. "Koppel Steel Union Approves New Pact," *American Metal Market* (hereafter *AMM*), Dec. 14, 1994; marketing information from author's commercial experience; capital expenditures in Sept. 1994 *Iron Age/New Steel* Capital Spending Annual Survey.
3. Bethlehem Steel produced rebar using electric furnace steelmaking, at Steelton, Pennsylvania. Its costs there were handicapped by the Steelton hot end's equipment being sized to produce the (larger and more metallurgically demanding) rail product line of that mill, rather than the "small and cheap" philosophy required in re-bar steelmaking. In 1986, it closed its 11-inch bar mill at Steelton and sold its rebar fabricating shops to a French-owned company, American Banaco.
4. Typically, those minimills that had not installed casters by 1980 did not survive the shakeout of minimill capacity in the early 1980s: for example, Penn-Dixie Corporation's Continental Steel (although a caster was belatedly installed in 1984); the John A Roebling Steel Corporation in New Jersey; and Texas Steel at Fort Worth, Texas. An exception to this as to other rules is Hawaiian Western Steel, still pouring ingots in 1996; there are also a number of specialty producers of ingots for forging operations.
5. *AMM,* Aug. 23, 1983, p. 1; Aug.31, p. 4; Dec.26, p. 3; June 27, 1984, p. 5.
6. Nucor's remarkable success story had attracted many writers and reporters. Richard Preston's best-selling *American Steel: Hot Metal Men and the Resurrection of the Rust Belt,* New York, 1991, tells much of the history of Nucor well, not just the story of the start-up of the pioneering Crawfordsville flat-rolled mill around which the book is structured. In addition, numerous stock analysts' reports have recited Nucor's history and economics, as the company's shares proved to be one of the most dramatic growth stocks of the 1980s.
7. Plants closed included Witteman Steel Mills, Fontana, California; Soulé Steel, Los Angeles; Roblin Steel, Dunkirk, New York; John A. Roebling Steel Corp., Trenton, New Jersey; Hurricane Steel, Sealy, Texas; and Continental Steel

(formerly Penn-Dixie Steel). The Joliet, Illinois, plant of Continental Steel was partly reopened, for rolling only, after it was purchased by Sheffield Steel of Sand Springs, Oklahoma. In addition to the new Quanex-MacSteel mill, a new rolling mill was built for plate at Tuscaloosa Steel in 1985.

8. Father Hogan, in his *Minimills and Integrated Mills,* Cambridge, Mass., 1987, pp. 48-49, lists 19,015,000 tons of U.S. minimill capacity at 50 mills. To his list should be added at least the following carbon steel electric furnace producers for a complete capacity total for the sector at the end of 1987: Northwestern Steel and Wire, 2.4 million tons; Quanex, two mills totaling approximately 700,000 tons; Phoenix/Citisteel, 400,000; Lukens, 650,000; Gilmore/Oregon Steel, 300,000; CSC Industries/Copperweld Steel Co. (estimated 500,000); and Laclede Steel (1 million). In 1987, I would not (yet) consider Lone Star or CF & I as minimills, but rather as formerly integrated mills in a state of transition. On this reckoning, the capacities of the major companies, in millions of tons, are Northwestern, 2.40; North Star, 2.355; Nucor, 2.075; Florida Steel, 1.585 and Chaparral, 1.50.

9. Plate mill closures were: Alan Wood, 1980; USS-South Works, 1982; Kaiser, 1983; Armco-Houston, 1984; USS-Homestead, 1986; USS-Baytown, 1986. In 1986, the USS-Geneva mill was closed during the U.S. Steel strike and only reopened when it was sold to Geneva Steel in 1987. LTV's former Republic mill at Gadsden was sold to Gulf States Steel in 1986 without ceasing operations. Phoenix Steel closed in 1986; the mill was bought by Citisteel in 1987 and resumed operations in 1988. The former Kaiser plate mill at Fontana, California, was bought by Oregon Steel in 1989 and operated until 1994 using outside slabs, primarily to supply skelp to Oregon's large-diameter line pipe mill in Napa, California.

10. Most welded pipe is produced by the ERW or electric-resistance welded method, by forming plate or strip "skelp" into pipe and electric-arc welding a continuous seam running the length of the pipe. Large-diameter pipe can also be formed by spiral welding, where the seam does not run lengthwise but spirally around the pipe; thus large-diameter pipes can be formed from narrower widths of skelp.

11. "Co-Steel Sees Bar, Rod as Market Opportunity," *American Metal Market,* Jan. 11, 1994; Qualitech: *AMM* articles, Jan. 19, Feb. 20, and Mar. 9, 1995; "Quanex Completes Projects," *AMM,* Apr. 3, 1995, reported Quanex's annual hot-rolled bar capacity increased from 500,000 to 550,000 tons per year with the addition of extra roll stands at both bar mills.

Chapter 6

1. The battles over iron and steel tariffs in the 1880s and 1890s, and the balance of trade in those products, are explained in detail in the Reverend William T. Hogan, *Economic History of the Iron and Steel Industry in the United States,* vol. 1, Lexington, MA, 1971, pp. 345-357. Quote is from p. 347.

2. *Iron Age,* Jan. 5, 1976, p. 20.
3. Announcements and commentary in *New York Times,* Feb.2, I, p. 1; Mar. 10, I, p. 1; Mar. 11, III, p. 2; Mar. 13, I, p. 1; April 25, IV, p.1.
4. For the company's operating problems, see *American Metal Market* (hereafter *AMM*), Jan. 31, 1994; executive changes, *AMM,* June 2, 1994; stock offering, *AMM,* Oct.19, 1994 and Feb. 9, 1995.
5. *AMM,* Nov. 22, 1988, p. 1; *New York Times,* Nov. 22, 1988, IV, p. 3; *AMM,* Dec. 5, 1988.
6. Speculation about a USS-Posco announcement is in *AMM,* Nov.14, 1985; the official announcement was reported in *AMM,* Dec. 20, 1985; speculation about the joint venture's impact on Geneva is in *AMM,* Mar. 12, 1986. The mill's hot band supply became controversial in 1988 when the Congressional Research Service issued a report recommending against expanding Korea's VRA quota to allow the import of hot bands; U.S. Steel charged that the report had been influenced by Utah's Congressional delegation, who were seeking to have the reopened Geneva Steel resume supplying Pittsburg. *AMM,* Dec. 16, 1988.
7. The Homestead mill in Pittsburgh had been closed three months prior to the strike. Speculation also focused on the future of the Edgar Thompson plant in the Pittsburgh area, although the future of this mill was secured (and the eventual closure of steelmaking at the Fairless Hills plant was made certain) by a commitment at the time of the strike's settlement to building a continuous caster at Edgar Thompson. U.S. Steel's threat to the Lorain hot end is in *AMM,* July 28, 1986.
8. Announcement of the joint venture: *New York Times,* Feb. 15, 1989, IV, p. 4; a good review of the mill's progress to 1993 is by Adrian Gardner, "East/West Joint Venture Begins to Make the Grade," in *Metal Bulletin Monthly,* May 1993.
9. *New York Times,* Mar. 24, 1983, IV, p. 4: Mar. 30, IV, p. 20; Mar. 31, IV, p. 20.
10. *New York Times,* Nov. 17, 1989, III, p. 12.
11. Major foreign investments in stainless steel include J&L Specialty, the second-largest stainless flat-rolled producer, owned by the Ugine division of Usinor-Sacilor; North American Stainless, a cold-rolling mill originally built in 1990 as a joint venture between equal partners Armco and Acerinox of Spain, but in which Acerinox owned 95 percent after 1994; Avesta-Sheffield, Inc., the U.S. arm of the Anglo-Swedish stainless group, with plate, bar, and pipe production in the United States; and two of the three largest stainless bar producers, Slater Steel (Canadian-owned) and Sammi Al Tech, owned by the Korean Sammi group.
12. Canadian mills acquired by international investors have included the minimills Courtice Steel and Manitoba Rolling Mills (MRM Steel), bought in 1989 and 1995 respectively by the Brazil's Grupo Gerdau; the specialty producer Atlas Stainless Steels, bought by Korea's Sammi; Sidbec-Dosco, with a 640,000-ton-per-year hot-strip mill as well as rod/bar and welded pipe mills, bought by the Indian-owned Ispat Group in 1994; and Sydney Steel, bought by China's Minmetals in 1994.

13. The closest thing to a U.S.-owned steel company in Canada is the bar cold-finisher Union Drawn Steel, once part of Republic Steel and now owned by the Pitterich group through Moltrup Steel Products. Oregon Steel also has a 60 percent stake in Camrose Pipe, a large-diameter pipe joint venture with Stelco.

Chapter 7

1. A good example of this was cited by John E. Jacobson of Chase Econometrics at Chase's World Steel Seminar, Chicago, Oct. 18, 1986. In 1984, Bethlehem Steel took a write-down of nearly $1 billion on the closure of its Lackawanna, New York, integrated mill. This made sense only if the expected future losses from continuing operations, plus the expected costs of necessary continuing investment to prevent the plant deteriorating further, had a net present value of $1 billion or more, meaning that the plant would be causing a drain of well in excess of $200 million or more each year, given the interest and inflation rates prevailing in 1984. The write-down might not have made short-term sense on this strict basis, although the financial community may have required Bethlehem Steel to take the step in the interests of the company's long-term financial viability.
2. National Steel Corporation, 1982 Annual Report; company press release, Mar. 2, 1982, quoted by the Rev. William T. Hogan, *Steel in the United States: Restructuring to Compete,* Lexington, MA, 1983, p. 74.
3. The history of CF & I from 1900 up to the mid-1980s, is handsomely covered in H. Lee Scamehorn, *Mine and Mill: The CF & I in the Twentieth Century,* Lincoln, NE, 1992.
4. "CF & I: Things Are Looking Up," *American Metal Market,* Sept. 28, 1994. Crane Corporation, Annual Report and Form 10-K, 1983, 1984.
5. Until 1995, CF & I was the only wire rod producer west of Kansas City, where the 700,000-ton-per-year rod mill of GS Industries (Armco until 1993) is located. The new CF & I rod mill, completed in late 1994, produces around 450,000 tons per year of rod and 150,000 tons per year of bar products, compared to 360,000 tons per year from the old rod mill. Two new producers entered the western wire market in 1995–96: Cascade Steel Rolling Mills of McMinnville, Oregon, a bar producer, built a new rod/bar mill which beginning in 1996 is expected to ship at least 200,000 tons per year of rod from a total capacity of 500,000 tons; and North Star Steel built a new greenfield bar/rod minimill in Kingman, Arizona, again with 500,000-ton-per-year capacity, completed in late 1995. The four mills—including the newly competitive GS Industries mill—looked set for a major battle for market share, which is likely to transform the region from an importer to an exporter of wire and wire rod.
6. The story of Geneva Steel's start-up and success has been told in a number of places, notably in *Metal Bulletin Monthly,* May 1994, pp. 24-27; *33/Metal Producing,* July 1994, pp. 21-24; and *Metal Center News,* January 1995, pp.

36-44. Perhaps the most interesting article, written from the perspective of the (rail) logistics of the mill, is by Mark W. Hemphill, "Taconite West, Coal East: How Wisconsin Central and Southern Pacific Snared the Big Geneva Steel Ore Haul," in *Trains,* Mar. 1995, pp. 36-47.

7. LTV Corporation, Annual Reports and Forms 10-K, 1985, 1986; *American Metal Market* (hereafter *AMM*), July 18, 1986.
8. *AMM,* Aug. 8 and Nov. 20, 1986; LTV Corporation, Annual Report, 1986; Form 10-K, 1987.
9. Quoted in "The New LTV Steel," *33/Metal Producing,* Aug. 1993, p.28.
10. Trico's critics are reported in *AMM,* April 19 and May 19, 1995.
11. "Low Electric Price Scrubs LTV's Corex," *AMM,* May 12, 1994.

Chapter 8

1. Richard Preston, *American Steel,* New York, NY, 1991.
2. Composite price of Number 1 heavy melting scrap in dollars per gross ton at Pittsburgh, Chicago and Philadelphia based on daily prices in *American Metal Market* (hereafter *AMM*), July 14, 1995.
3. American Iron and Steel Institute, *Annual Statistical Report,* various years, table, "Consumption of Scrap and Pig Iron By Types of Furnaces."
4. Stephen Wulff, speech to the Iron and Steel Scrap, Scrap Substitutes and Direct Steelmaking Conference, Atlanta, Mar. 22, 1995.
5. *American Metal Market,* Feb.8, 1995, p.15A.
6. *AMM,* Apr. 14, 1995. The British Steel units were to have supplied DRI to the Ravenscraig mill in Scotland, the subject of abortive negotiations with U.S. Steel in the early 1980s; when the proposed joint venture to supply U.S. Steel's Fairless Hills mill with slabs from Ravenscraig fell through, the decision was taken to close the Ravenscraig mill, thus making the unused DRI units available.
7. *AMM,* May 16, 1995. Georgetown Steel acquired the Kansas City mill from GST Technologies in late 1995, thus combining the two largest U.S. producers of high-carbon rod, used for such applications as tire cord, prestressed concrete strand, and upholstery spring wire; *AMM,* June 14, 1995.
8. Goldman Sachs research report, *Nucor,* Anthony H. Carpet, Oct. 4, 1993, p. 5. See also "Trinidad Iron Carbide Fares Just Fine: Nucor" in *AMM,* Feb. 13, 1995.
9. *AMM,* June 8 and July 20, 1995.
10. *AMM,* Nov. 16, 1994; July 12 and July 19, 1995.
11. Cost estimates for different stages of production at representative U.S. Class I integrated mills and flat-rolled minimills have been published by both Donald Barnett of Economic Associates, Inc., McLean, Virginia (for example, in his presentation to the Steel Survival Strategies IX conference, June 21, 1994) and by Peter Marcus and Karlis Kirsis in *World Steel Dynamics,* the series of cost, price, and output forecasts published by Paine Webber, New York.
12. The costs of the Crawfordsville mill are estimated in Preston's book *American Steel.* Perhaps the greatest bargains were Crawfordsville's two cold-rolling

mills, a used Voest-Alpine mill bought in 1990 from Klockner in Germany for $1 million, or scrap value, and a second mill bought from Sweden in 1994 for $4 million.

13. Gallatin and Steel Dynamics costs have been widely reported in press releases and statements by officers of the companies, as reported in *AMM* and elsewhere. For example, see Keith Busse's presentation on Steel Dynamics at the Steel Survival Strategies X conference, New York, June 21, 1995.
14. Industry capital expenditures are tracked in an annual survey by *Iron Age* magazine; these numbers are from the Sept. 1994 survey.
15. At the start of 1995 (before Gallatin Steel came on line) there were 35 hot-strip mills operated by 25 companies in the United States, and six operated by five companies in Canada. Of these, four produced exclusively stainless steel and two were used exclusively to provide skelp for pipemaking. The tinplate producers were Bethlehem, Dofasco, Inland, LTV, National, Stelco, U.S. Steel, Weirton, and Wheeling-Pittsburgh. The principal suppliers of auto body panels were AK Steel, Bethlehem, Dofasco, Inland, LTV, National, Rouge, Stelco, and U.S. Steel.
16. Comments by John Nolan, general sales manager of Steel Dynamics, at the AISI 1995 annual meeting, Chicago, reported in *AMM,* May 26, 1995.
17. Wilfried Bald, director of Schloemann-Siemag AG (SMS), to a press conference at the Steel Survival Strategies X conference, June 27, 1995, as reported in *AMM,* June 28, 1995.

Chapter 9

1. *Purchasing Magazine's* steel price track shows 1980 average prices of hot-rolled sheet at $360 a ton in nominal (1980) dollars, equivalent to $701 in 1994 dollars. In 1994, *Purchasing Magazine's* index reached a high for hot-rolled sheet of $379, while the average for the peak demand period of 1993 to 1995 has been around $350, exactly half the 1980 level.
2. Numbers for 1979 are from Paine Webber's *World Steel Dynamics, Core Report P,* 1982; 1994 numbers from *American Metal Market* (hereafter *AMM*), Feb. 20, 1995. In the first quarter of 1995, the peak for profitability in the cycle from 1993 to 1995, integrated steelmakers earned a record $50 per ton.
3. Figures from company annual reports. See also quoted remarks by Thomas C. Graham to steel analysts in *AMM,* Aug. 3, 1995.
4. McLouth's problems were spelled out in an *American Metal Market* interview with its CEO, Joseph Corso, in that newspaper's Aug. 25, 1994, supplement *Steelmaking.* The closure and sale of the mill were reported in the *AMM,* notably on Mar. 19 and June 28, 1996.
5. For reporting on National Steel's problems, leading to the management changes, see *Wall Street Journal,* Jan. 22, 1994 and *AMM,* Jan. 31, 1994.

6. See, for example, "Gulf States Steel Nearing Profits," in *AMM,* Apr. 4, 1986; "Gulf States Steel Needs $150M Help," in *AMM,* June 9, 1994. The political battle against Trico is described in, for example, *AMM,* June 21 and July 14, 1995.
7. See "WCI Offers Niche Products" in *AMM,* Mar. 3, 1995.
8. *AMM* supplement, *Flat Rolled Steel,* July 14, 1994, p. 5A. *AMM,* June 28, 1995, reports the doubts of Bruce Vahjen, can industry manager for Pepsi-Cola, about steelmakers' willingness to compete with aluminum.
9. Appliance shipments are tracked by the journal *Appliance,* which also publishes an annual report including ten-year reviews of the U.S. appliance industry; the 1995 annual report is *Appliance's* 43rd.
10. Two U.S. integrated flat-rolled companies, Geneva Steel and LTV Steel, still produce welded pipe from their own sheet. California Steel Industries at Fontana, California, also produces pipe from its own hot strip, but using imported slab. Integrated Bethlehem Steel (at Steelton) and nonintegrated Oregon Steel produce large-diameter line pipe from their own plate. Three nonintegrated companies, Laclede, Lone Star, and Newport Steel, operate relatively small hot-strip mills primarily to produce skelp for their own pipe and tube operations. These eight producers produce around 1 million tons of welded pipe and tubing a year, or around 25 percent of domestic production. In Canada, three flat-rolled steel producers, Ipsco, Sidbec-Dosco, and Stelco, make a much higher share of total pipe and tube production.

    A number of U.S. flat-rolled producers spun off or closed pipe and tubing operations in the 1980s and 1990s, including Bethlehem Steel (standard pipe, at Sparrows Point), National Steel, Sharon Steel, U.S. Steel, and Wheeling-Pittsburgh. A former National Steel subsidiary, Bull Moose Tube Co., is owned by the Caparo Group, which also acquired the former Sharon Steel hot-strip mill; it was reported in 1995 that the tube mill would in future be partly supplied from Sharon. Armco acquired Tex-Tube and Sawhill Tubular on its purchase of Cyclops in 1991 and still owns Sawhill Tubular; however, neither division primarily sourced its hot-rolled strip from Armco flat-rolled operations. Ipsco's new flat-rolled minimill at Montpelier, Iowa, is expected to supply that company's existing ERW pipe mill at Camanche, Iowa, and a further, large-diameter, pipe mill project announced in July 1996.
11. Independent galvanizing lines operating or under construction in 1996 included: BHP Coated Products division of BHP Steel (Rancho Cucamonga, California, and a second line under construction in Oregon); the Metaltech/NexTech group (three plants operating or under construction in the Pittsburgh area); Metro Metals (East Chicago, Indiana); Pinole Point Steel, Richmond, California; Precision Galvanizing (Ambridge, Pennsylvania); and Worthington Industries (Malvern, Pennsylvania).

    Mill-owned joint-venture galvanizers included: Double Eagle Coatings (Rouge Steel and U.S. Steel, Dearborn, Michigan); Double G Coatings (Bethlehem and National Steel, Jackson, Mississippi); DNN Galvanizing (Dofasco, National and NKK, Windsor, Ontario); L-S I and L-S II (LTV and Sumitomo, Cleveland and Columbus, Ohio, respectively); I/N Kote (Inland Steel and

Nippon Steel, New Carlisle, Indiana); USS-Posco Industries (the former U.S. Steel mill at Pittsburg, California); Walbridge Coatings (Bethlehem Steel and Inland Steel, Walbridge, Ohio); and Wheeling-Nisshin, Inc. (Follansbee, West Virginia).

Bethlehem also operates a galvanizing line at its former Lackawanna, New York, integrated mill as a unit of its Burns Harbor plant.

Chapter 10

1. "Acme Praised for Pollution-Reduction Efforts," *American Metal Market* (hereafter *AMM*), Feb. 7, 1995. Alternative approaches can be seen in integrated steelmakers' annual Form 10-K reports, where, for example, Bethlehem Steel's disclosure and discussion of environmental control and cleanup expenditures shows barely concealed hostility.
2. See, for example, Morgan Goodwin, "Dealing with the Very Dregs of Steelmaking," *AMM* supplement *Recycling Technology,* Aug. 24, 1995.
3. Review articles on the state of direct strip casting include articles by Jo Isenberg-O'Laughlin, *33/Metal Producing*: "Nearer to Net," in Jan. 1993, and "The Wheels Are Turning," in June 1994.
4. Stephen Baker, "The Odd Couple of Steel," *Business Week,* Nov. 7, 1994
5. Orders through 1995, in addition to Nucor's two furnaces at each of Hickman and Darlington, include new melt shops at Charter Steel in Saukville, Wisconsin; Gallatin Steel at Ghent, Kentucky; and North Star at Kingman, Arizona. DC furnaces were ordered as replacements for older AC furnaces at Bethlehem's Pennsylvania Steel Technologies subsidiary at Steelton, Pennsylvania; Border Steel in El Paso, Texas; North Star at St. Paul, Minnesota; and SMI in Birmingham, Alabama.
6. A good plain-language survey of developments in electric arc furnace technology is that by Jo Isenberg-O'Loughlin, "Power On!," in *33/Steel Producing,* May 1994, pp. 31-33, 64-71. See also "DC Arcs Spark US Imagination," *Metal Bulletin Monthly,* Mar. 1994, p.51.
7. 'The Demise of Pickled Steel,' *The Economist,* Mar. 4, 1995.
8. Frank Haflich, 'US Takes Mexican Steel Import Rise Quietly,' in *American Metal Market,* May 18, 1995, p.14A; for the Ispat–Wheeling-Pittsburgh deal, see WHX Corporation, Report on Form 10-K, 1995; the Chaparral-Ahmsa agreement is referred to in *AMM,* Apr. 18, 1995

APPENDIXES

INTRODUCTION

The following tables present the numerous facilities of the steel industries of the United States and Canada as of January 1, 1996. They are organized in two parts. Part I lists all ironmaking and steelmaking facilities. Part II lists steel producers by product—sheets, bar, pipe, and so on—and shows all facilities producing for a given product market with either capacity or estimated shipments data.

Most capacity in the steel industry is controlled by publicly owned companies, which publish significant process, capacity, and production data in annual reports, governmental regulatory filings (especially the U.S. Form 10-K), press releases, and marketing material. Much information is published elsewhere in specialist directories, such as the annual *Directory of Iron and Steel Plants* of the Association of Iron and Steel Engineers and the 1995 directory *Pipe and Tube Mills of the World* published by the journal *Preston Pipe Report*. In some cases where such information does not exist in published sources, and where companies have not revealed such information on request, the author has made estimates based on industry commercial knowledge. Responsibility for errors rests solely with the author.

LISTING OF APPENDIXES

PART I: IRON AND STEELMAKING

IRONMAKING:

STEELMAKING:

PART II: STEEL PRODUCERS BY PRODUCT

FLAT PRODUCTS:

BAR, ROD AND STRUCTURAL PRODUCTS:

12a Stainless, high alloy and tool steel producers
12b Carbon and alloy forging bar and ingot producers.

PIPE AND TUBING:

II.13 Structural Tubing and Piling Pipe
II.14 Carbon Steel Mechanical and Pressure Tubing (ERW)
II.15 Carbon Steel Standard and Line Pipe (CBW and ERW)
II.16 Large Diameter Carbon Steel Pipe (DSAW and ERW)
II.17 Oil Country Tubular Goods:
17a Seamless Oil Country Tubulars
17b Welded Oil Country Tubulars
II.18 Seamless Pipe and Tubing, other than stainless
II.19 Stainless Steel Pipe and Tubing:
19a Seamless pipe and tubing
19b Welded pipe and tubing

IRONMAKING

I.1: Iron Ore Producers

Integrated steelmaking, by definition, involves production of steel from virgin iron units—iron mined from the ground and not previously refined into steel. The term "integrated" refers to the backward integration of integrated steelmakers into, first, ironmaking (in the blast furnace) and ultimately into iron ore mining. Iron ore is now reduced to iron by a number of direct reduction processes (feeding electric furnace steelmaking) as well as by the blast furnace, thus creating a growing fusion of the former separate integrated and nonintegrated steelmaking sectors (see chapter 8).

Iron ores or, more accurately, highly concentrated iron pellets, have become a major globally traded commodity since the 1950s. Prior to that time, the major steelmaking regions of the world (Japan excepted) were largely self-sufficient in iron ore. In North America, however, the integrated industry is partly isolated from global trade because most integrated steel mills are located away from seaports. The Great Lakes form a distinct logistical basin for the iron and steel industry, with the small size of the St. Lawrence Seaway locks creating a cost barrier to the importation of iron ore from outside the lakes region. Large ore carriers operate within the upper Great Lakes (excluding Lake Ontario), and still larger ones operate on the worlds oceans; but only small (and therefore costly, on a per-ton basis) ships can pass from the ocean into the Lakes (or from Lake Erie into Lake Ontario).

Because of these freight cost differentials, operating mines are grouped into regions in the table below. Note that in most cases, a number of separate pits in a single mining property or district may feed one pellet plant; equipment and production may move between these from time to time. Here these are each treated as a single operating unit.

GREAT LAKES ORE PRODUCERS

Property, Pellet Plant Location, and Operator	Owners	Production Capacity [a]	Principal Customer Steel Mills
Empire Iron Mining, Palmer, MI (Cleveland-Cliffs)	Inland Steel, 40%; LTV, 25%; Wheeling-Pittsburgh, 12.5%; Cleveland-Cliffs, 22.5%	8,200,000	Inland Steel, LTV–Indiana Harbor, LTV–Cleveland, Wheeling-Pittsburgh
Eveleth Mines, Eveleth, MN (Oglebay Norton) [NOTE: Two properties, jointly operated: (A) Eveleth Taconite Co., (B) Eveleth Expansion Co.]	(A): Rouge Steel, 85%, Oglebay Norton 15%; (B): AK Steel, 35%; Stelco, 23.5%; Oglebay Norton, 41.5%.	(A): 2,300,000 (B): 3,600,000	Rouge Steel, Stelco–Nanticoke, AK Steel–Middletown
Hibbing Taconite, Hibbing, MN (Cleveland-Cliffs)	Bethlehem Steel, 70.3%, Stelco, 14.7%, Cleveland-Cliffs, 15%	8,400,000	Bethlehem–Burns Harbor, Stelco–Nanticoke
LTV Steel Mining Co., Hoyt Lakes, MN (Cleveland-Cliffs)	LTV Steel, 100%	10,600,000	LTV–Cleveland, LTV–Indiana Harbor
Minorca Mines, Virginia, MN (Inland Steel Mining Co.)	Inland Steel, 100%	2,750,000	Inland Steel
Minntac (Minnesota Taconite), Mountain Iron, MN (U.S. Steel)	U.S. Steel, 100%	18,000,000	U.S. Steel–Gary, U.S. Steel–Edgar Thomson, Geneva Steel, USS/Kobe
National Steel Pellet Co., Keewatin, MN (M.A. Hanna Co.)	National Steel, 100%	5,800,000	National Steel–Ecorse, National Steel–Granite City
Northshore Mining, Silver Bay, MN (Cleveland Cliffs)	Cleveland-Cliffs, 100%	4,800,000	AK Steel - Middletown, AK Steel–Ashland, Weirton Steel, WCI Steel
Tilden Mine, Tilden, MI (Cleveland-Cliffs)	Algoma Steel, 45%; Stelco, 15%; Cleveland-Cliffs, 40%	8,000,000	Algoma Steel, Stelco–Hamilton and Nanticoke

LABRADOR AND QUEBEC

Iron Ore Company of Canada, Labrador City, Labrador, and Sept-Iles, Québec (M.A. Hanna Co.)	Bethlehem Steel, 34.52%; M.A. Hanna Co., 28.15%; National Steel, 19.96%; Norcen, 11%; Dofasco, 6.4%	11,000,000 (pellets) [15,000,000 concentrates]	Bethlehem–Sparrows Point, Dofasco, exports
Québec-Cartier Mining, Port Cartier, Québec [b]	Dofasco, 50%; Mitsui, 25%; CAEMI, 25%.	8,000,000 (pellets) [20,000,000 concentrates]	Dofasco, Sidbec-Dosco, exports
Wabush Mines, Pointe Noire, Québec (Cleveland-Cliffs)	Stelco, 34.5%; Dofasco, 22.1%; Acme Steel, 13.75%; Inland Steel, 13.75%; Finsider, 8.89%; Cleveland-Cliffs, 7.01%	4,500,000	Stelco–Hamilton, Dofasco, Upper Lakes producers, exports

OTHER REGIONS

Algoma Steel, Wawa mine, Wawa, Ontario	Algoma Steel, 100%	[1,000,000 concentrates]	Algoma Steel
Geneva Steel, mines in Cedar City region of southwest Utah	Geneva Steel, 100%	[200,000 concentrates]	Geneva Steel

NOTES:

[a] **Tonnages of ores and pellets are normally measured in gross or long" tons of 2,240 pounds, as shown here, rather than in net tons of 2,000 pounds as used for measuring steel. Tonnages shown here are net tons of pellet plant production capacity except where specified.**

[b] **The pellet plant used by Québec-Cartier Mining (QCM) is leased from Sidbec-Normines, the original developer of part of the mining district at Fire Lake, Québec, operated by QCM; Sidbec-Normines is a partnership of Sidbec-Dosco and British Steel.**

IRONMAKING

I.2: Directly Reduced Iron Plants

At the start of 1996, there were only two operating direct-reduction ironmaking (DRI) plants in the United States and Canada, although significant production of DRI was undertaken in neighboring Mexico, Trinidad and Tobago, and Venezuela. However, a third was under construction, and four more iron or iron carbide plants were at an advanced stage of planning and site selection.

Additional DRI plants (other than prototype or pilot plants) have been operated by Armco at Houston, Texas; Oregon Steel at Portland, Oregon; and Stelco at Hamilton, Ontario. Each of these facilities has been permanently closed. Outside the United States and Canada, Nucor operates its pioneering iron carbide plant in Trinidad, where iron ore mining company Cleveland-Cliffs was also studying construction of a DRI plant in 1996.

I.2: DIRECT REDUCTION PLANTS—OPERATING AND PROPOSED—AT JANUARY 1996

Company and Plant Location	Process	Capacity, tons per year	Notes
British Steel, Mobile, Alabama	Midrex	2 of 550,000 each	Two modules relocated from Scotland, 1995-96
Georgetown Steel, Georgetown, South Carolina	Midrex	500,000	Built 1970
Georgetown Steel and Birmingham Steel joint venture, Louisiana	Midrex	1,200,000	To open 1997. World's largest single-module plant
KM Iron LLC (a joint venture of Kobe Steel Ltd. and Midrex Corp.)	Midrex - Fastmet	2 of 450,000 each	Decision due on site location in 1996 (Alabama or Louisiana)
Qualitech, Corpus Christi, Texas	Iron carbide	720,000	To open 1998. Steel Dynamics is a minority investor
Sidbec-Dosco Ispat, Inc., Contrecoeur, Québec	Midrex	1 of 850,000 1 of 500,000	Built 1969
Steel Dynamics, Inc., Ohio (site to be determined)	Inmetco	800,000	Go-ahead expected late 1996. To be sited either at SDI minimill or in Toledo, Ohio
Tondu Corporation, Burnside, Louisiana	To be determined	1,500,000	To open 1998

IRONMAKING

I.3: Blast Furnaces

At the end of 1995, 53 blast furnaces were operating at 25 integrated steel mills in the United States and Canada. Only 8 of these were less than 25 years old, and none were less than 15 years old. However, periodic relining, the replacement of major components, and the addition of upgrades such as increased operating pressures and the use of pulverized coal injection (PCI) mean that age is not in itself a good indicator of blast furnace productivity and life.

During 1995, the total number of operating furnaces was reduced by three, as Bethlehem Steel closed its Bethlehem, Pennsylvania, hot end and Wheeling-Pittsburgh moved from a three blast furnace operation to using two. Weirton Steel similarly moved from three to two furnaces in 1994, due to improved productivity from its principal furnaces. Numerous other small blast furnaces have been retired from service over the last decade but not demolished. Of the idle furnaces, some are available for restart in the event of major outages at their owners primary operating furnaces. Both Algoma Steel and Weirton Steel operated an idled furnace briefly in 1995-96 during a reline of a primary blast furnace. Other companies maintaining such "cold idle" furnaces include AK Steel (at Ashland), Acme Steel, McLouth, USS-Kobe, and U.S. Steel (at Gary). Time between relines varies with operating practice but is typically between 10 and 15 years. Partial or "mini relines" are used to extend this interval by an additional five to eight years.

I.3: BLAST FURNACES IN COMMISSION AT DECEMBER 1995

(output capacity in millions of net tons per year)

Plant and Furnace Identification	Hearth Diameter	Working Volume (cu. ft.)	Output Capacity	Notes
Acme Steel "A"	25'0"	41,100	0.9	
AK Steel, Ashland, "Amanda"	33'5"	70,500	2.0	
AK Steel, Middletown, # 3	29'4"	51,600	2.1	
Algoma Steel, # 6	27'0"	45,605	0.9	# 6 operating only during
# 7	35'0"	89,169	1.8	1995 re-line outage of # 7
Bethlehem, Burns Harbor "C"	38'3"	88,836	2.5	PCI. Re-lined 1994
"D"	35'9"	84,456	2.5	PCI
Bethlehem, Sparrows Point "L"	44'6"	130,000	3.3	New 1978; partial re-line 1993
"J"	30'0"	55,000	1.2	
"H"	30'0"	55,000	1.0	
Dofasco # 1	20'9"	31,800	0.8	
# 2	20'9"	32,600	0.8	
# 3	21'6"	31,900	0.9	
# 4	28'0"	56,320	1.4	
Geneva Steel # 1	26'6"	42,243	0.9	Re-line scheduled 1996
# 2	26'6"	42,243	0.9	
# 3	26'6"	42,243	0.9	
Gulf States # 2	26'0"	45,600	1.1	Re-lined 1995
Inland "A"	26'6"	47,883	1.2	
"B"	26'6"	46,053	1.2	
# 5	26'6"	46,049	1.2	PCI
# 6	26'6"	47,883	1.2	PCI
# 7	45'0"	123,897	3.2	PCI. New 1979; re-line 1993
LTV, Cleveland, C-1	27'6"	46,647	1.2	Partial re-line 1993
C-5	29'6"	55,203	1.6	Re-lined 1993
C-6	29'6"	56,441	1.5	Partial reline 1995
LTV, Indiana Harbor, H-3	29'6"	57,279	1.6	Partial re-line 1994
H-4	32'9"	68,584	1.8	Re-line scheduled 1996
McLouth Steel, # 2	28'6"	56,676	1.0	Idled April 1996
National Steel, Ecorse "A"	30'6"	62,434	1.2	
"B"	29'0"	55,468	1.2	
"D"	28'0"	53,252	1.1	Re-lined 1993
National Steel, Granite City "A"	27'3"	50,652	1.0	
"B"	27'3"	50,490	1.0	Re-lined 1995
Rouge Steel "B"	20'0"	27,609	0.8	
"C"	29'0"	54,987	1.6	
Stelco, Hamilton "D"	29'0"	52,866	1.2	PCI
"E"	29'0"	64,707	1.8	PCI
Stelco, Nanticoke # 1	33'9"	75,300	1.5	New 1978
USS-Kobe Steel # 3	28'6"	50,945	1.4	PCI. Re-lined 1992
# 4	29'0"	50,841	1.2	PCI
U.S. Steel, Fairfield # 8	32'0"	77,520	2.5	PCI
U.S. Steel, Gary # 4	28'10"	52,818	1.5	
# 6	28'0"	53,198	1.4	
# 8	26'6"	45,668	1.2	Re-lined after explosion 1995
# 13	36'6"	104,300	3.2	PCI. New 1977
U.S. Steel, Edgar Thomson # 1	28'10"	57,194	1.2	Re-line due 1996
# 3	25'3"	43,094	1.1	
WCI Steel "W1"	28'6"	54,000	1.5	Re-lined 1995
Weirton # 1	27'0"	54,072	1.3	Re-line due 1996
# 2	26'3"	45,960	1.0	Re-lined 1992
Wheeling-Pittsburgh # 3	23'2"	33,667	0.8	
# 5	23'4"	40,536	1.2	Re-lined and upgraded 1995

STEELMAKING

I.4: STEEL MILLS OF NORTH AMERICA
by Province and State, at January 1996 showing dates of (1) original construction and (2) present ownership

KEY TO ABBREVIATIONS:
Furnace/caster types:
BOF=basic oxygen furnace, EF=electric arc furnace, L=ladle metallurgy, BB=beam blank caster, BI=billet caster, BL=bloom caster, IN=ingot casting practice, SL=conventional slab caster, TS=thin slab caster.
Date (1): Date of first steelmaking at site.
Date (2): Effective date of current corporate ownership.
Principal products: HR=hot-rolled coil, CR=cold-rolled coil, HDG=hot-dipped galvanized (or similar coatings), EG=electrogalvanized (or similar coatings), TM=tin mill products, MBQ=merchant quality bar, SBQ=special quality bar, CF bar=cold-finished bar.
Excluded are castings and forgings plants, wire mills, and facilities limited to pipe and tube manufacture, and to the cold rolling of narrow strip under 36 inches wide.

CANADA

Company and Location (and ownership interests)	Furnace/ Caster	Raw Steel Capacity	Product Capacity	Date (1)	Date (2)	Principal Products
Alberta						
Altasteel, Edmonton (Stelco, Inc.)	EF/BI	325,000	325,000	1970	-	Rebar, MBQ
Manitoba						
Gerdau MRM Steel, Selkirk (Gerdau Group, Brazil)	EF/L/BI	310,000	310,000	1965	1995	MBQ, structurals, light rail
Nova Scotia						
Sydney Steel Co., North Sydney (Minmetals, China)	EF/L/BL/SL	600,000	500,000	1900	1995	Slab, rail
Ontario						
Algoma Steel, Sault Ste. Marie	BOF/L SL/BL/BB/IN	2,500,000	3,400,000	1934	1993	HR, CR, plate, rail, seamless, structurals
Atlas Specialty Steels, Welland (Sammi Group, Korea)	EF/L/BI/IN	125,000	70,000	1928	1990	Stainless bar
Canadian Drawn Steel, Hamilton (Bliss & Laughlin)	-	-	80,000	1911	1990	CF bar
Co-Steel Lasco, Whitby	EF/L/BI	900,000	1,400,000	1980	-	Rebar, MBQ, structurals
Courtice Steel, Cambridge (Gerdau Group, Brazil)	EF/BI	250,000	250,000	1982	1989	MBQ, rebar
DNN Galvanizing, Windsor (Dofasco, NKK, National Steel)	-	-	350,000	1993	-	HDG
Dofasco, Hamilton	BOF/L/SL	2,370,000	3,200,000	1898	-	HR, CR, HDG, TMP
Dofasco, Hamilton (new 1996)	EF/TS	1,350,000	450,000	1996	-	Slabs, internal use
Ivaco Rolling Mills, L'Orignal	EF/BI	450,000	650,000	1969	-	Wire rod
Slater Steels, Hamilton[a]	EF/L/BI/IN	650,000	400,000	1962	-	SBQ
Stelco, Hamilton	BOF/BL/SL	2,700,000	3,350,000	1905	-	HR, CR, HDG, TMP, plate, wire rod, SBQ
Stelco, Nanticoke	BOF/SL	1,700,000	1,900,000	1979	-	HR
Union Drawn Steel, Hamilton (Pitterich Group)	-	-	60,000	1905	1994	CF bar

[a] Capacity shown for Slater Steel is that upon completion of EF and bar mill upgrades in 1996.

Company and Location (and ownership interests)	Furnace/ Caster	Raw Steel Capacity	Product Capacity	Date (1)	Date (2)	Principal Products
Québec						
Atlas Specialty Steels, Tracy (Sammi Group, Korea)	EF/L/SL	115,000	135,000	1928	1990	Stainless sheet
QIT—Fer et Titane, Sorel	BOF/L/BI	800,000	-	1950	-	Billets
Sidbec-Dosco, Contrecoeur (Ispat, London)	EF/L/BI/SL	1,500,000	1.040,000	1928	1993	HR, wire rod, MBQ, skelp for pipe mill.
Sidbec-Dosco, Longueuil	-	-	350,000		1993	Rebar, MBQ
Sorel Forge, Sorel (Slater Industries)	EF/L/IN	30,000	30,000	1953	-	Ingots, forging bars, forged products
Sorevco, Coteau-du-Lac	-	-	125,000	1993	-	HD
Stelco-McMaster Ltée, Contrecoeur (Stelco)	EF/L/BI	480,000	300,000		-	SBQ, MBQ, rebar, tie plates
Saskatchewan						
Ipsco, Regina	EF/L/SL	1,000,000	900,000		-	Plate, pipe

United States

Company and Location (and ownership interests)	Furnace/ Caster	Raw Steel Capacity	Product Capacity	Date (1)	Date (2)	Principal Products
Alabama						
Birmingham Steel, Birmingham	EF/BI	425,000	425,000	1957	1984	Rebar, MBQ
Gulf States Steel, Gadsden	BOF/L/SL	1,300,000	900,000	1911	1986	HR, CR, plate, HDG
SMI Steel, Birmingham	EF/L/BI	450,000	450,000	1951	1983	MBQ, structurals
Trico Steel, Decatur (LTV, British Steel, Sumitomo)	EF/L/TS	2,200,000	2,200,000	1996	-	HR, CR
Tuscaloosa Steel, Tuscaloosa (British Steel)	EF/L/SL	1,000,000 (new 1996)	600,000	1984	1986	Coiled plate
U.S. Steel, Fairfield	BOF/L SL/BL	2,240,000	2,590,000	1898	1907	HR,CR, HDG, seamless pipe
Arizona						
North Star Steel, Kingman	EF/BI	500,000	500,000	1995	-	Re-bar, wire rod
Arkansas						
Arkansas Steel Assocs., Newport (Sumitomo, Yamato Kogyo)	EF/BI	300,000	300,000	1968	1989	Railroad tie plates
Nucor, Hickman	EF/L/TS	2,200,000	2,200,000	1992	-	HR, CR, HDG
Nucor-Yamato Steel, Blytheville (Nucor, Yamato Kogyo)	EF/L/BB	1,800,000	2,500,000	1988	-	Structurals, piling
Quanex MacSteel, Fort Smith	EF/L/BI	360,000	305,000	1982	-	SBQ
SMI Steel, Magnolia	-	-	60,000	1972	1992	Fence post "T" shapes
California						
BHP Steel, Rancho Cucamonga (BHP, Australia)	-	-	150,000	1995	-	HDG
California Steel Inds., Fontana (Kawasaki, CVRD [Brazil])	-	-	1,750,000	1943	1985	HR, CR, HDG, Pipe
Pinole Point Steel, Richmond	-	-	250,000	1966	1978	HDG
Precision Specialty Metals, Los Angeles	-	-	35,000	1980	-	Stainless CR sheet and strip
Tamco, Etiwanda[b] (Ameron; Mitsui; Tokyo Steel)	EF/BI	530,000	410,000	1957	1983	Re-bar
USS-Posco, Pittsburg (US Steel, Posco [Korea])	-	-	1,500,000	1930	1986	CR, HDG, TMP
Colorado						
CF&I Steel (New CF&I Steel LP, 95.2%; PBGC, 4.8%)[c]	EF/L/BI/BL	1,000,000	2,050,000	1880	1993	Rail, wire rod, rebar, MBQ, seamless pipe

[b] Raw steel capacity on completion of EF upgrade in 1995. Tamco is likely to increase its rolling capacity in 1996.

[c] The Pension Benefits Guarantee Corporations equity in CF & I was a condition of the companys 1992 emergence from bankruptcy. The New CF & I limited partnership includes Oregon Steel (87%), Nippon Steel (10%), and Nissho-Iwai (3%).

Company and Location (and ownership interests)	Furnace/ Caster	Raw Steel Capacity	Product Capacity	Date (1)	Date (2)	Principal Products
Connecticut						
Connecticut Steel, Wallingford (Von Moos, Switzerland)	-	-	250,000	1984	1987	Wire rod, wire mesh, rebar
Republic Engineered Steels, Willimantic	-	-	21,000	1962	1989	CF bar
Delaware						
Citisteel, Claymont (Minmetals, China)	EF/SL	400,000	400,000	1942	1988	Plate
Florida						
Ameristeel, Jacksonville[d] (Kyoei Steel, Japan)	EF/BI	500,000	380,000	1976	1992	Rebar
Georgia						
Atlantic Steel, Atlanta (Ivaco, Montréal, Québec)	-	-	550,000	1901	1979	Wire rod
Atlantic Steel, Cartersville	EF/L/BI	1,000,000	200,000	1975	1979	MBQ, SBQ
Bar Technologies, Cartersville	-	-	50,000	1991	-	CF bar
Hawaii						
Hawaiian Western Steel, Ewa (Ipsco, Regina, Saskatchewan)	EF/IN	60,000	60,000	1953	1988	Rebar
Illinois						
Acme Steel, Riverdale[e]	BOF/L/TS	1,200,000	750,000	1959	1986	HR, CR
Austeel Lemont, Lemont (Sumitomo, Kyoei Steel)	EF/BI	300,000	300,000	1958	1994	Rebar, MBQ, SBQ
Bar Technologies, Batavia	-	-	150,000	1955	-	CF bar
Bar Technologies, Harvey	-	-	150,000	1891	-	CF bar
Birmingham Steel, Joliet[f]	-	-	250,000	1870	1993	Rebar
Birmingham Steel, Kankakee[f]	EF/BI	750,000	500,000		1984	MBQ
Calumet Steel, Chicago Heights	EF/BI	150,000	120,000	1907	1985	MBQ, rebar
Chicago Heights Steel Co., Chicago Heights	-	-	140,000	1894	1985	MBQ, special sections
J-Pitt Steel, Chicago (Pitterich group)	EF/BI	100,000	-	1981	1994	Billets (to J-Pitt Steel Johnstown, PA)
Keystone Steel & Wire, Peoria	EF/BI	650,000	650,000	1910	1978	Wire rod
Laclede Steel, Alton (Ivaco, Montréal, 49%)[g]	EF/BI/IN	1,000,000	770,000	1911	-	HR strip/skelp, pipe, tubing, wire rod, SBQ
LTV Steel, Hennepin	-	-	1,350,000	1967	1984	CR, HDG
National Steel, Granite City (NKK Steel [Japan] 76%)	BOF/L/SL	2,400,000	2,600,000	1900	1971	HR, CR, HDG
Nelsen Steel & Wire, Franklin Park	-	-	50,000	1939	-	CF bar
Northwestern Steel & Wire, Sterling	EF/L/BB/BI	2,400,000	1,255,000	1912	-	Structurals, MBQ, wire rod
Republic Engineered Steels, Chicago	-	-	324,000	1905	1989	SBQ
Sheffield Steel, Joliet	-	-	216,000		1985	MBQ

[d] Ameristeels bar mill at Tampa was closed in 1995; the hot end of the same mill closed in 1993.

[e] On completion of a new thin-slab caster, 1997.

[f] The rod mill at Joliet, part of Birmingham Steels American Steel & Wire division, was to be converted by 1997 to produce coiled rebar, with the Kankakee mill to be devoted thereafter to MBQ products.

[g] Laclede Steel announced the closure of its wire rod mill in 1996.

Company and Location (and ownership interests)	Furnace/ Caster	Raw Steel Capacity	Product Capacity	Date (1)	Date (2)	Principal Products
Indiana						
Allegheny Ludlum, New Castle	-	-	150,000		-	Stainless CR sheet
Avesta Sheffield, New Castle (British Steel, 51%; Avesta, 40%)	-	-	30,000	1898	1989	Stainless plate
Beta Steel, Portage (Alphasteel Ltd., U.K.)	EF/SL (new 1996)	800,000	650,000 (in 1995)	1993	-	HR
Bethlehem Steel, Burns Harbor	BOF/L/SL/IN	5,200,000	5,300,000	1970	-	HR,CR, plate, HDG, EG
Chicago Cold Rolling, Portage (Bethlehem Steel, 45%)	-	-	350,000	1996	-	CR
Inland Flat Products Co., East Chicago [h]	BOF/L/SL/BI	5,400,000	4,800,000	1902	-	HR,CR, HDG
Inland Steel Bar Company, East Chicago	EF/L/BI	600,000	900,000	1902	-	SBQ
I/N Tek, New Carlisle (Inland Steel, 60%; Nippon Steel, 40%)	-	-	1,440,000	1992	-	CR
I/N Kote, New Carlisle (Inland Steel, 50%; Nippon Steel, 50%)	-	-	900,000	1993	-	HDG, EG
La Salle Steel, Hammond	-	-	50,000	1947	-	CF bar
LTV Steel, Indiana Harbor	BOF/L/SL	4,100,000	4,200,000	1916	1984	HR, CR, HDG, TMP
Metro Metals, East Chicago	-	-	200,000	1996	-	EG
National Steel, Portage (NKK Steel [Japan], 76%)	-	-	1,540,000			CR, HDG, TMP
Nucor, Crawfordsville	EF/L/TS	2,200,000	2,200,000	1988	-	HR, CR, HDG
Republic Engineered Steels, Gary [Dunes Highway plant]	-	-	84,000	1928	1989	CF bar
Republic Engineered Steels, Gary [Seventh Avenue plant]	-	-	55,000	1943	1993	CF bar
Slater Steel, Fort Wayne	EF/L/BI	75,000	75,000	1932	1980	Stainless bar (HR, CF)
Steel Dynamics, Butler	EF/L/TS	700,000	1,000,000	1995	-	HR, CR
U.S. Steel, Gary	BOF/L/SL	8,730,000	6,700,000	1908	-	HR, CR, plate, HDG, EG, terne plate
Iowa						
Ipsco, Montpelier	EF/L/TS	1,000,000	1,000,000	1994	-	Coiled plate. skelp
North Star, Wilton (Cargill)	EF/BI	330,000	330,000	1976	-	MBQ, rebar
Kentucky						
AK Steel, Ashland (Kawasaki, 22%)	BOF/L/SL	2,100,000	310,000	1916	1994	Slabs to Middletown; HDG
Green River Steel, Owensboro	EF/IN	140,000	150,000	1942	1988	Forging bars, SBQ
Kentucky Electric Steel, Ashland	EF/L/BI	300,000	300,000	1964	1993	SBQ, MBQ
Newport Steel, Newport (NS Group, Inc.)	EF/L/SL	700,000	560,000	1909	1981	HR (primarily skelp), pipe
North American Stainless (Acerinox, Spain) [i]	-	-	240,000	1990	-	Stainless CR sheet
North Star, Calvert City (Cargill)	-	-	250,000	1981	1985	Structurals
Louisiana						
Bayou Steel, La Place	EF/L/BI	800,000	600,000	1980	1985	MBQ, structurals
Maryland						
Avesta Sheffield, Baltimore (British Steel, 50%; Avesta, 40%)	EF/L/SL	120,000	200,000	1919	1995	Stainless plate
Bethlehem Steel, Sparrows Point	BOF/L/SL	3,600,000	3,200,000	1892	1915	HR, CR, plate, HDG, TMP
Republic Engineered Steels, Baltimore	-	-	70,000	1925	1994	Stainless bar

[h] After closure of Inlands plate mill in late 1995.

[i] North American Stainless installed a second cold-rolling mill in 1995, increasing its capacity from 120,000 to 240,000 tons per year. A hot-strip mill was due to be added by 1998. The mill was initially a joint venture owned 50 percent each by Armco, Inc., and Acerinox, but Armco sold 45 percent to Acerinox in 1994.

Company and Location (and ownership interests)	Furnace/ Caster	Raw Steel Capacity	Product Capacity	Date (1)	Date (2)	Principal Products
Massachusetts						
Teledyne Rodney Metals	-	-	60,000	1941	-	Stainless CR sheet
Michigan						
Double Eagle Steel Coating Co., Dearborn (Rouge Steel, 50%; U.S. Steel, 50%)	-	-	850,000	1989	-	EG
J & L Specialty Steel, Detroit (Ugine [France], 52%)	-	-	80,000	1950	1986	Stainless CR sheet
McLouth Steel, Trenton[j]	BOF/SL	1,500,000	2,400,000	1950	1991	HR
National Steel, Ecorse (NKK Steel [Japan], 76%)	BOF/L/SL	3,600,000	3,430,000	1929	1929	HR, CR, EG
North Star, Monroe (Cargill)	EF/L/BI	520,000	455,000	1980	-	SBQ, MBQ
Quanex MacSteel, Jackson	EF/L/BI	268,000	215,000	1969	-	SBQ
Rouge Steel, Dearborn[k]	BOF/L/SL	4,100,000	2,800,000	1930	1989	HR, CR
Minnesota						
North Star, St. Paul (Cargill)	EF/L/BI	800,000	500,000	1967	1974	MBQ
Mississippi						
Birmingham Steel, Jackson	EF/BI	450,000	425,000	1957	1985	Rebar, MBQ
Missouri						
GS Industries, Kansas City	EF/L/BI	1,000,000	700,000	1925	1995	Wire rod, grinding balls and rods, SBQ rounds
Nebraska						
Nucor, Norfolk	EF/L/BI	500,000	500,000	1977	-	MBQ, CF bar
New Jersey						
Co-Steel Raritan, Perth Amboy[l]	EF/L/BI	900,000	1,100,000	1980	-	Wire rod
New Jersey Steel, Sayreville (Von Roll [Switzerland], 60.7%)	EF/BI	500,000	500,000	1973	1977	Rebar
New York						
Allegheny Ludlum Corp., Special Materials Div., Lockport	EF/L/IN/SL	36,000	40,000	1922	1984	Stainless and high-alloy ingot, slab, strip
Al Tech, Dunkirk (Sammi Group, Korea)	-	-	85,000	1975	1990	Stainless bar, wire rod
Al Tech, Watervliet (Sammi Group, Korea)	EF/L/BI/IN	60,000	5,000	1989	1990	Stainless billets (to Dunkirk); seamless pipe
Auburn Steel, Auburn (Kyoei Steel, 50%; Sumitomo, 50%)	EF/BI	380,000	380,000	1976	-	MBQ, rebar, SBQ
Bar Technologies, Lackawanna[m]	-	-	730,000	1878	1994	SBQ (1)
Bethlehem Steel, Lackawanna	-	-	460,000	1878	1922	HDG; also coke ovens
Crucible Materials, Syracuse	EF/L/IN	65,000	75,000	1900	1985	Stainless and high-alloy HR and CF bar, tool steel
Niagara Cold Drawn, Buffalo	-	-	75,000	1940	1995	CF bar
North Carolina						
Ameristeel, Charlotte (Kyoei Steel, Japan)	EF/BI	360,000	300,000	1962	1992	Rebar, MBQ

[j] Filed for Chapter 11 bankruptcy protection, October 1995; the mill was closed April 1996 and purchased by Hamlin Holdings in June with the intention of reopening it in late 1996.
[k] Rouges raw steel capacity reflects the addition of a third caster strand in 1996.
[l] Co-Steel Raritans capacity is that upon completion of its 1996-97 expansion program.
[m] Bar Technologies acquired the former Bethlehem Steel 13-inch bar mill at Lackawanna in 1994. Production was to resume in 1996 using billets supplied from Johnstown, Pennsylvania.

Company and Location (and ownership interests)	Furnace/ Caster	Raw Steel Capacity	Product Capacity	Date (1)	Date (2)	Principal Products
Ohio						
A.B. Steel Mill, Cincinnati	-	-	75,000	1976	-	Re-bar, MBQ rounds
AK Steel, Middletown (Kawasaki, 22%)	BOF/L/SL	2,640,000	4,800,000	1900	1994	HR, CR, HDG, EG
Armco, Coshocton	-	-	200,000	1959	1992	Stainless CR sheet
Armco, Dover	-	-	600,000	1900	1992	HDG
Armco, Mansfield	EF/L/TS	750,000	750,000	1915	1992	Carbon/stainless HR,CR
Armco, Zanesville	-	-	165,000	1900	1905	Stainless CR sheet
Baron Drawn Steel, Toledo	-	-	75,000	1962	-	CF bar
American Steel & Wire, Cuyahoga Heights (Birmingham Steel Corp.)	-	-	900,000	1889	1993	Wire rod
Coil Coating Co., Howland [n]	-	-	125,000	1986	-	HD
CSC Ltd, Warren (formerly Copperweld Steel Co.)	EF/L/IN	550,000	550,000	1915	1988	SBQ, carbon and alloy
Cuyahoga Steel & Wire, Solon (Nissho-Iwai [Japan], 49%)	-	-	55,000	1984	-	CF bar, cold heading wire and wire rod
J & L Specialty Steel, Louisville (Ugine [France], 52%)	-	-	230,000	1943	1989	Stainless CR sheet
LTV Steel, Cleveland	BOF/L/SL	6,400,000	7,300,000	1868	1986	HR, CR, EG
Lukens, Inc., Washington Steel div., Massillon	-	-	200,000	1955	1992	Stainless CR sheet and plate finishing
Marion Steel, Marion	EF/BI	400,000	380,000	1916	1981	MBQ, rebar
McDonald Steel, McDonald	-	-	175,000	1917	1981	Special sections
North Star/BHP Steel, Delta (North Star, 50%; BHP Steel [Australia], 50%)	EF/L/TS	1,500,000	1,500,000	1996	-	HR, CR
North Star Steel, Youngstown (Cargill)	EF/BI/BL	450,000	270,000	1981	1985	Seamless OCTG; billets (to Calvert City, KY)
Ohio Coatings Co., Yorkville (Wheeling-Pittsburgh, 50%; Dong Yang, 25%; Nittetsu, 25%)	-	-	250,000	1996	-	TMP
Pittsburgh Canfield Corp., Canfield (Wheeling-Pittsburgh)	-	-	72,000			EG
Republic Engineered Steels, Canton (two plants)	EF/L/IN/BI	1,370,000	1,060,000	1889	1989	Ingot, billet, SBQ bar; stainless and alloy billets
Republic Engineered Steels, Massillon (two plants)	-	-	580,000		1989	SBQ – hot rolled and cold finished
Timken, Canton (Harrison plant)	EF/L/BL/IN	900,000	550,000	1899	-	SBQ, seamless tubing
Timken, Canton (Faircrest plant)	EF/L/IN	770,000	770,000	1985	-	SBQ and alloy bar
Timken, Gambrinus/Wooster	-	-	750,000	1925	-	Seamless pipe & tube
USS/Kobe Steel, Lorain (U.S. Steel, 50%; Kobe [Japan], 50%)	BOF/L/IN/ BI/BL	2,700,000	1,800,000	1895	1988	Seamless and welded pipe, SBQ, billets
WCI Steel, Warren	BOF/L/SL	2,040,000	1,500,000	1912	1988	HR, CR, HDG
Wheeling-Pittsburgh Steel, Steubenville	BOF/L/SL	2,400,000	2,850,000	1859	1968	HR, CR
Wheeling-Pittsburgh Steel, Yorkville	-	-	915,000	1929	1968	CR, TMP
Oklahoma						
Sheffield Steel, Sand Springs and Oklahoma City	EF/L/BI	530,000	386,000	1940	1982	MBQ, rebar
Southwest Steel, Tulsa (acquired by Niagara Corp., February 1996)	-	-	*40,000*	1970	1996	CF bar
Oregon						
Cascade Steel Rolling Mills, McMinnville [o] (Schnitzer Steel Industries)	EF/L/BI	700,000	900,000	1968	-	MBQ, rebar, wire rod
Oregon Steel, Portland [p]	EF/L/SL	800,000	1,200,000	1926	-	Plate; skelp to pipe mill at Napa, CA

[n] Coil Coating Co., part of bankrupt Sharon Steel, is closed and the subject of bids from potential buyers.
[o] On completion of second rolling mill in 1997.
[p] On completion of Steckel mill installation in 1996.

Company and Location (and ownership interests)	Furnace/ Caster	Raw Steel Capacity	Product Capacity	Date (1)	Date (2)	Principal Products
Pennsylvania						
Allegheny Ludlum, Breckinridge and W. Leechburg	EF/L/SL/IN	400,000	600,000	1936	-	Stainless HR, CR sheet
Allegheny Ludlum, Bagdad and Natrona	BOF/IN	600,000	150,000	1936	-	Silicon electrical steels
Allegheny Ludlum, Vandergrift	-	-	120,000	1956	1988	Stainless CR sheet
Allegheny Ludlum, Washington	EF/L/IN	60,000	62,000	1901	1990	Stainless plate, tool steel
Armco, Butler	EF/L/SL	860,000	700,000	1927	-	Stainless HR, CR sheet
Bar Technologies, Johnstown[q]	EF/L/BI/IN	1,300,000	400,000	1871	1994	SBQ, wire rod
Bethlehem Steel, Bethlehem [Structural Products Div.][r]	-	-	500,000	1873	-	Structurals, piling (using blanks from Steelton)
Bethlehem Steel, Steelton [Pa. Steel Technologies Div.]	EF/L/BB/BL	1,200,000	1,160,000	1867	1916	Beam blanks, rail, large-diameter pipe
Braeburn Alloy Steel, Lower Burrell (Carpenter Technologies)	-	-	*20,000*	1898	-	High alloy bars
Caparo Steel, Sharon[s]	EF/IN	600,000	1,350,000	1900	1994	HR, CR
Carpenter Technologies, Reading	EF/L/BI/IN	180,000	120,000	1989	1968	Stainless bar, wire rod strip, tool steel
Commercial Steel, Glassport	-	-	120,000	1992	-	Rebar, MBQ
Edgewater Steel, Oakmont	EF/IN	40,000	-	1916	-	Alloy ingot, forging bars
Electralloy, Oil City (G.O. Carlson, Inc.)	EF/L/IN	60,000	-	1967	1991	Stainless and nickel alloy ingots, billets
Ellwood Quality Steels, New Castle	EF/L/IN	300,000	-	1893	-	Alloy, stainless, tool steel ingots, forging bars
FirstMiss Steel, Hollsopple	EF/L/BI/IN	250,000	-	1988	-	Ingots, billets, tool steel
Franklin Steel, Franklin[t]	-	-	105,000	1985	-	Rebar (see note)
GalvTech, Pittsburgh	-	-	200,000	1996	-	HDG
GRD Steel, Monongahela (principals of Commercial Steel)	EF/BI	100,000	-	1992	-	Billets to Commercial Steel, Glassport
J & L Specialty Steel, Midland (Ugine [France], 52%)	EF/L/SL	400,000	400,000	1900	1990	Stainless CR sheet (hot band toll-rolled at LTV)
J & L Structural, Aliquippa[u]	EF/L/BI	300,000	440,000	1909	1987	Special shapes, MBQ
J-Pitt Steel, Johnstown (Pitterich group)	-	-	375,000	1871	1991	MBQ, SBQ, special shapes
Jersey Shore Steel, Avis	-	-	100,000			MBQ angles, flats
Koppel Steel, Ambridge (NS Group)	-	-	180,000		1989	Seamless pipe & tube
Koppel Steel. Koppel (NS Group)	EF/L/BL/BI	400,000	280,000 (bar mill)		1989	SBQ, tube rounds
Latrobe Steel, Latrobe (Timken Co.)	EF/IN	40,000	40,000	1913	1975	Alloy, stainless, tool steel wire rod and bar
LTV Steel, Aliquippa	-	-	460,000	1909	1984	TMP
Lukens Steel, Coatesville	EF/L/SL/IN	880,000	925,000	1810	-	Carbon & alloy plate
Lukens Steel, Conshohocken	-	-	445,000	1905	1983	Carbon & alloy plate
Lukens, Inc., Washington Steel div., Houston	EF/L/SL	220,000	-	1945	1993	Stainless hot band
Lukens, Inc., Washington Steel div., Washington	-	-	230,000	1946	1993	Stainless CR sheet
MetalTech, Pittsburgh	-	-	300,000	1989	-	HDG
Moltrup Steel Products, Beaver Falls (Pitterich group)	-	-	42,000	1914	1989	CF bar

[q] Bar Technologies numbers reflect the early 1996 start-up of the mill, including a new caster.

[r] Bethlehem Steels steelmaking facilities at Bethlehem, Pennsylvania, were closed at the end of 1995. They comprised both BOF steelmaking at the Structural Products Division and EF steelmaking at the BethForge division. Since late 1995, semifinished steel for the one remaining structural mill has been sourced from the Steelton mills caster, modified in 1995 to produce beam blanks.

[s] Caparo Steel numbers do not include proposed 1996-97 mill upgrades.

[t] Franklin Steel, a rail re-roller, closed in 1994 but was the subject of plans for re-opening during 1996.

[u] J & L Structural numbers reflect a proposed melt shop planned for 1996-97 construction.

Company and Location (and ownership interests)	Furnace/ Caster	Raw Steel Capacity	Product Capacity	Date (1)	Date (2)	Principal Products
Pennsylvania, continued						
NexTech, Turtle Creek	-	-	150,000	1992	-	HDG
North Star Steel, Milton [v]	EF/BI	150,000	175,000	1919	1988	Rebar
Republic Engineered Steels, Beaver Falls	-	-	45,000	1939	1989	CF bar
Standard Steel, Burnham (Freedom Forge Corp.)	EF/L/IN	290,000	290,000	1811	-	Rotary forged products
Teledyne Vasco, Latrobe	EF/IN	17,000	30,000			High alloy HR, CF bar
U.S. Steel, Braddock [Edgar Thomson Works]	BOF/L/SL	2,957,000	-	1875	1901	Slabs to Irvin hot-strip mill
U.S. Steel, Dravosburg [Irvin Works]	-	-	2,850,000	1937	-	HR, HDG, terne plate; hot bands to Fairless
U.S. Steel, Fairless Hills	-	-	1,800,000	1950	-	CR, HDG, TMP
Universal Stainless and Alloy, Bridgeville	EF/L/IN	150,000	150,000	1887	1994	Stainless, alloy, tool stl. Ingot, billet, plate
Universal Stainless and Alloy, Titusville	EF/IN	15,000	15,000	1887	1995	Stainless CR precision sheet, strip, bar
Wheeling Pittsburgh, Allenport	-	-	1,015,000		1968	CR sheet
WorldClass Processing, Ambridge [w]	-	-	400,000	1992	-	CR sheet
Worthington Steel, Malvern	-	-	400,000	1970	1985	CR sheet and strip
South Carolina						
Avesta Sheffield Bar Co., Richburg [x]	-	-	10,000	1994	-	Stainless bar
GS Industries, Georgetown	EF/L/BI (DRI plant)	1,000,000	750,000	1969	1995	Wire rod
Nucor, Darlington	EF/L/BI	800,000	800,000	1969	-	MBQ, structurals, CF bar
Nucor, North Charleston	EF/L/TS	1,800,000	1,800,000	1996	-	HR, CR
SMI Owen Steel, Columbia	EF/BI	350,000	250,000	1975	1995	MBQ, rebar
Talley Metals Technology, Hartsville	-	-	48,000	1985	-	Stainless bar
Tennessee						
Ameristeel, Jackson	EF/BI	550,000	400,000	1981	1992	Rebar, MBQ
Ameristeel, Knoxville	EF/BI	300,000	300,000	1950	1992	Rebar
Bayou Steel, Harriman [y]	-	-	250,000	1964	1995	MBQ
Birmingham Steel, Memphis [z]	EF/L/BI	2,000,000	-	1997	-	Billets
Niagara Cold Drawn, Chattanooga	-	-	40,000	1992	1995	CF bar

[v] North Stars former Milton Manufacturing mill was closed in 1991, and up for sale in the mid-1990s.

[w] WorldClass Processings plans for a minimill were terminated in late 1995 due to financing difficulties. It reportedly wished to proceed with cold-rolling facilities tied to its existing pickling and tempering lines.

[x] Avesta Sheffield toll-rolls stainless bar on the Richburg bar mill of Teledyne Allvac, a nickel alloy bar producer.

[y] The EF melt shop (capacity 175,000 tons per year) at the former Tennessee Forging Steel mill has not been re-started by Bayou Steel. The bar mill is supplied with billets from Bayous La Place, Louisiana, mill.

[z] Birmingham Steel announced the construction of its Memphis mill in 1995, to supply billets to its rod mill in Lorain, Ohio (American Steel & Wire division), and to its Joliet, Illinois, bar mill. Ultimate target capacity is shown.

Company and Location (and ownership interests)	Furnace/ Caster	Raw Steel Capacity	Product Capacity	Date (1)	Date (2)	Principal Products
Texas						
Border Steel Mills, El Paso	EF/BI	240,000	256,000	1961	-	Rebar, MBQ
Chaparral Steel, Midlothian	EF/L/BB/BI	1,550,000	1,500,000	1975	-	Structurals, MBQ, rebar
IRI International, Pampa	EF/IN	80,000	-	1980	-	Ingot, billet, forging bar
LeTourneau, Inc., Longview	EF/IN	75,000	100,000	1984	-	Ingot, plate, forging bar
Lone Star Steel, Lone Star	EF/IN	400,000	1,000,000	1942	1985	HR skelp, pipe
Lone Star Steel, Baytown [aa]	EF/SL	1,300,000	-	1971	1995	Slabs
North Star, Beaumont	EF/BI	900,000	700,000	1983	1985	Wire rod
Northwestern Steel & Wire, Houston	-	-	600,000	1943	1987	Wide flange beams
Nucor, Jewett	EF/L/BI	650,000	680,000	1975	-	MBQ, structurals
W. Silver & Co., El Paso	-	-	100,000	1971	-	Rebar
Structural Metals, Inc (SMI), Seguin	EF/L/BI	775,000	725,000	1949	-	MBQ, rebar
Utah						
Geneva Steel, Vineyard	BOF/L/SL	2,700,000	2,500,000	1943	1988	HR, plate, pipe
Nucor, Plymouth	EF/L/BI	600,000	600,000	1981	-	MBQ, rebar, CF bar
Western Cold Rolling, Vineyard	-	-	150,000	1994	-	CR
Virginia						
Roanoke Electric Steel, Roanoke	EF/L/BI	600,000	400,000	1954	-	MBQ, structurals, SBQ
Washington						
BHP Steel, Kalama	-	-	300,000	1996	-	CR, zincalume sheet
Birmingham Steel, Seattle	EF/L/BI	750,000	600,000	1931	1991	MBQ, rebar
West Virginia						
Steel of West Virginia, Inc., Huntington	EF/BI/IN	250,000	250,000	1907	1982	Special shapes, light rail
Weirton Steel, Weirton	BOF/L/SL	3,000,000	3,800,000	1909	1983	HR,CR, TMP, EG, HDG, chrome-plated sheet
Wheeling-Nisshin, Follansbee (Wheeling-Pittsburgh, 35.7%; Nisshin Steel [Japan], 64.3%)	-	-	600,000	1984	-	HDG, aluminized sheet
Wisconsin						
Charter Electric Steel, Saukville	EF/L/BI	250,000	250,000	1978	-	Wire rod

[aa] In 1995 Lone Star proposed to acquire and restart the former U.S. Steel melt shop at Baytown, to supply slab to its Lone Star mill and to sell slab on the world market through its partner in the venture, Metallica, Inc.

FLAT PRODUCTS

II.1: Plate: Flat and Coiled

Plate includes, strictly speaking, all flat rolled steel with a thickness of 0.1875 inches or greater. Traditionally it has been rolled from slabs on plate mills and is never coiled. However a certain amount of plate-thickness material—up to a quarter or even half an inch in thickness—has always been rolled in coiled form on hot-strip mills. Hot-strip mills dedicated principally to sheet production are not included in this list.

Since the early 1980s, the proportion of plate produced in coil form has increased, in part because distributors have acquired larger and heavier leveling lines to handle such material and in part because of the increased yields of such material compared to flat plate (both in rolling and in processing). A number of plate producers have reflected this change by installing Steckel mills to produce coiled products. Coiled plate is now produced in thicknesses up to 1 inch.

Narrow plates and wide flat bars, produced on universal mills, are included under the heading "Merchant Bar Quality (MBQ) Bars and Structurals," in table II.8.

II.1: Plate

Company and Plant Location	Max. Width Produced	Estimated Tons per Year Capacity	Flat or Coiled	Grades Produced
Algoma Steel, Sault Ste. Marie, Ontario	166"	550,000	Flat	Carbon
Allegheny Ludlum, Washington, PA	110"	70,000	Flat	Stainless, alloy
Armco, Inc., Butler, PA[a]	195"	[a]	Flat	Stainless
Avesta Sheffield, Baltimore, MD	96"	70,000	Flat	Stainless
Avesta Sheffield, New Castle, IN	108"	40,000	Flat	Stainless
Bethlehem Steel, Burns Harbor, IN	160"	1,140,000	Flat	Carbon
	110"	700,000	Flat	Carbon
Bethlehem Steel, Sparrows Point, MD	160"	600,000	Flat	Carbon
G.O. Carlsen, Coatesville, PA[a]	195"	[a]	Flat	Stainless
Citisteel, Claymont, DE	160"	400,000	Flat	Carbon
Geneva Steel, Vineyard, UT	126"	2,500,000[b]	Coiled	Carbon
Gulf States Steel, Gadsden, AL	134"	500,000	Flat	Carbon
Ipsco, Montpelier, IA	96"	1,000,000[c]	Coiled	Carbon
Ipsco, Regina, Saskatchewan	60"	900,000[c]	Coiled	Carbon
LeTourneau, Inc., Longview, TX	144"	100,000	Flat	Alloy
Lukens, Coatesville, PA	195"	600,000	Flat	Carbon, alloy, stainless
Lukens, Conshohocken, PA, Steckel mill	102"	325,000	Coiled	Carbon, alloy, stainless
Oregon Steel, Portland, OR, 106" mill	105"	450,000[d]	Flat	Carbon
Steckel mill	96"	1,200,000[d]	Coiled	Carbon
Stelco, Hamilton, Ontario	148"	600,000	Flat	Carbon
Tuscaloosa Steel, Tuscaloosa, AL	96"	1,000,000	Coiled	Carbon
U.S. Steel, Gary, IN	160"	1,000,000	Flat	Carbon, alloy

[a] Armco, Inc. and G.O. Carlsen toll-roll stainless plates at Lukens, Inc. Avesta Sheffield and Allegheny Ludlum also toll-roll a proportion of their stainless plate at Lukens, notably in sizes beyond their own mills capacity. Since 1994 Lukens has also melted stainless and rolled plate for its own Washington Steel division, to be finished (annealed and pickled) at Massillon, Ohio. Lukenss entry into the stainless plate business has led other producers seek alternatives to dependence on a competitor for rolling their plate.

[b] Approximately 500,000 tons of Geneva Steels 1995 production was in plate sizes, the balance in sheet.

[c] Approximately 75 percent of Ipscos capacity at Montpelier is dedicated to plate, 25 percent to sheet sizes. At Regina, Saskatchewan, up to half the mills production is used as skelp in the companys pipe and tube mills.

[d] Oregon Steels new Steckel mill will replace the companys 106" plate mill during 1996.

NOTE: Inland Steel left the carbon flat plate business in 1995.

FLAT PRODUCTS

II.2: Hot-Rolled Sheet

The basic form of sheet steel, from which all other sheet products (and welded pipe) are derived, is hot-rolled coiled sheet, produced from slab on a hot-strip mill. Over half of all steel is rolled on hot-strip mills—in North America in the 1990s, this means from 55 to 60 million tons in the United States, and from 8 to 9 million tons in Canada, varying over the economic cycle.

The 47 hot-strip mills listed do not include three Steckel mills dedicated to plate sizes, at Lukens Steel (Conshohocken, Pennsylvania), Oregon Steel (Portland, Oregon) and Tuscaloosa Steel (Tuscaloosa, Alabama). In addition, two narrow hot-strip mills at Acme Steel (due to be replaced by the new 60-inch mill) were operating in early 1996.

II.2: Hot-Rolled Sheet

Company and Plant Location	Hot-Strip Mill: Width	Built	Estimated tons per year capacity	Grades Produced
Acme Steel, Riverdale, IL	60"	1996	1,800,000	Carbon
AK Steel, Middletown, OH	86"	1968	4,000,000	Carbon
Algoma Steel, Sault Ste. Marie, Ontario	106"	1947	1,900,000	Carbon
Allegheny Ludlum, Brackenridge, PA	56"	1932	500,000	Stainless, silicon
Armco, Butler, PA	58"	1957	900,000	Stainless, silicon
Armco, Mansfield, OH	52"	1957	825,000	Carbon, stainless
Atlas Specialty Steels, Tracy, Québec	50"	1962	240,000	Stainless
Beta Steel, Portage, IN	60"	1991	800,000	Carbon
Bethlehem Steel, Burns Harbor, IN	80"	1966	4,100,000	Carbon
Bethlehem Steel, Sparrows Point, MD	68"	1948	2,600,000	Carbon
California Steel Industries, Fontana, CA	86"	1950	1,500,000	Carbon
Caparo Steel, Sharon, PA	60"	1935	1,200,000	Carbon
Dofasco, Hamilton, Ontario	68"	1966	3,200,000	Carbon
Gallatin Steel, Ghent, KY	62"	1995	1,800,000	Carbon
Geneva Steel, Vineyard, UT	132"	1944	2,500,000[a]	Carbon
Gulf States Steel, Gadsden, AL	54"	1957	900,000	Carbon
Inland Steel, East Chicago, IN	80"	1965	4,500,000	Carbon
	76"	1932	670,000	
Ipsco, Montpelier, IA	96"	1994	1,000,000[a]	Carbon
Ipsco, Regina, Saskatchewan	60"	1964	900,000[a]	Carbon (includes skelp)
Laclede Steel, Alton, IL	22"	1927	225,000	Carbon (skelp)
Lone Star Steel, Lone Star TX	73"	1944	800,000	Carbon (skelp)

[a] Capacity includes plate rolled on the same hot-strip mill.

[b] North American Stainlesss plans to build a new hot-strip mill were announced in December 1995. At that time, the mills size and capacity were not disclosed.

Steel Phoenix

ISBN 0-312-16198-0

Addendum

II.2: Hot Rolled Sheet (continued from p. 378)

LTV Steel, Cleveland, OH	80"	1964	2,000,000	Carbon
	84"	1970	3,800,000	
LTV Steel, Indiana Harbor, IN	84"	1939	4,200,000	Carbon
Lukens, Washington Steel Div., Houston, PA	56"	1945	225,000	Stainless
McLouth Steel, Trenton	60"	1954	1,200,000	Carbon
National Steel, Ecorse, MI	72"	1961	3,430,000	Carbon
National Steel, Granite City, IL	80"	1936	2,600,000	Carbon
Newport Steel, Newport, KY	50"	1930	560,000	Carbon (skelp)
North American Stainless, Carrollton, KY	6	1998	1,000,000	Stainless
North Star BHP Steel, Delta, OH	60"	1996	1,800,000	Carbon
Nucor, Crawfordsville, IN	53"	1988	1,800,000	Carbon
Nucor, Hickman, AR	61"	1992	2,200,000	Carbon
Nucor, North Charleston, SC	61"	1996	1,800,000	Carbon
Rouge Steel, Dearborn, MI	68"	1937	2,950,000	Carbon
Sidbec-Dosco, Contrecoeur, Québec	60"	1959	640,000	Carbon
Steel Dynamics, Butler, IN	60"	1995	2,000,000	Carbon
Stelco, Hamilton, Ontario	56"	1961	1,600,000	Carbon
Stelco, Nanticoke, Ontario	80"	1980	1,900,000	Carbon
Trico Steel, Decatur, AL	66"	1996	2,500,000	Carbon
U.S. Steel, Fairfield, AL	68"	1937	1,900,000	Carbon
U.S. Steel, Gary, IN	84"	1967	5,700,000	Carbon
U.S. Steel, Irvin, PA	80"	1938	2,850,000	Carbon
WCI Steel, Warren, OH	56"	1961	1,500,000	Carbon, silicon
Weirton Steel, Weirton, WV	54"	1927	3,800,000	Carbon
Wheeling-Pittsburgh Steel, Steubenville, OH	80"	1965	2,850,000	Carbon

II.8: MBQ Bars and Structurals (continued from p. 394)

		special shapes	
North Star, Kingman, AZ	500,000	Wire rod	[a]
North Star Steel, St. Paul, MN	500,000	MBQ	340,000
North Star Steel, Wilton, IA	330,000	MBQ	220,000
Northwestern Steel & Wire, Sterling, IL [14" mill]	405,000	MBQ	400,000
Nucor, Darlington, SC	650,000	MBQ	2,500,000
Nucor, Jewett, TX	680,000	MBQ	
Nucor, Norfolk, NE	700,000	MBQ	
Nucor, Plymouth, UT	800,000	MBQ	
Roanoke Electric Steel, Roanoke, VA	400,000	MBQ	350,000
Sheffield Steel, Joliet, IL	216,000	MBQ	150,000
Sheffield Steel, Sand Springs, OK	550,000	Rebar	200,000
Sidbec-Dosco, Contrecoeur, Québec	400,000	Wire rod	50,000
W. Silver, Inc., Vinton, TX	100,000	MBQ	50,000
St. Louis Steel Products, St. Louis, MO	50,000	MBQ	25,000
Steel of West Virginia, Huntington, WV	250,000	Special shapes	25,000
Stelco McMaster Ltée, Contrecoeur, Québec	300,000	MBQ	120,000
Stelco, Hamilton, Ontario [12" bar mill]	450,000	SBQ	200,000
SMI Steel, Birmingham, AL	450,000	MBQ	425,000
SMI–Owen Steel, Columbia, SC	330,000	Rebar	125,000
SMI Steel, Magnolia, AR	250,000	MBQ	150,000
SMI–Structural Metals, Inc., Seguin, TX	725,000	MBQ	500,000

FLAT PRODUCTS

II.3: Cold-Rolled Sheet (36 inches wide and over)

Of the steel rolled on hot-strip mills into the form of coiled sheets, relatively little is sold as a finished product in that hot-rolled form. Just over a quarter of North American hot-strip mill throughput—13 to 16 million tons in the United States and 2 million tons in Canada—is finally consumed as hot-rolled sheet. A further 4 million tons are converted to pipe and tubing; and additional tonnages are coated in hot-rolled form or are converted to strip products. However around half of all hot-rolled coils are sent for cold-rolling, for further reduction of their thickness and to achieve better surface quality and dimensional accuracy than possible in most hot-rolled products. It should be noted, though, that with improvements in the quality of light-gauge hot-rolled products and with growth in demand for coated steels, the share of total sheet shipments sold in uncoated cold-rolled form has declined in the last decade, after four decades of steady growth after 1945. Almost all stainless steel sheet, which is not normally coated, is sold in the form of cold-rolled coils.

Carbon steel cold-rolled coils are sold as a final product to end users, distributors, and coil coaters in tonnages approaching those of hot-rolled coils. These sales account for less than half the total tonnage of cold-rolled sheet steel. The balance of the cold mills throughput becomes the raw material for coated steels—galvanized sheets, tinplate, and similar metallic-coated sheet steel, plus a small proportion processed into specialty strip products. The degree of gauge reduction during cold-rolling depends on the final product application, but as a general rule coated steels are made from thinner gauges, with double-reduced tinplate requiring the thinnest sheet sizes commonly rolled at major mills. Most tin mills have dedicated cold-rolling mills and pickling and annealing lines.

Cold reduction of carbon sheet generally is undertaken on continuous (or "tandem") mills, with a number of four-high roll stands (each containing four rolls—two above and two below the strip, with smaller work rolls in contact with the strip able to be removed regularly for cleaning). The number of stands, and the power applied to each stand, determines the amount of size reduction and the speed of throughput of the strip. Some smaller single-stand reversing mills are also in operation. For stainless and some other specialty grades of steel, the force that must be applied to the work rolls to reduce the steels thickness is such that four-high mills are not practical. Instead, cluster mills—most often known after their inventor and patent-holder as Sendzimir or Z mills—are used. These are reversing mills with a large number of supporting rolls surrounding the pair of small work rolls, combining to apply far greater pressure through the work roll onto the strip. Tables II.3a and II.3b (on the following pages) show each mills' configuration.

The tables exclude temper/skinpass mills. These mills generally have only one or two stands, which may be two or four rolls high. Strictly speaking, these are cold-rolling mills but are used for surface conditioning of hot-rolled coil rather than for gauge reduction.

The tables also exclude narrow strip mills producing product widths narrower than 36 inches. Such mills, although part of the overall steel supply picture, have historically maintained a separate identity from the steel mill industry, reflecting the lower capital investment required and the very specialized niche markets served. Only in the stainless steel segment has there been significant overlap of ownership between cold-rolled sheet producers and cold-rolled strip.

II.3A Carbon and Alloy Sheet Cold Reduction Mills

[excluding Narrow Strip Mills and Temper/Skinpass Mills]

Company and Plant Location	Config-uration	Nominal Width	Tons per Year Capacity	Significant Sourcing or Supply Relationships
AK Steel, Middletown, OH	T5	80"	2,600,000	60%+ of output for in-plant coating
Algoma Steel, Sault Ste. Marie, Ontario	R	80"	306,000	
Allegheny Ludlum, West Leechburg, PA	T3	38"	80,000	Dedicated to silicon electrical steel
Armco, Mansfield, OH	T5	52"	450,000	Carbon CR production dedicated to Dover galvanizing plant
Bethlehem Steel, Burns Harbor, IN	T5	80"	1,500,000	70%+ to Lackawanna, Double G, and in-plant galvanizing lines
Bethlehem Steel, Sparrows Point, MD	T5	48"	660,000	Dedicated to tin mills
	T5	56"	530,000	Supplies four in-plant HD zinc/ aluminum lines, and Double G
	T4	66"	947,000	
BHP Steel, Kalama, WA (to open 1997)	*R*	60"	300,000	To supply Zincalume lines in-plant and at Rancho Cucamonga, CA
California Steel Industries, Fontana, CA	T5	43"	400,000	Up to 50% to in-plant HD line
	R	61	300,000	
Caparo Steel, Sharon, PA	Z	60"	180,000	
	T5	62"	380,000	In-house HD line
Chicago Cold Rolling, Portage, IN (open mid-1996)	R	60"	350,000	50% of capacity to be used by Bethlehem Steel; light gauges
Dofasco, Hamilton, Ontario	T5 P	68"	1,000,000	)
	T5	72"	1,400,000	) Mills supply four in-plant, DNN
	T5	56"	450,000	) and Sorevco joint venture HD
	R	66"	260,000	) galvanizing lines, plus tin mills
	R	56"	136,600	)
Gulf States Steel, Gadsden, AL	T4	54"	409,000	In-house hot-dip galvanizing
Huntco, Inc., Blytheville, AR	T4	60"	240,000	Hot band from Nucor, Hickman
Inland Steel, East Chicago, IN	T5	80"	1,750,000	Supplies Walbridge Coatings and in-plant coating lines
I/N Tek, New Carlisle, IN	T4 P	65"	1,500,000	Supplies I/N Kote
LTV Steel, Aliquippa, PA	T5	38"	600,000	Dedicated to tin mills. Hot band from Cleveland
LTV Steel, Cleveland, OH	T5	80"	1,450,000	Supplies L/S joint ventures and in-plant HD line
	T4	72"	960,000	
LTV Steel, Hennepin, IL	T5	84"	1,350,000	30% to in-plant HD line
LTV, Indiana Harbor, IN	T5	75"	1,500,000	50% to in-plant HD line
	T6	46"	680,000	Dedicated to tin mills
McLouth Steel, Gibraltar, MI	T4	60"	600,000	Hot band from Trenton mill
National Steel, Ecorse, MI	T5	80"	1,200,000	In-plant electro-galvanizing line, plus DNN Galvanizing joint venture
National Steel, Granite City, IL	T4	56"	700,000	In-plant HD lines.
National Steel, Portage, IN	T5	80"	1,400,000	Supplies in-plant tin, chrome, and HD lines, Double G joint venture
	T5	52"	700,000	
Nucor, Crawfordsville, IN	*R*	*55"*	400,000	In-plant HD line;. also rolls 409 stainless
	R	*55"*	500,000	
Rouge Steel, Dearborn, MI	T4	66"	1,224,000	Supplies Double Eagle EG line
Sidbec-Dosco, Contrecoeur, Québec	Z	52"	400,000	Supplies Sorevco HD joint venture
Steel Dynamics, Butler, IN (to open 1997)	*R*	*60"*	600,000	To supply in-plant coating line
Stelco, Hamilton, Ontario	T4	80"	1,150,000	) Four in-plant HD galvanizing
	T5	56"	500,000	) lines plus tin mill
USS-Posco, Pittsburg, CA	T5 P	56"	1,500,000	Hot band from Gary and Posco; in-plant HD and tin lines
U.S. Steel, Fairfield, AL	T6	52"	990,000	Two in-plant HD lines

II.3A Carbon and Alloy Sheet Cold Reduction Mills

[excluding Narrow Strip Mills and Temper/Skinpass Mills]

(continued)

U.S. Steel, Fairless Hills, PA	T4	80"	920,000	)
	T5	48"	710,000	) In-plant HD and tin lines
	T4	48"	240,000	)
U.S. Steel, Gary, IN	T5	80"	2,250,000	)
	T4	52"	750,000	) In-plant HD, EG, and tin lines
	T2	48"	240,000	)
U.S. Steel, Irvin, PA	T5	84"	1,490,000	In-plant HD and terne lines
WCI Steel, Warren, OH	T4	54"	576,000	In-plant HD and terne lines; also rolls silicon electrical sheets
Western Flat Rolled Steel & Processing, Lindon, UT	R	52"	500,000	Mill purchased and relocated 1995; adjacent to Geneva Steel
Wheeling-Pittsburgh Steel, Allenport, PA	T4	66"	1,015,000	Supplies Wheeling-Nisshin and Martins Ferry HD plants and Yorkville tin line
Wheeling-Pittsburgh Steel, Yorkville, OH	T5	45"	800,000	
	T3	35"	115,000	

Configuration codes: R = reversing mill, T = tandem (continuous) mill, number indicates number of stands in line, Z = Sendzimir cluster reversing mill, P = continuous pickling directly in-line with cold reduction mill.
Coating line abbreviations: HD = hot-dip galvanizing, EG = electrogalvanizing.

II.3B: Stainless Steel Cold-Rolling Mills

[Excluding Narrow Strip Mills under 36"]

Company and Plant Location	Configuration	Nominal Width	Tons per Year Capacity	Significant Sourcing or Supply Relationships
Allegheny Ludlum, Brackenridge, PA	T4	49.5"	300,000	
	R	51"	90,000	
	R	51"	108,000	
	Z	50"	33,000	
Allegheny Ludlum, New Castle, PA	Z	49"	120,000	Hot band from Brackenridge
Allegheny Ludlum, Vandergrift, PA	Z	52"	180,000	Hot band from Brackenridge
Allegheny Ludlum, West Leechburg, PA [a]	R	38"	40,000	Hot band from Brackenridge
Armco, Inc., Butler, PA	T4	51"	340,000	
	T3	52"	480,000	
	R	40"	140,000	
Armco, Inc., Coshocton, OH	Z	52"	90,000e	Hot band from Butler
	Z	40"	(combined)	
Armco, Inc., Mansfield, OH	Z	50"	90,000e	
Armco, Inc., Zanesville, OH	Z	44"	165,000	Hot band from Butler
J & L Specialty Products, Detroit, MI	R	50"	50,000e	Hot band toll rolled by LTV
J & L Specialty Products, Louisville, OH	R	44"	66,000	Hot band toll rolled by LTV
	Z	55"	66,000	Hot band toll rolled by LTV
J & L Specialty Products, Midland, PA	Z	55"	65,000	Hot band toll rolled by LTV
	T4 P [b]	60" [b]	275,000	Hot band toll rolled by LTV
Lukens, Inc., Washington Steel division, Washington, PA	Z	50"	75,000	Hot band from Houston mill
	Z	40"	38,000	Hot band from Houston mill
	Z	36"	3,000	Hot band from Houston mill
Lukens, Inc., Washington Steel division, Massillon, OH	Z	49"	105,000	Hot band from Houston and Conshohocken mills
North American Stainless, Carrollton, KY	Z	60"	170,000	[d]
North American Stainless, Carrollton, KY	Z	50"	120,000	[d]
Precision Specialty Metals, Los Angeles, CA [a, b, c]	Z	52" [a]	35,000	
Teledyne Rodney Metals, New Bedford, MA [a]	Z	42"	15,000	

[a] Additional Z mills for narrow-strip (under 36 inches nominal width) are operated at this location.

[b] New mills, due for completion late 1996-early 1997.

[c] Precision Specialty Metals, a stainless strip producer, does not have sheet-width annealing and pickling facilities to complement its new wide Sendzimir mill; likely the mill will be used initially to supply light-gauge coils for slitting and further processing.

[d] North American Stainless initially sourced most of its hot bands from Armco, Inc., Butler, PA. In 1996 it ordered a new hot-strip mill from Hitachi, to allow the mill to roll its own hot band from purchased slab. North Americans second Z mill was due to come in-line during 1996, and its hot-strip mill in 1997.

FLAT PRODUCTS

II.4: Galvanized Sheet (Including All Metal Coatings Other than Tinplate)

The coating of steel with zinc to resist corrosion in exposed applications dates from the nineteenth century, but in the last 30 years a wide range of new metal coatings and coating processes has been developed, largely in response to demands from automotive customers. A high proportion of wire is galvanized, and smaller quantities of pipe and structural products; however, by far the largest application of metallic coatings is to flat-rolled steel. While a wide range of specialty coatings are applied in small batches, the major coatings applied in the steel industry (other than tinplate) include:

- zinc
- galvannealed steel, a variant on zinc coating in which the strip is heated after coating to a temperature at which there is zinc and iron diffusion between the steel and its coating, creating a stronger zinc-iron alloy coating
- aluminum
- zinc-nickel
- Galvalume®, a proprietary coating of aluminum (55 percent), zinc (43.5 percent) and silicon, licensed by BIEC International, Inc., Bethlehem, Pennsylvania, a unit of Australias BHP Steel
- Galfan®, a proprietary zinc-aluminum-mischmetal alloy coating, licensed by the International Lead-Zinc Research Organization, Research Triangle Park, North Carolina
- lead-tin (known as terne plate, a product used in automobile fuel, brake, and exhaust systems but that is being displaced by stainless steel and other materials)

All of these types of coatings (sometimes excluding terne plate) often are grouped together into the broad category of galvanized steel, for convenience and to distinguish them from the other family of coated steels, tin mill products.

Two major processes are used for the application of coatings. In hot dipping (HD), the strip is passed after heating through a bath of the molten coating metal. In electrogalvanizing (EG), the strip is degreased and acid-pickled, to ensure a uniformly clean surface, and then passed though tanks in which the coating metal is passed through an electrolytic solution from anodes of the plating metal to the cathode of the steel strip. Electrogalvanizing is a much more expensive process than hot-dipping but has a number of advantages: thinner coatings are possible; coatings are more evenly distributed; the surface finish is more even; and by changing the density of the electric current, differential coating thicknesses can be applied, or coatings can be applied to one side of the strip only, with greater ease than with hot-dip processing.

North American demand for galvanized sheets has been growing steadily across economic cycles during the last 20 years, and has approximately doubled since 1985; in the mid-1990s, its level approaches 20 million tons a year. Capacity additions have reflected this growth, and further additions are likely as applications of galvanized steel in construction increase.

II.4: Galvanized Sheet Producers

Company and Plant Location	Tons per Year Capacity	Maximum width	Type of Coating
AK Steel, Middletown, OH	475,000	75"	HD zinc
	430,000	60"	HD aluminum
	150,000	51"	HD terne plate
	490,000	75"	EG zinc or zinc-nickel
AK Steel, Ashland, KY	312,000	60"	HD zinc or galvannealed
Armco Steel, Dover, OH	250,000	48"	HD zinc
	250,000	36"	HD zinc
Bethlehem Steel, Burns Harbor, IN	450,000	72"	HD zinc or galvannealed
	78,000	48"	EG zinc
Bethlehem Steel, Lackawanna, NY	460,000	72"	HD zinc
Bethlehem Steel, Sparrows Point, MD	170,000	48"	HD zinc
	170,000	48"	HD zinc or Galvalume
	170,000	49"	HD zinc or Galvalume
	260,000	49"	HD zinc
BHP Steel, Kalama, WA (start-up 1996)	150,000	48"	HD zinc-aluminum
BHP Steel, Rancho Cucamonga, CA	150,000	48"	HD zinc-aluminum
California Steel Industries, Fontana, CA	300,000	60"	HD zinc or galvannealed
Coil Coating Co., Howland, OH [a]	125,000	48"	HD zinc

[a] Coil Coating Co., a subsidiary of Sharon Steel, closed in 1992. The line was not part of the assets of Sharon Steel purchased and restarted by Caparo Steel but was the subject of a bid in 1995 by Wheeling-Pittsburgh Steel, which ultimately backed away from the transaction because of high environmental remediation costs. The plant was subject to interest from other potential purchasers and is likely to be reopened.

DNN Galvanizing, Windsor, Ontario [b]	400,000	72"	HD zinc (differential coating)
Dofasco, Hamilton, Ontario	170,000	48"	HD zinc or Galvalume
	320,000	60"	HD zinc or galvannealed
	254,000	52"	HD zinc or galvannealed
	305,000	60"	HD zinc
Double Eagle Steel Coating, Dearborn, MI [c]	850,000	72"	EG zinc
Double G Coatings, Jackson, MS [d]	260,000	49"	HD zinc or Galvalume
GalvTech, Pittsburgh, PA[e] (start-up 1996)	350,000	60"	HD zinc
Gulf States Steel, Gadsden, AL	140,000	48"	HD zinc
Inland Steel, East Chicago, IL	300,000	60"	HD zinc
	400,000	72"	HD zinc
	200,000	60"	HD aluminum
I/N Kote, New Carlisle, IN [f]	450,000	65"	HD zinc
	450,000	65"	EG zinc or zinc-alloy
L-S Electro-Galvanizing, Cleveland, OH [g]	420,000	72"	EG zinc
L-S II Electro-Galvanizing, Columbus, OH [g]	360,000	72"	EG zinc or zinc-nickel
LTV Steel, Cleveland, OH	144,000	60"	EG zinc
LTV Steel, Hennepin, IL	433,000	60"	HD zinc
LTV Steel, Indiana Harbor, IN	264,000	60"	HD zinc
	636,000	72"	HD zinc
Metaltech, Pittsburgh [e]	290,000	48"	HD zinc
Metro Metals, East Chicago, IN (start-up 1997)	200,000	72"	EG zinc
National Steel, Ecorse, MI	400,000	72"	EG zinc
National Steel, Granite City, IL	250,000	48"	HD zinc
	150,000	45"	HD zinc
(start-up 1997)	270,000	49"	HD zinc
National Steel, Portage, IN	265,000	48"	HD zinc or Galvalume
	488,000	72"	HD zinc
(start-up 1997)	270,000	49"	HD zinc
NextTech, Turtle Creek, PA	110,000	42"	HD zinc
Nucor, Crawfordsville, IN	200,000	48"	HD zinc
Pinole Point Steel Co., Richmond, CA	250,000	54"	HD zinc
Precision Galvanizing Inc., Ambridge, PA	150,000	36"	HD zinc
Pro-Tec Coating, Leipsic, OH [h]	600,000	72"	HD zinc or galvannealed
Sorevco, Coteau-du-Lac, Québec [i]	125,000	50"	HD zinc
Stelco, Inc., Hamilton, Ontario	135,000	46"	HD zinc
	240,000	48"	HD zinc
	229,000	56"	HD zinc

[b] DNN Galvanizing is a joint venture between Dofasco of Canada, National Steel of the United States, and NKK Steel of Japan, each with 33.3 percent; operations commenced in 1993.

[c] Double Eagle Steel Coating Co. is a joint venture between Rouge Steel (50%) and U.S. Steel (50%), located adjoining Rouges Dearborn plant. Double Eagle, which opened in 1985, has had its capacity uprated twice, most recently in 1994-95, to its current status as the worlds largest electrogalvanizing line.

[d] Double G Coatings is a joint venture of Bethlehem Steel (Sparrows Point division) and National Steel.

[e] GalvTech, MetalTech, and NextTech are owned and operated by a partnership of Pittsburgh area investors. MetalTech was a former LTV Steel facility coating heavier gauges of sheet, at the once-integrated Jones and Laughlin works on Pittsburghs south side. The other two lines have been newly built, NextTech (for light gauges) opening in 1992 and GalvTech (for medium gauges) in 1996.

[f] I/N Kote is a joint venture between Inland Steel and Nippon Steel.

[g] L-S Electrogalvanizing and L-S II Electrogalvanizing are joint ventures between LTV Steel and Sumitomo.

Stelco, Inc. and Mitsubishi, Hamilton, Ontario[j]	350,000	72"	HD zinc
U.S. Steel, Fairfield, AL	280,000	62"	HD zinc
(start-up 1997)	260,000	60"	HD zinc and Galvalume
U.S. Steel, Fairless Hills, PA	290,000	65"	HD zinc
U.S. Steel, Gary, IN	340,000	60"	HD zinc
	115,000	48"	HD zinc
	270,000	62"	EG zinc
U.S. Steel, Irvin Works, Dravosburg, PA	220,000	52"	HD zinc or Galvalume
	170,000	48"	HD zinc or Galvalume
	195,000	54"	HD terne plate
USS-Posco Industries, Pittsburg, CA	116,000	48"	HD zinc
	291,000	54"	HD zinc
Walbridge Coatings, Walbridge, OH[k]	400,000	60"	EG zinc or zinc-nickel
WCI Steel, Warren, OH	300,000 80,000	48" 48"	HD zinc HD terne plate
Weirton Steel, Weirton, WV	260,000	48"	HD zinc or Galfan
	140,000	42"	HD zinc or Galfan
	250,000	48"	HD zinc (differential coating)
	200,000	38"	EG zinc
Wheeling-Nisshin, Follansbee, WV	360,000	60"	HD zinc, alum., galvannealed
	240,000	50"	HD zinc, alum., galvannealed
Wheeling-Pittsburgh Steel, Canfield, OH	72,000	48"	EG zinc
Wheeling-Pittsburgh Steel, Martins Ferry, OH	133,000	36"	HD zinc
	227,000	48"	HD zinc
	454,000	60"	HD zinc

[h] Pro-Tec Coating is a joint venture between U.S. Steel and Kobe Steel of Japan.
[i] Sorevco is a joint venture between Sidbec-Dosco and Dofasco.
[j] The most modern of the four hot-dip galvanizing lines at Stelcos Hamilton mill, known as the Z line, is owned 60 percent by Stelco and 40 percent by Mitsubishi of Japan. It began operations in 1991.
[k] Walbridge Coating is a joint venture between Bethlehem Steel (Burns Harbor division), which supplies 75 percent of the steel inputs and markets 75 percent of the product, and Inland Steel (25 percent).

FLAT PRODUCTS

II. 5: Tin Mill Products

In North America, "tin mills" are electrolytic coating lines similar to those used for the production of electrogalvanized steel, in which tin or chrome is the metal coating applied to a cold-rolled steel coil substrate. A major difference, however, is that the matte surface finish achieved by electroplating alone is insufficient for the applications that use tin and chrome, in which a shiny or reflective surface is sought. The plated coil is therefore passed through an extra process, in which the metal is reheated briefly to melt the surface layer, which on cooling forms a shiny alloy layer. The coil may also be chemically treated to protect the surface finish.

Most tin mills produce electrolytic tinplate, feedstock for the container industry. In 1995 in North America, this was used almost exclusively for food cans, although steel may recover its position in other markets where it has been displaced by competing materials. A small number of lines produce a product known as tin-free steel, which is coated with chrome or chromium oxide. Tin-free steel was developed as a competitive response to the inroads of aluminum in beverage cans but has not been able to prevent aluminum taking almost 100 percent of that market in North America. A small amount of a third tin mill product, black plate, is also sold to the container industry. Black plate is an uncoated substrate, essentially the raw material for other tin mill products, which has been cold-reduced, annealed, and chemically surface treated so that it can accept organic or enamel coating (rather than metal) to protect and decorate the surfaces of the finished can.

The overall market for tin mill products has stagnated since a 1969 peak of over 6 million tons in the United States and over half a million tons in Canada. The chief end use, food containers, is not particularly cyclical and tends to vary with crop production rather than with the economy. In the mid-1990s, the U.S. market for tin mill products was a little over 4 million tons and the Canadian market remained at around 500,000 tons. North American producers have faced relatively little import competition, and the participants in the market have remained steady over the last twenty-five years. During this time two companies have left the market (Inland in 1970 and Kaiser in 1983) and none has entered. The first new tin mill during this entire period was announced in 1995 by Wheeling Pittsburgh, to be known as Ohio Coatings Company.

II.5: Tin Mill Products

Company and Plant Location	Tons per Year Capacity	Maximum Width	Products
Bethlehem Steel, Sparrows Point, MD	260,000	38"	Tinplate
	255,000	38"	Tinplate
	255,000	38"	Tin-free steel (TFS)
Dofasco, Hamilton, Ontario	144,000	40"	Tinplate
	273,000	48"	Tinplate/TFS
LTV Steel, Aliquippa, PA	210,000	38"	Tinplate
	252,000	38"	Tinplate
LTV Steel, Indiana Harbor	272,000	45"	Tinplate
	156,000	46"	TFS
National Steel, Portage, IN	334,000	38"	Tinplate
	285,000	38"	TFS
Ohio Coatings Co., Yorkville, OH [a]	250,000	42"	Tinplate
Stelco, Hamilton	250,000	42"	Tinplate/TFS
USS-Posco Industries, Pittsburg, CA	252,000	38"	Tinplate/TFS
	208,000	38"	Tinplate
U.S. Steel, Fairless Hills, PA	290,000	37"	Tinplate
	280,000	38"	Tinplate
U.S. Steel, Gary, IN	165,000	37"	Tinplate
	310,000	46"	Tinplate
	130,000	36"	TFS
Weirton Steel, Weirton, WV	342,700	39"	Tinplate
	308,500	39"	Tinplate/TFS
	335,700	39"	Tinplate
	298,400	38"	TFS
	234,100	39"	TFS / tinplate
Wheeling-Pittsburgh Steel, Yorkville, OH	490,000	42"	Tinplate
	160,000	48"	Tinplate

[a] Ohio Coatings is a joint venture announced in 1994 between Wheeling-Pittsburgh Steel (50%, and supplier of 100% of the substrate); Dong Yang Tinplate Ltd. of Korea (25%); and Nittetsu Shoji America, an affiliate of Nippon Steel (25%).

LONG PRODUCTS

II.6: Concrete-Reinforcing Bar (Rebar)

Concrete-reinforcing bars are the lowest priced of major steel mill products. With undemanding chemical specifications, they can be manufactured from the lowest-priced grades of ferrous scrap. Over the course of recent business cycles, North American demand has averaged a little under 6 million tons. Because of the low value of rebar in proportion to freight costs, relatively little is traded internationally (or even over long distances within North America).

Rebar was the first product to be produced solely by minimills in North America, after the exit of Bethlehem from the rebar business in 1986. Stelco, although an integrated company, produces rebar in Canada at its two minimills.

II.6: Concrete-Reinforcing Bar

Company and Mill Location	Bar Mill Capacity	Estimated 1994 Rebar Shipments	1994 Market Share, U.S. & Canada
A.B. Steel Mill, Cincinnati, OH [a]	100,000	25,000	
Altasteel, Edmonton, Alberta	240,000	180,000	2%
Ameristeel, Charlotte, NC	300,000	100,000	
Ameristeel, Jackson, TN	400,000	150,000	16%
Ameristeel, Jacksonville, FL	380,000	400,000	
Ameristeel, Knoxville, TN	300,000	250,000	
Auburn Steel, Auburn, NY	360,000	<50,000	
Austeel Lemont, Lemont, IL	300,000	<100,000	
Birmingham Steel, Birmingham, AL	500,000	400,000	
Birmingham Steel, Jackson, MS	400,000	200,000	21%
Birmingham Steel, Kankakee, IL	500,000	450,000	
Birmingham Steel, Seattle, WA	600,000	150,000	
Border Steel, Vinton, TX	256,000	200,000	3%
Cascade Steel Rolling Mills, McMinnville, OR	900,000[b]	310,000	6%
Chaparral Steel, Midlothian, TX	600,000	200,000	3%
Commercial Steel, Glassport, PA	120,000	100,000	
Connecticut Steel, Wallingford, CT [a]	150,000	<25,000	
Co-Steel Lasco, Whitby, Ontario	500,000	170,000	2%
Courtice Steel, Cambridge, Ontario	250,000	100,000	
Franklin Steel, Franklin, PA [a,c]	105,000	-	
Gerdau MRM Steel, Selkirk, Manitoba	310,000	<50,000	
Hawaiian Western Steel, Ewa, HA	50,000	25,000	
Marion Steel, Marion, OH	380,000	200,000	3%
New Jersey Steel, Sayreville, NJ	500,000	450,000	8%
North Star Steel, Milton, PA [c]	150,000	-	
North Star Steel, St. Paul, MN	500,000	100,000	4%
North Star Steel, Wilton, IA	330,000	100,000	
Northwestern Steel & Wire, Sterling IL	405,000	150,000	3%
Nucor, Darlington, SC	550,000	<100,000	
Nucor, Jewett, TX	280,000	<100,000	4%
Nucor, Norfolk, NE	400,000	<50,000	
Nucor, Plymouth, UT	400,000	<50,000	
Oregon Steel Mills, CF & I Division, Pueblo, CO [d]	600,000	25,000	
Roanoke Electric Steel, Roanoke, VA	400,000	25,000	
Sheffield Steel, Sand Springs, OK	550,000	250,000	5%
Sheffield Steel, Joliet, IL	216,000	50,000	
Sidbec-Dosco, Longueuil, Québec	400,000	50,000	
W. Silver, El Paso, TX	100,000	25,000	
SMI Steel, Birmingham, AL	450,000	<25,000	
SMI Owen Steel, Columbia, SC	330,000	200,000	7%
Structural Metals, Inc., Seguin TX	775,000	200,000	
Stelco-McMaster, Contrecoeur, Québec	300,000	120,000	2%
Tamco, Etiwanda, CA	410,000	400,000	7%

[a] Re-rollers without steelmaking capacity. May use either purchased billets or used railroad rails as feedstock.

[b] Cascade Steels rolling capacity is a management estimate for 1997 after a new, second rolling mill is worked up to full capacity. Output of rebar is expected to average 325,000 tons per year; the balance of shipments will include wire rod, fence posts and MBQ products.

[c] Mills mothballed at January 1996, but capable of being reopened.

[d] CF & I completed a new, 600,000-ton-per-year combined bar and rod mill in 1995, replacing two separate, old facilities with higher combined nominal capacities but high costs and low levels of output. However, it is not expected that CF & I will significantly increase its rebar production.

LONG PRODUCTS

II.7: Wire Rod

The steel industry historically regarded wire rod as a semifinished form of steel, most of which was converted into a finished form (that is, drawn into wire) within the steel mill. In the 1990s, however, over 70 percent of wire rods are shipped away from the producing mill, either to independent wire producers or to affiliated but distant wire mills operated as separate profit centers. Steel mills with in-house wire-drawing facilities may convert only a small proportion of their rod production internally. Therefore, steel wire production is now best regarded as a separate industry from steel production, and wire rod is considered a finished product of the steelmaking industry. It is invariably sold in coiled form.

North American demand for wire rod (including internally consumed wire rods) amounts to a little over 7 million tons per year, on average over the business cycle. The United States imported as much as 20 percent of its needs in the early 1990s, mainly from Canada. Capacity expansions in the United States between 1994 and 1996 are likely to reduce the proportion of imports, although Siderurgica de California, a new Mexican minimill in Mexicali, Baja California, began production of rod in 1994 aimed in large part at the western U.S. market.

Commodity or low-carbon (LC in table) grades account for about two-thirds of the total tonnage of wire rod production. They are used to produce familiar products such as fence wire, wire netting, concrete-reinforcing mesh, and nails. The remaining one-third of tonnage is divided between higher-value grades, including high-carbon (HC) rods (for spring wire, tire bead, prestressed concrete strand, etc.); cold-heading (CH) quality rod (for fasteners, automotive and other engineering applications), and smaller tonnage rod products for welding wire (WW), oil-tempered wire (OT), tire cord (TC), and fine wire (FW). Much carbon steel wire is annealed and/or galvanized before shipment. Alloy and stainless rods are produced in small tonnages (around 3 percent of the total) by specialty bar producers including Timken (alloy), CarTech (stainless for in-house wire drawing), Crucible, and Sammi Al Tech (both stainless).

Integrated mill production of wire rod is limited to a small amount of cold-heading grade rod produced on the 10-inch bar mill of USS/Kobe Steel, although billets from USS/Kobe also form a major part of the feedstock to the American Steel & Wire division of Birmingham Steel, pending the completion in 1997 of Birminghams new Memphis, Tennessee, melt shop.

II.7: Wire Rod

Company and Plant Location	Affiliated Wire Production	Principal Grades	Rod Mill Capacity
American Steel and Wire, Cuyahoga, OH and Joliet, IL [a]	In-house	HC, CH, WW, FW	1,050,000 [a]
Atlantic Steel, Atlanta, GA	Sivaco/National Wire (SNW Group)	LC, TC	300,000
Bar Technologies, Johnstown, PA and Lackawanna, NY [b]	-	[b]	390,000 [b]
Cascade Steel Rolling Mills, McMinnville, OR [c]	-	LC	200,000 [c]
Charter Steel, Saukville, WI	In-house	CH	250,000
Connecticut Steel, Wallingford, CT	In-house	LC	150,000
Co-Steel Raritan, Perth Amboy, NJ	-	HC	850,000
Georgetown Steel, Georgetown, SC	Andrews Wire; Florida Wire & Cable; Tree Island Industries.	HC	750,000
GS Industries, Kansas City, MO	-	HC, CH	700,000
Ivaco, L'Orignal, Ontario	Sivaco/National Wire (SNW Group)	LC	650,000
Keystone Steel & Wire, Peoria, IL	In-house	LC	650,000
Laclede Steel, Alton, IL	Plants at Fremont, IN, and Memphis, TN	HC, LC, OT	200,000
North Star Steel, Beaumont, TX	-	LC	900,000
North Star Steel, Kingman, AZ	-	LC	500,000[d]
Northwestern Steel & Wire, Sterling, IL	In-house	LC	410,000
Oregon Steel Mills, CF & I division, Pueblo, CO	In-house	LC	600,000
Sidbec-Dosco, Contrecoeur, Québec	Plants at Etobicoke, Ont., and Montréal, Qué.	LC, HC	400,000
Stelco, Hamilton, Ontario	Stelwire; Frost Wire Products	LC, HC, CH	700,000
USS/Kobe Steel, Lorain, OH	-	CH	[e]

[a] American Steel and Wire, the former wire rod and wire operations of U.S. Steel, has since 1993 been a division of Birmingham Steel. A second rod mill at Cuyahoga, installed in 1995, adds 550,000 tons per year of capacity to the existing 495,000-ton-per-year-rated mill. Birmingham Steel plans, the new mill achieving full production, to convert the Joliet mill (360,000 tons per year) to rebar production. Both plants have been dependent on purchased billets, a situation that will change in 1997 once Birmingham Steels new Memphis steel mill is completed.

[b] Bar Technologies purchased the former Bar, Rod and Wire division of Bethlehem Steel in 1995 and restarted operations at Johnstown in early 1996. Initial production was of special quality bar products; however, the company was reported to be planning to add a rod block to the Johnstown 11-inch bar mill (rated at 390,000 tons per year) and dedicate that mill to rod, while using the 13-inch bar mill at Lackawanna, New York, for bar production. Bar Technologies did not acquire Bethlehem Steels two idle rod mills, at Johnstown and Sparrows Point.

[c] Cascade Steel Rolling Mills is a new entrant into the rod market, with the completion of a new bar mill including a rod block in 1995. Production on the new mill was planned to average 300,000 tons of rebar and 200,000 tons of rod per year.

[d] Initial target capacity on start-up in 1995. Potential ultimate capacity (bar and rod products) of up to 900,000 tons.

[e] USS/Kobe Steel installed new reducing/sizing and coiling equipment at its 10-inch bar mill in 1995 that allows it to roll small products traditionally considered to be wire rod sizes.

LONG PRODUCTS

II.8: Merchant Bar Quality (MBQ) Bars and Structurals, Including Flat and Round Bar, Angles, Channels, and Light Beams

As the name suggests, merchant bar products are general-purpose steel shapes sold primarily through stocking distributors. They are used primarily in construction and maintenance, but are also—especially flat, square, and round bars—consumed in every type of metal fabrication and many manufacturing industries.

Published statistics for bars and merchant products in both the United States and Canada tend to lump MBQ products together with special-quality bars. In addition, in the U.S. statistics lose merchant light structural shapes such as angles and channels within the larger category of structural shapes of 3 inches or greater cross-section. Estimates of the market for merchant bars and shapes, excluding wide flange beams, which constitute the classic "heavy structural" product, tend therefore to vary, but average around 6 million tons—a little over 5 million tons a year in the United States and a little under 1 million tons a year in Canada.

Production of MBQ products is usually undertaken on the same rolling mills used for rebar (at the smaller end of the size range) or wide flange beams (at the heavy end). They also overlap in some cases with special bar quality (SBQ) production, especially where the bars are destined for cold finishing, and in certain cases with the production of special shapes. Because MBQ products are used so universally and are easy to manufacture (undemanding physical and chemical specifications), they can be rolled as a "fill-in" product on mills primarily devoted to another long product. For this reason, mills are identified below as to whether MBQ bars or another class of bar product—rebar, SBQ, wide flange beams (WF), special sections—is the principal product of that mill.

Merchant bar products are no longer produced at integrated mills in the United States. The last integrated producer, Bethlehem Steels Structural Products division in Bethlehem, Pennsylvania, which is primarily a producer of wide flange beams but also produces certain sizes of standard beam, channel, and angle, ended integrated steel production in 1995 and now sources its steel from the nonintegrated Steelton mill. In Canada Stelco remains a producer of some merchant bar sizes at its integrated Hilton Works in Hamilton, Ontario.

II.8: MBQ Bars and Structurals

Company and Plant Location [and bar mill identification if appropriate]	**Bar Mill Capacity**	**Principal Product**	**Estimated 1995 MBQ Tons**
Altasteel, Edmonton, Alberta	240,000	Rebar	100,000
Ameristeel, Charlotte, NC	300,000	MBQ	
Ameristeel, Jackson, TN	400,000	MBQ	360,000
Ameristeel, Jacksonville, FL	500,000	Rebar	
Ameristeel, Knoxville, TN	300,000	Rebar	
Atlantic Steel, Cartersville, GA [12" mill]	185,000	MBQ	150,000
Atlantic Steel, Atlanta, GA [13" mill]	280,000	SBQ	100,000
Auburn Steel, Auburn, NY	360,000	MBQ	300,000
Austeel Lemont, Lemont, IL	300,000	MBQ	150,000
Bayou Steel, La Place, LA	600,000	MBQ	500,000
Bayou Steel, Harriman, TN [a]	260,000	MBQ	[a]
Bethlehem Steel, Bethlehem, PA [42" mill]	600,000	WF Beams	50,000
Bethlehem Steel, Steelton, PA [20" mill]	280,000	Wide flats	25,000
Birmingham Steel, Birmingham, AL	500,000	Rebar	450,000 [b]
Birmingham Steel, Jackson, MS	400,000	MBQ	
Birmingham Steel, Kankakee, IL	500,000	Rebar	
Birmingham Steel, Seattle, WA	600,000	Rebar	
Calumet Steel, Chicago Heights, IL	120,000	MBQ	100,000
Cascade Steel Rolling Mills, McMinnville, OR	900,000 [c]	Rebar [c]	160,000
Chaparral Steel, Midlothian, TX [23" mill]	900,000	MBQ/WF	800,000
Chaparral Steel, Midlothian, TX [12" mill]	600,000	MBQ/Rebar	
Chicago Heights Steel Co., Chicago Heights, IL	140,000	MBQ	120,000
Co-Steel Lasco, Whitby, Ontario [three mills]	1,430,000	MBQ	900,000
Courtice Steel, Cambridge, Ontario	250,000	MBQ	200,000
Gerdau MRM Steel, Selkirk, Manitoba	310,000	MBQ	250,000
J-Pitt Steel, Inc., Johnstown, PA	96,000	SBQ/ special shapes	20,000
Jersey Shore Steel, South Avis, PA	80,000	MBQ	60,000
J & L Structural, Aliquippa, PA	390,000	Special shapes	50,000
Kentucky Electric Steel, Ashland, KY	260,000	SBQ	50,000
Marion Steel, Marion, OH	380,000	Rebar	150,000
New Jersey Steel, Sayreville, NJ	500,000	ReBar	20,000
North Star Steel, Calvert City, KY	250,000	MBQ/	200,000

[a] Bayou Steel acquired the Harriman, Tennessee, plant of the former Tennessee Valley Forging Steel in 1995. Bayou intended to restart the bar mill there (but not the melt shop) to roll rebar and small merchant bars up to 3 inches cross-section, that is, products smaller than Bayous production range at La Place, Louisiana.

[b] Birmingham Steel intended to make changes in its Kankakee and Joliet, Illinois, mills in 1996-97. Announced plans included the conversion of the Joliet mill from rod to coiled rebar production, transferring all rebar production at Kankakee to Joliet, and expanding the range of MBQ products rolled at Kankakee.

[c] Cascade Steel Rolling Mills installed a second bar mill in 1995, expanding its total rolling capacity to an estimated 900,000 tons. The planned output of the combined mills by 1997 was expected to include around 200,000 tons per year of MBQ products, including fence post.

[d] New mill, built 1995.

LONG PRODUCTS

II. 9: Special Bar Quality (SBQ) Bars

Special Bar Quality (SBQ) products are a class of bars produced for two major uses. In the hot-rolled form, they may be used for engineering applications requiring more exacting specifications (usually for strength) than merchant quality bars. Examples of such applications are axles, steering columns, and suspension springs in vehicles; fasteners; and the forging industry. Second, they may be used as feedstock for the production of cold-finished bars, which are cold-worked after rolling to give extra dimensional accuracy or surface quality. SBQ bars are sometimes produced on the same mills as MBQ bars, especially if they are destined for cold-finishing. They can be distinguished from MBQ bars by the fact that they are normally produced to customer order and are sold directly to the user rather than through distributors ("merchants"). The U.S. and Canadian market consumes about 5.5 million tons of SBQ bars a year, including bars further processed into cold-finished bars.

SBQ products tend to overlap with the category of "special shapes," which could be considered a subcategory of SBQ production. Special shapes, meaning long products with nonstandard profile sizes or cross sections, are also produced to customer order for specific applications. They are, however, generally treated as a separate niche within the steel bar industry and are listed separately here. At the upper end of the size range, SBQ producers also tend to overlap and compete with forged bars: forging producers tend to be competitive with SBQ mills on small production runs, where the cost of setting up a rolling mill for small tonnages does not pay. Forges are also customers of SBQ mills, however, buying large-diameter primary bars for conversion into forged shapes.

Three integrated steelmakers produce SBQ bars in North America: Inland Steel Bar Company, which uses billets from both its own electric furnaces and from its parent companys integrated mill; USS/Kobe Steel; and Stelco, which produces SBQ products at both its Hilton Works integrated plant and its Stelco-McMaster minimill.

(See table II.9 on next page)

II.9: Special Bar Quality (SBQ) Bars

Company and Plant Location [mill identified where multiple mills exist]	Product Range	Bar Mill Capacity	Est. 1995 SBQ Tons Sold
Atlantic Steel, Atlanta, GA [13" mill]	Flats to 8" wide, rounds to 2"	280,000	175,000
Atlantic Steel, Cartersville, GA [12" mill]	Squares, rounds to 2"	185,000	50,000
Bar Technologies, Johnstown, PA [11" mill]	[a]	390,000	0
Bar Technologies, Lackawanna, NY [13" mill]	[a]	730,000	0
Bethlehem Steel, Steelton, PA [20" mill]	Flats to 14" wide	280,000	50,000
Chaparral Steel, Midlothian, TX [12" mill]	Rounds to 2.5"	600,000	100,000
Copperweld Steel Corp., Warren OH [21" and 12" mills]	Carbon and alloy rounds, squares, hexes, flats	440,000	350,000
Inland Steel Bar Co., East Chicago, IN [21" and 12" mills]	Flats, squares, rounds	900,000	750,000
J-Pitt Steel, Johnstown, PA [14", 12", and 9" mills]	Flats, hexes, rounds, round-cornered squares	375,000	100,000
Kentucky Electric Steel, Newport, KY	Flats to 12" wide, especially spring steel	260,000	200,000
Koppel Steel, Koppel, PA [22" mill]	Rounds 2.875–6"	280,000	150,000
North Star Steel, Monroe, MI	Rounds to 3.25"	500,000	450,000
North Star Steel, Wilton, IA	Flats to 4"	330,000	100,000
Nucor, Darlington, SC	Rounds - feed to Nucor Cold Finish division	650,000	Internal use only—see CF bar
Quanex MacSteel, Fort Smith, AR	Rounds and RCS to 6"	345,000	475,000 [plus CF bar]
Quanex MacSteel, Jackson, MI	Rounds and RCS to 5.5"	215,000	
Republic Engineered Steels, Canton, OH [12" and 8" mills; 8" closed 1996]	Rounds to 3", squares, flats, hexes, octagons.	580,000	725,000 [plus 300,000 CF bar]
Republic Engineered Steels, Massillon, OH [18" mill]	Rounds to 6.25", squares, flats	320,000	
Republic Engineered Steels, Chicago, IL [11" mill]	Rounds, hex, flats	288,000	
Roanoke Electric Steel, Roanoke, VA	Flats to 6", rounds	400,000	50,000
Sidbec-Dosco, Contrecoeur, Québec [12" mill]	Flats to 6", squares, rounds to 2.5"	400,000	50,000
Slater Steels, Hamilton Specialty Bar Div., Hamilton, Ontario	Flats to 6", sqaures, rounds to 2.5"	308,000	275,000
Stelco, Hamilton, Ontario [12" mill]	Rounds to 2.438", hexes	450,000	375,000
Stelco-McMaster Ltéé, Contrecoeur, Québec	Rounds to 4.5", spring flats	300,000	120,000
Timken Co., Faircrest and Harrison Plants, Canton, OH [22" and 14" mills]	Carbon & alloy rounds, squares	580,000	400,000 [plus CF bar]
USS/Kobe Steel, Lorain, OH [38" primary mill, 12" & 10" bar mills]	Rounds to 13.5", hexes	1,240,000	700,000

[a] Bar Technologies was due to resume SBQ shipments from the former Bethlehem Steel Bar, Rod and Wire (BRW) division in 1996. The size range from each mill was still to be determined.

LONG PRODUCTS

II.10: Wide Flange Beams, Piling, and Rails

The heaviest "long products" include wide flange beams, used for major load-bearing columns and cross-members in construction; piling, including both H-piles (bearing piles with similar cross-sections to wide flange beams) and sheet piling (used for temporary retaining walls, flatter products with interlocking couplings at their sides); and railroad rails. These are typically produced on similar mills, although in North America today the four rail producers roll the product on dedicated mills.

Annual consumption of beams and piling varies cyclically with the level of nonresidential construction. Beam shipments are mixed together with other merchant structurals over 3 inches cross-section for reporting purposes in the United States, and with rail in Canada. However, industry estimates indicate that U.S. demand for wide flange beams varies across the business cycle from around 3 to 4 million tons per year, with a further 250,000 to 500,000 tons in Canada. Rail demand in the two countries has ranged over the last decade between 500,000 and 1 million tons, while piling demand is typically around half a million tons. Structural tubing (among steel products) and reinforced concrete are substitutes for, and competitors of, beams in construction. Steel piling pipe and wood are substitutes for H-piles and sheet piling.

Canada's Algoma Steel is the last North American integrated mill producing both rails and structurals, after Bethlehem Steel closed its Bethlehem, Pennsylvania, integrated steelmaking operation in 1995.

II.10: Wide Flange Beams, Piling, and Rails

Company and Plant Location	Products	Mill Capacity	Estimated 1995 Shipments
Algoma Steel, Sault Ste. Marie, Ont. [50" mill]	WF to 24"	600,000	180,000
Algoma Steel, Sault Ste. Marie, Ont. [30" mill]	Rail	combined	150,000
Bayou Steel, La Place, LA	MBQ, WF to 8"	600,000	50,000
Bethlehem Steel, Bethlehem, PA [42" mill]	WF to 27", H- and sheet-piling	500,000	650,000 [a]
Bethlehem Steel, Steelton, PA [28" mill]	Rail	1,160,000	300,000
Chaparral Steel, Midlothian, TX [23" mill]	WF to 14", MBQ	900,000	500,000
Chaparral Steel, Midlothian, TX [heavy beam mill]	WF to 24"	combined	combined
Co-Steel Lasco, Whitby. Ontario [16" mill]	MBQ, WF to 10"	350,000	50,000
Northwestern Steel & Wire, Sterling, IL	WF to 18", MBQ	440,000	900,000
Northwestern Steel & Wire, Houston, TX	WF to 27", H-piling	600,000	combined
Nucor, Darlington, SC	MBQ, WF to 8"	650,000	50,000
Nucor-Yamato, Blytheville, AR [52" mill]	WF to 24", H-piling	1,100,000	1,700,000
Nucor-Yamato, Blytheville, AR [59" mill]	WF to 40"	700,000	combined
Oregon Steel Mills, CF & I Division, Pueblo, CO [45" mill]	Rail	1,250,000	250,000
Sydney Steel, Sydney, Nova Scotia	Rail	500,000	150,000

[a] Bethlehem Steel operated a second mill, producing beams to 40 inches, until late 1995.

LONG PRODUCTS

II.11: Cold-Finished Bars

Cold-finished bars are generally special bar quality (SBQ) bars that have been cold-worked by drawing, grinding, and other operations to enhance the bars dimensional accuracy and/or surface quality. Cold-finished bars are produced in round, square, hexagonal, and (occasionally) octagonal shapes. The market for carbon steel CF bars in the United States and Canada has averaged around 1.5 million tons in the 1990s.

The largest two producers, Republic and Nucor, combine hot-rolling and cold-drawing bar production at certain of their bar mills, although the two products are marketed separately and the products are treated as stand-alone profit centers. The next two largest producers are also affiliated with hot-rolled bar producers, but the cold-finished bar operations are geographically separate as well as operationally at arms-length.

II.11: Cold-Finished Bars

Company and Plant Location(s)	Estimated 1994 CF Bar Shipments
Baron Drawn Steel, Toledo, OH	<40,000
Bliss & Laughlin Steel Co., Harvey, IL; Batavia, IL; Cartersville, GA [a]	130,000
Canadian Drawn Steel, Hamilton, Ontario [div. of Bliss & Laughlin] [a]	50,000
Corey Steel, Cicero, IL	<40,000
Cuyahoga Steel & Wire, Solon, OH	42,000
La Salle Steel [div. of Quanex], Hammond, IN	160,000
Moltrup Steel Products, Beaver Falls, PA [b]	40,000
Nelsen Steel and Wire, Franklin Park, IL	<50,000
Niagara Cold Drawn Corp., Buffalo, NY and Chattanooga, TN [c]	60,000
Nucor Cold Finished, Darlington, SC, Jewett, TX, Norfolk, NE	250,000
Plymouth Steel, Warren, MI	<40,000
Republic Engineered Steels, Massillon, OH; Gary, IN (2 plants); Beaver Falls, PA; Willimantic, CT.	290,000
Southwest Steel, Catoosa, OK [c]	40,000
Taubensee Steel & Wire, Wheeling, IL	<40,000
Union Drawn Steel II Ltd., Hamilton, Ontario [b]	45,000

[a] Bliss & Laughlin was acquired by hot-rolled bar producer Bar Technologies after a bidding contest with International Metals Acquisition Corporation (now Niagara Industries) in 1995.
[b] Moltrup Steel Products and Union Drawn Steel are owned by the same principals as hot-rolled producer J-Pitt Steel.
[c] Niagara Cold Drawn and Southwest Steel are divisions of Niagara Industries, New York (formerly International Metals Acquisition Corporation).

LONG PRODUCTS

II.12: Stainless and Specialty Producers

II.12a: Stainless Steel [SS], High Alloy and Tool Steel [TS] Producers

Company and Plant Location	Products	Bar Mill Capacity [a]
Avesta Sheffield Bar Co., Richburg, SC	SS bar	[b]
Carpenter Technology, Reading, PA [2 mills]	SS, TS, and high alloy hot-rolled and cold-finished bar, rod, etc.	118,000
Copperweld Steel Corp., Warren, OH	Tool steel	440,000 [c]
Crucible Materials Corp., Syracuse, NY	SS, TS, titanium, and high alloy hot-rolled and cold-finished bars	65,000
Electralloy, Oil City, PA	SS and alloy ingots, billets, rounds	N.A.
Republic Engineered Steels, Baltimore, MD	SS bar	40,000
Sammi Al Tech, Dunkirk, NY	SS and TS bar and rod	60,000
Sammi Al Tech, Watervliet, NY	SS and TS billets, extrusions	N.A.
Sammi Atlas, Welland, Ontario	SS, TS, and high alloy hot-rolled and cold-finished bar	60,000
Slater Steels, Fort Wayne Specialty Alloys Div., Fort Wayne, IN	SS hot-rolled and cold-finished bars and angles	75,000
Talley Metals Technology, Hartsville, SC	SS bar and rod	45,000
Teledyne Allvac, Richburg, SC	TS and high alloy ingot, billet, bar	40,000
Timken Co., Canton, OH	SS and high alloy bars, bearings	580,000 [c]
Universal Stainless & Alloy, Bridgeville, PA	SS and TS ingot, billet, plate	N.A.

N.A. = Not applicable.
[a] Tons per year
[b] Uses toll rolling at Teledyne Allvac.
[c] Capacity predominantly devoted to carbon steel production.

II.12b: Carbon and Alloy Forging Bar and Ingot Producers

Company and plant location	Products	Primary Melt Capacity [a]
Edgewater Steel, Oakmont, PA	Hot-rolled circular products	41,600
Electralloy, Oil City, PA	Ingots, billets, round bar 5–26"	60,000
Ellwood Quality Steels, New Castle, PA	Ingots	300,000
A. Finkl & Sons, Chicago, IL	Ingots, forgings	30,000
FirstMiss Steel, Hollsopple, PA	Ingots, billets, forged bars	250,000
Green River Steel, Owensboro, KY	Ingots, bars 3–9", squares 3–12"	140,000
IRI International, Pampa, TX	Ingots, billets, bars, forgings	27,600
Latrobe Steel [division of Timken], Latrobe, PA	Ingots, billets	33,000
Marathon LeTourneau, Longview, TX	Ingots and plate	120,000
National Forge, Irvine, PA	Forging ingots, 24–40" dia.	100,000
Sorel Forge, Sorel, Québec	Forgings, forged bars	30,000

a Tons per year.

PIPE AND TUBING

II.13: Structural Tubing and Piling Pipe Electric-Resistance Welded (ERW) Square, Rectangular, and Round Tubing for Structural Applications

Structural tubing and piling pipe are the two major load-bearing uses of tubular steel in construction. They are distinguished from mechanical tubing, which is also used in load-bearing applications, by (1) being produced in standard sizes and therefore stocked and sold through distributors; and (2) being used in buildings and other fixed structures, rather than in machinery, equipment, and other manufactured goods.

Most structural tubing is sold with square or rectangular cross sections, for rigidity in load-bearing applications in the construction of buildings, plant, and heavy equipment. Some round tubing is also sold as or described as structural tubing, although this is often simply line pipe or mechanical tubing used in structural applications.

True piling pipe is a type of round structural tubing, although relatively small tonnages are manufactured as such. Between 30,000 and 40,000 tons are reported as produced in a typical year, or less than 10 percent of the total tonnage of steel sold in all shapes for piling and less than 1 percent of the total sales of pipe. However, at least as much unreported material manufactured as standard or line pipe is also used in piling, often when written down in value and classed as secondary or used (salvaged) material. Piling pipe is normally filled with concrete when buried, becoming in effect the casing of cast-in-ground concrete piling.

(See table II.13 on next page.)

II.13: Structural Tubing and Piling Pipe

Company and Plant Location	Min. Width Produced	Max. Width Produced	Estimated Capacity, Tons per Year
Alpha Tube/Beta Tube, Holland, Ohio	0.75"	6"	120,000
American Tubular Products, Lindon, UT	2"	8"	120,000
Atlantic Tube & Steel, Mississauga, Ontario	1.5"	6.25"	42,000
Atlas Tube, Harrow, Ontario	1.25"	9"	150,000
BMF Condel, Inc., Bromont, Québec	0.725"	3"	24,000
Beck Corporation, Elkhart, IN	2.375"	5"	20,000
Bull Moose Tube, Burlington, Ontario	0.5"	4"	45,000
Bull Moose Tube, Elkhart, IN	1.5"	16"	200,000
Bull Moose Tube, Gerald, MO	0.5"	3.5"	120,000
Bull Moose Tube, Trenton, GA	0.5"	3"	40,000
Copperweld Corp., Birmingham, AL	5"	12.5"	112,000
Copperweld Corp., Chicago, IL	4"	12.5"	200,000
Dallas Tube and Rollform, Dallas, TX	0.5"	8"	15,000
Delta Tube & Fabricating, Holly, MI	1.5"	2.5"	12,000
Hanna Steel, Fairfield, AL	1.315"	7"	140,000
Hanna Steel, Gadsden, AL	0.625"	2"	12,500
Hanna Steel, Northport, AL	1"	5"	12,500
Hannibal Industries, Los Angeles, CA	0.375"	5"	100,000
Independence Tube, Chicago, IL	1.5"	7	130,000
Ipsco, Geneva, NE	2.5"	7"	50,000
Ipsco, Red Deer, Alberta	2.875"	12.75"	140,000
James Steel and Tube, Madison Heights, MI	1.5"	6.625"	70,000
Laclede Steel, Benwood, WV	0.5"	4.5"	200,000
Lindsay Manufacturing Co., Lindsay, NE	5.563"	8"	150,000
Mariuchi America Corp., Santa Fe Springs, CA	0.5"	6"	75,000
Maverick Tube, Hickman, AR	3.0"	10.75"	180,000
Northwest Pipe & Casing, Atchison, KS	8.725"	16"	180,000
Olympic Tube, Cleveland, OH	0.625"	4.5"	100,000
Philips Mfg. & Tower Co., Dothan, AL	0.5"	3.125"	45,000
Philips Mfg. & Tower Co., Shelby, OH	0.5"	2.5"	75,000
Reinke Manufacturing Co., Deshler, NE	4.5"	6.725"	35,000
Sonco Steel Tube, Brampton, Ontario	0.375"	15"	325,000
TMP Division, Norcross, GA	0.725"	3"	20,000
UNR - Leavitt, Chicago, IL	3.5"	12.75"	160,000
Unistrut Diversified Products, Wayne, MI	1"	3.5"	12,000
United Tube Corp., Medina, OH	0.5"	2.375"	35,000
U.S. Metal Forms and Tubes, Muirkirk, MD	0.375"	5"	60,000
Valmont Industries, Brenham, TX [a]	N.A.	N.A.	150,000
Valmont Industries, Tulsa, OK	14"	48"	400,000
Valmont Industries, Valley, NE	0.84"	16"	300,000
Welded Tube of America, Chicago, IL	0.75"	20"	600,000
Welded Tube of Canada, Concord, Ontario	1.5"	10.75"	300,000
Western Tube & Conduit, Long Beach, CA	0.5"	4.5"	150,000

N.A. = not applicable.

[a] Valmont Industries produces tapered tubing at its Brenham, Texas, plant. Much of this is finished as lighting and traffic poles at Valmonts plant at Springville, Utah.

II.14: Carbon Steel Mechanical and Pressure Tubing:

Electric Resistance Welded (ERW)

Mechanical tubing is produced to customer order (rather than in standard sizes) in round, square, and rectangular cross sections, for use as components in the manufacture of machinery, plant, and equipment including cars, aircraft, farm machinery, appliances, and the like. In most uses, mechanical tubing does not carry fluids. It is used for load-bearing or reinforcing components, to transmit or absorb energy, or to contain or protect other components. Pressure tubing, on the other hand, is used in similar applications but to carry fluids (liquids or gases), usually at higher than atmospheric pressure.

Producers and products in these categories often overlap with other categories, notably (round) structural tubing, standard pipe, and conduit, which can also be used in such applications. However, the key element distinguishing them from other pipe and tubing products is that they are made-to-order, manufactured to the precise specifications required for the manufacturing application.

Depending on the application, ERW mechanical and pressure tubing can be used as-welded, annealed, cold-drawn, and/or galvanized. Mechanical tubing for applications requiring precise inside or outside diameters, such as in hydraulic cylinders, will normally be redrawn using the drawn-over-mandrel (DOM) method. See also "Seamless Pipe and Tubing," table II.18, for producers of seamless mechanical tubing, normally used in applications requiring heavy wall thicknesses, such as in the production of bushings, bearings and shafts, and for seamless pressure tubing.

(See table II.14 on next page.)

II.14: Carbon Steel Mechanical and Pressure Tubing

Company and Plant Location	Minimum Diameter	Maximum Diameter	Redraw Facilities	Estimated Capacity, Tons per Year
Acme Roll Forming, Sebewaing, MI	1.75"	7.625"		50,000
Alliance Tubular Products, Alliance, OH	0.75"	10.75"	Yes	60,000
Allied Tube & Conduit, Harvey, IL	0.625"	5"		180,000
American Roll Formed Products Corp., Painesville, OH	0.625"	2.375"		15,000
American Tube Co., Kokomo, IN	0.75 "	2.875"		30,000
American Tube Co., Phoenix, AZ	1"	4"		50,000
American Tubing Products, SC [a]	0.5"	2.5"		
AP Parts Co., Toledo, OH	1.75"	6"		70,000
Arc Tube, Inc., Sault Ste. Marie, Ontario	0.375"	0.5"		10,000
Arizona Iron Supply, Inc., Phoenix, AZ	0.725"	1.875"		7,500
Automax Mfg., Staten Island, NY	0.375"	0.725"		20,000
Berne Tube Products Co., Berne, IN	0.25"	0.375"		10,000
Blazon Tube Co., West Point, MS	0.5"	6"		50,000
Bull Moose Tube, Chicago Heights, IL	0.5"	3.5"		75,000
Bundy Corp., Cynthiana, KY	0.1875"	0.75"	Yes	80,000
Bundy of Canada Ltd., Bramalea, Ontario	0.725"	3"		25,000
Caine Steel Co., East Chicago, IN	0.75"	2.25"		60,000
California Steel & Tube, Industry, CA	0.5"	3.5"		50,000
Central Nebraska Tubing, Waverly, NE	0.75"	2.375"		50,000
Century Tube Corp.. Pine Bluff, AR	0.725"	2.875"		70,000
Copperweld Corp., Piqua, OH	0.375"	4"	Yes	60,000
Copperweld Corp., Shelby, OH	1.25"	12"	Yes	103,000
Cosco, Inc., Columbus, OH	0.5"	1.125"		36,000
Delhi Solac Ltée, Delhi, Ontario	0.625"	3"		18,000
Delhi Solac Ltée, St.-Jerome, Québec	0.5"	2"		15,000
Detroit Tubing Mill, Inc., Detroit, MI	0.5"	1.5"		20,000
Diversified Products Inc., Opelika, AL	0.75"	3.5"		25,000
Dundee Products, Dundee, MI	0.75"	3"		30,000
Edna Tubing Corp., Lorain, OH	0.375"	3"		45,000
Eugene Welding Co., Marysville, MI	2"	6"		125,000
Ex-L Tube, Inc., Kansas City, MO	1.25"	7.5"		50,000
Hannibal Industries, Vernon, CA	0.375"	0.5"		100,000
Hickory Springs Mfg., Birmingham, AL	0.5"	3"		40,000
Hoffman Industries, Sinking Spring, PA	0.3125"	2.5"	Yes	80,000
Indiana Steel Co., Seymour, IN	1"	2"		25,000
Indiana Tube Corp. Evansville, IN (div. of Handy & Harman Co.)	0.1875"	0.625"		25,000
International Specialty Tube, Detroit, MI	0.5"	3"		10,000
ITT Automotive Co., Archbold, OH	0.1875"	0.375"	Yes	10,000
ITT Automotive Co., New Lexington, OH	0.25"	0.375"	Yes	15,000
ITT Automotive Co., Rochester, NY	0.1875"	0.75"	Yes	50,000
ITT Automotive Co., Searcy, AR	0.1875"	0.75"	Yes	20,000
Jackson Tube Service, Inc., Piqua, OH	0.875"	2.5"		85,000
K-W Tube, Inc., Seymour, IN	0.625"	2"		25,000
Kirk-Eastern, Inc., Gardner, MA	0.375"	3.25"		35,000
Lock Joint Tube Co., South Bend, IN	0.725"	2.5"		70,000

[a] New producer, to commence shipments 1996.

II.14: Carbon Steel Mechanical and Pressure Tubing

LTV Steel, Cedar Springs, GA	0.375"	3"		40,000
LTV Steel, Cleveland, OH	0.5"	4.5"		70,000
LTV Steel, Elyria, OH	0.75"	3"		50,000
LTV Steel, Ferndale, MI	0.5"	6.625"		90,000
Markin Tubing, Inc., Wyoming, NY	0.1875"	1"		20,000
Metal-Matic, Inc., Minneapolis, MN	0.25"	3.5"		60,000
Michigan Tube, Inc., Eau Claire, MI	0.375"	3"		30,000
Middletown Tube Works, Middletown, OH	0.375"	3"		20,000
Mid-States Tube Corp., Kenosha, WI	1.875"	4"		50,000
Mid-West Company, Chicago Heights, IL	2.375"	6.725"		25,000
National Metalwares, Inc., Aurora, IL	0.5"	1.5"		20,000
National Metalwares, Inc., LaSalle, IL	0.75"	1.5"		20,000
Opelika Welding Machine, Opelika, AL	0.75"	3"		25,000
Pacific Tube Co., Los Angeles, CA	0.5"	4.5"		50,000
Paragon Tube Corp., Fort Wayne, In	0.84"	3"		10,000
Parthenon Metal Works, Laverne, TN	0.5"	1.9"		45,000
Pittsburgh Tube, Darlington, PA	1.05"	4"	Yes [b]	65,000
Pittsburgh Tube, Fairbury, IL	0.5"	5"	Yes [b]	40,000
Pixley Tube Co., Marlow, OK	0.725"	2"		20,000
Plymouth Tube Co., West Monroe, LA	1"	1.75"		
Plymouth Tube Co., Winamac, IN	0.75"	5"		
Precision Tube Technology, Houston, TX	1"	5"		25,000
Quality Tube, Houston, TX	0.875"	4.5"		15,000
Sawhill Tubular, Warren, OH	0.5"	6.625"		175,000
Sawhill Tubular, Wheatland, PA	0.5"	3.25"	Yes	25,000
Searing Industries, Rancho Cucamonga, CA	0.5"	2.5"		12,000
Sonco Steel Tube, Mississauga, Ontario	0.5"	3"		25,000
Southwestern Pipe, Houston, TX	0.5"	4"		70,000
Southwestern Pipe, Bossier City, LA	0.5"	3"		50,000
Standard Tube Canada, Inc., Woodstock, Ontario	0.5"	8.625"		125,000
Standard Tube Canada, Inc., Winnipeg, Manitoba	0.625"	2.5"		15,000
Stelpipe, Welland, Ontario	0.5"	4.5"	Yes	120,000
Sterling Pipe & Tube, Toledo, OH	1.312"	4"		
Techtron Tube, Depere, WI	0.5"	3"		25,000
Tektube Co., Tulsa, OK	2"	3"		15,000
Troxel Co., Moscow, TN	0.5"	3"		30,000
True Temper Corp., Armory, MS	0.725"	1.5"		10,000
TubeTech, Inc., Palestine, OH	0.5"	1.5"		35,000
Tubular Products, Birmingham, AL	0.5"	3"		25,000
UNR Industries, Hammond, IN	0.375"	3"		150,000
Union Tubular Products, Torrington, CT	0.94"	2"		10,000
United Tube, Medina, OH	0.5"	2.375"		35,000
U.S. Metal Forms & Tubes, Beltsville, MD	0.375"	5"		60,000
Vanex Tube Corp., Niles, OH	2"	6"		50,000
Vest, Inc., Los Angeles, CA	0.5"	7.5"		150,000
Webco Industries, Oil City, PA	0.625"	5"	Yes	30,000
Webco Industries, Sand Springs, OK	0.625"	5"	Yes	60,000
Welded Tube of Canada, Concord, Ontario	0.5"	2.75"		50,000
Welded Tubes, Inc., Orwell, OH	0.375"	2.125"	Yes	6,000
Western Tube & Conduit, Long Beach, CA	0.5"	4.5"		150,000
Wheatland Tube, Chicago, IL	0.5"	2"		200,000
Wheatland Tube, Omega Division, Little Rock, AR	1.125"	3"		100,000

[b] Redraw facilities located elsewhere, at Chicago, Illinois, Jane Lew, West Virginia, Monaca, Pennsylvania, and Monroe, New York.

II.15: Carbon Steel Standard and Line Pipe:

Continuous Butt Welded (CBW) and Electric-Resistance Welded (ERW)

Standard pipe, as the name suggests, is general-purpose welded pipe used in almost every application for steel, although the grade is primarily intended for carrying low-pressure fluids in construction applications. It is the pipe usually specified for plumbing and heating, and is used in many ways in the manufacture of industrial plant, machinery, and equipment. "Sprinkler pipe" is a term used for those light-wall standard pipe sizes used primarily in building fire-protection systems. Externally, it may be used in irrigation systems and in water well casing. A small amount of seamless pipe is also produced to the ASTM A-53 standard pipe specification.

Line pipe is general-purpose, standard-size pipe produced for external applications—typically, oil, gas, and water pipelines, thus the term "line pipe." Line pipe is produced up to very large diameters, but the effective economic size limit of ERW pipe production is about 24 inches diameter. For larger sizes of line pipe, produced by the submerged-arc and spiral-weld processes, see table II.16.

Until the 1980s, welded standard pipe was produced almost entirely by the CBW process, while line pipe (with a slightly more rigorous specification set by the American Petroleum Institute, API 5L) was produced by the more expensive ERW process. In recent years, producers of ERW pipe have increasingly offered their product as an economic alternative to both CBW and seamless standard pipe. Much ERW pipe is dual-stenciled with both the ASTM and API specifications. (Line pipe may be substituted for standard pipe, although not vice-versa.) Most standard pipe, however, is used in sizes from ¼ inch to 8 inches, while most line pipe is used in sizes from 4 inches upward.

(See table II.15 on next page.)

II.15: Carbon Steel Standard and Line Pipe

Company and Plant Location	Process	Minimum Diameter	Maximum Diameter	Estimated Capacity, Tons per Year
American Tube Co., Phoenix, AZ	ERW			
Camrose Pipe, Camrose, Alberta [a]	ERW	4.5"	16"	100,000
CSI Tubular Products, Fontana, CA	ERW	4.5"	16"	100,000
Hickman Pipe, Hickman, KY	ERW			
Imperial Steel Products, Winnipeg, Manitoba	ERW	3"	10.75"	40,000
Ipsco, Camanche, IA	ERW	2.375"	8.625"	210,000
Ipsco, Geneva, NE	ERW	2.5"	7"	100,000
Ipsco, Edmonton, Alberta	ERW	4.5"	16"	110,000
Ipsco, Regina, Saskatchewan	ERW	1.5"	2.375"	30,000
Ipsco, Regina, Saskatchewan	ERW	14"	24"	500,000
Laclede Steel, Alton/Vandalia, IL	CBW	0.5"	4"	160,000
Laclede Steel, Fairless Hills, PA	CBW	0.5"	4"	240,000
Prudential Pipe, Calgary, Alberta	ERW	2.375"	12.75"	200,000
Sawhill Tubular, Sharon, PA	CBW	0.5"	4"	150,000
Sawhill Tubular, Warren, OH	ERW	2"	8"	150,000
Sharon Tube, Sharon, PA	CBW	0.125"	3"	90,000
Sharon Tube, Sharon, PA	ERW	0.5"	3.5"	40,000
Sidbec-Dosco, Montreal, Québec	CBW	0.5"	4"	70,000
Southwestern Pipe, Houston, TX	ERW	0.5"	4.5"	
Stelpipe, Welland, Ontario	CBW	0.5"	4"	100,000
Stelpipe, Welland, Ontario	ERW	0.5"	16"	250,000
Tex-Tube, Houston, TX	ERW	2.5"	8.625"	100,000
Western Tube and Conduit, Long Beach, CA	ERW	0.5"	3"	100,000
Wheatland Tube, Wheatland, PA	CBW	0.5"	4"	150,000

[a] Camrose Pipe is owned by Oregon Steel (60 percent) and Stelco (40 percent).

II.16: Large-Diameter Carbon Steel Pipe:

Double-Submerged-Arc Welded (DSAW) and Spiral Welded (SPI)

The effective economic limit of production by the electric-resistance welding process (ERW) is between 16 and 24 inches in diameter. Above these sizes, pipe production today is generally by either the double-submerged-arc welding (DSAW) process for longitudinally welded pipe, using skelp wide enough to form the necessary circumference, or the pipe is spiral welded from narrow skelp. As a general rule, spiral weld pipe is less expensive but less robust than DSAW pipe.

Most large-diameter pipe is used in as line pipe in pipelines, although smaller tonnages are also used as piling pipe (chiefly spiral weld pipe) and in structural and mechanical uses such as cylinders (generally DSAW pipe). Capacity figures in this table are theoretical maximum output numbers for the mills concerned. Few large-diameter pipe mills operate at anything like these numbers over lengthy periods, as they depend on the receipt of infrequent large-tonnage orders as and when major pipelines are constructed.

Producers of seamless pipe over 16 inches, and of large-diameter stainless pipe, are listed separately in tables II.18 and II.19.

II.16: Large-Diameter Carbon Steel Pipe

Company and Plant Location	Process	Minimum Diameter	Maximum Diameter	Estimated Tons per Year Capacity
Berg Steel Pipe, Panama City, FL	DSAW	24"	64"	250,000
Bethlehem Steel, Steelton, PA (Pennsylvania Steel Technologies division)	DSAW	20"	42"	240,000
Camrose Pipe, Camrose, Alta.	DSAW	20"	42"	184,000
Canadian Phoenix Steel Products, Toronto, Ontario	Spiral	10"	86"	36,000
Cappco Tubular Products, Cartersville, GA	Spiral	8.625"	84"	25,000
L.B. Foster Co., Savannah, GA	Spiral	8.725"	120"	110,000
L.B. Foster Co., Parkersburg, WV	Spiral	8.725"	120"	185,000
Geneva Steel, Vineyard, UT	DSAW	20"	40"	120,000
Ipsco, Regina, Saskatchewan [a]	Spiral	18"	72"	200,000
Labarge Pipe & Steel, Wagoner, OK	DSAW	17"	144"	200,000
Northwest Pipe & Casing, Adelanto, CA	Spiral	18"	154"	70,000
Northwest Pipe & Casing, Portland, OR	Spiral	18"	146"	200,000
Oregon Steel, Napa Pipe Corp. division, Napa, CA	DSAW	16"	42"	350,000
Progressive Fabricators, St. Louis, MO	Spiral	12"	144"	250,000
Saw Pipes Ltd., Baytown, TX [b]	DSAW	24"	48"	300,000
Skyline Steel, Camphill, PA [c]	Spiral	8.725"	72"	40,000
Skyline Steel, Scooby, MS [c]	Spiral	8.725"	24"	25,000
Steel Forgings, Inc., Shreveport, LA	DSAW	20"	56"	130,000
Thompson Pipe & Steel, Denver, CO	Spiral	18"	123"	95,000
Thompson Pipe & Steel, Princeton, KY	Spiral	18"	123"	40,000
Welland Tube (div. of Stelco), Welland, Ontario	DSAW	20"	36"	200,000
Welland Tube (div. of Stelco), Welland, Ontario	Spiral	36"	60"	300,000

[a] In June 1996, Ipsco announced plans to build a large-diameter ERW pipe mill in Iowa, close to the companys new Montpelier plate minimill.
[b] Marketed by U.S. Steel.
[c] A subsidiary of Arbed S.A., Luxembourg.

II.17: Oil Country Tubular Goods:

Seamless and Welded Drill Pipe, Production Tubing, and Casing

Casing, the largest tonnage category of oil country tubular goods (OCTG), is the structural retainer for the walls of oil and gas wells. It is generally not removed after a well is completed. Production tubing is installed inside the casing to bring oil and gas to the surface. It may be removed when a well is being worked upon or closed down. Drill pipe is normally reused many times; it requires extreme strength to transmit torque from the surface rig to the drill bit.

The bulk of OCTG shipments are by producers that specialize in the market, often with in-house or captive pipe finishing operations to perform the operations necessary to meet American Petroleum Institute (API) specifications and industry requirements. OCTG finishing includes heat-treating, upsetting, straightening, threading, and coating operations. Independent OCTG finishers perform these operations for nonspecialized producers and for imported pipe. A number of welded pipe mills that primarily specialize in line pipe do produce OCTG, mainly for casing. Of these, mills with significant annual OCTG tonnage shipments are shown in table II.17 below as well as in either table II.15, "Carbon Steel Standard and Line Pipe," or table II.18, "Seamless Pipe and Tubing."

(See tables II.17a and II.17b on next page.)

II.17a: Seamless Oil Country Tubulars

Company and Plant Location	Minimum Diameter	Maximum Diameter	Estimated Tons per Year Capacity	Est. 1994 OCTG shipments
Algoma Steel, Sault Ste Marie, Ontario [a]	2.375"	7"	260,000	250,000
	4.5"	12.75"	290,000	
C F & I Steel, Pueblo, CO [b]	5"	10.75"	200,000	120,000
Koppel Steel, Ambridge, PA	1.875"	8.5"	300,000	160,000
Lone Star Steel, Lone Star, TX	5.5"	10.625"	200,000	20,000
North Star Steel, Youngstown, OH	5.5"	10.75"	270,000	120,000
Prudential Steel, Calgary, Alberta	2.375"	8.625"	200,000	50,000
Quanex – Gulf States Tube division, Rosenberg, TX [a]	0.313"	2.375"	20,000	10,000
Timken Co., Canton, OH [a]	1.75"	11"	230,000	50,000
Timken Co., Gambrinus, OH [a]	2.375"	12.5"	750,000	
U.S.S./Kobe Steel, Lorain, OH [a, c]	1.9"	4.5"	200,000	
U.S.S./Kobe Steel, Lorain, OH [a, c]	10.625"	26"	540,000	300,000

[a] Mills also listed in table II.18, Seamless Pipe and Tubing."
[b] Majority-owned subsidiary of Oregon Steel.
[c] USS/Kobe Steels tubulars are marketed by U.S. Steel.
Other seamless mills capable of producing OCTG but producing primarily for non-oilfield markets, include Quanex–Michigan Seamless Tube, South Lyon, Michigan, and Timken at Wooster, Ohio.
LTV Steel maintains a mothballed seamless OCTG mill at the site of its former Campbell Works integrated steel mill near Youngstown, Ohio.

II.17b: Welded Oil Country Tubulars

Company and Plant Location	Minimum Diameter	Maximum Diameter	Estimated Tons per Year Capacity	Est. 1994 OCTG Shipments
Camp-Hill Corporation, McKeesport, PA a, b	8.625"	20"	200,000	25,000
Ipsco, Calgary, Alberta	4.5"	10.75"	175,000	100,000
Ipsco, Edmonton, Alberta [a]	4.5"	16"	120,000	
Lone Star Steel, Lone Star, TX	2.375"	16"	500,000	325,000
LTV Steel, Counce, TN [a]	4.5"	8.625"	180,000	50,000
LTV Steel, Youngstown, OH [a]	6.625"	16"	380,000	
Maverick Tube, Conroe, TX	2.375"	8.625"	250,000	50,000
Newport Steel, Newport, KY	4.5"	13.375	580,000	300,000
Paragon Industries, Sapulpa, OK [a]	4.5"	16"	400,000	75,000
Quanex – Gulf States Tube Division, Rosenberg, TX [a]	0.313"	2.375"	20,000	5,000
Stelpipe, Welland, Ontario [a]	2.375"	16"	200,000	25,000
U.S.S./Kobe, Lorain, OH [a, b]	2.375"	6.725"	150,000	30,000

[a] Mills also listed in table II.15, Carbon Steel Standard and Line Pipe."
[b] Marketed by U.S. Steel.
Other ERW mills capable of producing pipe to API standards for welded OCTG, but whose shipments to this market are limited, include Ipsco at Regina, Saskatchewan; Northwest Pipe and Casing at Portland, Oregon; Prudential Steel at Calgary, Alberta (also a producer of seamless OCTG); Quanex–Gulf States Tube Division, Rosenberg, Texas (also seamless OCTG); and Sawhill Tubular, Sharon, Pennsylvania.

II.18: Seamless Pipe and Tubing

(Other than Mills Producing Exclusively Stainless Steel or OCTG)

Seamless pipe and tubing, produced from solid, cast steel rounds, is usually manufactured in two stages. A hot-piercing operation rolls the round shape over a mandrel to form a rough tube, after which the hollow shape is finished either by rolling down the outside diameter (while the mandrel keeps the inside diameter fixed) or by rotary milling to increase the inside of the tube (while the outside diameter is held constant by rolls). Much seamless pipe is also cold-drawn to produce precise outside diameter (OD) and inside diameter (ID) dimensions. Smaller quantities of seamless, including some large-diameter and specialty tubing, are produced by extrusion and forging processes using hydraulic presses.

Seamless pipe is more expensive and capital-intensive to produce than welded pipe, but is sought after for applications requiring great strength and structural integrity relative to the size of the pipe. The lack of a weld seam means the absence of the weak points inherent in other tubulars.

Seamless pipe mills producing exclusively for the OCTG market are listed separately in table II.17b, "Seamless Oil Country Tubulars." Seamless stainless is found in table II.19b, "Stainless Steel Seamless Pipe and Tubing."

(See table II.18 on next page.)

II.18: Seamless Pipe and Tubing, other than Stainless

Company and Plant Location	Minimum Diameter	Maximum Diameter	Estimated Tons per Year Capacity	Principal Markets
Algoma Steel, Sault Ste. Marie, Ontario	2.375" 4.5	7" 12.75"	260,000 290,000	OCTG, line pipe OCTG, line pipe
Associated Tube Industries Ltd., Markham, Ont.	0.1875"	6.725"	10,000	Pressure tubing
CF & I Steel, Pueblo, CO	5"	10.75"	200,000	OCTG, standard pipe
Copperweld Corp., Shelby, OH	1.438"	7"	70,000	Mechanical tubing
Koppel Steel, Ambridge, PA	1.875"	8.5"	300,000	OCTG, line pipe
Kubota Metal Corp., Orillia, Ontario	2"	25"	2,000	Mechanical tubing
Lone Star Steel, Lone Star, TX	5.5"	10.625"	200,000	OCTG, mechanical tubing
LTV Steel, Campbell, OH [a]	6.05"	14.375"	300,000	OCTG
North Star Steel, Youngstown, OH	5.5"	10.75"	270,000	OCTG, standard pipe
Prudential Steel, Calgary, Alberta	2.375"	8.625"	200,000	OCTG, mechanical, pressure, line pipe
Plymouth Tube Co., Winamac, IN	1.75"	5"	50,000	Mechanical, pressure
Quanex – Gulf States Tube Division, Rosenberg, TX	0.313"	2.375"	20,000	Mechanical, pressure
Quanex, Michigan Seamless Div., So. Lyon, MI	0.5"	4.125"	40,000	Mechanical, pressure
Sharon Tube Co., Sharon, PA (redraw only)	0.125"	2"	10,000	Mechanical, pressure
Stelpipe, Welland, Ontario	1.23"	2.375"	20,000	Standard, line pipe
Timken Co., Canton, OH	2.25"	5.5"	230,000	Mechanical, pressure
Timken Co., Gambrinus, OH	2.375"	12.5"	750,000	Mechanical, pressure
Timken Co., Wooster, OH	1.725"	3.5"	75,000	Mechanical, pressure
U.S.S./Kobe, Lorain, OH [b]	1.9"	4.5"	200,000	Line, standard, OCTG
U.S.S./Kobe, Lorain, OH [b]	10.75"	26"	540,000	Line pipe, OCTG
U.S. Steel, Fairfield, AL	3.5"	9.625"	600,000	OCTG, line pipe

[a] Not operating
[b] Marketed by U.S. Steel.

II.19: Stainless Steel Pipe and Tubing:

Seamless and Welded, for All Applications

Tables II.19a and 19b show the major North American stainless pipe and tube manufacturers as of January 1996. They exclude a number of specialty redraw mills that make tubing for the medical, aerospace, instrumentation, and similar small-diameter markets, but do not manufacture their own redraw tube hollows. Some of these redraw mills, such as Teledyne Rodney Metals, are major factors in the high-value end of the specialty tubing market.

Stainless steel seamless pipe and tubing markets in North America are dominated by imports, both of finished products and of redraw hollows for finishing in the United States. Two of the major seamless producers listed—Sandvik and TAD—import redraw hollows from their foreign parent companies.

Caution should be taken with stainless capacity numbers. Many stainless tubular mills, if they declare capacity at all, do so in terms of feet of output, not tons. The annual North American market for stainless steel tubulars is a little over 100,000 tons, and most producers operate at a fraction of their theoretical potential capacity. Few mills, for example, run at more than five turns per week. The capacity figures in this category, therefore, should be taken more as a guide to relative throughput and position in the marketplace than as true capability numbers.

II.19a: Stainless Steel Seamless Pipe and Tubing

Company and Plant Location	Minimum Diameter	Maximum Diameter	Capacity, Tons per Year	Principal Markets
American Extrusion Products, Beaver Falls, PA	1.66"	4.5"	6,000	Mechanical tubing
Curtiss-Wright, Buffalo, NY	3"	18"	2,500	Large-diameter pipe
DMV Stainless, Houston, TX	0.5"	4"	5,000	Standard pipe
Kaiser Electroprecision, Irvine, CA	4"	30"	10,000	Mech. tubing, cylinders
Plymouth Tube, Hopkinsville, KY	0.125"	1.25"	5,000	Pressure tubing
Sammi Al Tech, Watervliet, NY	0.375"	5.5"	7,200	Mechanical tubing
Sandvik Tube Ltd., Amprior, Ontario	0.25"	2"	1,500	Pressure tubing, pipe
Sandvik Tubular Products, Scranton, PA including Pennsylvania Extrusion Company (PEXCO) joint venture	0.125"	2"	10,000	Pressure tubing, pipe
Wyman Gordon Forgings, Houston, TX	6"	48"	100,000	Cylinders

II.19b: Stainless Steel Welded Pipe and Tubing

Company and Plant Location	Minimum Diameter	Maximum Diameter	Estimated Tons per Year Capacity	Principal Markets
Accumetrics Ltd., Royersford, PA	0.125"	0.25	2,500	Instrumentation
Accu-Tube, Englewood, CO	0.006"	0.375	2,500	Instrumentation
Acme Tube, Mansfield, LA	0.5"	7.5	10,000	Ornamental, structural
Acme Tube, Somerset, NJ	0.5"	4	5,000	Ornamental, structural
Alaskan Copper & Brass, Seattle,WA	3"	36	50,000	Corrosive process plants
Allegheny Ludlum, Claremore, OK	0.625"	3.5	6,600	Pressure tubing
AP Parts Co., Toledo, OH	1.375"	3.5	5,000	Mechanical tubing
Associated Tube Industries, Markham, Ontario	0.1875"	6.725	10,000	Mechanical, pressure tubing
Avesta Sheffield, Inc., Wildwood, FL	0.84"	60	10,000	Standard pipe, pressure, & mechanical tubing
Bristol Metals, Bristol, TN	0.5"	36	18,000	Corrosive process plants
Consolidated Stainless, Orlando, FL	0.5"	4.5"	2,500	Corrosive process plants
Damascus Bishop Tube, Malvern, PA	0.187"	4.5"	2,500	Ornamental tubing
Damascus Bishop Tube, Sharon, PA	0.125"	8.625"	12,000	Corrosive process plants
Davis Pipe & Metal, Blountville, TN	2"	48"	3,000	Standard, mechanical
Douglas Brothers, Portland, ME			2,500	Pulp & paper, power
Felcker Bros. Corp., Marshfield, WI	3"	12.75"	2,500	Pulp & paper, power
Fischer Canada, Waterloo, Ontario	0.5"	3"	3,000	Mechanical, ornamental
Gibson Tube, Inc., Bridgewater, NJ	0.1875"	1.5"	2,500	Mechanical, pressure
Greenville Tube, Clarkville, AR	0.125"	1.375"	2,000	Instrumentation
Handy & Harman, Norristown, PA	0.1875"	2.5"	3,000	Instrumentation, pressure
Henderson Barwick Inc., Brockville, Ontario	3"	96"	100,000	Corrosive process plants
ITT Sterling Stainless, Englewood, CO	0.125"	0.375"	1,000	Instrumentation
Lee Wilson Engineering, Toledo, OH	4.5"	6"	3,000	Standard pipe
LTV Steel Tubular Products, Cleveland, OH	0.75"	6.625"	72,000	Standard pipe, pressure & mechanical tubing
Oakley Industries, Englewood, CA	0.125"	1"	3,000	Mechanical tubing
Oakley Industries, Niles, Il	0.25"	0.5"	3,000	Mechanical tubing
Phoenix Tube, Bethlehem, PA	1.5"	6"	5,000	Ornamental tubing
Plymouth Tube, West Monroe, LA [a]	1"	1.75"	5,000	Pressure, mechanical
Rath Manufacturing, Janesville, WI	0.5"	4"	15,000	Ornamental, pressure
Romac Tube, Sparks, NV	1.5"	5"	2,000	Ornamental, structural
Romac Tube, Troutman, NC	0.5"	8"	5,000	Ornamental, structural
Salem Tube, Greenville, PA	0.625"	3.5"	4,000	Pressure, mechanical
Scientific Tube, Addison, Il	0.25"	1.75"	2,000	Pressure tubing
Superior Tube, Collegeville, PA	0.125"	2.5"	5,000	Mechanical, pressure
Swepco Tube, Clifton, NJ	4"	48	10,000	Corrosive process plants
Teledyne Metal Forming, Elkhart, IN	0.1875"	3.5"	2,500	Mechanical
Trent Tube Division, Crucible Materials Corp., East Troy, WI	0.125"	60"	15,000	Mechanical, pressure tubing
Uniform Tubes, Collegeville, PA	0.25"	0.75"	1,000	Mechanical tubing
United Industries, Beloit, WI	0.5"	5"	2,500	Mechanical, pressure
Webco Industries, Mannford, OK	0.25"	1.25"	5,000	Mechanical, pressure
Wheatland Tube, Little Rock, AR	0.75"	3"	4,000	Mechanical, pressure

[a] Also stainless redraw mills at Horsham, Pennsylvania; Salisbury, Maryland; and West Monroe, Louisiana.

INDEX

C

J

K

L